THE

SAINTS ABROAD

Missionaries Who Answered Brigham Young's
1852 Call to the Nations of the World

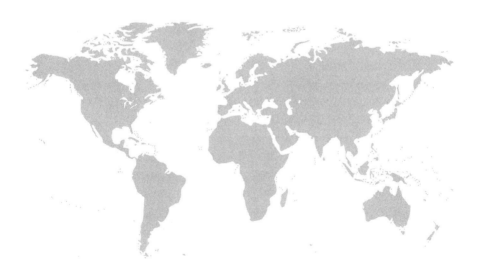

Edited by Reid L. Neilson and R. Mark Melville

RSC
BYU

DESERET
BOOK

Published by the Religious Studies Center, Brigham Young University, Provo, Utah, in cooperation with Deseret Book Company, Salt Lake City.
Visit us at rsc.byu.edu.

Printed in the United States of America by Sheridan Books, Inc.

DESERET BOOK is a registered trademark of Deseret Book Company.
Visit us at DeseretBook.com.

Cover and interior design by Emily V. Strong.
Cover painting by Clark Kelley Price.
Chapter page map images courtesy of freevectormaps.com.

ISBN 978-1-9443-9472-1

Library of Congress Cataloging-in-Publication Data

Names: Neilson, Reid L., 1972- editor. | Melville, R. Mark, 1988- editor.
Title: The Saints abroad : missionaries who answered Brigham Young's 1852
   call to the nations of the world / dc edited by Reid L. Neilson and R.
   Mark Melville.
Description: Provo, Utah : Religious Studies Center, Brigham Young University
   ; Salt Lake City : Deseret Book, [2019] | Includes bibliographical
   references and index.
Identifiers: LCCN 2018045883 (print) | LCCN 2018054152 (ebook) | ISBN
   9781944394721 (ebook) | ISBN 9781944394721 (print)
Subjects: LCSH: Mormon missionaries--History--19th century. | Mormon
   missionaries--Biography. | LCGFT: Biographies.
Classification: LCC BX8661 (ebook) | LCC BX8661 .S25 2019 (print) | DDC
   266/.9309034--dc23
LC record available at https://lccn.loc.gov/2018045883

For Ned L. and Carla M. Christensen
—RLN

For David R. Clark and S. Mark Palmer
—RMM

"Song for the Missionaries of 1852"

Come brethren let us sing a song of praise unto the Lord,
Who hath chosen us and sent us forth to preach his holy word,
'Mong distant nations far away, where sin and sorrows reign—
Where dire commotion fills the land with wretchedness and pain.
Chorus—Then brethren let us not forget to work, and watch, and pray;
Our God will never us forsake, but guard us night and day.

We go to teach eternal truth, to saints and sinners too,
To tell the world the glorious things the saints have got in view;
No doubt temptations deep and strong, will often us assail,
And satan will his cunning use to cause our faith to fail.
Chorus—Then brethren let us not forget, &c.

We go to tell the saints abroad, how they may all secure
Succession of eternal lives, to those who will be pure;
How thrones and principalities, dominions and powers,
They may obtain eternally, with other friends of ours.
Chorus—Then brethren let us not forget, &c.

We leave behind us, those we hold most sacred, fond and dear;
We know they're in the hands of God, and what have we to fear:
The joys of home we now forgo our mission to fulfil,
And go to do what God requires—we have no other will
Chorus—Then brethren let us not forget, &c.

And when our work abroad is done, and we are called home,
O may our hearts be pure as gold, fit for the world to come;
May thousands saints accompany us, when west our steps we bend,
Whose praises to the God we love, forever will ascend.
Chorus—Then brethren let us not forget, &c.

—William Clayton, "Song for the Missionaries of 1852."[1]

---

1. William Clayton, "Song for the Missionaries of 1852," *Deseret News*, November 27, 1852. Clayton composed these lyrics at Black's Fork of the Green River on the Mormon Trail on September 23, 1852, in honor of his fellow missionaries called at the special August conference. It was sung to the tune of "My Heart and Lute."

CONTENTS

ILLUSTRATIONS

EDITORIAL METHOD

THERE ARE THREE MAJOR TYPES OF NOTES OR AIDS that documentary editors can provide their readers: provenance, textual, and contextual notes.[1] To make this rich assemblage of missionary letters and reminiscences more comprehensible, we have employed all three categories of annotation to illuminate the people, places, and things the eight representative Latter-day Saint elders referenced in their letters. We have generally followed the same style used in Reid L. Neilson and Nathan N. Waite, eds., *Settling the Valley, Proclaiming the Gospel: The General Epistles of the Mormon First Presidency* (New York: Oxford University Press, 2017), a companion volume to the present book.

---

1. Stevens and Burg, *Editing Historical Documents*, 158–70; see also Kline and Perdue, *Guide to Documentary Editing.*

Provenance Notes

Our goal is to make these letters more accessible to our twenty-first-century audience. We want our readers to be aware of where they can find the original documents, better understand their genre, and come away with a greater appreciation of their publication history. To this aim we offer the following notes on the documents' provenance or history.

Repository information. Original printings of all the missionaries' letters contained herein can be found in the archival collections of the Church History Library, The Church of Jesus Christ of Latter-day Saints, Salt Lake City, as detailed in the source notes at the beginning of each chapter.

Publication history. Nineteenth-century missionaries often wrote letters to church leaders, and their accounts were published in various Latter-day Saint periodicals. We have included letters from a variety of sources. Dan Jones and Jesse Haven wrote to Presidents Franklin D.[2] and Samuel W. Richards[3] of the European Mission, and their correspondence was published in the *Latter-day Saints' Millennial Star*, which long served as an official publication of The Church of Jesus Christ of Latter-day Saints in England.[4] Orson Spencer's letter to Brigham Young was published as a

2. Franklin D. Richards (1821–99) was baptized in his home state of Massachusetts in 1838. He served several missions in the midwestern United States before laboring in the British Isles from 1846 to 1848, again from 1849 to 1852 (part of that time as mission president), and again from 1854 to 1856 (again as mission president). He became an Apostle in 1849. Jenson, *Latter-day Saint Biographical Encyclopedia*, 1:115–21; Early Mormon Missionaries database, s.v. "Franklin Dewey Richards."

3. Samuel W. Richards (1824–1909), the brother of Franklin D., was baptized in 1838. Like his brother, he served three missions to the British Isles (1846–48, 1852–54, and 1857–58), twice as mission president. He served several other missions to the United States throughout his life. Jenson, *Latter-day Saint Biographical Encyclopedia*, 1:718–19; Early Mormon Missionaries database, s.v. "Samuel Whitney Richards."

4. The *Millennial Star* was a church periodical published in England beginning in 1840. Like other church periodicals of the day, it printed extracts from the Doctrine and Covenants and other scriptures, reported on significant events in the church, and provided other items of interest to Latter-day Saints. Usually the president of the British Mission was the editor. The *Millennial Star* was published until

stand-alone pamphlet by Samuel W. Richards in 1853. Thirty years after his mission, Edward Stevenson wrote a reminiscent account to Apostle George Q. Cannon,[5] editor of the *Juvenile Instructor*, a magazine for young Latter-day Saints. Benjamin Johnson wrote a handwritten memoir several decades after his own missionary service; his is the only holograph item featured as a chapter in this book. James Lewis and Chauncey West both had their letters printed in the *Deseret News*, the church-operated frontier newspaper in Salt Lake City.[6] Augustus Farnham had letters published in the *Millennial Star*, the *Deseret News*, and the *Western Standard*, a Latter-day Saint newspaper published by George Q. Cannon in San Francisco.[7]

1970. Alan K. Parrish, "*Millennial Star, The*," in *Encyclopedia of Latter-day Saint History*, 752; Parrish, "Beginnings of the *Millennial Star*," 133–49.

5. George Q. Cannon (1827–1901) was born in Liverpool, England, and was baptized there in 1840. He traveled to Utah in 1847 and worked in the California gold fields before serving a mission to Hawaii from 1850 to 1854. He became an Apostle in 1860 and edited several Latter-day Saint periodicals throughout his life, including the *Western Standard*, *Juvenile Instructor*, and *Deseret News*. Cannon became a Utah territorial delegate to US Congress and served as counselor to church presidents Brigham Young, John Taylor, Wilford Woodruff, and Lorenzo Snow. Journal of George Q. Cannon, Chronology.

6. The *Deseret News* functioned as both a conventional newspaper, reporting on the news of the day, and a religious newspaper, with articles from a Latter-day Saint viewpoint. The Saints had published a newspaper since 1832 in Independence, Missouri. In 1847, Brigham Young asked William W. Phelps to buy a printing press to take to the Salt Lake Valley. The press arrived in Utah in 1849, but it was not until June 15, 1850, that the first issue of the *Deseret News* was published. Willard Richards was the first editor of the paper. Paper shortages were a constant problem during the paper's first decade. The *Deseret News* is still in publication. Dennis L. Lythgoe, "The *Deseret News*," in *Utah History Encyclopedia*, 140; Hunter, "Starting a Pioneer Newspaper," 8–17.

7. The *Western Standard* was published in San Francisco by George Q. Cannon between February 1856 and November 1857. It joined the ranks of other Latter-day Saint periodicals, such as the *Mormon* and the *Seer*, intended to defend the church and its people from the criticisms of other local presses. Cannon, "George Q. Cannon and the *Western Standard*," 22–25.

Textual Notes

Transcription method. Scholars engaged in documentary editing employ a variety of transcription methods. Editors make choices on the kinds of editorial apparatus they will use based on the types of documents they are featuring and their anticipated readership. Most of the letters in this book were written to church leaders and then published in periodicals.

We have used a conservative "expanded transcription" method of displaying the printed text. This editorial approach "encompasses a wide spectrum of editing styles, all of which standardize accidentals, datelines, and signatures; mark paragraphs with indentations; and do not attempt to reproduce the excessive spacing and physical layout of the text of documents."[8] We have occasionally bracketed clarifications to the text and made any other corrections according to the seventeenth edition of *The Chicago Manual of Style* and the eleventh edition of *Merriam-Webster's Collegiate Dictionary*.

Indecipherable characters or words. Occasionally a pioneer press error or the age of the printed page renders a letter or word indecipherable. When the missing text could be deduced from its context, we have filled the letter in without brackets.

Names of people. We chose to clarify the names of people, since some of our readers may be family historians searching for their ancestors. Aside from standard abbreviations such as "Wm.," we have used brackets to expand abbreviated or partial names in the text and correct misspellings; thus, "elder Barnes" becomes "elder [Lorenzo] Barnes," and so forth. We have included a biographical register of all the missionaries called in 1852. Other people have been identified in footnotes when possible; many, however, were impossible to find.

Spelling variants and misspelled words. Many of the original words in the missionaries' correspondence do not conform to modern spelling conventions. Some of these words are nineteenth-century spelling variations (such as "proceedure" instead of "procedure"), and we have retained them because they convey the historical nuances of the letters. We have, however, silently corrected words that were simply misspelled

---

8. Stevens and Burg, *Editing Historical Documents*, 76–77.

(such as "precisely") or that were typographical errors (such as "psesiding" or "deprepation"). At times, it has been difficult to discern whether a given spelling was a nineteenth-century variation or a simple misspelling, so we have had to use our best judgment. The *Oxford English Dictionary* has been an invaluable resource in historic spellings, as have the linguistic corpora of Mark Davies of Brigham Young University.[9]

One chapter is an exception to this convention. Chapter 5, Benjamin Johnson's account of his mission to the Sandwich Islands, is a handwritten reminiscence that was not printed during his lifetime. We have kept misspellings in his chapter to preserve the character of his writing. When he inserted words above the main line of text, we have added them in <angle brackets>. When he underlined words, we have changed them to *italics*. Although he frequently superscripted abbreviations, we have not retained superscript text.

Punctuation. Punctuation has generally been retained from the original. It was often difficult to tell whether a particular mark was a period or a comma, or whether it was a colon or a semicolon; these unclear punctuation marks have been silently changed to whatever makes the most grammatical sense. Sometimes we have added punctuation marks in brackets when necessary to improve readability, but we have not used brackets for periods. Square brackets in the original are rendered as {braces}.

Formatting. When the letters were originally published, they used a variety of formatting methods in the greetings and signatures (including letters embedded within the longer letters), such as all caps, small caps, italics, bold, and line breaks. The introductory and closing materials have been standardized and set in roman in the published accounts. However, we have retained small caps and italics when they occur in the body of the text, since the missionaries used them for emphasis. Sometimes, ordinal numbers or abbreviations used superscripts, especially in Johnson's reminiscence. We have decided not to use any superscript characters.

---

9. Davies, *Google Books Corpus*; Davies, *Corpus of LDS General Conference Talks*.

Contextual Notes

We also provide informational or contextual footnotes to help readers better understand the historical setting of the elders' correspondence. We want our audience to appreciate the individuals, scriptural passages, geographical features, and events mentioned in the letters. We also hope to clarify obscure references and correct any erroneous details featured in the texts that readers might find confusing.

Biographical references. To help readers know something of the lives and times of the men whose names were called at the August 1852 conference, we have provided biographical information about every missionary announced at that meeting. We have provided outlines of their lives in our biographical register. We have also provided footnotes for many of the individuals mentioned by the missionaries when we could identify them, whether they were Latter-day Saints or not. Patricia L. Spilsbury and her team of volunteers have done an astounding job of identifying the wives and families who were left behind in fledgling Utah Territory. The files used to compile each biography, as well as information about the wives and children of the eight featured missionaries, are available in the General Epistles biographical collection at the Church History Library in Salt Lake City.

Scriptural references. Like other Christians in antebellum America, the Latter-day Saints lived in a biblical culture, where the Bible greatly influenced written language and spoken rhetoric. But unlike their counterparts who only accepted the Old and New Testaments as the word of God, the Latter-day Saints also considered the Book of Mormon (1830), the Doctrine and Covenants (1835), and the Pearl of Great Price (published in 1851 but not canonized until 1880) as scripture. Canonical allusions and quoted Bible passages readily understood by nineteenth-century readers may be more obscure and hidden to modern readers. We have attempted to explicate these scriptural references in notes.

Geographic references. We have attempted to identify many of the locations mentioned in the elders' writings. Some of the geographical descriptions that were so evident to the writers and intended recipients of the missionaries' correspondence will likely be confusing without explanatory notes. Maps and endnotes are intended to assist the reader. However, some places referenced in the letters have undergone name changes or have ceased to exist, so they have been difficult to locate.

We are hopeful that our provenance, textual, and contextual notes, together with the assembled images, map, and appendixes, make the past more accessible and friendly. Although the Latter-day Saints lived differently in pioneer Utah and the nineteenth-century world, why and how they did so should be made more understandable by our editorial apparatus.

Acknowledgments

We are grateful for the support of the executive leadership of the Church History Department, including Elder Steven E. Snow, Elder J. Devn Cornish, and Elder LeGrand R. Curtis Jr. Moreover, the librarians and staff members of the Church History Library of The Church of Jesus Christ of Latter-day Saints, Salt Lake City, provided helpful guidance and access to primary source documents and secondary research. These professionals and volunteers have been delightful to work with and learn from during this project. Thanks are due to Julie Marie Cropper, Jo Lyn Curtis, Jessica Porter King, Kelley Konzak, and Carson V. Teuscher, who assisted with transcribing and verifying the text as well as the endnotes. We also show appreciation for the professional reviewers of our manuscript, including R. Lanier Britsch, Peter Crawley, Ronald D. Dennis, and Scott D. Marianno. They each gave important feedback as seasoned historians. But any errors that remain are our own.

We are also thankful for the contributions of the Church History Department biographical team led by the remarkable Patricia L. Spilsbury, including missionaries Marlene N. Breti, Patsy Hendrickson, James A. Jacobs, Beverly K. Jones, Shirley L. Romney, Paul D. Simpson, Devin M. Teichert, Laura J. Tropple, Judith A. Wight, Nola R. Wilkinson, and Kathleen Williams. This outstanding group researched and drafted the biographical register. Spilsbury also proposed the idea of researching the wives and families that the missionaries left behind while they served their missions. Information about the missionaries' family lives, particularly the sacrifices made during the years of their missions, was researched and drafted by her team of volunteers: Deborah L. Means (researched Dan Jones), Shirley L. Romney (Orson Spencer and Edward Stevenson), Judith E. Wight (Jesse Haven), Patricia L. Spilsbury (Benjamin F. Johnson),

Katelyn Stevens (James Lewis), Kathleen Williams (Chauncey W. West), and Eileen S. Carlston (Augustus Farnham).

We appreciate BYU Studies and the Mormon Historic Sites Foundation for allowing us to reprint updated versions of the following essays that appeared in their periodicals: Reid L. Neilson, "Proselyting on the Rock of Gibraltar, 1853–55: The Letters of Edward Stevenson to the *Juvenile Instructor* in 1885," *BYU Studies Quarterly* 55, no. 1 (2016): 95–132; and Reid L. Neilson, "Early Mormon Missionary Work in Hong Kong: The Letters of James Lewis to Apostle and Church Historian George A. Smith, 1853–1855," *Mormon Historical Studies* 17, nos. 1 and 2 (Spring and Fall 2016): 1–35.

We express thanks to the Religious Studies Center team of Thomas A. Wayment, Scott C. Esplin, Joany O. Pinegar, R. Devan Jensen, Brent R. Nordgren, Emily V. Strong, Ashlin Awerkamp, Petra Javadi-Evans, Megan Judd, and Michael R. Morris Jr., who turned this manuscript into a beautiful book.

Finally, Reid dedicates this volume to his late mission president Ned L. Christensen and his mission mom Carla M. Christensen. He served with them in the Japan Sapporo Mission between 1991 and 1993, when he lived in the cities of Otaru, Sapporo, Kitami, Asahikawa, and Shinoro as a young missionary.

Mark dedicates this book to his mission presidents, David R. Clark and S. Mark Palmer, who oversaw Latter-day Saint missionary work in the region of Spokane, Washington. They themselves served as missionaries along the trails blazed by Jesse Haven and Augustus Farnham in South Africa and New Zealand, respectively.

Reid L. Neilson
Assistant Church Historian and Recorder
Bountiful, Utah

R. Mark Melville
North Salt Lake, Utah

INTRODUCTION

WHEN MOST SCHOLARS OF RELIGION IN NORTH AMERICA and historians of the American West envision The Church of Jesus Christ of Latter-day Saints in the mid-nineteenth century, they conjure up images of a martyred Joseph Smith buried in Nauvoo, Illinois, and his prophetic successor, Brigham Young, leading the beleaguered vanguard company of Latter-day Saint pioneers to the Great Salt Lake Valley by ox-drawn wagons. The Exodus, ultimately numbering about seventy thousand pioneers over two decades, has become an American epic of biblical proportions. But by 1852, just five years after the "American Moses" and his fellow Latter-day Saints had begun settling the valleys of the Intermountain West, the global distribution of members of the church was much more European than American.

Beginning in 1837, Latter-day Saint missionaries evangelized in England and the surrounding countries, where they enjoyed tremendous conversion results. Smith later charged members of the Quorum of the Twelve in Nauvoo, Illinois, the year before his martyrdom, "Don't let a single

Portrait of Brigham Young. Courtesy of Church History Library.

corner of the earth go without a mission."[1] Before his death, he had called a handful of elders to evangelize in the nations of Australia, India, South America, Germany, Russia, Jamaica, and Tahiti; some fulfilled their missions, while others did not. It would be Smith's successor and his fellow apostles who largely expanded missionary work beyond the British Isles. They were responsible for personally leading the Latter-day Saint errand to the world over the ensuing decades. Between 1849 and 1851, Young assigned church leaders and laity to preach in Italy, France, Scandinavia, the Sandwich Islands, and Chile for the first time. "While most of these initial attempts had limited success, they do reveal that Brigham Young and his associates took very seriously the scriptural injunction to carry the gospel" to all the world, argues historian David J. Whittaker.[2]

By the end of 1852, just fifteen years after the first Latter-day Saint apostles traveled to England, the 50,000-member American sect had evolved into a largely British religious tradition. Its center of gravity, although not its headquarters, had shifted across the Atlantic Ocean to the potteries and industrial centers of the United Kingdom. That year there were at least 10,000 Latter-day Saints in Utah Territory, 1,000 in eastern North America, and 900 in the California Mission. In contrast, there were three times as many members in Europe: about 32,500 in the British Mission, 1,100 in the Scandinavian Mission, 60 in the German Mission, 300

1. Smith, History, vol. D-1, 1539; Smith, journal, April 19, 1843, in Hedges et al., *Joseph Smith Papers, Journals, Volume 2*, 370.
2. See Whittaker, "Brigham Young and the Missionary Enterprise," 90–91; see also Neilson and Waite, *Settling the Valley, Proclaiming the Gospel*, 114.

in the French Mission, and 200 in the Italian Mission. (Additionally, there were 950 in the Sandwich Islands Mission [Hawaii], 1,500 in the Society Islands Mission [French Polynesia], 70 in the Australia Mission, and some converts in the East India Mission.)[3]

The church's shift into a transnational spiritual movement further accelerated in the summer of 1852 in dramatic fashion. Young and his counselors in the First Presidency planned a special missionary conference in the newly constructed adobe Salt Lake Tabernacle on the temple block. Over the weekend of August 28–29, church leaders made two landmark announcements over the pioneer pulpit: a flurry of global mission assignments and a spirited defense of plural marriage.

Church leaders strategically held their conference in the summer heat to help the newly called missionaries travel over the mountain passes to the west and east before the winter snows. "We have come together to day," President Heber C. Kimball explained to the gathered Latter-day Saints that Saturday morning, "to hold a special conference to transact business, a month earlier than usual, inasmuch as there are elders to be selected to go to the nations of the earth, and they want an earlier start than formerly. There will probably be elders chosen to go to the four quarters of the globe to transact business, preach the Gospel, &c."[4] During the Saturday afternoon session, the First Presidency assigned one hundred men to proselytize in distant lands, the largest cohort of full-time elders in the church's three-decade history, as documented in the special conference meeting minutes featured in appendix 1.[5] Men (and their wives and children) were surprised to learn that they had been called to preach in the distant lands of Europe, Africa, Asia,

3. Plewe, "State of the Church in 1852," 234–36.

4. Church leaders also held their regular fall general conference meetings on October 6–8, 1852. See "Minutes of the General Conference . . . ," *Deseret News*, October 16, 1852.

5. *Minutes of Conference* was initially published as a *Deseret News* extra in Salt Lake City, Utah, September 14, 1852. See appendix 1, 285–316 herein. Ten days earlier, the first newspaper mention of the historic gathering was printed: "The Special Conference," *Deseret News*, September 4, 1852. The initial "extra" was republished in a regular newspaper edition as "Minutes of Conference," *Deseret News*, September 18, 1852, about three weeks after the event.

and the Pacific Isles, as documented in the missionary register found in appendix 2. "That was the way things happened in Utah. You could be an ordinary man," historian Laurel Thatcher Ulrich explains, "then, all of a sudden, you were sent off to save the world."[6]

On Sunday morning, August 29, Apostle Orson Pratt publicly acknowledged and defended the church's practice of polygamy for the first time. It had been instituted by Joseph Smith more than a decade earlier and was conducted with increasing openness by Latter-day Saint patriarchs in the intervening years.[7] Though polygamy was no secret to the nation, the church's open admission helped ratchet up tension that would lead to conflict with the United States government for more than fifty years. "From then on, church leaders publically endorsed the practice as a fundamental, even defining, aspect of Mormonism and integrated the practice into a broader vision of Mormon political philosophy," historian Christine Talbot argues. "The open practice of plural marriage added new dimensions to Mormon doctrine that, combined with earlier controversies, produced an insurmountable distance between Mormon and white middle-class Protestant Americans."[8] The doctrine's public promulgation would also present long-term challenges to Latter-day Saint elders called to preach during the second half of the nineteenth century—a painful theme that emerges often in their personal letters and subsequent narratives.[9]

These missionary assignments came at a tenuous time, while the pioneers were still literally trying not to starve to death in their desolate Great Basin kingdom.[10] Limited financial and human resources, coupled with competing institutional projects, forced church leaders to make heart-wrenching decisions. How to fulfill their divine mandate to "build Zion" at home and to "warn the nations" abroad, while at the same time

6. Ulrich, *House Full of Females*, 239.

7. Crawley, *Descriptive Bibliography of the Mormon Church*, 2:354–57. See Whittaker, "Bone in the Throat," 293–314; Daynes, *More Wives Than One*; and Gordon, *Mormon Question*, 22–23.

8. Talbot, *Foreign Kingdom*, 33.

9. In addition to the narratives featured in this volume, see Ulrich, *House Full of Females*, chapter 10.

10. Neilson and Waite, *Settling the Valley, Proclaiming the Gospel*, 11–13.

meeting the temporal and spiritual needs of the Saints and the entire human family across time and space, weighed heavily on the hearts of Latter-day Saint authorities settled in the Great Salt Lake Valley.

Literary scholar Terryl L. Givens, in his history of church culture, argues that Latter-day Saints may be best understood historically as a paradoxical people. "A field of tension seems a particularly apt way to characterize Mormon thought," he explains. "Mormonism, a system in which Joseph Smith collapsed sacred distance to bring a whole series of opposites into radical juxtaposition, seems especially rife with paradox—or tensions that only appear to be logical contradictions." Givens insightfully frames his cultural study around four of the most prominent of these pairs: authoritarianism versus individualism, certainty versus learning, sacred versus quotidian, and exile versus integration.[11] His resulting study is illuminating and demonstrates how these ongoing oppositions have helped shape Latter-day Saint culture since the antebellum age in America.

As we have immersed ourselves intellectually into the nineteenth-century world of the church, we have come to appreciate that there were at least two additional paradoxes pressing on the minds of Latter-day Saint leaders and laity during the first decade of pioneering in Utah. As Reid L. Neilson and Nathan N. Waite document in their companion volume to this book, there was an ongoing tension between the prophetic priorities to settle the valley in Utah and simultaneously proclaim the gospel abroad during this pioneer era.[12] "Missionaries were expanding the work worldwide, opening one new land after another, although long-term efforts were gradually focusing on a few fruitful countries," cartographer Brandon Plewe similarly describes this paradox. On the other hand, groups of Latter-day Saints increasingly immigrated to relatively isolated Utah Territory. "These competing efforts would continue throughout the rest of the nineteenth century."[13]

Brigham Young and his fellow church leaders struggled to find the proper balance between their church's competing (and complementary) colonization and evangelization programs. Prioritizing temporal and

---

11. Givens, *People of Paradox*, xiii–xvii.
12. Neilson and Waite, *Settling the Valley, Proclaiming the Gospel*, 1–31.
13. Plewe, "State of the Church in 1852," 243.

spiritual imperatives with limited human and financial resources required the wisdom of biblical Solomon. Any adult men they assigned to help settle the villages springing up throughout the Intermountain West meant fewer missionaries they could send abroad to teach and gather new converts to Zion. The Latter-day Saints considered anyone who had not received baptism under proper priesthood authority, at home or abroad, among those needing salvation. Young's calling of over one hundred men in August 1852 to cross geographical space across the globe to win converts exemplifies this missionary impulse. Ideally, their converts would then gather with their families to Zion, bringing with them the means to help colonize in Utah and aid their fellow pioneer Saints. These new immigrants could later serve as missionaries themselves, often to their former homelands, and convert others, ensuring that there was always a growing number of settlers at home and missionaries abroad.

An additional tension that emerges during this frontier era was the church leadership's wrestle with eschatological time and evangelistic priorities. To whom should they first offer the message and ordinances of salvation in the last days: *the living or the dead*? This was not a question that their fellow Christians were asking themselves. Despite the Apostle Paul's reference to his fellow Saints "who are baptized for the dead" (1 Corinthians 15:29; see also Doctrine and Covenants 128), the Latter-day Saints became the first (and only) Christians in the modern age to institutionally shoulder the divine responsibility to redeem the entire human family.[14] For believers, it was not "salvation of the living" or "salvation of the dead" but both. The only question was timing.

Church members felt compelled theologically to cross earthly time and this mortal sphere, which added an additional dimension to their already complicated evangelistic outreach. Smith first taught this distinctive Latter-day Saint doctrine in August 1840, while preaching at a public funeral in Nauvoo, Illinois. According to Smith's dictated revelations, all of God's earthly offspring—alive or dead—would be held to the same standards and be given equal opportunities to learn the commandments and accept the priesthood ordinances required for salvation in the mortal or postmortal

---

14. See Paulsen, Cook, and Mason, "Theological Underpinnings of Baptism for the Dead," 101–16.

Christen Dalsgaard, *Mormons Visit a Country Carpenter*. © Intellectual Reserve, Inc.

life, prior to the Final Judgment and Resurrection. Months later the prophet reasoned, "If we can, by the authority of the Priesthood of the Son of God, baptize a man in the name of the Father, of the Son, and of the Holy Ghost, for the remission of sins, it is just as much our privilege to act as an agent, and be baptized for the remission of sins for and in behalf of our dead kindred, who have not heard the Gospel, or the fullness of it."[15] Early Latter-day Saints rejoiced at this expansive theology, which permitted them to redeem vicariously their kindred dead. Since the Nauvoo period, Latter-day Saints have not struggled theologically with the destiny of the unevangelized, unlike their fellow Christians.

While the living could participate in these salvific ordinances for themselves, the dead would have to depend upon the living to act as proxy for them in the same ordinances. Moreover, all rituals for the salvation of the dead would have to be performed in Latter-day Saint temples, consecrated for that very purpose, the prophet taught. Latter-day Saints

15.   Smith, History, vol. C-1, 61.

constructed a specially made font in the Nauvoo Temple's basement to perform proxy baptisms for the dead, to aid in their work for the salvation of the dead. This doctrinal innovation has proven to be both a blessing and a burden for believers. Latter-day Saints are expected to become "saviors on Mount Zion" for their ancestors reaching back to the original family in Eden during their mortal or millennial estate.[16]

This redemptive work for the dead was resumed in Utah during the same years that the "missionaries of 1852" went out to the nations of the world. Just as they had embraced the opportunity to baptize their kindred dead in the Nauvoo Temple, the Latter-day Saints in Utah regularly participated in proxy baptisms for their deceased loved ones. Brigham Young and the First Presidency desperately needed more people to build another temple in the West, but on this August occasion, they prioritized the competing value of missionary work for the living. But living and breathing converts from Europe, Asia, and Africa promised to be future participants in the work for the salvation of the dead, just as they would help build Zion in Utah upon their arrival. It proved to be a virtuous cycle in the future, to be sure, but it was one fraught with tension in the present moment.

Within two months of the August 1852 conference, nearly all the missionaries embarked for their respective fields of labor. Unable to highlight their hundred-plus individual stories, we have relied upon the autobiographical writings of eight men to illuminate their shared and disparate experiences, including how the news of polygamy impacted their proselytizing. In part 1, "Evangelizing in the Atlantic World," we focus on the narratives of Dan Jones and the Wales Mission, Orson Spencer and the Prussia Mission, Edward Stevenson and the Gibraltar Mission, and Jesse Haven

---

16. After Smith's murder, Young performed the final ordinance work in the Nauvoo Temple on February 8, 1846, just as the Latter-day Saints began their Exodus to the American West. On July 28, 1847, days after he arrived in the Great Salt Lake Valley, he marked the location for a new temple where they could resume their work for the salvation of the living and the dead. The Salt Lake Temple, begun in April 1853, took four decades to complete before it was dedicated in April 1893. In the meantime, leaders performed temple ordinances in the public Council House (1851–55) and the private Endowment House (1855–89), both located in downtown Salt Lake City, a stone's throw from the temple building site. Berrett, "Endowment Houses," in *Encyclopedia of Mormonism*, 2:456.

and the Cape of Good Hope Mission. Part 2 tells the story of "Evangelizing in the Pacific World," through the records of Benjamin Johnson and the Sandwich Islands Mission, James Lewis and the China Mission, Chauncey West and the Siam and Hindoostan Missions, and Augustus Farnham and the Australia Mission.

This volume brings to the forefront the paradoxes and challenges Latter-day Saint leaders faced during the early 1850s, as they sought to both settle the valley and proclaim the gospel, as well as provide salvation for both the living and the dead. While chronicling the first century of the restored church of Jesus Christ in 1930, Assistant Church Historian Brigham H. Roberts made an audacious declaration about the missionaries called in August 1852: "Thus did the Church of the Latter-day Saints in these years . . . seek to fulfill the initial obligation given to that church in the very opening of the New Dispensation, namely, to preach the gospel of the kingdom to every nation, and kindred, and tongue, and people." He continued his claim with one long laudatory sentence, which begs contemplation (and challenge) by anyone studying nineteenth-century Christian missiology in America:

> And if the numerical and financial strength of the church be taken into account, or rather its weakness in these respects be taken into account, and if the circumstance of the location of the saints in an undeveloped and comparatively isolated country in the mountain interior of America be also considered, the splendor of this missionary spirit, and the wonder of the journeys of these missionaries to such distant lands, and their achievements in the face of all the hardships and hindrances to be endured and overcome—if all this be considered, it will render these missionary enterprises the most wonderful manifestations of Christian zeal and enthusiasm—the largest and most earnest service undertaken, within the same space of time, for God and man, since the days of the apostles of the early Christian church.[17]

---

17. Roberts, *Comprehensive History of the Church*, 4:75–76.

Part 1

EVANGELIZING IN THE ATLANTIC WORLD

1

DAN JONES AND
THE WALES MISSION

Historical Introduction

"IN NO PLACE HARDLY HAVE I PREACHED without a few hundreds of attentive hearers, and not unfrequently a couple of thousands," Dan Jones reported on his second mission to Wales in September 1853. Jones, a native Welshman, had been sent to preach the restored gospel in Wales between 1845 and 1849, and he exhibited a natural talent for preaching in a nation that was especially receptive to the message of the Latter-day Saints. So prosperous was this mission that church leaders called him to serve there again in 1852, and of the eight missionaries featured in this volume, Jones saw by far the greatest number of converts. Over the course of his mission, he visited various church conferences, preached to densely packed crowds, organized branches of the church, responded to attacks by local clergy and others, and published tracts. He had a major role in bringing a sizable group of Welsh converts into the church and subsequently into Utah Territory, both in 1849, when he returned from his first mission, and in 1856, when he returned from his second.

Dan Jones. Courtesy of Church History Library.

The Early Life of Dan Jones, 1810–44

Dan Jones was born in 1810 in Flintshire, Wales, to Thomas and Ruth Jones. He went to sea by age seventeen and became a mariner, perhaps even traveling around the Cape of Good Hope in South Africa and visiting India, among other places. After marrying Jane Melling in 1837, he immigrated to the United States about 1840 and became a boat captain, earning the title "Captain Dan Jones." In 1842, he became part owner of a steamboat called the *Maid of Iowa*, and as its captain, he would transport Latter-day Saints from a sawmill in Wisconsin to Nauvoo via the Mississippi River. After hearing unfavorable reports of the Saints, Jones investigated church doctrines and was baptized on January 19, 1843. That April, the *Maid of Iowa* carried a group of Saints to Nauvoo, and according to tradition, upon their arrival, Joseph Smith stepped aboard, put his hand on the head of small-statured Dan Jones, and reportedly proclaimed, "God bless this little man."[1]

The prophet subsequently purchased a half interest in the *Maid of Iowa* and became a joint owner of the steamboat, which Jones piloted frequently on church business.[2] Jones spent the nights of June 25 and 26, 1844, with Joseph and Hyrum Smith in Carthage Jail. In a letter to Thomas Bullock, Jones reminisced that on the last night in jail, Joseph Smith told him, "You

1. Dennis, *Call of Zion*, 1, 79n6; Jones, "Martyrdom of Joseph Smith and His Brother Hyrum," 79; Jenson, *Latter-day Saint Biographical Encyclopedia*, 3:658; Christensen, "Life and Contributions of Captain Dan Jones," 4–14.
2. Christensen, "Life and Contributions of Captain Dan Jones," 7–10; Leonard, *Nauvoo*, 150–51.

will see Wales and fulfill the mission appointed you ere you die."[3] The next morning, on June 27, Jones visited Governor Thomas Ford and asked for better military protection. When Jones returned to the jail, the guards denied him entry. He was given a letter by Almon Babbitt with a request from Smith to take it to Mr. Browning in Quincy, Illinois. As Jones was about to depart on his horse, which he had previously arranged to be ready for him, a mob surrounded him, but he managed to escape and departed on the wrong road, fortuitously avoiding a dozen soldiers sent to waylay him. Jones was away from Carthage when the mob murdered Joseph and Hyrum Smith.[4] Jones boarded a boat traveling on the Mississippi River; when it stopped near Warsaw, Illinois, he hid under a mattress and remained concealed from a mob that intended to hang him.[5] To Jones and other Latter-day Saints, these narrow escapes from death were a fulfillment of prophecy that enabled him to later labor in Wales, just as Smith had said.

First Mission to Wales and Settlement in Utah, 1845–52

In 1837, Joseph Smith called Apostle Heber C. Kimball to open missionary work across the ocean in the British Isles. As the work progressed, missionary efforts expanded into Wales, with Henry Royle and Frederick Cook being the first officially assigned to the country. By the end of 1840, there were more than one hundred converts in North Wales. Thanks to the efforts of William Henshaw and others in South Wales, branches of the church were organized in 1843, and on April 6, 1844, the Merthyr Tydfil Conference[6] was organized, the country's first. But Henshaw spoke only

---

3. Jones, "Martyrdom of Joseph and Hyrum Smith," 10; see also Jones, "Martyrdom of Joseph Smith and His Brother Hyrum," 101; Smith, History, Vol. F-1, June 26, 1844, 173.

4. Jones, "Martyrdom of Joseph Smith and His Brother Hyrum," 79–109; "Home Intelligence—Wales," *Millennial Star* 16, no. 26 (July 1, 1854): 414; Christensen, "Life and Contributions of Captain Dan Jones," 15–18; Jenson, *Latter-day Saint Biographical Encyclopedia*, 3:658–59; Leonard, *Nauvoo*, 384–90.

5. Jones, "Martyrdom of Joseph Smith and His Brother Hyrum," 80, 107–8.

6. A conference was a geographical ecclesiastical unit consisting of several branches. Merthyr Tydfil is an ancient town in southern Wales. It was the country's industrial

English and not Welsh, and he and many of the other missionaries were limited in their efforts.[7]

When Dan Jones arrived in January 1845, there were already two hundred converts in South Wales. But Jones initially labored in North Wales, where he witnessed the conversion of only three people during his first year.[8] However, at the end of 1845, he was transferred to Merthyr Tydfil in South Wales. There in the heartland of the country, Apostle Wilford Woodruff put him in charge of all the country's missionary work. As part of his proselytizing efforts, Jones authored and published many tracts and other works, including a periodical called *Prophwyd y Jubili* (Prophet of the Jubilee).[9] Jones also called for the new converts to gather to Zion, though "Zion" had switched from Nauvoo to Utah during his absence. As many of the Welsh planned to leave their native country, antagonistic publications and sentiments raged, often taking aim at Dan Jones specifically. "You would have thought that I had seven horns, if not as many heads," Jones reported. "The scenes here are very like the continental rabbles of Missouri, &c., and still raging worse and hotter daily. You need not be surprised should you hear of Carthage tragedies ere long."[10] Nevertheless, he was a dynamic speaker and seemed to relish the sense of battle between him and the local clergy. Despite opposition, Jones's efforts were fruitful: by the time

center in the mid-nineteenth century. *Merriam-Webster's Geographical Dictionary*, s.v. "Merthyr Tydfil"; Dennis, *Call of Zion*, 1.

7. Jenson, *Encyclopedic History of the Church*, 936–37; Dennis, *Call of Zion*, 1; Christensen, "Life and Contributions of Captain Dan Jones," 20–22.

8. Dennis, *Zion's Trumpet: 1854 Welsh Mormon Periodical*, xiii.

9. On his first mission to Wales, Dan Jones published *Prophwyd y Jubili* (Prophet of the Jubilee), a periodical in Welsh, from 1846 to 1848. As Jones prepared to leave his mission, he established the *Udgorn Seion* (Zion's Trumpet) to replace *Prophwyd y Jubili* and to be published by John Davis. Both papers promoted and defended the Restoration as official church publications for Welsh readers. Davis oversaw the publication of *Udgorn Seion* until 1854, when Jones succeeded him as editor; Daniel Daniels took over in 1856, Benjamin Evans took over in 1858, and George Q. Cannon took over in 1861. The periodical ceased publication in 1862. Dennis, *Zion's Trumpet: 1856 & 1857 Welsh Mormon Periodical*, xix–xxx.

10. Dan Jones, "Letter to Elder Orson Spencer," *Millennial Star* 9, no. 20 (October 15, 1847): 318–19.

he departed Wales after laboring there for four years, the Latter-day Saint population of the country exceeded three thousand. In February 1849, Jones led a few hundred Saints aboard the *Buena Vista* to depart for their new home in America.[11]

After arriving in the port city of New Orleans in 1849, Jones led his group up the Mississippi and Missouri Rivers to Kanesville (Council Bluffs), Iowa, where he established a Welsh enclave called Cambria's Camp for those who could not afford to go to Utah at that time. Jones, along with the approximately eighty Welsh pioneers who were financially able to travel to Salt Lake City that year, became part of the George A. Smith wagon company that arrived in Salt Lake City in late October 1849.[12] Weeks after his arrival, he entered into plural marriage by marrying his second wife, Elizabeth Jones Lewis, who had been part of the George A. Smith company with him. In late 1849 and early 1850, President Brigham Young asked Apostle Parley P. Pratt to oversee an expedition to southern Utah to find new places for settlement. Jones was one of many men assigned to the journey; part of his purpose on the trip was to search for a rumored Welsh Indian tribe.[13] After returning to his home in Salt Lake City, Jones finished constructing a sailing vessel, the *Salicornia*, used by Howard Stansbury and the United States Army of Topographical Engineers to survey the Great Salt Lake.[14] In September 1850, Isaac Morley chose a hundred men, including Jones and his family, to help settle the town of Manti. Jones was elected as its mayor in April 1851, serving in this capacity until he left on his second mission to Wales in the fall of 1852.[15]

---

11. Dennis, *Call of Zion*, 1–31; Jenson, *Encyclopedic History of the Church*, 936–37; Christensen, "Life and Contributions of Captain Dan Jones," 19–31.

12. Dennis, *Call of Zion*, 36–69; Christensen, "Life and Contributions of Captain Dan Jones," 46–55.

13. Smart and Smart, *Over the Rim*, 124–26, 227–28. According to Welsh folklore, a prince named Madoc sailed from Wales in 1170 AD and landed in America, and his descendants survived and carried on Welsh language and tradition somewhere on the continent. The legend became vastly popular in America in the eighteenth and nineteenth centuries, as various groups tried to identify Welsh Indians. See Williams, *Madoc*.

14. Van Alfen, "Sail and Steam," 207.

15. Christensen, "Life and Contributions of Captain Dan Jones," 53–72.

UDGORN SEION,

NEU

SEREN Y SAINT;

YN CYNNWYS

EGWYDDORION "GORUCHWYLIAETH CYFLAWN-DER YR AMSEROEDD,"

MEWN

TRAETHODAU, LLYTHYRON, HANESION, PRYDYDDIAETH, &c.

" A mi a osodais wylwyr arnoch chwi, gan ddywedyd, Gwrandewch ar sain yr udgorn."—JER. VI, 17.

" Holl drigolion y byd, a phreswylwyr y ddaear, gwelwch pan gyfodo efe faner ar y mynyddoedd, a chlywch pan udgano ag udgorn."—ESA. XVIII, 3.

CYFROL VII.

ABERTAWY:

ARGRAFFWYD, CYHOEDDWYD, AC AR WERTH GAN D. JONES.

1854.

Title page of *Udgorn Seion* (Zion's Trumpet), edited by Dan Jones.

6

Second Mission to Wales, 1852–56

When Dan Jones was called on his second proselytizing mission in August 1852, it was under more difficult circumstances. Whereas his first mission permitted him to bring his wife Jane along, for his second mission he had to leave behind not one but two wives, Jane and Elizabeth, and several children, many of them Elizabeth's children from her first marriage. Jones headed across the eastern United States before sailing to the United Kingdom in company with Thomas E. Jeremy and Daniel Daniels.[16] These two companions had been baptized in Wales while Jones was serving his first mission, and both had previously sailed with him on the *Buena Vista*.[17] When Jones arrived in Wales in December, local Saints flocked around to welcome him back. He served as second counselor to mission president William S. Phillips before becoming president of the mission again in January 1854, at which time he also became editor of *Udgorn Seion*.[18] He also resumed publishing missionary pamphlets and tracts.[19]

On this second mission, Jones found the Welsh less receptive to his message. Persecutions raged, with one particular factor being especially significant: polygamy. His first mission had taken place before the 1852 public announcement of plural marriage, but Jones's second call came at the same time the Latter-day Saints' unconventional marital practice was announced to the world. On his way to Wales, Jones translated Joseph Smith's 1843 revelation on plural marriage into Welsh, which was

16. The *Millennial Star* in November 1852 also mentioned an Edward Griffin in the list of missionaries called to Wales, but the list was compiled from various letters and not from official sources. The conference minutes and the First Presidency's Eighth General Epistle, both published in the *Deseret News*, did not mention Edward Griffin. "Important Special Conference," *Millennial Star* 14, no. 38 (November 13, 1852): 600; "Minutes of Conference," *Deseret News*, September 18, 1852; "Eighth General Epistle," *Deseret News*, October 16, 1852.

17. See "Jeremy, Thomas Evans," and "Daniels, Daniel," in appendix 2, pp. 337, 325–26 herein.

18. Dennis, *Zion's Trumpet: 1853 Welsh Mormon Periodical*, xvi; Christensen, "Life and Contributions of Captain Dan Jones," 31–35.

19. Dennis, *Defending the Faith*, xv.

published in the January 1, 1853, issue of *Udgorn Seion*.[20] The practice generated significant disapproval among those of other faiths. "The capital which the priests make of the 'plurality' has prevented the people investigating heretofore, although it has had a salutary influence upon the Saints, and it is getting old and forgotten by the world gradually," Jones wrote.[21]

Despite the public opposition from many, Jones had incredible missionary success. People crowded into buildings and followed him from town to town to hear him speak.[22] "The increasing audiences the Elders obtain generally, and the lively interest which the public manifest in the all-absorbing topic of 'Mormonism,' more than intimate that it is neither dead nor dying; . . . a thousand-and-one other sweet-scented nosegays, may divert their attention a while, but, like 'Jonah's gourd,' they fade and perish, and, when the Spirit of truth, like a breeze from Paradise, blows away their stench, 'Mormonism'—the same impregnable and ever-living theme, still haunts them closer than ever before; . . . hundreds, if not thousands, now stand aghast on the brink, with nothing apparently withholding but shame that they have been so long scared by the baseless bug-bears of their clerical hob-goblin story-tellers."[23] Two thousand Welsh were baptized into the church between 1853 and 1856, when Jones returned to Utah.[24]

During his presidency, Jones also helped with collecting money for the Perpetual Emigrating Fund, which provided loans to needy Latter-day Saints traveling to Utah, and oversaw another migration of Saints to the Salt Lake Valley. He was delighted to see these converts' enthusiasm to gather: "I beg to assure you that I would not wish to see a greater desire for that than is evidently pervading every class, in every locality. 'Do help *me* to go to Zion;' 'When shall I go home?' 'Oh, do try to help me off this

20. Revelation, July 12, 1843 [Doctrine and Covenants 132], at Joseph Smith Papers website, josephsmithpapers.org; Dennis, *Zion's Trumpet: 1853 Welsh Mormon Periodical*, xvii, 8–16.

21. "Home Correspondence," *Millennial Star* 16, no. 48 (December 2, 1854): 766; p. 19 herein; Christensen, "Life and Contributions of Captain Dan Jones," 31–34.

22. "Home Intelligence," *Millennial Star* 15, no. 45 (November 5, 1853): 733–34; pp. 13–14 herein.

23. "Home Correspondence," *Millennial Star* 17, no. 34 (August 25, 1855): 539–40.

24. Christensen, "Life and Contributions of Captain Dan Jones," 31–35.

time,' are so often reiterated in my hearing, and plead with such anxiety and earnestness, that they tingle in my ears, asleep as well as awake."[25] From April to May 1856, Jones oversaw more than seven hundred Saints, organized into eleven wards, aboard the *S. Curling*,[26] sailing from Liverpool[27] to Boston.[28] These Welsh converts then made their way to Iowa by rail, where they outfitted before crossing the plains to Utah. Most of them joined the Edward Bunker handcart company, the third company to test the inexpensive handcart experiment, arriving safely in Salt Lake City in early October.[29] Jones did not travel with this company; he had been assigned to head a wagon company, but due to illness, John Hunt instead headed the wagon company, and Jones joined Apostle Franklin D. Richards's group. Richards and his companions moved swiftly across the plains, passed the ill-fated Willie and Martin companies, and brought word of their plight to Salt Lake City in time for the October 1856 general conference. Jones did not participate in the rescue of these groups because of sickness.[30]

Postmission Life, 1856–62

After returning to Utah, Dan Jones spent the remainder of his life less dynamically. He married a third wife, Mary Matilda LaTrielle, and lived in Salt Lake City, where he continued to minister among the local Welsh

---

25. "Report of the Church in Wales," *Millennial Star* 18, no. 16 (April 19, 1856): 242.

26. The *S. Curling* was built in Thomaston, Maine, in 1854 and was owned and piloted by Captain Sanders Curling, also of Thomaston. In 1855, the ship and Captain Curling transported 581 Latter-day Saints, under the leadership of Israel Barlow, from Liverpool to New York. Dan Jones led the second group of Latter-day Saints on this ship; the *S. Curling* departed Liverpool on April 19, 1856, and arrived in Boston on May 23. Sonne, *Ships, Saints, and Mariners*, 178–79.

27. Liverpool, on the northwestern coast of England, was the nation's primary port in the 1800s. The first missionaries to England arrived there in 1837. John Taylor began preaching in Liverpool in 1840, and there were many converts in the ensuing years. Between 1850 and 1869, more than 30,000 Latter-day Saints departed from Liverpool. *Merriam-Webster's Geographical Dictionary*, s.v. "Liverpool."

28. "Foreign Correspondence," *Millennial Star* 18, no. 27 (July 5, 1856): 427–30; p. 29 herein.

29. Mormon Pioneer Overland Travel database, s.v. "Edward Bunker Company (1856)."

30. Christensen, "Life and Contributions of Captain Dan Jones," 78–82.

population, rather than returning to Manti.[31] In 1857, he began sailing the *Timely Gull*, a ship belonging to Brigham Young, to transport cargo to sell at various spots on the Great Salt Lake.[32] He moved to Provo, Utah, by 1859. His first wife, Jane, died on February 24, 1861, and Jones passed away from tuberculosis in Provo on January 3, 1862, at age fifty-one.[33]

Dan Jones's missionary companions likewise served in the church for the remainder of their lives. Daniel Daniels took over Jones's duties as mission president and editor of *Udgorn Seion* from 1856 until 1857. He moved to Salt Lake City and later Brigham City, Utah, and Malad, Idaho, where he served as bishop from 1866 to 1877 before dying in 1879.[34] Thomas Jeremy departed from Wales in 1855 and sailed back to the United States with Edward Stevenson.[35] He served a second mission, acting as president of the Welsh Mission from 1860 to 1864, and he labored again in the British Isles from 1875 to 1876. He served on the high council of the Salt Lake Stake for nearly twenty-three years, from 1864 to 1887, before dying in Salt Lake City in 1891.[36]

Dan Jones's Family Life

Dan Jones married Jane Melling in 1837 in Denbigh, Wales, and she immigrated to America with him. Jane accompanied Jones on his first mission to Wales. When he was instructed to return to Utah and to bring a group of Welsh Saints with him, he planned to leave Jane and their new little daughter Claudia in the care of the Saints in Wales until he could return on a second mission. However, Jane, not wanting to be left behind, traveled

31. Christensen, "Life and Contributions of Captain Dan Jones," 82–84.
32. Jenson, *Latter-day Saint Biographical Encyclopedia*, 3:660; Christensen, "Life and Contributions of Captain Dan Jones," 85; Dennis, *Zion's Trumpet: 1856 & 1857 Welsh Mormon Periodical*, 204. Brigham Young had the *Timely Gull* built in 1854; it was wrecked at Antelope Island in late 1858. Morgan, *Great Salt Lake*, 253–57.
33. Christensen, "Life and Contributions of Captain Dan Jones," 86–88; Jenson, *Latter-day Saint Biographical Encyclopedia*, 3:660.
34. Dennis, *Zion's Trumpet: 1856 & 1857 Welsh Mormon Periodical*, xviii.
35. See chapter 3, "Edward Stevenson and the Gibraltar Mission," herein.
36. Jenson, *Latter-day Saint Biographical Encyclopedia*, 2:653.

with her four-week-old infant daughter on board the *Emblem*, a ship that left Liverpool on March 12, 1849, two weeks after Jones had left on the *Buena Vista*.[37]

During that first mission, Jones met Elizabeth Jones Lewis, a Welsh convert. Elizabeth sold property to her brother-in-law for three thousand pounds to finance many of the Saints' travel expenses.[38] Jones and Elizabeth departed from Wales in 1849. Elizabeth wrote: "I had paid the passage of forty persons across the ocean and up to Council Bluffs, and from there I provided for and paid the expenses of thirty-two to Salt Lake City. Having every comfort that could be obtained, we perhaps made the trip under as favorable circumstances as any company that has ever accomplished the journey."[39] Jane and her newborn, Claudia, caught up with Jones and Elizabeth at Council Bluffs, Iowa. The company reached Salt Lake City in October of 1849, and on November 8, two weeks after their arrival in Salt Lake, Dan Jones was sealed to both Jane Melling Jones and Elizabeth Lewis.

In 1851, Jones traveled with his wives, Jane and Elizabeth, to settle in Manti, Utah. When Jones left on his mission in 1852, he had two daughters living: Claudia, Jane's daughter, and Ruth, Elizabeth's daughter. Jane bore a son, Joseph Dan, the following May. During this period, Jane would drive an ox team from Manti to Salt Lake to exchange butter, cheese, grain, and other goods for cloth, thread, and other things not obtainable in Manti.[40]

Elizabeth was caring for six children from her first marriage. She and Jones had a daughter, Ruth, and after she moved to Provo, Utah, she also gave birth to a son, Brigham, just barely after Jones had left Utah.[41] She appears to have struggled to support her family during this time, as referenced in a discourse in which Brigham Young reproved the Saints for not paying debts: "There is a sister from Wales, the wife of brother Dan Jones, who has expended thousands of pounds to help the poor to this place, and they have cursed her all the day long, and she has now to labor hard for the

---

37. Dennis, *Call of Zion*, 112.
38. Nash, "Isaac B. Nash Family Histories & Documents," 11–12.
39. Tullidge, *Women of Mormondom*, 460.
40. "Jones, Claudia—History of Claudia Jones Dennis," Welsh Mormon History.
41. Josephine Lewis Anderson, "Elizabeth Jones Lewis Jones—Biography," Welsh Mormon History.

support of herself and children."[42] During his mission, Elizabeth requested and was given a bill of divorcement from Jones. The reasons for her request are unknown. She remarried Dan four months before his death and was appointed the administrator of his estate when he died.[43] She continued living in Salt Lake City until her death in 1895.

On February 18, 1857, Dan married a third wife, Mary Matilda LaTrielle, who had traveled in the company Jones temporarily captained in 1856.[44] They had two children,[45] and Mary died in 1916.[46]

Source Note

While on his second mission, Dan Jones wrote seven letters that were published in the *Millennial Star*, the official church publication of the British Isles. These were addressed to President Samuel W. Richards and his brother Franklin D. Richards, who succeeded him as mission president.[47] We have herein reproduced four of the letters, which recount the mission's remarkable successes in the face of significant opposition. The letters describe masses of people gathering to hear Jones speak, converts being baptized, mobs and clergymen persecuting the Saints, and Jones

42. Brigham Young, "Necessity of Home Missions, Etc.," *Journal of Discourses*, 3:121.
43. Christensen, "Life and Contribution of Captain Dan Jones," 89–90.
44. Mormon Pioneer Overland Travel database, s.v. "John A. Hunt Company (1856)"; Welsh Mormon History, Immigrants, s.v. "Mary Matilda LaTrielle."
45. Christensen, "Life and Contribution of Captain Dan Jones," 88–89.
46. Welsh Mormon History, Immigrants, s.v. "Mary Matilda LaTrielle"; "Service Tuesday for Mary M. Vincent," *Salt Lake Tribune*, March 13, 1916.
47. "Home Intelligence," *Millennial Star* 15, no. 45 (November 5, 1853): 733–34; "Home Intelligence," *Millennial Star* 16, no. 17 (April 29, 1854): 269–70; "Home Correspondence," *Millennial Star* 16, no. 48 (December 2, 1854): 766–68; "Foreign Correspondence," *Millennial Star* 18, no. 27 (July 5, 1856): 427–30. We did not include the other three letters because of space limitations and because their contents were less relevant or less informative of Jones's mission experience. See "Home Intelligence—Wales," *Millennial Star* 16, no. 26 (July 1, 1854): 413–14; "Home Correspondence," *Millennial Star* 17, no. 34 (August 25, 1855): 538–40; "Report of the Church in Wales," *Millennial Star* 18, no. 16 (April 19, 1856): 241–45. Jones also wrote a letter to church president Brigham Young from Wales in 1855, which includes additional details about his mission. Dan Jones to Brigham Young, March 27, 1855, Incoming Correspondence, Brigham Young Office Files.

publishing defensive tracts. The final letter describes the journey of the seven hundred Welsh converts aboard the *S. Curling* as they sailed from Liverpool to Boston.

DOCUMENT TRANSCRIPTS

Dan Jones to Samuel W. Richards, September 29, 1853[48]

Merthyr Tydfil, September 29, 1853.
President S. W. Richards—

Dear Brother—I have had the pleasure of visiting a Conference every Sunday since I saw you, and have preached in the most populous places some four or five times every week besides. I am happy to say that the Lord in His goodness has bestowed His good Spirit upon me to overflowing. I was very kindly received by the Saints and the world everywhere, and I had the great pleasure of leaving the Saints in union, and fully determined to be up and doing, while the day lasted. In many places I found people who had travelled from twenty to thirty miles across hills and dales, purposely to meet me. I do believe that with the blessing of Him who owns the vineyard, it will blossom like the rose, so that it will bear a better crop than ever. In no place hardly have I preached without a few hundreds of attentive hearers, and not unfrequently a couple of thousands. For instance—in Bethesda, Carnarvonshire,[49] on a Sunday afternoon, a very large barn was prepared for the occasion, with a pulpit, &c. When I came in sight of the place, behold! a small field adjoining was nearly full, so that I had to crowd my way, and O! the eyes that stared at the "man of forty wives," they were like truckle

---

48. "Home Intelligence," *Millennial Star* 15, no. 45 (November 5, 1853): 733–34.

49. Bethesda is a town located in the former boundaries of Caernarvonshire, which used to be a county in northwest Wales. *Merriam-Webster's Geographical Dictionary*, s.v. "Caernarvonshire."

berries in milk! "Where will you preach?" inquired a loud voice from the far end. "In that big barn, if I can ever get there," was the reply. "You can't get in, for that was crammed full of people long ago," cried many voices. And so it was, pulpit and all! What a chance, thinks I! "Fetch a cart to the middle," was the next invention, which was scarcely said than done. Into the cart I mounted, and who that has not experienced the like can imagine the "glorious heaven below" which I realized the next two hours? Heaven's floodgates were thrown open, Pentecostal like![50] With open mouths, and tears of joy glistening in their eyes, did the mass unmoved drink down with greediness eternal truths. They were reluctant to have an intermission, many followed me, and the world contended who should have me to tea. Several promised to be baptized soon. That over, and six o'clock come, again they were there, and some congregations had brought their preachers with them—more than one got converted, too, as they admitted to me. Again over the mass I mounted my scaffold, and had as good attention as before, and as much power of the Spirit as I wished to have, for a couple of hours more; in fact, 'twas difficult to find a place for the "Amen." All were astonished, all believed, methinks! at least, if there was an unbeliever left he dared not say so. Till dark they stood there, and several voices begged of me to "preach to-morrow," saying, that "thousands more would come." I told them that I had an appointment in Bangor[51] then, five miles off. A general shout was heard—"Let us follow him to-morrow," and many of them did. I left six there to be baptized next day by the Elders. The Calvinistic Association[52] was commencing at Bangor then, but I sent the bell-man round,

---

50. In Acts 2, the followers of Jesus were gathered on the day of Pentecost, "and they were all filled with the Holy Ghost, and began to speak with other tongues, as the Spirit gave them utterance" (Acts 2:4). After the Apostle Peter preached, three thousand people were baptized.

51. Bangor is a city in northwest Wales. *Merriam-Webster's Geographical Dictionary*, s.v. "Bangor."

52. The Calvinistic Methodist Church, known today as the Presbyterian Church of Wales, grew out of eighteenth-century preaching by Griffith Jones, Howel Harris, and Daniel Rowland. The movement seceded from the Church of England in 1795 and became formally established in 1811. Proselytizing for the religion grew in the ensuing decades. *Oxford Dictionary of World Religions*, s.v. "Calvinistic Methodists"; Dennis, *Prophet of the Jubilee*, xxi.

and got hundreds of their hearers, and five at the close said they would be baptized. From there I had to be on the lope to Carnarvon,[53] &c., to enjoy similar scenes of blessedness. If I had had time to stay, I might have done more; but a streak of fire is kindled, and the Elders are blowing the bellows. God bless them.

Your affectionate brother,

D. Jones.

Dan Jones to Samuel W. Richards, April 3, 1854[54]

Merthyr, April 3, 1854.

President S. W. Richards—

Dear Brother—On the 25th and 26th ult. we enjoyed a good meeting of the East Glamorganshire Conference here.[55] All was peace and goodwill with the Priesthood and the Saints, much of the Spirit of God was enjoyed, all seeing eye to eye in all matters of business done; many responded to the call to go and open new places of preaching, two new Branches were organized, and fifty baptisms reported.

The Priesthood generally are realizing their duty of saving souls; they take hold with zeal in reformation, out-door preaching, tract distributing, and, better than all, they manifest a determination generally to *live* their religion before the world; the results are, that the Lord rewards their diligence by copious out-pourings of His Holy Spirit, nearly all the Branches in this Conference have received the various gifts of the Spirit, of late;[56] and I am cheered with similar good news from all the Conferences. Present prospects

---

53. Caernarfon is a port town in northwest Wales. It is home to a thirteenth-century castle. *Merriam-Webster's Geographical Dictionary*, s.v. "Caernarvon."

54. "Home Intelligence," *Millennial Star* 16, no. 17 (April 29, 1854): 269–70.

55. Glamorganshire was a county on the southern coast of Wales. It contained the cities of Cardiff and Swansea. *Merriam-Webster's Geographical Dictionary*, s.v. "Glamorganshire."

56. Gifts of the Spirit are "heavenly endowments" given by God through the Holy Ghost. These gifts include "tongues, prophecy, revelation, visions, healing, interpretation of tongues," and others. H. George Bickerstaff, "Gifts of the Spirit," in

flatter me that, by the aid and blessing of Him who owns the work, much good will be done, and there will be a great gathering into His fold.

The Presidents of other Conferences are alive to the importance of faithfully warning men this coming summer, and are preparing for the campaign with energy.

I have just returned from attending a Conference in Brecknockshire,[57] and I am happy to say that truly the Spirit of the Lord is there, and the prospects are cheering; love and union abound generally.

I intend visiting Monmouthshire[58] Conference next Sunday, where they have lately baptized about fifty.

I learn that the circulation of the *Star* and the *Udgorn* is increasing gradually, although the agents do not order more from the offices.

A few days ago, we had the pleasure of baptizing a neighbouring Baptist minister, and one of his local preachers.[59] Many of their former members came to witness their confirmation, when I had a good opportunity of laying the truth before them. They listened attentively and respectfully, and I believe that the spirit of truth impressed an unvarnished testimony upon their minds. The two brethren have received testimonies of the truth, and are zealously testifying unto others.

Encyclopedia of Mormonism, 2:544–46; Joseph Smith, "Church History," March 1, 1842, in Davidson et al., *Joseph Smith Papers, Histories, Volume 1*, 500.

57. Brecknockshire was a mountainous county in southeast Wales. *Merriam-Webster's Geographical Dictionary*, s.v. "Brecknockshire."

58. Monmouthshire was a county in southeast Wales, bordering England and right below Brecknockshire. *Merriam-Webster's Geographical Dictionary*, s.v. "Monmouthshire."

59. The Reverend John James was baptized "together with a young preacher who belonged to the same house of worship" in Cefn-coed-y-cymmer on March 19, 1854, by Thomas Jones, himself a convert from the Baptist faith. Thomas Jones recorded, "Brother J. James met with the people, in the Chapel of the Baptists, the next morning, for the purpose of terminating their obligation with one another; and a host came together in the afternoon, to witness the confirmation of the two brothers. My prayer henceforth is to God, for them to receive a solid witness for themselves, so they may call on all their old friends to come and seek the same blessing, and to rejoice together with them in this great grace." Thomas Jones, "Baptism of a Preacher," *Zion's Trumpet* 7, no. 12 (March 25, 1854), in Dennis, *Zion's Trumpet: 1854 Welsh Mormon Periodical*, 191.

The same day and hour, at another place, a Unitarian minister was baptized, who is a promising young man also. He never ceased praying for forty-nine hours after baptism, until the Lord blessed him with His Spirit in much power and demonstration.

The young man straightway went amongst his old associates, and testified of the truth. Instead of converting all before him, as he had anticipated, he was expelled from a college where he had been sometime graduating, his friends scorned and his parents disowned him, but he came here in good cheer, and says that he has found a better Father than the one he lost, and better friends.[60]

May the Lord bless the three with perseverance to endure all things, and make them a blessing to many of their old associates, many of whom are not far behind, they say.

Thus, you see, dear brother, that the Lord is crowning our labours with some success, although but preludes to a spontaneous harvest of souls, I trust. A spirit of inquiry is manifest in the world, and the crowds who come to hear preaching, indicate that the Lord has many more children in Wales yet.

I crave an interest in your prayers, to rightly administer the word of life to Saint and sinner, and for the prosperity of the kingdom of God in Wales.

With kind regards to yourself, brother [James] Linforth,[61] and the brethren in the office, and ever praying for your success in all things pertaining to your high and responsible calling, I am truly your brother, &c.,

D. Jones.

---

60. Thomas Jones wrote, "I am pleased to inform you that I received a letter from Carmarthen, last week, notifying me, after I had left my home, that they baptized a young Student enrolled in the School, where preachers are taught by men. He was confirmed at the water's edge; he gave himself to earnest prayer; and within forty-eight hours, he had a clear witness; but, because he spoke of what the Lord had done to his soul, he was turned out of the School, the Chapel, and the house of his father! Is it not strange, how the professors of Christianity hate the religion of Christ?" Jones, "Baptism of a Preacher," 191–92.

61. James Linforth (1827–99) served as assistant editor of the *Millennial Star* beginning in 1851, traveled to Utah in 1856, and was living in California by 1860. Crawley, *Descriptive Bibliography of the Mormon Church*, 1:111, 393; Mormon Pioneer Overland Travel database, s.v. "James Linforth."

Dan Jones to Franklin D. Richards, October 26, 1854[62]

Udgorn Seion Office, Swansea,[63] October 26, 1854.
President Richards.

Dear Brother—In accordance with your request through the *Star*, to be advised of the state of the work of God amongst the various nations over which you have the high honour to preside, I embrace this opportunity to inform you of the general features of the Church in Wales.

During the summer season the Priesthood have been diligent in out-of-door preaching, and have had more numerous and attentive audiences than heretofore; "camp meetings" have been the order of the season, especially where much opposition has been presented; and the combined influence of the Saints so assembled has never failed so far to move the prejudice, storm the strongest ramparts, and win conquest to the kingdom of God.

The weaker Conferences have been much strengthened by the aid of Elders and Priests from the stronger, who, together with many "volunteers" labouring in new grounds, sustained principally by tracts, have done much towards the spread of the Gospel; and I am pleased to see, by the renewed vigour of the officers generally, that they realise their responsibilities, and the importance of faithfully warning their fellow beings of impending dangers.

You can anticipate our future prospects of success when I say, what I have not been able to say so unexceptionably heretofore, that officers and Saints are united, so far as I know; and I have had the pleasure of visiting the majority of the Conferences of late; everywhere the Saints evince an increasing desire to excel in *living* their professions, which to me is a certain forerunner of paramount success.

Now, the weather being unfavourable to out-door preaching, the brethren manifest no less zeal to water the seed so profusely sown, by distributing tracts from house to house and selling them to the world, each having

---

62. "Home Correspondence," *Millennial Star* 16, no. 48 (December 2, 1854): 766–68.
63. Swansea is a coastal city in southern Wales. Many emigrating Welsh Latter-day Saints left from Swansea before going to Liverpool, England, to sail to America. *Merriam-Webster's Geographical Dictionary*, s.v. "Swansea."

his sphere appointed him weekly;[64] and truly it does the Saints, as well as the world, much good, because, as they say, the Lord blesses them with His Spirit abundantly in so doing. So that "Mormonism," so far from being in a dying or dead state, as many have flattered themselves, is humming about the ears of the priests and people, who feel quite alarmed already, and admit that this "imposture" threatens to be more dangerous than ever. You would be pleased to see the diligence of the Saints, in following the tracks of the clergy, priests, and Scripture readers, and all sorts of pedlars, with "Replies" to the falsehoods which they spread abroad, sometimes meeting in the same house, and then I leave you to judge who finds the door first! Truly their zeal is worthy of a better cause. But through the blessings of Him who owns the work, all their efforts are abortive to retard its onward march. The capital which the priests make of the "plurality" has prevented the people investigating heretofore, although it has had a salutary influence upon the Saints, and it is getting old and forgotten by the world gradually.

Baptisms have not been as numerous as we expect them to be shortly, although a few individuals are still being baptized everywhere. I will merely recite one out of many instances—even in Merthyr, the place where the very stones might have denounced a Gospel-hardened race,[65] the seed is sprouting like a tulip bed after a summer's shower—seventeen baptized and twenty backsliders returning in one Branch in one week. That most popular of preachers—the Cholera,[66] which has swept off hundreds in that vicinity of late, may have contributed some to accomplish the above; but I am glad to learn, that out of the many attacked by that "king of terrors,"

---

64. Nineteenth-century Latter-day Saint missionaries would publish pamphlets and other tracts to spread their message and to respond to criticisms from outsiders and former members. Distributing the tracts became an important part of the proselytizing effort. Whittaker, "Early Mormon Pamphleteering," 15–26, 85–99.

65. Jones might have taken the imagery of stones preaching from Luke 19. As Jesus was coming into Jerusalem, his followers praised God. The Pharisees told him to rebuke his disciples, and he responded, "I tell you that, if these should hold their peace, the stones would immediately cry out" (Luke 19:40).

66. At the time these missionaries visited, the world was suffering from the third cholera pandemic, which originated in India. Unsanitary conditions and global trade led to widespread cholera, a disease that dehydrates and can be particularly lethal if left untreated. Hays, *Epidemics and Pandemics*, 227–37.

no Saints have died there, and only two or three have I heard of elsewhere, the ordinance being their only antidote.[67]

In regard to myself, I never did feel a greater desire to further the purposes of God, so far as I understand them, nor more pleasure in it; I never fancied that I could do much, but my mite is as willing as the much of my brethren. My Counsellors—Elders [Thomas] Jeremy and [Daniel] Daniels, are very efficient and zealous men, of one heart and soul with myself in all things, and they are a great blessing to the Saints. May the Lord bless them for it.

I have lately published upwards of 50,000 Welsh tracts on the first principles, "Replies," and "Invitations," with the addresses, time of preaching, &c., for every Branch of note throughout the Principality, nearly all of which are in circulation, at the lowest rates, besides other Welsh tracts previously on hand, and a fair proportion of English, so that taking all into consideration we have a reasonable prospect for success when the spirit of truth accompanies them home to the honest heart.[68] The problem is solved, that tract distributing, so far from augmenting, is the best method of liquidating "old book debts,"[69] by winning new coworkers to that, as well as to every other laudable work; proving the force of the expression of

---

67. James 5:14 in the New Testament says, "Is any sick among you? let him call for the elders of the church; and let them pray over him, anointing him with oil in the name of the Lord." Since the beginning days of the church, elders placed oil on the head of the sick, put their hands on the afflicted's head, and offered a blessing, similar to a prayer. Bruce B. Clark, "Blessings," in *Encyclopedia of Mormonism*, 1:129.

68. Dan Jones authored more than a dozen pamphlets on his first mission to Wales and nearly two dozen on his second. This was in addition to *Prophwyd y Jubili*, *Udgorn Seion*, a hymnal, and a book of scriptural commentary. Dennis, *Defending the Faith*, xv.

69. In the 1850s, new publications printed at the *Millennial Star* office were given out on credit. This practice allowed more books and pamphlets to be printed and distributed, but debts for these works accumulated. Sometimes a missionary would incur a debt but not remain long enough to repay it, and local leaders often issued reports and lectures requesting payment. Whittaker, "Early Mormon Pamphleteering," 21–22.

one of old—"He which soweth sparingly shall reap sparingly;"[70] whereas, the liberal mind deviseth liberal means, and by his liberality shall he live.[71]

The old debts have been considered quite an impediment to the progress of the work in all the Conferences, but I am pleased that, of late, a new era has dawned upon us in that respect, by the abundant blessings manifestly poured upon the faithful minority in proportion to their exertions in paying the debts, so that by far the majority are now convinced that the Lord pays better interest on their loans than they had conceived of; nor is it new or strange to hear them detail in the meetings how the Lord has repaid them for "days' work" contributed, but the fact engenders faith in Him and in His promises, in proportion to its use.

Without particularizing on incidents, you will be able, by the above representation, to delineate the general features of the work in Wales at the present time; and while your superior judgment may deliberate over the scene, that the Spirit of inspiration may dictate amendments, alterations, new means, or anything, anyhow, to give the Gospel a greater impetus in our midst, is the heart's desire of him who has no higher ambition.

I will detain you to state one instance, which occurred lately, to show the rage of the adversary, and you may have a suggestion on the subject.

While two Elders were preaching in Caermarthenshire[72] a few Sundays ago, a gang of thirty or forty, led on by a tavern keeper, commenced shouting and hallooing, professedly to drown the voice of the brother who was preaching. Their lungs failing before they accomplished their object, the stones came next; one struck the other brother in the face, until his blood was streaming; others whizzing by their heads, failed to dislodge them, so the mobs rushed upon them, forced them to flee, and pursued them for a long way, until one succeeded in gaining the woods; the other was knocked down by a stone, and brutally kicked while bleeding on the ground, the timely aid of a generous stranger saving his life, when they had pronounced him dead. The stranger carried him to a house, and he so far recovered as to be able to ride back with a guard next day to detect the mob, when the

---

70. 2 Corinthians 9:6.

71. See Isaiah 32:8.

72. Carmarthenshire was a county in southern Wales. *Merriam-Webster's Geographical Dictionary*, s.v. "Carmarthenshire."

tavern keeper openly avowed the deed, and declared that "the next time, instead of stones they would use guns;" and he subsequently, when arraigned before the authorities, reiterated the threat with impunity, and without the least prohibition, fine, or censure on their part. The highest dignitaries have written abusive letters to our attorney for defending the brethren. These are the third and fourth Elders whom this man has attempted to murder; one, an old man over sixty years of age, was struck down by a stone hitting him on the head, thrown by this same villain, a year ago, abused, and left for dead. When he recovered so as to be able to prosecute him, the Court fined the defendant 6d!⁷³ The plaintiff had the costs to pay, and had a severe reprimand for preaching, with threats if he continued. Another Elder, having called at this fellow's house on business, he came in with a club, and beat him so brutally that he barely escaped with his life.

There are those in that vicinity who believe, and some desire baptism, but this roaring lion threatens the life of any Saint he meets, and we can get no protection. But I have probably written enough these busy times, hoping this long history will remind you of that long letter promised me long ago.

With congratulation upon your safe return, and continual prayer for you in every good, and with my kind respects to yourself, to President [Daniel] Spencer, if there (heaven alone can reward him for the good he has done here—universally and deservedly beloved and esteemed), also to the brotherhood in the Office, I bring my epistle to a close.

From your brother in the Covenant,
D. Jones.

Dan Jones to Franklin D. Richards, May 21, 1856⁷⁴

Boston.
Ship "S. Curling," May 21st, 1856.
President [Franklin D.] Richards.

---

73. British currency consisted of twenty shillings (s) per pound (£) and twelve pence (d) per shilling. *Oxford English Dictionary*, s.v. "pound."
74. "Foreign Correspondence," *Millennial Star* 18, no. 27 (July 5, 1856): 427–30.

My dear Brother—While the passengers are on tip-toe, stretching their necks over the bow of the ship, watching for Cape Cod[75] to raise his hoary head above the blue lip of ocean, I, though no less anxious than they to see the long looked-for welcomer of all pilgrims to "the land of the free and the home of the brave,"[76] retire to my cabin to inform you of some of the incidents of our voyage.

In a few hours after I was loosed from your parting grip, and that of the other faithful and highly esteemed brethren at your Office door, on April 19, which parting has not yet been or will be for some time forgotten, I found myself mustering the passengers on board the *S. Curling*, in the open sea, being towed out by a steamer. All this over, to the astonishment of the inspecting officers, in less time and with less trouble, they said, than they ever had with any other ship; and after the tug had taken our worthy brother Daniels and other faithful escorters back home, I availed myself of the first opportunity to organize the passengers.

Having conversed with my counsellers, J[ohn]. Oakley and D[avid]. Grant, and some dozen presiding Elders, brother [Patrick Twiss] Birmingham[77] was chosen Secretary; the ship was divided into eleven wards, and suitable Presidents appointed to each, whose duties, although defined to them emphatically, would only be a repetition to you of what you have often heard.[78]

---

75. Cape Cod is a curved peninsula in southeast Massachusetts. European travelers landed on the cape beginning in the early seventeenth century. *Merriam-Webster's Geographical Dictionary*, s.v. "Cape Cod."

76. Francis Scott Key coined the United States' nickname "land of the free and the home of the brave" in "The Star-Spangled Banner," written in September 1814 after the Battle of Baltimore in the War of 1812. The song, set to the tune of the anthem for England's Anacreontic Society, gained steady popularity in the decades preceding the Civil War. Ferris, *Star-Spangled Banner*, 14–25.

77. Patrick Twiss Birmingham (1830–?) was from Ireland and traveled to Utah in 1856. Mormon Pioneer Overland Travel database, s.v. "Patrick Twiss Bermingham."

78. The elders presiding over the eleven wards were Thomas Thomas, John Edwards, John Perry, Job Welling, John McDonald, James Thomas, Evan Evans, Richard Williams, William Butler, John Lewis, and John Walters. Sonne, *Ships, Saints, and Mariners*, 178.

For the first three days gentle breezes and tides wafted us to Cape Clear;[79] four days more of strong north east wind hurried us at the rate of twelve or more knots per hour to the westward, which had so flattered us with a speedy passage, that it took two weeks of adverse winds to erase it from our minds. During this time the S. *Curling*, though called a mammoth of her species, with her 700 passengers and luggage, crew, and withal 2,000 tons of iron in her bowels, rocked like a crow's-nest on a lone sapling in the gale, nor paid deference to Saint more than to sinner, all in turn.

Amidst the wreck of berths, wholesale, the passengers grappled to be uppermost, which position was no sooner gained, than they were again reversed with beds uppermost. Of course pots, pans, kettles, and every thing that could make a noise, joined as usual in the music, and the medley dance. Upon the deck, also, where we enticed, helped, carried or hoisted all we could, true affection bound them in heaps or piles to each other; all had one leg too short or too long every step, but amid such a throng 'twas as difficult for one to fall alone as it would be for a ten pin to fall alone amidst its tottering throng; and here, before they learned to *walk alone*, all felt the power of the adage, "Once a man and twice a child." More than once, in the mean time, the power of the Priesthood curbed the fury of old Boreas, who, as soon as the bits were out of his mouth, like a prancing steed, again would snort in the gale, requiring all the faith on board to rein him in, until, at length a *certain few*, in an indescribable *circle*, fettered him, and ever since stubborn old Boreas has been more tractable to his riders, and promises to continue so until he lands them.[80]

Notwithstanding the roughness of this wintry passage, we continued to be quite a devotional people. At 5 a. m. each day the bugle called the men out to clean their wards, and then to retire on deck while the ladies were dressing for morning prayers, at a quarter to six o'clock. At dusk the bugle called all hands to prayer again, by wards, and it pleased me much to see, by the almost universal willingness to go below, that the call was duly appreciated, nor was the scene less interesting to see seven hundred Saints on their way to Zion, pent up in so small a space, all bow the knee, and,

---

79. Cape Clear is part of Clear Island off the southwest coast of Ireland. *Merriam-Webster's Geographical Dictionary*, s.v. "Clear Island."

80. Boreas was the Greek god of the north wind. *Oxford English Dictionary*, s.v. "Boreas."

with their hearty Amen, lift their hearts in aspirations of praise to Him who deserves our all. Instructions suitable to the circumstances were freely given, at such times, by the presiding Elders; and, to their praise be it said, were as freely received and promptly carried out.

Our evenings, after meetings until bedtime, were spent in singing the songs of Zion;[81] after which the men retired on deck, while the females retired to a better place.

Sundays, at 10 a. m., I have enjoyed myself much in council with the presiding Elders, where undisturbed union has always reigned. At 2½ p. m., we held public meetings on deck, where we had Captain and crew among the audience. The sisters, especially through the various wards, being ever preaching their favourite topic—the celestial order of marriage[82]—it was deemed ungenerous in the Elders not to help them in such a laudable undertaking. Consequently, according to previous announcement, myself and counsellors volunteered our services to help them, and did our best for a couple of hours, the two last Sundays; in return we received the thanks

---

81. The Welsh were known for their tradition of singing. Bathsheba Smith traveled across the plains in 1849 with some of Jones's converts, and she recorded, "Maney of the Welch Saints were excelent singers, which afforded us assistance in our public meetings, and helped to enliven our evenings." After the Saints from Wales arrived in Utah, Brigham Young asked John Parry to organize a choir of the immigrants, and this choir evolved into the Tabernacle Choir. Smith, "Autobiography," 24; Dennis, *Call of Zion*, 60.

82. Marriages properly performed through the priesthood were known by church members as sealings, in which men and women were sealed together for eternity. Today sealings occur in temples, but during early pioneer Utah times they were performed in the Endowment House in Salt Lake City. Marriage sealings performed by proper authority are viewed by church members as one of the crowning ordinances of their religion. Doctrine and Covenants 132 taught that under certain circumstances, Latter-day Saint men could be "sealed" to more than one wife. Plural marriages, or "celestial marriages," required the approval of ecclesiastical leaders and had to be performed by priesthood authority. Revelation, July 12, 1843 [Doctrine and Covenants 132], at Joseph Smith Papers website, josephsmithpapers.org; Bennett, "Nature and Development of Latter-day Saint Temple Work," 22–33; Paul V. Hyer, "Temple Sealings," in *Encyclopedia of Mormonism*, 1:1289–90; Campbell, *Establishing Zion*, 170.

of the sisters for doing it so much better, they say, than they could do it themselves.

At 8 p. m. the bugle again called to sacrament meetings[83] in the wards, when many could not refrain from testifying of the goodness of God and their love of "Mormonism." Tuesday and Thursday evenings, prayer meetings convened in the wards.

Thus, from day to day, blow high, blow low, in the bonds of love and union, whether English, Irish, or Britons—of the latter we had about 560—has this noble band of Zion's pilgrims served their God, on the wide ocean; nor do I believe that any people could do better, under the circumstances, than they have done.

In the cooking department, where I have seen in the experience of years, others, "whose God is their belly," have a "bone of contention" in every kettle, and fight with bones, kettles, and pans, these quiet and self-denying people have sanctified even the galley—the seat of war—with their harmony. Two wards at a time have half an hour for cooking breakfast, three quarters for dinner, and half an hour for supper, reversing alternately, and the intervals between meals for baking, &c. This dispenses with the throng around the galley, and each know his turn by seeing the number of his ward over the door.

The health of the passengers, although good in the main, considering the weather, has not been without grievous exceptions. I regret to say that, notwithstanding myself, counsellers, and others devoted all our time to nourish the sick, especially the old, and the mothers of infants, by preserves, soups, sago, arrowroot,[84] and all the well assorted stock you furnished, owing to a lack of energy in some to contend with and overcome sea-sickness, by coming to the air, themselves and babes suffered much, six

---

83. Sacrament meetings are Sunday gatherings of Latter-day Saints in which they commemorate the sacrament of the Lord's Supper by partaking of bread and water (or wine, in the nineteenth century). The practice dates to the very beginning of the church. C. Robert Line, "Sacrament," in *Encyclopedia of Latter-day Saint History*, 1050–51.

84. Sago and arrowroot are starches obtained from tropical plants. They are used as thickening agents, but by themselves they are nutritionally deficient. *Second Supplement to the Penny Cyclopædia*, 237.

of the latter have died, namely Joseph J. Davies, son of George W. Davies, of Cardiff,[85] aged one year and five months, of inflammation of the lungs, on 28th of April; Hyrum Bassett, son of John Bassett, of Wales, 29th of April, aged ten months, of inflammation of the lungs; Joseph Thomas, son of William Thomas,[86] of Milfordhaven,[87] on the 8th of May, aged nine months and five days; Parley R. Lewis, son of John Lewis,[88] of Tredegar,[89] of cancer in the breast, aged seven months, on the 9th of May; John Davies, son of Evan D. Davies, of Glamorganshire, of consumption,[90] on the 17th of May; and Joseph Price, son of John Price,[91] of Pembrokshire, May 21st, of consumption, aged twelve months. Three of the former, however, were so weakly, that the doctor said while inspecting them at Liverpool, they would not live ten days. Mothers might prolong the lives of their babes, did they keep them half the time on the deck in the fresh air, but they keep them smothered up in their arms in the blankets, inhaling each other's breath. Owing principally to this the chicken-pock[92] broke out among the children, and in despite of all efforts to check its progress, in which the doctor of the ship and Captain Curling distinguished themselves, it spread throughout the whole of the ship, yet, by steady perseverance, and the

---

85. Cardiff is a seaport city in southeast Wales. A castle was built in the eleventh century, and it became the capital of Wales in 1955. *Merriam-Webster's Geographical Dictionary*, s.v. "Cardiff."

86. William Thomas (1805–?) was a Welsh farmer and arrived in Utah in 1856. Mormon Pioneer Overland Travel database, s.v. "William Thomas."

87. Milford Haven is a seaport town on the southwest coast of Wales. *Merriam-Webster's Geographical Dictionary*, s.v. "Milford Haven."

88. John Lewis (1824–?) arrived in Utah with his family in 1856. Mormon Pioneer Overland Travel database, s.v. "John Lewis."

89. Tredegar is a town in southeast Wales that was important in the coal industry. *Merriam-Webster's Geographical Dictionary*, s.v. "Tredegar."

90. *Consumption* was an older word for tuberculosis, so called because it led to weight loss. *Oxford English Dictionary*, s.v. "consumption."

91. John Price (1820–83) arrived in Utah with his family in 1856. Mormon Pioneer Overland Travel database, s.v. "John Price."

92. "Chicken pock" was a variant for "chickenpox" and also sometimes referred to the individual pustules of the disease. Chickenpox usually infects children and is an airborne contagion. *Oxford English Dictionary*, s.v. "chicken pock."

blessing of God upon the ordinance of His Gospel, it has not proved fatal, but by this time all have either recovered or are recovering.

To change the topic from our decrease to our *increase*, I have the pleasure of saying, that our company has been augmented by the inauguration of two little cherubs from the spirit world,[93] who are already the favourites of all, and all say, they must come to Zion with us. They would have one called Dan Curling Dee, son of Thomas Dee,[94] Llanelly,[95] Wales. The other is called Claudia Curling Reynolds, daughter of brother Reynolds, England; mothers and babes are doing well, and the former say they would come a long way again to be rocked in so easy a cradle with their infants, and especially so as to bequeath upon their infants the rights of cosmopolites or citizens of the world. We are kept on the alert, *by the signs*, waiting for Neptune[96] in his carriage to bring us some more sea-born "Mormons."

But, hark! What means the tumultuous throng of hasty feet that press along? The word is passed—Land oh! Land oh! I cannot stay, I must up to see it too. Well, there it is sure enough, the grey old Cape Cod, some dozen miles to the windward; passengers, old and young, lame, maimed, halt, and blind, shouting out, "There it is! There it is! There are houses, and trees, and men walking!" Some wish for wings to fly to it, yet they have to wait for them to grow.

It affords me much pleasure to say, that my gratitude to you is still increased, commensurate with the able and efficient aid I have received, in all things, from the good men whom you gave me to be counsellors—ever ready, always willing, and one in all things, I cannot speak too highly of them; nor will the services they have rendered to this people be soon forgotten.

The conduct of Captain Curling has demanded our praise; generous, courteous, and philanthropic, he has shared his commiseration indiscrim-

---

93. In Latter-day Saint theology, all people existed as spirits and lived with God before they were born. Gayle Oblad Brown, "Premortal Life," and Walter D. Bowen, "Spirit World," in *Encyclopedia of Mormonism*, 3:1123–25, 1408–9.

94. Thomas Dee (1832–1906) and his wife Ann arrived in Utah in 1856. Mormon Pioneer Overland Travel database, s.v. "Thomas Dee."

95. Llanelly can refer to an inland town in southeast Wales or a larger seaport town, Llanelli, further to the west. *Merriam-Webster's Geographical Dictionary*, s.v. "Llanelli."

96. Neptune is the Roman god of the sea. *Oxford English Dictionary*, s.v. "Neptune."

inately among the greatest sufferers, and all have received comforts from his liberal hand. He has vouchsafed to us the freedom of his commodious and splendid ship, fore and aft, both in our devotions as well as our amusements and recreations, for which, as well as for his gentlemanly, humane, and parental conduct, the Saints, in public meeting assembled, of all people first and foremost to appreciate and reciprocate favours, were pleased with the privileges given them, to express, with an uplifted hand, their gratitude to him; and many are the invocations for their Father to repay him with the blessings he merits. As for myself, we have spun yarns together for hours, as we paced the quarter deck eagerly scrutinizing the horizon, lest a treacherous squall should take us unawares, and disturb the repose of the sleepers below. At home among the stars, born in a storm, cradled on the ocean, few things escaped his eagle eye, with such a one, hours have I spent with a pleasure known only to weather beaten old tars. May he moor his barque, yes, his *fleet* in Zion's snug harbor, ere the equinoctial gales of life beset him.

I ought to further add, that the provisions you furnished were of a superior quality, and so abundant that few drew their rations. You would be reminded, by the meat, &c., which was hung up to the deck below, of a huge butcher's shop, and, sometimes, when the overstrained cords gave way beneath the ponderous mass, some felt the strength and hardness of bones, which did not, luckily, however, prove fatal.

Boston, May 25th. On the 22nd, pilot boarded us; light winds off shore kept us off until daylight of the 23rd, when the tug, *Enoch Train*, came alongside and towed us to Quarantine Ground. In a few hours the Inspectors came aboard, welcomed by the spontaneous three cheers of 700 people, and, strange as it may seem, called the names of all, and passed them, in less than one hour and a half, without any further complaint than that "I was taking all the handsome ladies to Utah." The passengers were all remarkably clean, as well as the ship, which commanded the admiration of all. In proof of the latter I would say, that I had made a wager with Captain Curling, upon leaving Liverpool, that the lower decks would be whiter than his cabin floor, and the Quarantine Doctor decided in my favour.

Noon, we moored alongside the wharf, and had the great pleasure of meeting my worthy friend N[athaniel]. H. Felt,[97] whose judicious counsels I had learned to appreciate before, while taking a company through St. Louis, but now more welcome than ever.

24th. Concluded a contract with the Railway, to take about 400 to Iowa city[98] direct, fare $11, under 14 half-fare, and under 6 years free, with 100 lbs of luggage free: $3.50 per cwt[99] for freight; to leave Monday, 11 a.m. Got the privilege from our ever kind Captain Curling, to remain on board until that time. Sent all luggage except bedding up to the station in safety, and without aid of either mates, loafers, or any but ourselves. Our arrival created quite an excitement through the City, and the wharf is thronged with inquisitive and astonished spectators, including reverends, ladies, officials, and editors. A delegation from the tract society waited on me, petitioning the privilege of distributing Testaments, tracts, &c., to enlighten the benighted "Mormons," and they were as much astonished as pleased when informed that their charity was highly appreciated, and that they were at perfect liberty to say or introduce anything they pleased, to any and all of the passengers—that we could investigate, and, if they could decoy any away from "Mormonism" I would thank them for it, and be glad to get rid of them.[100] They gazed wildly when informed that these people's

97. Nathaniel Felt (1816–87), a tailor, was born in Salem, Massachusetts, and was baptized there in 1843. After fleeing Nauvoo in 1846, he settled in St. Louis and assisted emigrating Saints who were traveling through that city. He relocated to Salt Lake City in 1850 and became a legislator. From 1854 to 1856, he served a mission in New York City and the surrounding region; he returned to Utah in 1856 but served additional missions to Britain and New England later in life. He died in Salt Lake City in 1887. Woods, "Nathaniel H. Felt," 219–36; Jenson, *Latter-day Saint Biographical Encyclopedia*, 2:380–83.

98. Iowa City is located in eastern Iowa and was the original capital of Iowa Territory and the state of Iowa. The University of Iowa, located in Iowa City, was founded in 1847. *Merriam-Webster's Geographical Dictionary*, s.v. "Iowa City."

99. "Cwt" is an abbreviation for hundredweight, a unit of measurement equal to 112 pounds in the United Kingdom and 100 pounds in the United States. *Oxford English Dictionary*, s.v. "hundredweight."

100. Church leaders often said it was better if people who were weak in their faith would leave the church before traveling to Utah. In 1855, the First Presidency stated, "If any apostatize in consequence of this regulation [regarding handcart travel], so

actions were predicated upon actual *knowledge*, by the revelations of God to each for *himself*, and not upon mere belief. I informed them that if they would pronounce in their churches, and attend to-morrow on the wharf at 11 a.m., and at 5 p.m., I would endeavour to tell them what "Mormonism" *really* is, and invited all the Bostonians to come and hear our *own* representations of ourselves, which seemed to please them much, and by all prospects there will be a good turnout. May the spirit of "Mormonism" manifest its wonted power for their good.

I have been treated very respectfully, even courteously, by your Consignees, officials of the city, and government, and in fact, without exception, and even after critical examination on principle, have been highly complimented. Thank the Lord that "Mormonism" is looking and marching upwards through the snares of darkness with which hireling priests and editors have endeavoured to ensnare it.

The *Enoch Train*[101] arrived 12 days before us, and the company is highly spoken of for cleanliness and order, the best ever here, *ourselves* excepted of course!

---

much the better, for it is far better that such deny the faith before they start than to do so, for a more trifling cause, after they get here; and if they have not faith enough to undertake this job, and accomplish it too, they have not faith sufficient to endure with the saints in Zion, the celestial law which leads to exaltation and eternal lives." See "Thirteenth General Epistle of the Presidency of the Church of Jesus Christ of Latter-day Saints," *Deseret News*, October 31, 1855, in Neilson and Waite, *Settling the Valley, Proclaiming the Gospel*, 249.

101. The *Enoch Train* was built in Boston, Massachusetts, in 1852. On March 23, 1856, it departed Liverpool, England, with more than five hundred Latter-day Saints, including Truman Leonard, returning from his mission to India, and converts from Switzerland, South Africa, Denmark, and India. It landed in Boston on May 1, 1856, and some of its passengers were among the first handcart pioneers. Sonne, *Ship, Saints, and Mariners*, 71; Knoblock, *American Clipper Ship*, 69.

I was much disappointed in my expectation of meeting Presidents [John] Taylor[102] or [Daniel] Spencer, here, they are both out west, I am informed.[103]

I am endeavouring to dispose of the surplus provisions to the best advantage, but have not as yet had an offer to my mind.

Having said so much hurriedly, brother Franklin, and being called upon by an assembled throng to preach for them, I bid you, and the beloved brethren in the Office adieu, praying the Lord to bless you with health, influence unbounded, and all your heart's desires in time and eternity, and beg to remain as ever, truly your brother in the Gospel,

D. Jones.

102. John Taylor had been sent to New York to print a paper and to oversee Latter-day Saint emigration through New York City. He established the *Mormon*, which ran from February 17, 1855, to September 19, 1857. The office of the *Mormon* was located within two blocks of three dozen newspapers, including the *New York Tribune* and the *New York Herald*, and it published numerous articles defending Latter-day Saint doctrines and addressing misinformation. It also provided emigration guides to members traveling west and information on places they could find jobs in New York. Taylor edited the *Mormon* until May 1857, when he left New York to return to Utah. Woods, "Gifted Gentleman in Perpetual Motion," 177–92; Crawley, *Descriptive Bibliography of the Mormon Church*, 3:203–5; "Our Last Issue," *Mormon*, Sept. 19, 1857.

103. Daniel Spencer had arrived in Boston on March 30, 1856, and in April he did some business with John Taylor in New York. He made his way to Iowa City that month, but in early May he returned to Boston and New York via railroad. He went back to Iowa City that May before Jones had arrived. Spencer, diary, April–May 1856.

2

ORSON SPENCER AND
THE PRUSSIA MISSION

Historical Introduction

AFTER ORSON SPENCER AND JACOB HOUTZ WERE BANISHED from preaching in the kingdom of Prussia in early 1853, they questioned their own efforts. "Had we done all that we could to plant the Gospel in the hearts of the people to whom we were sent?" they wondered.[1] It was Spencer's third mission, and after serving as president of the British Mission for a year and a half, he found it difficult to be evicted from Berlin after less than two weeks. One can infer the reasons for his insecurities: his call had come from the leaders of the church in 1852, and he had sacrificed to leave his young family behind in Utah Territory, so why were his efforts so fruitless? Spencer and Houtz concluded, however, that the problem was not because they had done too little, but because the national laws were intolerant of new religions and because Satan had a great influence in the world: "I

---

1. Spencer, *Prussian Mission*, 12; p. 60 herein.

Orson Spencer. © Intellectual Reserve, Inc.

do exceedingly marvel at the great power of the Devil among the nations. The extent of the oppressions, cruelties, abominations, and miseries, is greater than my heart ever conceived before."[2] Having done all they felt they could do, Spencer and Houtz departed for England, and Spencer detailed their experience in a letter to Brigham Young before returning home to America.

Orson Spencer's Early Life and Church Service, 1802–52

Orson Spencer was born March 14, 1802, in West Stockbridge, Massachusetts, the eleventh of his family's children. After an illness in his teenage years left him with a disabled leg for life, he pursued a life of intellect, education, and religion. He graduated from Union College and the Theological College at Hamilton, both in New York, in 1824 and 1829, respectively. After his 1829 graduation, Spencer began work as a Baptist minister, and in 1830, he married Catharine Curtis. Ten years later, while still living in Massachusetts, his brother Daniel Spencer brought the message of the restored gospel to Orson's home.[3] Spencer and his family were baptized and subsequently moved to Nauvoo, Illinois, in 1841, where he became an alderman and taught at the University of Nauvoo, a fledgling institution that oversaw education in the community.[4] In the summer of

---

2. Spencer, *Prussian Mission*, 14; p. 64 herein.
3. Rogers, *Life Sketches of Orson Spencer and Others*, 9–15; Spencer, *Life Summary of Orson Spencer*, 9–27; Sadler, "Life of Orson Spencer," 1–5.
4. The University of Nauvoo operated from 1841 to 1845 to encourage education among Latter-day Saints. Classes in secular subjects—science, writing, foreign languages, arithmetic, and so forth—were taught to adults in the community, and

1843, he served a mission to the eastern states, where he ministered to his wife's family before bringing his own parents back to Nauvoo with him; they died within a few years. As the majority of the Saints were driven out of Nauvoo in early 1846, Catharine died along the trail thirty miles out of Nauvoo.[5]

As a new widower, Orson Spencer was called on a mission for the church in 1846. He was asked to leave his six living children, all under the age of fourteen, behind in Winter Quarters in present-day Nebraska so that he might take over Apostle Orson Hyde's duties to preside over the British Mission. Before Spencer reached Liverpool on January 23, 1847, erroneous word arrived in England that he had died. In reality, it was his brother Hyrum Spencer who had died, but the message was taken as fact, and Apostle Franklin D. Richards departed from his labors in Scotland to take over Spencer's intended post in Liverpool.[6] "Few men in the 19th century possess that degree of longevity which enables them to read in the public prints their own obituary notice, but it has been Elder Spencer's privilege to read the feelings of his brethren concerning him, when they expected never to see him again in mortality," Richards quipped when he found Orson very much alive.[7] As president of the mission, Spencer's duties included editing and writing for the *Millennial Star*, the official church publication in Britain; he also published two widely circularized tracts[8] and a theological treatise consisting of letters between him and a Baptist minister in Massachusetts.[9] Additionally, he enjoyed success as a preacher: "Wherever I go, the Saints gather around me as though they would worship me. They often walk ten or twenty miles to see me and hear me preach. . . . The gospel is

the university oversaw the local common schools, intended for children. Black, "University of Nauvoo," 189–206.

5. Rogers, *Life Sketches of Orson Spencer and Others*, 15–41; Spencer, *Life Summary of Orson Spencer*, 28–32; Sadler, "Life of Orson Spencer," 5–49.

6. Rogers, *Life Sketches of Orson Spencer and Others*, 47–84; Spencer, *Life Summary of Orson Spencer*, 32–38; Sadler, "Life of Orson Spencer," 50–52.

7. Franklin D. Richards, "Address," *Millennial Star* 9, no. 3 (February 1, 1847): 42.

8. Orson Spencer, *The Gospel Witness* (Liverpool: R. James, 1848); Orson Spencer, *Character!!* (Liverpool: R. James, 1848).

9. Orson Spencer, *Letters Exhibiting the Most Prominent Doctrines of the Church of Jesus Christ of Latter-day Saints* (Liverpool: Orson Spencer, 1848).

THE

LATTER-DAY SAINTS'

MILLENNIAL STAR.

VOLUME IX.

"AND THEY THAT BE WISE SHALL SHINE AS THE BRIGHTNESS OF THE FIRMAMENT;
AND THEY THAT TURN MANY TO RIGHTEOUSNESS AS THE STARS FOR EVER AND
EVER."—*Daniel* xii, 3.

LIVERPOOL:
EDITED AND PUBLISHED BY ORSON SPENCER,
39, TORBOCK STREET, SOHO STREET.

MDCCCXLVII.

The title page of a volume of the *Millennial Star*, "edited and published by Orson Spencer."
Courtesy of Church History Library.

spreading wonderfully, probably not less than five thousand will be added to the Church this year."[10]

In August 1848, Apostle Orson Pratt replaced Spencer as president of the British Mission (the third "Orson" in a row to hold the calling), so Spencer was free to return to his family in America.[11] For the next few years, Spencer was involved in local politics in Utah and became chancellor of the University of Deseret, which later became the University of Utah.[12] As chancellor, he lectured on the value of education, donated books, and oversaw the primary schools in the territory.[13] He was serving in this capacity when he was called on another mission in August 1852. His companion was to be Jacob Houtz, no stranger to the Spencer family: after being baptized in 1844, Houtz traveled in Daniel Spencer's company to arrive in Salt Lake City in 1847. Beginning in 1851, Houtz relocated from Salt Lake City to Springville, Utah, where he established a farm and built a gristmill.[14] Moses Clough was also called to labor in Prussia, but he couldn't obtain a passport and instead spent three years in England.[15] Spencer and Houtz departed from their homes to begin their new mission to Prussia, only three years after Orson had returned from his earlier mission to England.

10. Rogers, *Life Sketches of Orson Spencer and Others*, 63.

11. Spencer, *Life Summary of Orson Spencer*, 39–42; Rogers, *Life Sketches of Orson Spencer and Others*, 108; Early Mormon Missionaries database, s.v. "British Mission."

12. The General Assembly of Deseret established the University of Deseret in 1850. It was nicknamed the "Parent School," as it was intended as the guardian of all of Utah's educational endeavors. Due to the lack of financial support, classes were discontinued in 1852. The university opened again in the 1867, and in 1894 it became the University of Utah. Davis Bitton, "University of Utah," in *Encyclopedia of Latter-day Saint History*, 1275–76.

13. Rogers, *Life Sketches of Orson Spencer and Others*, 122–23; Spencer, *Life Summary of Orson Spencer*, 94–97; Sadler, "Life of Orson Spencer," 63–69.

14. Whitney, *History of Utah*, 4:108; "Houtz, Jacob," in appendix 2, p. 336 herein.

15. Crawley, *Descriptive Bibliography of the Mormon Church*, 3:55–56.

History of the German Mission and Orson Spencer's Attempt in Prussia, 1852–53

Daniel Carn (or Garn) arrived in Hamburg, Germany,[16] in April 1852 and officially opened the German Mission of the church. However, due to its proximity to other nations, Latter-day Saints had been spreading the gospel in the country on a limited basis throughout the previous decade. In September 1840, English convert James Howard became the first Latter-day Saint to visit the country, but he did little, if any, preaching. The following year, Apostle Orson Hyde stopped in Germany on his way to Palestine and began studying German. On his way back in 1842, he returned to the country and published a Latter-day Saint tract in German, *Ein Ruf aus der Wüste* (A Cry from the Wilderness). These early efforts had little or no impact on conversions in Germany itself, but there were many Germans who were baptized in the United States or England.[17] In the fall of 1851, George Parker Dykes, who had been laboring in Denmark, and Apostle John Taylor, who had been serving in France, arrived in Hamburg and began publishing a German periodical, *Zions Panier*. Taylor brought with him George Viett, a German schoolteacher, who had started to translate the Book of Mormon into German, and he and Dykes joined forces in the translation, which was published in 1852.[18] Carn entered Hamburg on April 3, 1852, and in the coming months he organized the Hamburg Branch. However, he was imprisoned in January 1853; after an American

---

16. Hamburg is an important port city on the Elbe River in northern Germany. It was originally built around 825. *Merriam-Webster's Geographical Dictionary*, s.v. "Hamburg."

17. Scharffs, *Mormonism in Germany*, 1–8.

18. Five men assisted with the German translation of the Book of Mormon between 1851 and 1852: John Taylor, the president of the French Mission; George P. Dykes, a missionary who knew some German and was asked by Taylor to assist; George Viett, a German schoolteacher who had been baptized in France; John Miller, a convert who was baptized during the translation project; and Daniel Carn (or Garn), who was called as president of the German Mission and replaced John Taylor. Dykes and Viett were mainly responsible for the translation. The translation was completed April 1852 and published in Hamburg the following month. Scharffs, "*Das Buch Mormon*," 35–39; Crawley, *Descriptive Bibliography of the Mormon Church*, 2:322–25.

consul negotiated his release, he was banished from the city.[19]

Such were the conditions when Orson Spencer and Jacob Houtz arrived in Hamburg to begin their efforts in the neighboring kingdom of Prussia[20] in January 1853.[21] But religious tolerance in Prussia was even worse than that in Germany. On January 20, Spencer and Houtz visited American consul Samuel Bromberg[22] in Hamburg to have their passports endorsed. Bromberg was skeptical that they would

Portrait of Jacob Houtz. Courtesy of Church History Library.

be permitted to preach in the Prussian capital, Berlin: "Prussia will not treat you as the Syndic of Hamburg has Elder Carn, debating a long time whether they will allow you to operate there—their course will be prompt and energetic, probably setting you out of their kingdom *immediately.*"[23] Subsequently they traveled to Berlin and met with American envoy Daniel D. Barnard,[24] who informed the missionaries that minority religions were not well tolerated, with foreign ministers being ejected from the

---

19. Carn did return to Hamburg, and in December 1853 he arrived in Liverpool with thirty-three emigrating German Saints. Scharffs, *Mormonism in Germany*, 1–13; Jenson, *Encyclopedic History of the Church*, 280.

20. Prussia, a kingdom that included parts of present-day northern Germany and western Poland, was a powerful state of the German Confederation. It was abolished in the twentieth century. *Merriam-Webster's Geographical Dictionary*, s.vv. "Germany," "Prussia."

21. George C. Riser, Jacob F. Secrist, George Mayer, and William Taylor also arrived to preach in Germany. Mayer soon transferred to Switzerland, while Riser, Secrist, and Taylor all went back to England within four months after arriving in Germany, due to problems with local governments. Scharffs, *Mormonism in Germany*, 11–12.

22. Samuel Bromberg (about 1805–1880s?) was born in Hamburg and was an American consul from 1849 to 1853. He later moved to New York City.

23. Spencer, *Prussian Mission*, 3; p. 46 herein.

24. Daniel D. Barnard (1797–1861) was a US representative from New York and American envoy to Prussia from 1850 to 1853. See Penney, *Patrician in Politics.*

country. In addition, Prussian laws forbade people to emigrate unless they had performed mandatory military service, so Latter-day Saints, with their doctrine of "gathering," would be considered "obnoxious to the policy and laws of the Government."[25] Spencer and Houtz considered preaching in "a secret, unobserved course of introducing the Gospel," but they recognized that the only practical method was to be direct and request permission from "the powers that be."[26] On January 29, they wrote a letter to Karl Otto von Raumer,[27] the minister of public worship, requesting an audience with the king and permission to preach in the country. On February 1, they met with the police, who told them: "You, Orson Spencer and Jacob Houtz, are hereby commanded to depart out of this kingdom to-morrow morning, under the penalty of *transportation*; and you are also forbidden ever to return to this kingdom hereafter, under the penalty of being transported."[28]

Spencer and Houtz were disappointed to be banished, but at the same time, they relished the persecution: "My heart inwardly rejoiced, and I said to myself, our religion is good, and pure, and faultless, having come from the holy heavens; and having spoken against that, you will have to answer it to Him, who revealed it from the Heavens for the blessing and salvation of all those who should receive it."[29] Less than two weeks after their arrival in Germany, Spencer and Houtz obediently left Prussia and proselytized in England, which was considerably more receptive to their message than Prussia had been.[30] After a few months in England, Spencer led a group of Latter-day Saints across the plains and arrived in Utah in August 1853.[31]

---

25. Spencer, *Prussian Mission*, 5; p. 49 herein.
26. Spencer, *Prussian Mission*, 6; p. 51 herein.
27. Karl Otto von Raumer (1805–59) was appointed as minister of religious affairs by King Frederick Wilhelm IV in 1850. Mitchell, "Mormons in Wilhelmine Germany," 21–22.
28. Spencer, *Prussian Mission*, 10–11; p. 58 herein.
29. Spencer, *Prussian Mission*, 11; p. 59 herein.
30. Spencer, *Life Summary of Orson Spencer*, 75; Sadler, "Life of Orson Spencer," 70–71; Spencer, *Prussian Mission*, 16; p. 68 herein.
31. Spencer, *Life Summary of Orson Spencer*, 75; Sadler, "Life of Orson Spencer," 71; Rogers, *Life Sketches of Orson Spencer and Others*, 133; Mormon Pioneer Overland Travel database, s.v. "Orson Spencer/Joel J. Terrell Company (1853)."

Continued Church Service

In April 1854, just eight months after returning from his Prussian mission, Orson Spencer was called on yet another mission, this time within the United States. He left his wives and children, never to see them again. First he labored in Cincinnati, Ohio, along with Apostle Orson Pratt, in part to establish a waystation for Latter-day Saint emigrants from Europe.[32] In July 1855, Apostle Erastus Snow, president of the mission at St. Louis, Missouri, called him to edit the *St. Louis Luminary*, a church periodical; Spencer agreed to take the position, but as it turned out, he would never take over the editorial duties of the paper.[33] Soon after arriving in St. Louis, he was sent to preach to the Cherokee Nation, but there is no evidence of him being successful in ministering to them.[34] In September 1855, he returned to St. Louis with a fever. He never recovered and died there on October 15, 1855.[35] His body was transported to Utah and interred in the Salt Lake City Cemetery the following summer. Spencer's daughter, Aurelia Spencer Rogers, later reminisced, "The hardest thing for me to bear, was the thought of my father dying away from home, with none of his family near to comfort him in his last moments; although he had kind friends to minister to his wants, which was quite a satisfaction. My father could be counted as one who had left father and mother, wives and children and all

---

32. Spencer, *Life Summary of Orson Spencer*, 76–78; Sadler, "Life of Orson Spencer," 73.

33. "Obituary of Orson Spencer," *St. Louis Luminary*, October 20, 1855. The *St. Louis Luminary* ran from November 22, 1854, to December 15, 1855. Apostle Erastus Snow bought a press and printing supplies and set up the printing office in the local meetinghouse. In January 1855, he assigned James H. Hart to edit and take charge of the paper. Before departing for Utah in August 1855, Snow appointed Orson Spencer as the new editor, but Spencer fell ill and later died, so Hart continued to edit the paper. Subscriptions were doing quite well in late 1855, but John Taylor advised that the *Luminary* be discontinued, since Snow was back in Utah and Spencer had died. Crawley, *Descriptive Bibliography of the Mormon Church*, 3:163–65. See also Black, "*St. Louis Luminary*: The Latter-day Saint Experience at the Mississippi River, 1854–1855," 157–73.

34. Spencer, *Life Summary of Orson Spencer*, 79–82; Sadler, "Life of Orson Spencer," 75–76.

35. "Obituary of Orson Spencer."

that he held dear, for the gospel's sake."[36]

Jacob Houtz likewise continued to serve the church after his unsuccessful Prussian mission. On his way back from Europe in 1853, he stopped in the eastern United States, where he converted his sister Catharine Boyer and brought her to Utah. He constructed mills in Springville, where he spent most of the remainder of his life. He served another mission to the eastern United States in 1869, and he died in Springville on December 11, 1896.[37]

Orson Spencer's Family Life

As noted earlier, Orson Spencer married Catharine Curtis in 1830, but she died in 1846 while the family was relocating from Nauvoo. In January 1846, before Catharine died, Spencer married Eliza Ann Dibble, but they never lived together or had children; their marriage was canceled in 1849.[38] Spencer and Catharine had eight children, with two of them dying at a very young age, so six were living when Spencer left to preside over the British Mission.[39] Despite the intense demands of presiding over the mission, Spencer did not neglect his family duties. He frequently sent money and letters of advice and encouragement to his children. He married a second wife, Martha Knight, while he was in England.[40]

In 1848, the Spencer children traveled from Winter Quarters to Salt Lake City with Brigham Young's company. Daniel Spencer, their uncle, had prepared a room in a fort for the children to occupy. Orson arrived in the Salt Lake Valley in September 1849 and was reunited with his children, who met their new stepmother and little half sister.[41] He married three additional women in the ensuing years in Salt Lake City: Margaret Miller in October 1849, Mary Jane Burn Davis (known simply as Jane) in February

---

36. Rogers, *Life Sketches of Orson Spencer and Others*, 148–49.
37. Whitney, *History of Utah*, 4:108–9; "Houtz, Jacob," in appendix 2, p. 336 herein.
38. Smith, "Story of Eliza Ann Dibble," 12.
39. Spencer, *Life Summary of Orson Spencer*, 106.
40. Rogers, *Life Sketches of Orson Spencer and Others*, 52–75; Spencer, *Life Summary of Orson Spencer*, 43–63; Sadler, "Life of Orson Spencer," 52–59.
41. Rogers, *Life Sketches of Orson Spencer and Others*, 76–122; Spencer, *Life Summary of Orson Spencer*, 72–73; Sadler, "Life of Orson Spencer," 60–62.

1852, and Mary Hill Bullock in September 1852.[42] It is not clear what kind of relationship there was between Spencer and Mary Bullock: they were sealed days before Spencer departed for his mission to Prussia, they had no children, and Aurelia Spencer Rogers makes no mention of Mary as a wife. The sealing might have been done in gratitude for Mary and her late husband, James Bullock, caring for the Spencer children during Spencer's first mission.[43]

After Spencer left in 1852, Martha spent the duration of his absence caring for many of his children, only three of them her own. Margaret might have also helped out in the home, though she had no children of her own. Jane gave birth to her only child with Spencer in December 1852, after he had already departed.[44] It is not clear what these families did to support themselves during his absence, though it is reasonable to suppose that he sent them funds, as he had done on his previous mission.

Spencer and Jane were divorced about the time Spencer left on his third and final mission, and Martha had a daughter after he left. He continued to write letters of encouragement home: "We are separated, too, for a little season, in order that we may better understand each other's value, and love more fervently and serve one another more patiently."[45] In his last letter to his family, he wrote, "Let me die many deaths before I turn away from such a God or from such a people. . . . I feel to bless you, and hope that you will have many things next winter that will make you comfortable."[46] The next message to his family was written by someone else, informing them that he had died.[47]

Source Note

After retreating from Prussia to England in 1853, Orson Spencer recounted his failed attempts in a letter to President Brigham Young. "After some

42. Spencer, *Life Summary of Orson Spencer*, 105.

43. Spencer, *Life Summary of Orson Spencer*, 106; Rogers, *Life Sketches of Orson Spencer and Others*, 130.

44. Spencer, *Life Summary of Orson Spencer*, 106.

45. Rogers, *Life Sketches of Orson Spencer and Others*, 137.

46. Rogers, *Life Sketches of Orson Spencer and Others*, 141.

47. Rogers, *Life Sketches of Orson Spencer and Others*, 142.

careful hesitancy," Spencer agreed to have the letter "printed in the British Isles, before its perusal by him for whom it was primarily designed. . . . The British Saints had always manifested a deep interest in all the foreign missions, and have recently made frequent and particular inquiry after the result of the mission to Berlin. . . . The Author has concluded to furnish the public with the full report of the mission in pamphlet form, feeling that a mere abstract, printed in the *Millennial Star*, would not be as satisfactory."[48] Spencer's letter is herein reproduced as published in the pamphlet *The Prussian Mission of the Church of Jesus Christ of Latter-day Saints* (Liverpool: S. W. Richards, 1853). He describes his impressions of the country during his brief time there, his interactions with local officials before they banished him and Houtz, and his unfavorable opinion of European governments.

DOCUMENT TRANSCRIPTS

Orson Spencer to Brigham Young, February 8, 1853[49]

To President Brigham Young.

Honoured and Beloved Brother,—I feel it my pleasure and duty at this time and place, to advise you of my doings, touching the Mission to the kingdom of Prussia, which I have had the honour to undertake according to the appointment of the Church. With the exception of a few of the first days of my journey from Great Salt Lake City, I have enjoyed good health—abating sea-sickness always. For this I am grateful to God, and to the Priesthood in Zion, whose intercessions are ever effectual in behalf of the faithful. The toils and difficulties of crossing the plains were measurably forgotten through the delightful union and rich heavenly instruc-

---

48. Spencer, *Prussian Mission*, 2.
49. Orson Spencer, *The Prussian Mission of the Church of Jesus Christ of Latter-day Saints* (Liverpool: S. W. Richards, 1853).

tions of the large company of Elders with whom I was happily associated. I pass over many striking incidents attendant upon our journey through the States and across the Atlantic Ocean, by briefly saying, the good and mighty hand of our God was strikingly made manifest in our comfort, preservation, and prosperity up to the time of our arrival in Liverpool. All our brethren appointed on Missions to England and Europe have now safely arrived, except brothers Lamoreaux, Pitt, and Toner, whom we soon expect.[50] The elements have combined to give them a very astonishingly swift passage. One company of Elders crossed the Atlantic in 15 days, by a sailing packet, and one or two others in 18 days.

On the 20th January, brother Jacob Houtz and myself sailed from Hull for Hamburg; brother Moses Clough being detained in England for want of a passport. On our arrival in Hamburg, we found Elder Daniel Carn just expelled from that city by an order of the government. He has retreated to Altona,[51] a Danish dominion, for the present, but he feels very uncertain whether he will be allowed to continue his labours in that region to any good purpose much longer.[52] The other portions of the German Mission who have reached Hamburg are no less unsettled as to their prospective field of labour. The former, accompanied us to the American Consul, a native German, Mr. Bromberg, in order to get our passports endorsed;

---

50. William Pitt arrived in Liverpool on March 9, 1853, aboard the *William Nelson*. Daniel Toner arrived in Liverpool on April 1 aboard the *Roscius*. Andrew L. Lamoreaux arrived in Liverpool on April 26 aboard the *Kossuth* and left two days later for France. "Arrival," *Millennial Star* 15, no. 13 (Mar. 26, 1853): 202; "Arrival," *Millennial Star* 15, no. 16 (April 16, 1853): 250; "Arrival," *Millennial Star* 15, no. 19 (May 7, 1853): 296.

51. Altona was a city next to Hamburg, Germany, but it belonged to Denmark from 1640 until 1864. It became part of Hamburg in 1937. *Merriam-Webster's Geographical Dictionary*, s.v. "Altona."

52. Daniel Carn arrived in Hamburg in April 1852 as president of the German Mission. He began making a few converts, but in January 1853, he was confronted by government officials, who objected to his preaching. He refused to leave Hamburg because he had not broken any laws, but he was arrested for a few hours before he moved to Altona, which then belonged to Denmark. Carn participated in Latter-day missionary endeavors in Altona and continued to oversee proselyting in Hamburg. He was again arrested in October 1853 and permanently left Germany thereafter. Scharffs, *Mormonism in Germany*, 9–13.

Mr. Bromberg expressed some surprise at our presumption in undertaking to carry the Gospel to the kingdom of Prussia. Says he, Prussia will not treat you as the Syndic of Hamburg has Elder Carn, debating a long time whether they will allow you to operate there—their course will be prompt and energetic, probably setting you out of their kingdom *immediately*. But, he continued, if you should find it otherwise, I earnestly request that you will please to inform me. He renewed the same request at a still later interview. He observed that American citizens had frequently suffered imprisonment and abuse in Germany, and the American government had been distinctly informed of the same, but the information lay upon the files of Congress without ever being even called up. Hamburg is sexually corrupt, like other nations of Europe, and it is said, not only to license 15,000 females to transgress the laws of virtue and of God, the revenue of which goes to support the army, but the columns of the German newspapers contain notices, advertising for the company of females, naming what hour of the day the gentleman will admit them to his apartment. Oh earth! how shameless! The secretary of the American Legation, Mr. Fay,[53] residing at Berlin, told me that the prostitution of the sexes in that city was greater than we should dare to *think;* and the Sabbath, says he, is a holiday.[54]

Upon our arrival at Berlin we were, in company with other railway passengers, immediately surrounded with a moveable fence or paling, and guarded by soldiers armed with guns and bayonets, until our examination was finished. We then took a carriage, and were soon set down at a respectable hotel, within five to eight minutes' walk of the king's palace. Our passports were demanded and taken to the police-office. We accordingly soon secured a neat, well furnished room in the hotel, which we soon dedicated to God and the service of the Mission during our residence in it.

53. Theodore Sedgwick Fay (1807–98) was born in New York and was Secretary of the American Legation in Berlin from 1837 to 1853. He was also a prolific writer. *New International Encyclopædia*, s.v. "Fay, Theodore Sedgwick," 8:409.

54. Prostitution was legally tolerated in Hamburg as a "necessary evil" that "must be endured under strict supervision of the authorities." As long as prostitution was legal, it could be monitored and regulated so that human trafficking and venereal diseases could be kept in check, they argued. In Berlin, prostitution had been alternately tolerated and forbidden, but an ordinance in 1851 tolerated it again after it had been illicit for a few years. Sanger, *History of Prostitution*, 189–252.

The next day we went to visit the American Legation, for the purpose of securing any useful information as to the laws and usages of the Prussians, and also what toleration or religious restrictions existed among them, and further, what would be a proper method of securing an interview with the king, if we should seek it.[55] We gave our names to the American minister, Mr. Barnard, but not having a card of introduction at hand, we were not admitted to his presence. We then sought an interview with his secretary, Mr. Fay, residing in another street, where we obtained ingress, his dignity being more accessible. Mr. Fay hailed us as American citizens very familiarly, and readily put many pointed questions concerning our Mission, and especially the nature of our religion; as, Do not your people totally reject christianity? No, we do not reject true christianity; no, by no means. But do your people believe in polygamy? Most assuredly, we believe in the Patriarchal Order of a Plurality of Wives, as taught·in the Old and New Testament.[56] I wish to be open to conviction of truth, how can you prove the doctrine of Plurality from the Scriptures? it is not at all congenial with my feelings. I waived such an abrupt and hurried investigation, and sought to turn the conversation by promising at another time to put some books into his possession, that might satisfy his mind better than a hasty conversation could do. Mr. Fay politely proffered to give us a card to the Hon. Mr. Barnard, for which we thanked him kindly, and promised

55. Frederick William IV (1795–1861) was king of Prussia from 1840 to 1861.

56. After the public announcement of polygamy, Latter-day Saints justified the practice as not only acceptable but in many ways superior to monogamy. They often used biblical arguments, including the fact that numerous patriarchs had many wives and that God had commanded Adam and Eve to multiply. Orson Pratt claimed that polygamy had been practiced in the early Christian Church, but secular Roman law forbade it, and Christianity abandoned the practice. Benjamin Johnson also argued that the New Testament taught that the gospel of Christ was the same gospel of the Old Testament polygamists, and that Paul's admonition for bishops to be "the husband of one wife" (1 Timothy 3:2) implied that polygamy was practiced in his day. Latter-day Saints reasoned that monogamy led men to engage in various immoral activities, so polygamy would solve that problem as well. There were also several other physiological and sociological reasonings offered in support of the practice. Whittaker, "Early Mormon Polygamy Defenses," 43–63; "Christian Polygamy in the Sixteenth Century," *Seer* 1, no. 12 (December 1853): 177–83; Johnson, *Why the "Latter Day Saints" Marry a Plurality of Wives*, 12.

to call upon him again soon. We then soon had the pleasure of being admitted into the presence of Mr. Barnard, who was once a citizen of New
York State, near Rochester. Mr. Barnard, apparently at the age of 55 or 60,
seemed intelligent and dignified, but rather disposed to have our interview
brief, saying that he was very busy just then; upon which intimation I
immediately arose, and said to brother Houtz, Then let us leave—giving
him to understand that we were not so dull that we could not appreciate a
hint. Upon this he immediately said, O, no, sit a little. Accordingly we sat
down, and broached our business. We wished an interview with the King
of Prussia, and such a knowledge of the laws as would best subserve the
interests of our Mission. He responded, I can render you no aid whatever in
getting access to the king—perhaps Mr. Fay may inform you how the king
is likely to be approached by strangers. We had not however asked his aid
in any way, but said incidentally that we had yet to learn how his majesty
could be approached. He said there was but one Church known in the laws
of Prussia, and that was the Evangelical Church, of which the king was the
acknowledged head, and the king felt it his duty to protect their religious
order as much as any other interest pertaining to the people.[57] The Evangelical Lutheran Church was the only established religion of the kingdom, but
as there were some whole provinces that adhered to the Roman Catholic
faith, that religion existed by *permission* of Government, under the special and personal supervision of the king's police. The Jews also have some
shadow of religious privilege. The Baptists have a secret and unobserved
existence in Prussia; but Baptist missionaries from other countries were not
allowed to remain in the kingdom of Prussia. Professor Oncken, a Baptist, was immediately ejected from Prussia. And many highly respectable
sectarian ministers have been unceremoniously ejected from Prussia. The
Baptists are not permitted to hold public meetings in any public place, or
to baptize, or to administer the rites of marriage. Their meetings are held in
an unobserved stolen manner; and their baptisms practised after the same

---

57. The king of Prussia was head of the country's state church. In 1817, King Frederick William III united the Reformed and Lutheran churches in Prussia. Some
Lutherans objected, and in 1841, King Frederick William IV permitted a group
of Lutherans to break off and form the Evangelical Lutheran Church in Prussia.
"Light on the Lutheran Church in Germany," 260–61.

manner.[58] I inquired of Mr. Barnard, if there was anything in the policy of the Government, or in their existing laws, that would forbid persons to emigrate from Prussia to other countries. He replied, that both the policy and the existing laws of the Government distinctly forbad emigration. The law, continues he, forbids any man to leave this kingdom until he has performed service in the army during a given number of years. And if any citizen of Prussia, after returning from a foreign land, (though he may have been absent twenty years,) is proved not to have served in the royal army of Prussia, he is immediately forced into the army, until the law which he has violated is magnified. The labouring poor are regarded as constituting an essential part of the support of Government, and any religion that favours emigration is obnoxious to the policy and laws of the Government.[59]

Seeing no poor persons in the streets, as in England, I inquired the cause. My interpreter and guide replied, If a poor person were to lisp any expression of his wants or sufferings, he would be immediately seized and put into the custody of the Government officers, and put out of sight, and disposed of in a manner quite unwelcome to a freeman. An intelligent gentleman, who had been a student of the University of Berlin,[60] told me that thousands died of starvation; and the oppression of the people was wholly beyond endurance, and insurrection and rebellion would inevitably take place soon. The rebellion of 1848[61] humbled the King, insomuch that he granted the people, in the language of Mr. Barnard, the shadow of a

58. The Prussian constitution of 1850 nominally provided for religious freedom, but various articles in it contained exceptions to religious liberty that were open to interpretation. It stated, "The exercise of religious liberty shall not be permitted to interfere with the civil or political duties of the citizens." Thus state-recognized religions, such as Catholics and Lutherans, were granted more liberty than nonrecognized religions, such as Baptists. Mitchell, "Mormons in Wilhelmine Germany," 19–22.

59. In Prussia in the 1840s, citizens were permitted to leave the country as long as they did not owe military duty, after stricter emigration laws had been in place during earlier decades. Torpey, "Leaving: A Comparative View," 16–18.

60. The University of Berlin, known today as Humboldt University of Berlin, was founded in 1811 under the auspices of Frederick William III of Prussia by Wilhelm von Humboldt.

61. In the 1840s, reforms raged in Paris, and in March 1848, crowds of protestors similarly gathered in Berlin. King Frederick Wilhelm IV surprisingly responded to

constitution; but though the spirit of tyranny was forced to go abroad for a little season, seeking rest, yet it has returned to the breast of the King of Prussia, with seven other spirits worse than the first. As in the empire of France, the efforts of Prussians to mollify the rigors of despotism have only resulted in multiplying those rigors tenfold. And the King's little finger in the year 1853 is thicker than his thumb was previous to 1848. And this retrograde tendency to absolutism is supposed to be universally prevalent on the whole continent of Europe.

We readily ascertained from the American Legation, that our arrival in Berlin was looked for[,] and the object of our mission was no secret. That Legation was familiar with the fact, that the King had sought an acquaintance with the history of the Church of Jesus Christ of Latter-day Saints. We found our appointment had been published in German newspapers, also a notice of the Danish emigration. An exaggeration of the number of the Danish emigration, and also a misrepresentation of the design of our people in obtaining emigrants from Europe, in order to become a state and subserve political ends, were quite apparent in the different public German prints. On Thursday, the 27th January, we again called upon the secretary, Mr. Fay, not knowing whether we should be allowed to remain in Berlin long or short, but desirous to make as many acquaintances as possible, and glean from the whole a knowledge of the best possible course to pursue, not forgetting to humble ourselves before the Lord for all our unworthiness. But from some cause our reception with the secretary was decidedly different from what it was the day before. Cool and reserved, he had concluded that his mind ought to be established in matters of religion, at the age of 45 years, and he declined reading the books which he had previously requested the pleasure to see. He gave his opinion, that if we wished to communicate with the King, he was only accessible through some prime minister, or leading officer in the state department. He named the Secretary of Foreign Affairs, and also his excellency the State's Minister of Public Worship, V. Raumer.

Now, after retiring to our room, and calling upon the Lord, according

their demands by promising a constitution and election reform, but he changed his plans in April 1849. A constitution was created in December 1848 and revised in 1850. Barclay, "Revolution and Counter-revolution in Prussia," 73–85.

to the privilege of the priesthood in days of revelations from the heavens, we deemed it necessary to mark out some course of conduct to be pursued in our mission, not knowing whether we should be permitted to stay a day or a year. Only two methods of proceedure seemed to present to our minds from which we might select one. One method was, to adopt a secret, unobserved course of introducing the Gospel, without excitement or much notoriety, until we could gain a foothold. We, however, soon came to the conclusion that this method, however desirable, would be wholly impracticable. We could not even stop an hour in any person's house, private or public, without sending our passport to the police-office, to give notice of our whereabouts. There was danger of hiring any one to secrecy that might harbour us, lest he should prove to be a minion of Government in disguise. For, we were most credibly informed that a system of secret espionage was continually practised, and the minions of Government, unobserved, were operating in every sphere—in domestic and private life, as well as public, and yet unknown, except to the authorities of the Government. This fact was most abundantly confirmed to us. The question then arose in our minds—is it the design of the Apostolic power that sent us, that we should undertake to introduce the Gospel in this manner where such a rigid police ordeal exists, with all these liabilities and contingencies. Our conclusion was in the negative. The time has not yet come in this way to fish and hunt in order to save the souls of men, as the spies in Canaan saved Rahab and her house.[62] But the powers that be, shall be honored according to their station, firstly, in order that sovereigns and rulers may be proved in their official responsibilities, knowing full well that they, too, have a Sovereign and Ruler in the eternal heavens, who will judge both the prince and the peasant by one impartial scale of unerring justice. On the other hand, we had received encouragement from his Majesty the King of Prussia that he would maintain an honourable bearing towards a deputation from a

---

62. Jeremiah 16:16 speaks of the gathering of Israel: "Behold, I will send for many fishers, saith the Lord, and they shall fish them; and after will I send for many hunters, and they shall hunt them from every mountain, and from every hill, and out of the holes of the rocks." In Joshua 2, Joshua sends spies to Jericho, and the harlot Rahab takes them in; in Joshua 6, Jericho is destroyed, but Rahab and her family are saved for her treatment of the spies.

numerous and worthy people, whose history and doctrines he had officially inquired after, through our honourable delegate at Washington, J. M. Bernhisel;[63] and whose inquiry had been promptly responded to by an early transmission of all the information which our best books could furnish. The Prussian Ambassador, residing in London, had forwarded to his Majesty, at Berlin, a full and complete set of books from the Church's Branch Office, in Liverpool (England). We concluded that we had a right to anticipate at least a respectable reception, until our mission could be fairly and honourably disposed of, on principles of civility at least. Accordingly our reflections finally balanced in favor of addressing a request to one of the highest officers of the Government of Prussia for to grant us an interview with his Majesty the King of Prussia, and also the privilege of preaching and publishing the Gospel of Jesus Christ in his dominions. Accordingly, we drew up the following letter, addressed to his excellency V. Raumer, State's Minister of Public Worship. Here I insert an exact transcript of the original letter:—

"To His Excellency Mr. V. Raumer, State's Minister of Public Worship.

"The undersigned Ministers of the Gospel of the Church of Jesus Christ, from the United States of America, constitute a deputation from the Church of Jesus Christ of Latter-day Saints (commonly called Mormons), bearing credentials from Brigham Young, Governor of the Territory of Utah, United States of America.

"Your excellency is doubtless aware that his Majesty the King of Prussia, not long since, instructed his Majesty's Minister at Washington, Baron V. Herolt, to inquire of the delegate in Congress from Utah Territory, the Hon. J. M. Bernhisel, what were the distinguishing tenets and doctrines of the Church of Jesus Christ of Latter-day Saints (*alias* Mormons). In response to that inquiry, the books best calculated to give the information desired by his Majesty the King of Prussia, were promptly forwarded to his Majesty from the Church's Office, in Liverpool (England).

"Further action was also taken by the Church of Jesus Christ of

---

63. In 1851, John Milton Bernhisel (1799–1881) was appointed as a Utah territorial delegate to Congress in Washington, DC. He served from 1851 to 1859 and again from 1861 to 1863. Barrett, "Dr. John M. Bernhisel," 159–63.

Latter-day Saints at their late General Conference, held at Great Salt Lake City, September 1st, 1852, to send the undersigned as a chosen deputation, whose duty it should be to seek, in the most respectful manner, an interview with his Majesty the King of Prussia, and with his excellency the State's Minister of Public Worship, in order to answer any interrogations that might be propounded by his Majesty, or by his Majesty's Minister of Public Worship, whereby the marvellous work which has been wrought by the God of our fathers, Abraham, Isaac, and Jacob, in the land of America, and in the islands of the sea, and in remote parts of the earth, may be conveyed to all sovereigns and all subjects, who are meekly and humbly waiting for the salvation of the true Israel of God, scattered abroad among every nation, kindred, tongue, and people.[64]

"The undersigned deputation do also most respectfully solicit the royal favor of being permitted to preach and publish to his Majesty's subjects, in the kingdom of Prussia, the prominent doctrines of the Church of Jesus Christ of Latter-day Saints, as set forth in the publications previously forwarded to his Majesty, at the instance of the Hon. J. M. Bernhisel.

"The undersigned have taken the liberty to address your Excellency in the use of the English language, being but imperfectly skilled in the knowledge of the German tongue.

"And the undersigned will await the reply of your Excellency at Hotel Zur Stadt, Magdeburg, Monstrasse, No. 11.

"In the meantime, supplicating grace, mercy, and peace from the God of Heaven to rest upon his Majesty the King of Prussia, and upon his Majesty's State's Minister of Public Worship, for ever, we have the honor to subscribe ourselves your humble servants in the Gospel of Jesus Christ,

"Orson Spencer.

"Jacob Houtz.

"Berlin, January 29th, 1853."

---

64. Acts 3:13 uses the phrase "the God of Abraham, and of Isaac, and of Jacob, the God of our fathers"; the expression "every nation, and kindred, and tongue, and people" originated in Revelation 14:6.

The foregoing letter having been dedicated to God, we took particular pains to deliver into the residence of His Excellency, with our own hands; the porter of his Excellency received the same, and said that the delivery was right. When this duty was discharged, we felt perfectly tranquil, and satisfied that we had done the best that we could. This letter was delivered to His Excellency on Saturday, the 29th January. On Monday, the 31st, at night, we received a summons signed by the President of the king's police, requiring our attendance at the police office, on Tuesday, the 1st February, at 11 o'clock, a.m.

The night previous to our examination before the king's police, I told Elder Houtz that we would prepare ourselves again to call upon the Lord, and I assured him that we should have some intimation from our Heavenly Father concerning our true position, that night. Here allow me to say, that in all our decisions and doings, there existed the most perfect union of spirit and effort between myself and brother Houtz.

We laid ourselves down to sleep, full of praises, and confidence in our God, neither knowing nor fearing any harm.

That night, I had a dream, which I trust you will allow me to relate. I saw myself on the platform of a scaffold of a barn—the rails and poles laid across from one great beam to another. On the verge of this scaffold of rails and slabs lying far aloft, above the barn floor, in a scattered relation, I saw myself leading the way, and a companion following, the latter saying, this will be a precarious matter to walk on such a scaffold, from one great beam to the other. Yes, said I, but we shall *go* it. Another companion did not seem to reach the height of the scaffold before he went back. A few other men seemed to be sitting hard by the border of the same scaffold, but not exactly upon it. I succeeded in reaching the opposite great beam, in one or two instances however, fixing a place for my companion to step with caution. But after I reached the opposite beam I had yet to make two or three steps, solely upon the beam about twelve inches wide, which seemed the most difficult part of the whole matter. But these steps I was bound to take at all hazards. It occurred to me that it would ill become me to stoop or crawl on my hands and knees, and accordingly I made the attempt to walk the short distance that remained, in a perfectly upright position of the body. But while I was making the requisite steps, I found that I *must* go off. And having gone as far as I could, I made a virtue of necessity, and jumped barely in time to secure my feet under me, and alighted upon some old hay, without any injury, to the gratification of some that were looking on from the side which I had departed from. I joined in the congratulation, and said it was a quick movement indeed. I awoke, and discovered that it was a dream, and immediately exclaimed, From whence is this dream? Is this from God? Lord, how shall I know whether this is from thee or from some other source? The reply then came to me, quick as thought, in an easy manner, as though it had been read from some printed book—"Mine Angel hath stood by your bed-side, to keep all foul spirits away from you, in order that my Spirit might indite the truth upon your mind, even as a fond and tender mother watches over her sleeping child to brush the flies away, and to prevent its being disturbed when it needs refreshing: and this is the way that I revealed myself to my servant Jacob at Bethel, while he slept upon a stone for a pillow: and this is the way that I revealed my will to Solomon in a dream."[65] Then it was, as the foregoing dream and answer to my enquiry flowed into my mind, like honey and oil, that my heart melted within me, and my soul rejoiced in praises to my Heavenly Father. And I exclaimed, has the Lord even spoken to me, and His Angel, like the police of Heaven, stood by my bed-side, while I was unconscious of it, and knew not the glory that surrounded me? This testimonial of the divine guidance and protection, to me, a stranger, in a strange land, afforded me ample compensation for all the travel of a long journey through sea-sickness and frosty deserts, and the privation of family, of home, and of the priesthood of Zion—and the expense of time and means. Many are the testimonies of the Lord to them that keep His commandments, but the richest of all his testimonies are those which come when they are most needed. In the morning I communicated the dream to Elder Houtz, and told him at the same time, that I did not know how long we should be in crossing the scaffold, but probably we might have to jump in order to escape something worse. It occurred to me that it would be best to employ a licensed inter-preter of the English and German languages to act for us before the police

---

65. In Genesis 28:11–19, the patriarch Jacob rests on stone pillows and has a dream of angels ascending and descending on a ladder, and God promises land for his pos-terity. In 1 Kings 3:5–15, the Lord appears to Solomon in a dream and promises him a wise heart.

court, although brother Houtz had a passable knowledge of the German. My object was, to have a private interpreter in disguise, that could oversee both the public interpreter and the Prussian judges, without himself being known as an interpreter. Upon our admission into the presence of the court, however, the court whispered to the public interpreter, and he was detained and not suffered to be present at our examination. Either the clerk of the court or one of the judges acted as interpreter, mangling the English, however, rather disagreeably. After some interchanges of words among themselves, in a low tone, and while passing from one court room to another, they at length commenced the examination, which I will relate with as much accuracy as my memory will permit:—

What is your object in coming to the city of Berlin?

We came here to obtain permission of the authorities of Prussia to preach the Gospel of Jesus Christ, the fundamental doctrines of which are set forth in printed books, which have been sent to his Majesty your King. I then interposed and asked the Court, if we were summoned before that Court in answer to a letter bearing our signatures, addressed to his Excellency V. Raumer, in which letter the object of our visit to the city of Berlin was distinctly explained. The answer of the Court was in the negative. Still, certain questions and concurring circumstances led us to scruple the veracity of the reply. Court.—Will you state what was your object in coming here? or what religion do you teach? Is it the Evangelical religion? Is it the Catholic or the Protestant religion you wish to teach? Answer.—I will tell you in few words. We wish to teach the Gospel as revealed to the Church of Jesus Christ of Latter-day Saints, from the Heavens. This Church of Jesus Christ of Latter-day Saints was organized in the year 1830, in America, by Joseph Smith, a Prophet sent of God, and ordained by the ministry of an Angel from Heaven to reveal and preach salvation to the inhabitants of the earth. Court.—Who is this Jesus Christ? and who is Joseph Smith? Answer.—{Before we could answer the last questions we had to indulge a smile, that authorities high in the established Evangelical Church of Prussia should be troubled with such a weak memory as to forget who Jesus Christ was. They might forget and lose the spirit of Christ, but how should they forget his name?} How, said the Court again, does your religion differ from the Evangelical or Lutheran Church? Reply.—Our Church is an exact likeness to the Primitive Church, having in it Apostles, Prophets,

&c., with the gifts of miracles, healings, &c., enjoying the ministry of angels from heaven. Court.—You have some order of marriage—what is your order of marriage, and how does it differ from that of the Evangelical Church? Answer.—If two persons are mutually agreed, and there are no known obstacles to their union, they are married for time and for all eternity. Court.—Well, that is our method of marriage. I then said, then you marry for time and for all eternity, do you? Yes. Here I take occasion to remark, that the Court did not seem to rest satisfied with the inquiry about marriage, and the answer. They either had a vague and imperfect idea of our system of plurality of wives, or they had forgotten something perhaps which they had been instructed to inquire after, or they could not express their question in English, according to their wish. They undoubtedly conceived that there was something objectionable in our system of marriage, which they wanted to use to our disadvantage, but could not get at it. Have you any secret signs and tokens among you, like unto the Catholics? No, not to my knowledge, for I do not know what secret signs the Catholics have.[66] I asked, if they knew before of our coming, and the object of it. They replied, they suspected our business. Again, I inquired if Mr. V. Raumer, the State's Minister of Public Worship, was the most suitable government officer to apply to, in order to get access to the King, and also to decide the question whether we might preach and publish the Gospel in the Kingdom of Prussia? The Court replied in the affirmative, and said that our application to preach the Gospel would then be handed over to his Excellency Mr. V. Raumer, for his sanction or rejection. This led us most assuredly to believe not only that his Excellency Mr. V. Raumer had received our letter of the 29th January, 1853, and instigated the summons which had brought us before the King's Police, February 1st, but also that Mr. V. Raumer was actually in session with the President of the King's Police in an adjoining room, and did *dictate* the order for our banishment out of the kingdom, which followed the investigation. After we had borne testimony

---

66. Spencer conveniently used his lack of knowledge of Catholic symbols to skirt the issue, as Latter-day Saints do use "signs and tokens" in temple rituals. In Spencer's time, these practices were done in other buildings, since the Latter-day Saints did not then have a temple. Bradshaw, "Freemasonry and the Origins of Modern Temple Ordinances," 159–237.

to the work of the Lord, and the organization of the Church by his Prophet Joseph Smith, and also to the doctrines of the Church, they took our declarations in writing, and requested us to sign the same, which we did do with all readiness, being glad to leave upon their public records a knowledge of the fundamental principles of salvation, with the testimony of two witnesses bearing the eternal Priesthood of God signed to the same. And I verily believe our testimony will remain against them to the final reckoning of the judgment day. Our testimony was then translated into the German for the comprehension of the whole Court, and transferred into another room for the inspection and action of some higher powers. During this period we held some little conversation with that member of the Court, who could speak imperfect English, concerning the relative populations and products of Berlin and New York. I never was more sensible of the instruction given by Jesus Christ to his disciples—when you are brought before governors and kings, "take no thought how or what ye shall speak, for it shall be given you in that same hour what ye shall speak."[67] While we were going to the place of trial, I repeated aloud to Brother Houtz the foregoing passage of Scripture, feeling to rejoice abundantly in the assurance that the precious promise of Christ would in very deed be perfectly fulfilled. Surely the Lord is a God of Truth, and let all people trust in his most holy and unerring word.

After the lapse of some time, the decision of the higher authorities was returned from some distant apartment or office, and we were permitted to read our destination in the English language. The decision of the Court was in substance as follows:—You, Orson Spencer and Jacob Houtz, are hereby commanded to depart out of this kingdom to-morrow morning, under the penalty of *transportation*; and you are also forbidden ever to return to this kingdom hereafter, under the penalty of being transported. After perusing the order, I requested the Court to give me a copy of it, in order that I might have some written instrument to show the authority that had sent me. My request was denied, and I was given to understand that we would have to obey the order without any copy being given. This denial was *significantly* expressed. I then said, have we committed any fault, or any crime whatever, that we should be subjected to such abrupt and rigid

---

67. Matthew 10:19.

banishment? The reply was, No! but it is your religion that has caused it. When this declaration was made, imputing the only fault to our religion, my heart inwardly rejoiced, and I said to myself, our religion is good, and pure, and faultless, having come from the holy heavens; and having spoken against that, you will have to answer it to Him, who revealed it from the Heavens for the blessing and salvation of all those who should receive it. I next sought to have them protract the time of our departure, alleging that we had some unfinished business that would detain us a week, or at least two or three days, in order to finish it, &c. No; was the peremptory reply, you cannot have it; you must go, to-morrow morning. Finding them inexorable, I then said, I suppose the morning means any time till evening. The reply was, you must go to-morrow morning at eight o'clock, at the same time using some contemptuous expression in the German, which was understood by Elder Houtz to be uttered in some anger. The ruling judge, then got the railway time-table, after which he said, that we must depart at half-past seven o'clock the next morning.

The court next asked, if we fully understood our destination and their decision, and if we did, they wished we would sign a declaration that we were not ignorant of the decision, but fully understood it, which we consented to sign. Finding, that the more we said to them, so much the more they endeavoured to thrust us away in a barbarous manner, we ceased our efforts. They then passed us into two other rooms, in each of which we underwent a minute and distinct inspection, the object of which appeared to be, to take a registry of the description of our persons, and perhaps another object was to overawe us with a sense of our danger if ever we were found again in the precincts of that kingdom. But we looked down upon them as being as much beneath us as the very dust of our feet: and they had no power but from God, who was our friend by covenant, and not theirs. Therefore we felt more contempt for them, than they possibly *could* feel *for us*, because we had knowledge from whence all power emanates, and they were ignorant. Poor wretches! our souls were full of blessings and heavenly desires for their good, and the good of their king and all his subjects, up to the very day that they thrust us from their presence, and would not hearken to the great tidings which we had brought to them over seas and continents, and Angels had brought from the distant realms of glory. The heavens will bear an eternal record that we loved their souls, and poured out our hearts night and day that peace and salvation might come unto them; but now our desires are turned to other people who are more worthy of the kingdom of God. They took the precaution so to mark our passport, that when we had occasion to show it, some significant marks would show policemen that we were under sentence of expulsion from the kingdom. It was now past two o'clock in the afternoon, and we still desired to see if the American Minister, or his Secretary, could or *would* do anything expressive of his disapprobation of such proceedings towards American citizens. We knew that such treatment was undoubtedly in violation of the comity of civilized and friendly nations. Our next object was to prove the fidelity of our own Ambassador towards American citizens. We however found that both the members of the Legation had gone out upon a riding excursion, and would not return to their office till evening. Although the time allowed to us to tarry was inadequately short, still we called again, and with some difficulty obtained a few moments of the Secretary's time in signing our passports, and the meagre consolation from him that many others, and some of the best men, had been as abruptly driven from the city as we had been. We then resigned ourselves submissively to the decree that thrust us out, being abundantly assured that there was no probable chance to evade it. Reflections, of course, arose in our minds—had we done all that we could to plant the Gospel in the hearts of the people to whom we were sent? Would it have been wisdom in us to have remained beyond the time stipulated by the government for our departure, and thereby put the validity and efficacy of their order to the test? Was there a reasonable hope that we could have set down with impunity in any other part of the Prussian dominion? Was it possible that the king himself (living in close proximity with the State's Minister of Public Worship, and the President of Police) had not been a co-worker in the expulsory order, and perhaps would have countermanded the order of his State's Minister and the President of Police? These were questions that passed and repassed through our minds with as deep considerations as the circumstances of the case would allow. We felt the importance of the mission, its bearing upon the destinies of a great and precious people, and the lamentation that must follow any neglect or mismanagement on our part. The repulse was sudden, and, so far as we knew, unparalleled in the history of the missions of this Church. For the success of this mission, prayer had probably been offered up to God daily from the hearts of the best of men in many lands. As yet, however, up to the date of this letter, we have not been able to discover any essential error in our proceedings. Our minds have enjoyed quietude and satisfaction in the endeavour to do the best that we could, and we have been enabled, in all meekness and faith, to wash our feet clean from the condemnation that may attend the inhabitants of Prussia. And should you, dear President, upon the reception of this letter, think proper to give us your approbation for having gone to the full extent that our wisdom and ability would permit in righteousness, it will tend greatly to confirm our joy and satisfaction in the important mission assigned us. A careful observer of signs and circumstances might feel prompted to conjecture several reasons, or rather causes, why the message of heaven has been so abruptly and deplorably spurned, and rejected by the authorities of the kingdom of Prussia. The genius of the Prussian Government is widely different from what many living in the free United States, might suppose it to be.

There are two classes of men, who are in some measure qualified to form a tolerably correct estimate of the nature and character of the governments of Europe, or more especially of the Western parts of Europe. One class is, those who have travelled or lived under these governments; another is, those who have seen the condition of these nations, in the visions of the Spirit of God. But one abatement should enter into the calculation of those who have travelled into the nations of Europe, only a few years since; and that is this: Europe is not now what it was only a year or two since. The bias and wane to Democracy which existed a few years since, is now making an accelerated retrograde movement back to the most rigid despotism. Where revolutions have recently occurred,[68] the people themselves have proved to demonstration that they cannot abide either freedom, or blessing, or salvation. They cannot endure the simplest principles of self-preservation and order, saying nothing of the purer and higher order and organization

---

68. In 1848, numerous revolutions occurred throughout Europe, including in France, Prussia, Italy, Poland, Romania, and Hungary. Discontent with feudal systems and other issues sparked upheavals in France, and the revolutionary spirit spread across the continent. Additionally, the infamous Irish Potato Famine created turbulence in the British Isles at this time. Some Latter-day Saints viewed these events as heralding in the second coming of Jesus Christ. Revolutions would lead to religious

of the Gospel. Southern Slaves are better qualified to appreciate blessings (aside from the curse upon them) than the great mass of white subjects in Western Europe.[69] Consequently, like the dog, the latter return to their own vomit, and like the sow that was washed, they return with ten-fold greediness to their wallowing in the mire.[70] The freest and most intelligent nation of Europe, except England, has made a most palpable *demonstration* towards popular freedom. The result has been, that the people themselves could not abide any thing but high-handed despotism. Their hearts are so full of filthiness, abomination, and every deceitful and wicked thing, that nothing but the fetters of despotism, drawn tighter and tighter, until they actually perish in their chains, will meet the exigency of their case. This demonstration in favour of a sort of *telestial* salvation,[71] has been made by the most inviting and promising part of all Continental Europe. France is the flower and pride of the Continent of Europe. But France cannot abide even the twilight that shoots up from the Western horizon. She recoils back

---

freedom, which in turn would lead to Mormon converts who could gather to Zion. Jews would also be freed from oppression and thereby be able to fulfill prophecies about their role in Palestine. See Livingston, *From Above and Below*, 35–70.

69. Most nineteenth-century Protestant whites held a belief that black Africans and African-Americans descended from biblical Cain, and this tradition likewise permeated Latter-day Saint ideas. Some blacks were ordained to the priesthood during the lifetime of Joseph Smith, but after the Latter-day Saints migrated to Utah, Brigham Young banned those of black African descent from receiving the priesthood and participating in temple ordinances, a practice that was in place until 1978. Mauss, "Casting Off the 'Curse of Cain,'" 82–83; Reeve, *Religion of a Different Color*, 106–39, 259; Allred, "Traditions of Their Fathers," 34–49.

70. In the New Testament, 2 Peter 2:22 reads, "But it is happened unto them according to the true proverb, The dog is turned to his own vomit again; and the sow that was washed to her wallowing in the mire."

71. In Latter-day Saint theology, God will ultimately judge all people and assign them a degree of glory based on their actions. These glories are the celestial, terrestrial, and telestial, *telestial* being a uniquely Latter-day Saint word. The telestial kingdom is the lowest of the three, and its inhabitants are described as "liars, and sorcerers, and adulterers, and whoremongers, and whosoever loves and makes a lie." Larry E. Dahl, "Degrees of Glory," in *Encyclopedia of Mormonism*, 1:367–69; Revelation, 16 February 1832, in Godfrey et al., eds., *Joseph Smith Papers, Documents, Volume 2*, 191 [Doctrine and Covenants 76:103].

towards her own nocturnal darkness, as more congenial to the abominations that have long been growing sturdy and invincible with the duration of many ages. How then shall the nations dwelling in exterior darkness, without even the faint radiations of twilight, abide any thing but the vials of wrath, and those without mixture. Western Europe, including Prussia, Austria, Greece, Russia, and Turkey, are, in comparison with France, as huge beasts likened to some slender animals whom some effort has been made to tame: the grisly bear, tiger, and lion, in other words, compared with the deer or antelope. But if my information be correct, even France is far deeper in the pit of horrid abomination than Sodom ever dared to be.[72] What then must Western Europe be? Here, similitudes fail. The despotism and slavery of Western Europe is like the darkness of ancient Egypt, more capable of being felt than described. The lips of the populace are sealed, and the province of their *thoughts* is confined to the narrow, dark chambers of their natal embryo. Long-continued estrangement from natural rights and privileges has rendered even conscience their enemy, and a despot accusing and menacing them for presuming to think or speak in matters of freedom and salvation. The spirit of truth has been so belied, and so ingeniously transformed and depicted for many ages as an enemy to the popular masses, that it is regarded as a visitant of hideous designs, and no matter in what form it comes, it is looked upon as full of "fire-brands, arrows, and death;" and the people flee before the first symptoms of its approach, as they would from the pestilence, and myriads of forked-tongued serpents. But are the rulers happy who have reduced the people to this sad and hopeless dilemma? No, far from it. That which they have sown, they stand in momentary and awful fear of reaping. They have reduced and subjugated the people through lies, bribery, sensuality, imprisonment, tortures, murders, and, worse than all, pious dogmas that doubly kill. Those are happy, like robbers, whose immense, blood-bought treasures have to be watched with incessant and fearful anxiety. But though you, dear brother, may not ask, yet some will doubtless ask, how can all these things be and continue in countries where there exist such splendid and richly endowed Universities of learning, and where religion is not only universal, but established by

---

72. *Sodom* alludes to a biblical city known for its wickedness, described in Genesis 18–19. *Oxford English Dictionary*, s.v. "Sodom."

law, and the sovereigns themselves are the pious heads of the Church, and profess and solemnly avow that they receive continued revelations from the God of Heaven, to direct them in all their ways? Universities have schooled the people, and law-established Churches have prayed and preached the people into the nethermost corners of hell. But for these, the people would not, and could not, have been subjugated and reduced to such impotence, wretchedness, and abomination.

I do exceedingly marvel at the great power of the Devil among the nations. The extent of the oppressions, cruelties, abominations, and miseries, is greater than my heart ever conceived before. If these be the fruits of early apostacy and transgression of the laws, covenant, and ordinances of God, then my heart exclaims, how terrible are thy judgments against evil doers, Oh, thou Holy One of Israel! Oh, thou righteous ruler of heaven and earth, suffer not men to continue in their wickedness, and corrupt the whole earth; but cut off the wicked speedily, before they multiply and increase their wicked ways upon the earth.

The condition of the wicked nations of the earth is so complicated, so full of entanglement, so hopelessly corrupt, that it really seems bordering upon unkindness and want of fatherly compassion not to allow them to make a speedy end of themselves, and sweep the earth clean of such unspeakable pollution. When I have stood by the bedside of a fellow-man suffering excruciating agonies from some mortal and incurable disease, I have most heartily wished that death might hasten to his release, and rescue the sufferer. When I contemplate the condition of many nations of Europe, as beyond the pale of recovery to righteousness, and as led captive to the Devil, and a prey to every deceitful and hurtful lust—shut out from knowledge—all domestic and social ties sundered, even as the precious growing corn is rent and trampled under foot of swine[73]—all offices of humanity abolished or banished—the cries of starvation, excessive and rewardless toil, the wailings of calamity, and the groanings of oppressed innocence, are hushed at the point of the bayonet, or by the gloom of the dungeon—and the light of eternity is not permitted to reflect a ray of consolation upon the benighted mind—my heart exclaims, Oh Lord, hasten to reap down the

---

73. Compare Matthew 7:6, which speaks of pearls, rather than corn, being trampled by swine.

earth, and suffer not the miseries of the human race to linger. Let the strong be dispossessed of his ill-obtained goods. But, after the testimony of Thy servants has gone forth to all nations, let righteousness be laid to the line, and judgment to the plummet; and sweep away the refuges of lies; and abolish the covenant with death; and break up the agreement with hell.

Now, dear sir, that there is an agreement between some of the potentates in high places, and the satanic rulers of the darkness of this world, suffer me to give a very reliable account of some extraordinary features in the character of the Czar of Russia.[74] My information comes through an intimate friend of the Emperor Nicholas, said to be a philosopher of considerable distinction. Nicholas, the Emperor of Russia, claims that he receives revelations from God continually, and that he has been raised up by the God of heaven for the express purpose of uniting the Catholic, and Greek or Protestant, Churches into one Church. By him the long lamented breach between these adverse religious powers is to be healed. The reins of authority and power are given to him for this express purpose and end. He regards the Pope of Rome to be a usurper and impostor; and he, Nicholas, is ordained of God to destroy the power of the Pope, and unite the two great contending religious powers into one. Now, the Emperor Nicholas is the brother-in-law of Frederick William, the King of Prussia; that is, the Empress of Russia, the wife of Nicholas, is the sister of Frederick, the King of Prussia. Now, the King of Prussia is said to be a very pious man, and his brother-in-law, Nicholas, must be equally pious, seeing that he receives revelations from God, and is ordained to so great a work of restitution in the affairs of Europe. And there is ample proof that the latter couples works with his faith, in that he musters the largest and most effective military force now known in Europe. *Par nobilium fratrum*,—a pair of noble brothers![75]

The Emperor of Austria,[76] too, for the first time, it is said, has paid a very friendly and familiar visit to Berlin to see King Frederick. Each of these sovereigns, it will be recollected, claims to be the representative of adverse religions. Catholics, Greeks, and Lutheran Protestants here seem

---

74. Emperor Nicholas I (1796–1855) reigned from 1825 to 1855.
75. Nicholas I was married to Alexandra Feodorovna, or Charlotte of Prussia (1798–1860), the daughter of Frederick Wilhelm III.
76. Emperor Franz Joseph I (1830–1916) reigned over Austria from 1848 to 1916.

inclined to dip their several spoons into one common soup-dish,—

> "How pleasant 'tis to see
> Kindred and brethren all agree."

It only needs the Sublime Porte, or the Mahometan Ottoman, to cast *his* spoon into the same soup-dish, and the holy quadrangle will be nearly complete enough to take peace from a fourth part of the earth, and carry out the *consumption* decreed of heaven, and make an end of many nations. No doubt, these pious personages will do up their work religiously, according to their holy profession and calling. They already know how to use the sword, in order to back up their revelations, and, if other things are lacking, to make out their full equipment, I think the arsenal of heaven can furnish a ready supply of such effective instruments as plague, pestilence, and famine, by which the *consumption decreed* will be accomplished. And if the straggling dissenters, under the name of "spiritual rappers," who have fled to the United States, do not hail from the ensign of Western Europe for their license to preach and reveal the things of the "Spirit World," they are in danger of being hurled into oblivion by the greater works of the authorities at their fountain head on this side the Atlantic.[77] The people of the Continent are living in fearful apprehension of revolutions and wars; and the suspense, jealousy, and vigilance consequent upon such a state of things, are like the precursory pangs of dissolution. The first shadow of suspicious appearances is readily magnified and changed into real form and substance, and summary execution nips the germ before any development of the bud can designate to what class or genus it belongs. The rulers fear the people, and the people hate the rulers.

The last desperate effort is now making of trying to unite the different sovereigns against the people, under the sway of their respective sceptres.

---

77. Spiritualism began in New York in the late 1840s and then spread rapidly across the country, including among some Latter-day Saints in the San Bernardino colony in California. Spiritualists believed they could contact the spirits of the dead, who would respond by knocking or by manifesting themselves through a medium, a living person. Apostle Amasa Lyman opposed spiritualism in San Bernardino in the 1850s, but in the late 1860s and 1870s, he and other disaffected members became involved in the spiritualist Godbeite movement. Bitton, "Mormonism's Encounter with Spiritualism," 39–50.

This is a *dernier resort*;[78] necessity alone dictates it, and necessity may perhaps bring this union of rulers into a temporary completion. The channels of intercommunication among the people are measurably closed or abolished, through a system of espionage that has reached the zenith of perfection. Consequently the people cannot know their own strength, neither can they consolidate their energies into any position of self-defence against the shameless aggressions of despotic rulers. No plans can be concerted or even discussed with safety; no whispers can reach the ceiling of midnight privacy, but the spirits of air will convey the same to their antagonistic oppressors. Therefore the people are being prepared to be led forth to the slaughter, by despots, even as the ox that knows not his bloody destination. They cannot help themselves; they have neither knowledge nor power to help themselves. The chains of darkness hold them fast. There is none to deliver—no arm to bring salvation. But some one may say, is there none of Heaven's Police to guard the way of the righteous—to open the window-shutters of the soul—to cleanse the avenues of intelligence, and let in the redeeming light of eternity, except for those who dwell in Zion? Yes, it may be there is all this, and more; but seemingly not now. Is not the Lord beginning to say to many nations, "this is your hour, and the power of darkness"?[79] and as he said to Judas when Satan had entered into him, "what thou doest, do quickly"?[80] Do not the powers of darkness prevail over all flesh, excepting but a small portion? And is not that wicked revealed in high places (though in lying wonders) so effectively as to ensnare the nations, and ultimately to execute the *decree of consumption*, when few men shall be left. But if judgments are permitted to go forth, and wars are allowed to make many nations desolate, in order to gratify the evil propensities of despotic rulers, may we not fondly hope that many millions, now groaning under the iron hand of their oppressors, will make a happy exchange of their condition? They are not voluntary and intelligent agents in these prospective scenes of carnage and human slaughter, and are therefore comparatively innocent. And though swept off this earth by appalling calamities, and the ambitious schemes of blood-guilty rulers, yet they will go to that land where the "weary

---

78. *Dernier resort* (or *ressort*) means "last resort." *Oxford English Dictionary*, s.v. "dernier."
79. Luke 22:53.
80. See John 13:27.

will be at rest, and where the wicked will cease from troubling." In that land to which the signs of the times seem to indicate that they are hastening, they will become accessible to the servants of God and to the glorious light of truth, which are now withheld from them by the cunning craft of men, and by rulers who make merchandise of the souls of men, and sacrifice millions upon the bloody altar of their ambition.

But I have already protracted this letter beyond my original design, and must now close. The work of the Lord is very prosperous in Great Britain, under the able Presidency of Elder Samuel W. Richards. The Saints are progressing in knowledge, union, and the power of the spirit of truth. I have had the pleasure to preach to several large meetings of different Conferences, and find that the revelation concerning the New and Everlasting Covenant is not only happily and gratefully received, but it is also inspiring the thousands of British Saints with the most ardent desires to be gathered to the valleys of the mountains. On account of the great length of time required in order to get your instructions relative to my future movements, and that of those associated with me in the Prussian Mission, I have written to President Orson Pratt for his earliest advice as to the propriety of my laboring in the United States, together with Elder Jacob Houtz, until you think proper to call me to my family and the bosom of the Church.[81] A homeward mission is always acceptable, when it is followed with your approbation and blessing. Elder Clough is advised to stop in England at present. Any advice that your multiplied engagements may suffer you to give my dear family in my absence will be most sensibly appreciated.

That you may long live to feed the Church of Christ with knowledge and understanding, and hold the sceptre of righteousness on the earth, and enjoy the fruits of your abundant labors, is the unceasing prayer of your humble servant, and truly affectionate brother in the Gospel of Jesus Christ,

Orson Spencer.
Liverpool, England, February 8th, 1853.

---

81. Orson Spencer and Jacob Houtz left England on April 2, 1853, aboard the ship *America*, and Spencer returned to Utah later that year. "Departure of Elders Spencer and Houtz," *Millennial Star* 15, no. 16 (April 16, 1853): 250; Jenson, *Latter-day Saint Biographical Encyclopedia*, 1:338.

3

EDWARD STEVENSON AND THE GIBRALTAR MISSION

Historical Introduction

IN JANUARY 1885, THE *JUVENILE INSTRUCTOR* MAGAZINE ran a short cover story on the history of Gibraltar, known as "the Rock," the British overseas territory located on the southern tip of the Iberian Peninsula bordering Spain. The editor, George Q. Cannon, wrote, "When Elders Edward Stevenson and N[athan] T. Porter arrived in Gibraltar in March, 1853, to preach 'Mormonism,' they were immediately taken before the police to plead their cause. Elder Porter was required to leave and the only thing which saved Elder Stevenson from sharing the same fate was the fact that he had been born on the Rock; still he was forbidden to preach his religion. He, however, during his labors of one year, and amid great privations and trials, succeeded in bringing several persons into the Church."[1]

Another article on Gibraltar or even a mention in the future pages of

---

1. "Gibraltar," *Juvenile Instructor* 20, no. 2 (January 15, 1885): 18.

Edward Stevenson. © Intellectual Reserve, Inc.

the *Juvenile Instructor* would have been highly unlikely had the cover story not caught the eye of Stevenson, by then sixty-four years old and living in northern Utah. Desiring that his fellow Latter-day Saints in the Intermountain West might better appreciate the secular history of his British homeland, Stevenson drafted a seven-letter secular history of the Rock, which ran for months in the magazine.[2] Beginning with his eighth letter, Stevenson's ten subsequent missives (for a total of seventeen letters to the *Juvenile Instructor*) chronicle his "missionary experience"[3] as a young elder in Gibraltar in 1853 and 1854. Stevenson narrates his mission to Gibraltar with great passion and some prejudice: the Latter-day Saints, whom he sees as righteous, are constantly trying to build Zion at home and abroad, while the Protestants and Catholics he encounters, whom he sees as less than righteous, are trying to thwart their progress at every turn. His story is filled with black and white characters and organizations—there is little gray in his reminiscent account—like the memoirs left by so many Latter-day Saint missionaries during the nineteenth century. Still, Stevenson's detailed account of his experiences in Gibraltar is significant because he was one of

2. Edward Stevenson, "Gibraltar [Letter 1]," *Juvenile Instructor* 20, no. 4 (February 15, 1885): 55; Edward Stevenson, "Gibraltar, Letter 2," *Juvenile Instructor* 20, no. 5 (March 1, 1885): 66; Edward Stevenson, "Gibraltar, Letter 3," *Juvenile Instructor* 20, no. 6 (March 15, 1885): 93–94; Edward Stevenson, "Gibraltar, Letter 4," *Juvenile Instructor* 20, no. 7 (April 1, 1885): 100; Edward Stevenson, "Gibraltar, Letter 5," *Juvenile Instructor* 20, no. 8 (April 15, 1885): 118; Edward Stevenson, "Gibraltar, Letter 6," *Juvenile Instructor* 20, no. 9 (May 1, 1885): 130–31; and Edward Stevenson, "Gibraltar, Letter 7," *Juvenile Instructor* 20, no. 10 (May 15, 1885): 159.

3. Unlike letters 1–7, letters 8–17 all have "missionary experience" in their subtitles.

only two Latter-day Saints to ever proselytize and temporarily establish the church on the Rock during the first 140 years of the church's history.

Stevenson and Porter's Early Years, 1820–48

Stevenson was uniquely suited by nativity to serve as a missionary in the British colony of Gibraltar. As later experiences made clear, only a native Gibraltarian would be allowed to proselytize on the Rock in the mid-nineteenth century. Stevenson was born on May 1, 1820, in Gibraltar, the fourth son of Joseph Stevenson and Elizabeth Stevens. In 1827, at the tender age of seven, he immigrated with his family to the United States, settling first in New York and then in Michigan. In 1831 his father passed away, leaving him in the care of his mother and siblings. In 1833, three years after The Church of Jesus Christ of Latter-day Saints was organized in upstate New York, missionaries Jared Carter and Joseph Woods evangelized in Michigan. Although still a young man, Stevenson believed their words and embraced their teachings. He was baptized on December 20, 1833, and his mother and several siblings also joined the church. As a family they gathered with the Latter-day Saints in Missouri and endured the trials that followed the church and its members across that state. While living in Far West, Stevenson became more acquainted with Joseph Smith, having first met him while living in Michigan. Stevenson was eventually exiled from Missouri with the body of the church and moved to the temporary safety of Nauvoo, Illinois. There he married his first wife, Nancy A. Porter (the sister of his future missionary companion Nathan T. Porter), in 1845 and was endowed in the Nauvoo Temple in 1846. He crossed the plains in the Charles C. Rich company in 1847, his first of nearly twenty crossings over the plains on behalf of the church as a leader and missionary.[4]

Stevenson's brother-in-law, Nathan Tanner Porter, was born on July 10, 1820, in Corinth, Vermont, to Sanford and Nancy Porter. A decade later, Lyman Wight and John Corrill preached to the Porter family in Illinois, and they were baptized in August 1831. The Porters joined the main body of Saints, first moving to Independence, Missouri, in 1832 and then to

---

4. "Three-Quarters of a Century," *Deseret Evening News*, May 1, 1895; Jenson, *Latter-day Saint Biographical Encyclopedia*, 1:214–16; Stevenson, "Life of Edward Stevenson."

Nauvoo, Illinois, in 1839. Porter was called on missions to the eastern states in 1841 and 1844, but he returned early from his 1844 mission because of the martyrdom of Joseph and Hyrum Smith. In 1847, the Sanford Porter family left Nauvoo and arrived in the Salt Lake Valley that October. Nathan married Rebecca Ann Cherry on November 12, 1848. He was called to accompany Stevenson to Gibraltar in 1852.[5]

Precursor to the Restoration in Gibraltar

Latter-day Saint evangelism in the Mediterranean world began several years before church leaders assigned Edward Stevenson and Nathan T. Porter to Gibraltar in August 1852. Apostle Lorenzo Snow and his companions arrived in Italy in June 1850 to begin proselytizing. Struggling to find a foothold in Italy, Lorenzo Snow determined to expand his Italian Mission into the larger Mediterranean world and even into British India to the east. In 1851, he called William Willes and Hugh Findlay to India,[6] and Thomas Lorenzo Obray to Malta.[7] In the spring of 1852, Snow was called back to church headquarters in Utah along with the other Apostles evangelizing in Europe. Before he left, however, he expressed his hope that missionary work might spread to the Iberian Peninsula. That May, Snow issued a call from the mission headquarters in Malta for elders to begin proselytizing work in Gibraltar. Sharing his desires with President Samuel W. Richards of the British Mission, he explained: "The English and Italian languages are much spoken at Gibraltar as well as the Spanish, and we are anxious to see the kingdom of God beginning to spread its light if possible through the Spanish dominions, and feel to do all in our power to effect so desirable an object. We cannot help but believe that the Lord has some good people in that place." Snow himself was apparently planning to visit Gibraltar to observe conditions firsthand.[8] "In a few days I will have

---

5. Porter, "Record of Nathan Tanner Porter"; Early Mormon Missionaries database, s.vv. "Lyman Wight," "John Corrill."

6. See Britsch, "East India Mission of 1851–56," 150–76; Britsch, *Nothing More Heroic*; Crawley, *Descriptive Bibliography of the Mormon Church*, 2:362.

7. Jenson, *Encyclopedic History of the Church*, 465–66; Crawley, *Descriptive Bibliography of the Mormon Church*, 2:328.

8. The first foreign Latter-day Saint missions were created in Great Britain, and from

completed my arrangements here and shall then, the Lord willing, take my departure for that country, and spend there what little time yet remains at my control, with a view of making an opening as wisdom may direct." The Apostle then asked for a "wise, energetic, faithful, and experienced Elder" to begin proselytizing on the Rock, as well as additional missionaries for India.[9]

Samuel Richards published Snow's letter in his mission's periodical, the *Millennial Star*, and added his own letter of endorsement to open the Rock to missionary work. "The letter of Elder Lorenzo Snow, published in the last Number of the STAR, contains an important call for Elders, to assist in moving on the work in Gibraltar and Bombay, to which we cheerfully respond, and hope the Presidents of Conferences will report to us, without delay, such Elders as they may be acquainted with, who are suitably qualified for those important stations." Richards suggested that single elders or those married men who "can provide for their families" would be excellent choices. "An Elder with some knowledge of the French, Spanish, and Italian languages, would be peculiarly adapted to fill the call for Gibraltar."[10] With his three-year mission complete, Snow departed from Malta and the Italian Mission, stopping over in Gibraltar for several days on his way to Liverpool, England. After crossing the Atlantic to New York City, he arrived in Salt Lake City on July 30, 1852.[11] One month later, Snow's hopes of opening Gibraltar to missionary work and sending more elders to India were realized when the First Presidency called a special missionary conference in Salt Lake City. Edward Stevenson and Nathan Porter, the only two men assigned to Gibraltar, were as stunned at their assignment as the other newly called missionaries were at theirs.

there missionaries were sent throughout the British Empire. The plan to start a mission in Gibraltar fits this pattern. See for example "The Church in 1870," in Plewe, *Mapping Mormonism*, 120–21.

9. Lorenzo Snow to Samuel W. Richards, May 1, 1852, published as Lorenzo Snow, "The Malta Mission: Letter from Elder Lorenzo Snow," *Millennial Star* 14, no. 15 (June 5, 1852): 236–37.

10. Samuel W. Richards, "Editorial: Call for Elders for Gibraltar and Bombay," *Millennial Star* 14, no. 16 (June 12, 1852): 250.

11. Snow Smith, *Biography and Family Record of Lorenzo Snow*, 230–32.

Stevenson's Experience in Gibraltar, 1852–55

Stevenson and Porter departed from Utah in September 1852 and traveled through St. Louis, New York City, and Liverpool before reaching their destination. When Stevenson and Porter arrived at Gibraltar on March 8, 1853, they followed a newfound friend, Mr. Willis, into the garrison. The colony was very strict on allowing visitors, but since Willis was a Gibraltarian resident, the guards did not question Stevenson and Porter upon their entry. One of their first tasks was to climb the Rock of Gibraltar, where they "erected an altar of loose stone and dedicated ourselves and the mission unto the Lord." Days later, they visited Stewart Henry Paget, the police magistrate, who was amazed that they had made it into the port without identification. He told them, "You [Stevenson] will be allowed, as native born to remain on the rock, but if caught preaching will be made a prisoner immediately. And you, Mr. Porter, by this permit will be allowed to remain fifteen days; your permit will not be renewed, and if you preach you will be cast outside our gates."[12] True to local officials' words, Porter was shipped out of Gibraltar on April 1, leaving Stevenson to spread the gospel message by himself.[13]

Stevenson faced considerable opposition from clergy and government officers. On one occasion, an officer who happened to be Methodist put him "under guard, saying that my religion was one that could not be tolerated in that place. For the first time in my life I was marched into the guard house a prisoner." Stevenson was soon released after explaining what he had been doing.[14] Stevenson's worldview included heavenly vengeance against those who opposed the Latter-day work. He met a man who said that "Joe Smith was served just right and ought to have been killed long before he was." The next day, this man "began vomiting blood, and before he could be carried to the hospital he was dead. . . . Thus did the judgment of God speedily follow him."[15] Stevenson also met some people he had

---

12. Edward Stevenson, "Gibraltar, Letter 9, Missionary Experience," *Juvenile Instructor* 20, no. 12 (June 15, 1885): 191; p. 87 herein.

13. Edward Stevenson, "Gibraltar, Letter 10, Missionary Experience," *Juvenile Instructor* 20, no. 13 (July 1, 1885): 196; pp. 88–89 herein.

14. Stevenson, "Gibraltar, Letter 10," 196; p. 91 herein.

15. Edward Stevenson, "Gibraltar, Letter 13, Missionary Experience," *Juvenile Instruc-*

known from his youth in Gibraltar. One Mr. Smith, a Methodist friend of his father, wanted him to preach in their local church, but he rescinded his enthusiasm upon learning he was a Latter-day Saint. Smith's family began reading the Book of Mormon, but Smith opposed the church. Like the man who vilified Joseph Smith, "the poor man was very soon again confined to his bed, but not long this time, for he soon died."[16] Another family friend, Mr. Gilchrist,

Portrait of Nathan Porter. Courtesy of Church History Library.

regarded the church as an "imposture," but he offered to help Stevenson with fifty cents, which Stevenson declined.[17] Despite the antagonism of many of the Gibraltarians, he managed to baptize several converts, and on January 23, 1854, he organized the Rock Port Branch of the church.[18] Not all family friends opposed Stevenson and his doctrines as Mr. Smith and Mr. Gilchrist had done; Stevenson baptized a woman who had dandled him on her knee when he was a child.[19] In May 1854, however, several of his new converts, members of the British military, were sent away to Eastern Europe to fight in the Crimean War.[20] "A solemn

    tor 20, no. 16 (August 15, 1885): 252; p. 100 herein.

16.   Edward Stevenson, "Gibraltar, Letter 12, Missionary Experience," *Juvenile Instructor* 20, no. 15 (August 1, 1885): 229; p. 98 herein.

17.   Stevenson, "Gibraltar, Letter 13," 252; p. 99 herein.

18.   Stevenson recorded twenty-one individuals in his journal whom he baptized or blessed as members of the Rock Port Branch. See Stevenson, diary, table after the March 31, 1854, entry; Neilson, "Proselyting on the Rock of Gibraltar," 130–31.

19.   Stevenson, "Gibraltar, Letter 12," 229; p. 98 herein.

20.   The Crimean War began in 1853, when Russia tried to take over land from the Ottoman Empire, in part so they could have access to the Black Sea. The United Kingdom objected to this, joining French and Ottoman forces in the fight against Russia. Most of the fighting occurred in the Crimean Peninsula, and many soldiers died from disease rather than from fighting. In 1856, all countries involved signed

reflection crossed my mind," Stevenson recorded, "who of this one thousand will ever return home again to fathers, mothers, brothers, sisters or wives?"[21] One of these converts, John McLean, preached his new faith to fellow soldiers and established the Expeditionary Force Branch of the church.[22]

Stevenson was discouraged when these members left Gibraltar, "thus depleting [his] hard earned little branch."[23] Two weeks later, Stevenson recorded his frustration and expressed his wish for divine punishment on Gibraltar: "There is no chance in this garrison under those adulterers <authorities> without permission from the colonial secretary of foreign affairs so I shall soon leave them to their own distruction for it is bound to come on this place. . . . This place neads a scourge to soften the hearts of the rulers & people & I feel to say in the name of the Lord Wo Wo Wo be unto this city."[24] Sometime between May 1854 and April 1855, Stevenson left Gibraltar for England. He oversaw a group of Saints departing from Liverpool aboard the ship *Chimborazo*, aided by Elders Andrew Lamoreaux and Thomas Jeremy, who were also returning from their 1852 missions.[25] Stevenson arrived home in Utah in September 1855.[26]

---

the Treaty of Paris, which created some compromises, including making the Black Sea a neutral zone. Jones, "Wars and Rumors of Wars," 30; Temperley, "Treaty of Paris of 1856 and Its Execution," 387–414.

21.   Edward Stevenson, "Gibraltar, Letter 15, Missionary Experience," *Juvenile Instructor* 20, no. 18 (September 15, 1885): 279; p. 103 herein.

22.   John McLean was baptized on January 6, 1854, and became the president of the LDS Expeditionary Force Branch in Turkey. His division fought in the Battle of Inkerman in November 1854, in which he was wounded by a bayonet. He attempted to preach to fellow soldiers in the war and was mainly unsuccessful, but there were a few converts. Jones, "Wars and Rumors of Wars," 32–34; LeCheminant, "Valiant Little Band," 20–21; Stevenson, diary, table after the March 31, 1854, entry.

23.   Edward Stevenson, "Gibraltar, Letter 14, Missionary Experience," *Juvenile Instructor* 20, no. 17 (September 1, 1885): 262.

24.   Stevenson, diary, May 15, 1854.

25.   Sonne, *Ships, Saints, and Mariners*, 42.

26.   Mormon Pioneer Overland Travel database, s.v. "Seth M. Blair/Edward Stevenson Company (1855)."

Additional Church Service, 1855–97

Stevenson's proselytizing efforts in his native Gibraltar mark just the beginning of his remarkable missionary legacy for the church. After Gibraltar, Stevenson served nine additional proselytizing missions in North America and Europe and helped lead four emigrating companies from the East to Utah. He was also responsible for bringing Book of Mormon witness Martin Harris to Utah and for encouraging his rebaptism in September 1870. Three years after he detailed his missionary experiences in Gibraltar to George Q. Cannon and the readers of the *Juvenile Instructor* in 1885, he joined historian Andrew Jenson and Joseph S. Black on a special church history mission to visit many of the early historic sites of the Restoration.[27] In October 1894, Stevenson was called to serve as one of the first seven presidents of seventies,[28] a position he honorably fulfilled until his passing on January 27, 1897, in Salt Lake City, Utah. He never did return to his birthplace in Gibraltar following the close of his mission in 1855.[29]

Nathan Porter also continued to serve in the church. After being forced out of Gibraltar in 1853, he labored in England until January 1856. While returning to Utah, he traveled with the Hodgetts company, a wagon company that somewhat shepherded the ill-fated Martin handcart company, and they arrived in Salt Lake City in December 1856. He married his second wife, Eliza Ford, in 1857. Nathan Porter and Edward Stevenson were mission companions two more times, in 1869 and 1872, when they traveled to the eastern states. Both Stevenson and Porter were born in 1820, and they both died in 1897 (Porter died April 9, 1897).[30]

---

27. See Neilson, Bray, and Johnson, *Rediscovering the Sites of the Restoration.*

28. Seventy is a Latter-day Saint priesthood office below that of Apostle. The organization and functions of the seventy have changed significantly since the church's beginning, but per Doctrine and Covenants 107:93–94, there have consistently been seven presidents who preside over the other members of the seventy. Both the Old and New Testaments speak of groups of seventy men performing ecclesiastical duties. Alan K. Parrish, "Seventy: Overview," in *Encyclopedia of Mormonism,* 3:1300–1303.

29. "Three-Quarters of a Century," *Deseret News,* May 1, 1895; and Joseph Grant Stevenson, "Stevenson, Edward," in *Encyclopedia of Latter-day Saint History,* 1192.

30. Porter, "Record of Nathan Tanner Porter"; Mormon Pioneer Overland Travel

Edward Stevenson's Family Life

Edward Stevenson married Nancy Areta Porter on April 7, 1845, in Nauvoo, Illinois, and they were sealed in the Nauvoo Temple the following year. When Stevenson left on his mission in 1852, they had four children, ages six and younger.[31] His mother, Elizabeth Stevens Stevenson, moved in with Nancy during his absence, and Stevenson made preparations for his family financially: "I have rented my set of tin tools & shop to Brother Whitehouse for one third of the prophits & the adjoining room for 18 dollers for the year as the man is poor for I was offered 36 dollers the same day for the same room for the same time this with 36 dollers for the other building & the rent of my 5 acre lot will help take care of my familey. I leave them with plenty of provisions for this year and 25 dollars cash so this is grattifying to me to think of though deprived of each other's society & I feel as though they will be blest in my absence."[32] Stevenson was heartbroken when he learned that their infant daughter died while he was away from home: "Rec[eive]d a letter this day from home anounceing the death of my youngest daughter Nancy Elizabeth Stevenson who departed May 5, which takes me rather on surprise haveing recd a letter last month dated Apr. 29th & that stated all well and little Nancy E. was then about 9 months old & could nearly run alone. But, oh, the sudden change the Monster Death can make in only 8 days."[33]

After his Gibraltar mission, Stevenson married three additional wives: Elizabeth DuFresne in 1855, Emily Williams in 1857, and Louisa Yates in 1872. He had another child with Nancy, eight children with Elizabeth, eleven with Emily, and three with Louisa. Practicing polygamy came with substantial challenges: Nancy divorced him in 1869, and Stevenson had to hide from federal prosecution of polygamists during the 1880s, just as many others did.[34]

---

database, s.v. "Nathan Tanner Porter."

31. Stevenson, "Life of Edward Stevenson," 119.
32. Stevenson, diary, September 15, 1852.
33. Stevenson, diary, August 4, 1853.
34. Stevenson, "Life of Edward Stevenson," 138–40, 199.

Source Note

Edward Stevenson wrote the featured seventeen letters to George Q. Cannon, editor of the *Juvenile Instructor*, in response to a short cover story on the history of Gibraltar, which ran in January 1885. The January article barely made mention of Stevenson's missionary sojourn there in 1853–54, nearly thirty years earlier. Cannon published Stevenson's detailed letters in his magazine over a nine-month period, beginning on February 15 and ending on November 15, 1885. Historians are reliant on Stevenson's personal writings and his reminiscent accounts for the history of the Gibraltar mission field in the mid-1850s. Nathan Porter later wrote an autobiographical account of his life, but besides his account and what Stevenson personally recorded at the time, there are no corroborating accounts or documents. Stevenson did send a number of letters back to Utah during his early mission, and their contributions to our understanding of what he experienced as a young missionary in Gibraltar during 1853 and 1854 are noted below. It appears that Stevenson relied heavily on his 1850s writings (such as his letters, *Deseret News* correspondence, and regular diary entries) when he wrote his 1885 letters to Cannon.

DOCUMENT TRANSCRIPTS

Edward Stevenson to George Q. Cannon, June 1, 1885[35]

At a special conference held in Salt Lake City, August 28, 1852, I was called to take a mission to Gibraltar in company with Elder N[athan]. T. Porter. It was at this conference that the revelation on celestial marriage was first made public, and was taken to the world by the greatest number of Elders

---

35. Edward Stevenson, "Gibraltar, Letter 8, Missionary Experience," *Juvenile Instructor* 20, no. 11 (June 1, 1885): 175. Compare with Edward Stevenson, "Gibralter [*sic*] Mission, Letter No. 1," *Deseret News*, January 2, 1856.

that had ever been called on missions at any one time before.

It was agreed that the company going east should meet on the Weber River, forty-five miles from the city, and we would proceed from that point across the plains together. Daniel Spencer was elected captain of the company; Orson Spencer, chaplain; and Orson Pratt, preacher and general instructor. Our company consisted of eighty-four Elders, who had twenty carriages and eighty-eight horses and mules.

In crossing over the Little Mountain our carriage was broken down, and we left our baggage there, covered up with a buffalo robe, while we returned to the city to have the vehicle repaired. After getting the necessary repairs done we again started, but on account of storms were compelled to camp out at the mouth of Emigration Canyon. The next day we arrived at our camp outfit on the Little Mountain just in time to save it from a band of roving Indians. That night we camped all alone on the Big Mountain and were disturbed in our slumbers by the howling of the wolves. We slept very well, however, after having commended ourselves to the care of the Lord.

On the 20th of September, 1852, the whole company began to move and on the 1st of October we arrived at the Missouri River in the best of health and spirits. Our evenings on the journey had been spent around the camp fire discussing religious subjects and often being instructed by Apostle O. Pratt.

Our company now began to scatter to go to their various fields of labor. I joined a company and took steamer for St. Louis. We were kindly treated on board. A discussion took place in the cabin between Elder O. Pratt and Mr. Storon, president of the Missouri College, resulting in a Bible triumph in favor of Apostle Pratt.

In St. Louis, Elder Wm. Pitt found himself without sufficient money for his passage to his field of labor and was walking down the street with his head bowed down, wondering what he should do to obtain the necessary means. Suddenly he saw before him, on the walk, a ten-dollar bill, the exact amount required. He picked it up and after searching in vain for the owner, used it for procuring his passage to England. On November

11th,[36] twenty-one of us, who had engaged passage to Liverpool on a sailing vessel of 1,800 tons burden, set sail, and arrived at our destination on January 5th, 1853.[37] We buried one passenger, a Catholic, in the open sea. He was sewed up in a blanket and some weights were attached to the feet. Burial services, in the absence of one of their priests, were read by Elder Perigreen Sessions,[38] and he was then slid off a plank into the blue waters of the ocean. The usual customhouse overlooking of our baggage took place at Liverpool. A French stranger was detected with a crust surrounding a quantity of tobacco, making it look like a loaf of bread. The experiment cost him $250.00.

While in New York our whole company were provided with passage and provisions with the exception of one Elder, who did not have sufficient money to buy food. A stranger came along and passed several of us, enquiring concerning our missions. But when he came to the only one not yet provided with his outfit, he dropped five dollars into his hand. With a tear of gratitude the stranger was blessed and God praised.

After visiting Prest. S. W. Richards at 15 Wilton Street, Liverpool, and my friends in Leicester, London, Southampton and the Isle of Wight, myself and companion took passage from Southampton on her majesty's steam packet, *Iberia*,[39] on February 28th, 1853.[40] We had enjoyed many

36. Stevenson's letter to the *Deseret News* as well as his personal diary indicate the missionaries actually boarded their ship on November 17. Stevenson, "Gibralter Mission, Letter No. 1"; Stevenson, diary, November 17, 1852.

37. The missionaries sailed from New York to Liverpool, England, aboard the *American Union*, a Yankee ship that was built in 1851. The ship operated in various lines until it became a transient in 1877. Sonne, *Ships, Saints, and Mariners*, 13.

38. Perrigrine Sessions was on his way to preside over the Manchester Conference in 1852; he got sick on the journey and never recovered, so he was sent home in 1854.

39. The *Iberia* was built in England in 1835 and had some of the best passenger accommodations of the period. It had three masts and was owned by the P. & O. Line. Sonne, *Ships, Saints, and Mariners*, 102.

40. Nathan Porter had this to say about their time in Southampton: "On the 11th (February 1853) we took the cars for South Hampton, the point of our embarkation for Gibraltar. Here we met with Elder James Wille, who also came with us across not only the plains but the sea also. He was now President over the Southampton Conference. We stopped in this conference until the 29th [*sic*] (February 1853), visiting the branches of the saints who contributed in furnishing means for

excellent and profitable meetings with the many churches in England, holding before them the new revelation on the eternity of marriage.[41]

On the morning of March 3rd we cast anchor in Vigo Bay,[42] Spain, after sailing 663 miles over the rough Bay of Biscay.[43] This is a lovely bay, abounding with a variety of fish. Its borders abound with oranges, figs, grapes and nuts. Sixty-eight miles more and we pass Oporto,[44] on the coast of Portugal. The next city was Lisbon,[45] the capital of Portugal. It lies two miles up the Tagus River,[46] and is very strongly fortified. The queen's palace and garden are worthy of attention; the remainder of the city is very filthy. On March 6th we left Lisbon and cast anchor in Cadiz Bay, Spain.[47] We were now about 9,000 miles from our Utah home.

our passage. Having now sufficient means we engaged passage on the steam Packet Iberia." Porter, "Record of Nathan Tanner Porter," 57.

41. "While waiting for passage, we visited Portsmouth Dockyard and the Isle of Wight, and went on board the Duke of Wellington, a three decker of 131 guns, many of which were very heavy. This splendid ship is propelled by steam and sail, and has been the flag ship of the British fleet in the recent war with Russia. While on the Isle of Wight we were invited to preach in a sectarian chapel; the people were much taken up with our doctrine, not knowing that we were Mormon elders." Stevenson, "Gibralter Mission, Letter No. 1."

42. Vigo is a seaport on the northwest coast of Spain. *Merriam-Webster's Geographical Dictionary*, s.v. "Vigo."

43. The Bay of Biscay is a gulf of the Atlantic Ocean north of Spain and west of France. *Merriam-Webster's Geographical Dictionary*, s.v. "Biscay, Bay of."

44. Oporto, or Porto, is a seaport city in northwest Portugal. *Merriam-Webster's Geographical Dictionary*, s.v. "Porto."

45. Lisbon has been inhabited for millennia and is located on the coast of the country's southern half. *Merriam-Webster's Geographical Dictionary*, s.v. "Lisbon."

46. The Tagus River originates in eastern Spain and drains into the Atlantic Ocean in Portugal, where it forms a lagoon at Lisbon. *Merriam-Webster's Geographical Dictionary*, s.v. "Tagus."

47. Cádiz, a seaport on the southwest coast of Spain and about sixty miles northwest of Gibraltar, is an ancient city dating back to the Phoenicians around 1100 BC. The Bay of Cádiz is the city's harbor. *Merriam-Webster's Geographical Dictionary*, s.vv. "Cádiz," "Cádiz, Bahía de."

Edward Stevenson to George Q. Cannon, June 15, 1885[48]

On the morning of March 8th, 1853, we were anchored under Gibraltar and heard the morning gun fired as the signal for opening the gates of the fortress, raising the drawbridges, lowering rope ladders and opening up the garrison generally.

The picturesqueness of the rock and garrison from the waters of the bay, especially when illuminated, on a dark night was a grand scene. The houses of both the north and south towns are terraced one above the other on the rock.[49]

Small crafts soon placed us and our luggage on the rock. The guard was ordered to allow no one to pass the portals without proper credentials. One gentleman who was not prepared for this was turned away. My American passport[50] did not reach me at Liverpool as expected, and President Richards failed to influence the American consul and minister at London to supply the deficiency, and I was therefore in danger of being turned away. But strange to say, myself and companion passed into the garrison unchallenged, which afterwards surprised the officers.[51]

---

48. Edward Stevenson, "Gibraltar, Letter 9, Missionary Experience," *Juvenile Instructor* 20, no. 12 (June 15, 1885): 191. Compare to Edward Stevenson, "Gibralter Mission, Letter No. 6," *Deseret News*, April 16, 1856; and "Gibralter Mission," *Millennial Star* 15, no. 17 (April 23, 1853): 266–67.

49. "The morning was fair and beautiful. My feelings were peculiar as I gazed upon the stupendous rock of Gibralter rising from the Mediterranean Sea to the height of 1400 feet. And was it strange to have those feelings, as it was not only the land of my birth, but the field of my future labors in the ministry?" Edward Stevenson, "Gibralter Mission, Letter No. 2," *Deseret News*, January 23, 1856.

50. In the nineteenth century, passports were not as reliable as they are today, and government officials would often permit or forbid people based on subjective judgments, such as class distinctions. At this time, the population of Gibraltar was rapidly increasing, and the area's officials tried to confront the problem by limiting the number of foreigners who visited or lived there. Even visitors needed permits. Robertson, *Passport in America*, 15; Constantine, *Community and Identity*, 93–131.

51. Porter had this to say about how they got into Gibraltar without identification: "We disembarked with our friend Mr. Willis, he having ordered a conveyance to take him to his residence. He invited us to put our luggage in with his and accompany him to his home. We gladly accepted the invitation, and thus made our way

The Rock of Gibraltar. Courtesy of Pixabay.com.

While passing along the narrow streets and sidewalks only paved with cobble stone, but scrupulously clean, and on seeing so many people of different nationalities, there being twelve different languages spoken by the people living here, we began to realize with what kind of a spirit we had to contend, and it produced peculiar emotions best known to those who feel the worth of souls and are placed in a strange land thousands of miles from home. It truly made us feel to put our trust in the Lord.

After getting something to eat we walked up to the summit of the rock and erected an altar of loose stone and dedicated ourselves and the mission unto the Lord, and we were comforted.[52] The scenery from this spot was

into the garrison with our friend as a guide, which deluded the guards and sentinel at the gate from recognizing us as strangers from any foreign land or clime. So we were permitted to enter through the gate without any questions being asked as to our nativity, who we were or from whence we came, and so we were not under the necessity of obtaining a pass, which is required of all foreigners who wish admittance into the Fortress." Porter, "Record of Nathan Tanner Porter," 59–60.

52. Climbing mountains and dedicating the land for the preaching of the gospel was a common occurrence at the time. In September 1850, Apostle Lorenzo Snow and his companions climbed a mountain in Italy and there offered a prayer dedicating the land to the preaching of the gospel. In December 1850, the missionaries in Hawaii climbed a mountain near King's Falls, built a three-foot

sublime. Spain lies to the north; Morocco on the coast of Africa, fifteen miles to the south; the Mediterranean on the east, and the straits and bay on the west. It was dusk when we wound our way down the rock to the town and secured lodgings at the house of a Spanish lady whose husband was a convict keeper.

On the Sabbath we visited the Methodist[53] church and were introduced to Rev. Mr. George Alton.[54] Subsequently we made an effort to obtain the

altar, and knelt in prayer to dedicate the land. Jesse Haven and his companions, who had been called on missions during the same 1852 meeting as Stevenson, climbed the mount called Lion's Head in South Africa in April 1853 to dedicate the area to receive their message. James A. Toronto, "Italy," in *Encyclopedia of Latter-day Saint History*, 556–58; Britsch, *Moramona*, 4–5; Monson, "History of the South African Mission of The Church of Jesus Christ of Latter-day Saints," 18–19; chapter 4, "Jesse Haven and the Cape of Good Hope Mission," p. 125 herein.

53. Roman Catholicism eventually overtook Islam as the dominant religion of Gibraltar. Methodism, an eighteenth-century break-off from the Church of England, was planted in Gibraltar in 1769, when it was established by British soldiers. Missionaries and preachers for the movement were continually sent to the area in the ensuing years. A formal society was established on the Rock by the early 1800s, and the first official chapel was completed in 1810. Methodist schools were established in the 1830s, and many families, even non-Methodists, began sending their children to those schools, an action that concerned the Roman Catholic priests. The Methodist missionaries regarded these schools as an essential aspect of converting people, but most students became Catholics. Methodism struggled against the Church of England, and missionaries to Spain fought against Catholicism, but Methodism retained a presence. See Jackson, "Methodism in Gibraltar."

54. Reverend George Alton arrived in Gibraltar in 1847. In addition to overseeing his Methodist religion in Gibraltar, he also attempted to distribute tracts and Bibles in heavily Catholic Spain. By 1854 he was in charge of all Methodist work in Gibraltar and was able to negotiate the Methodist Church through clashes with the Anglican Church. In 1855, he relocated to Madrid to supervise the printing of Bibles but still oversaw Methodism in Gibraltar. He left Spain in 1856 because of social upheaval there and went back to England in 1858, but he returned to Gibraltar in 1862. Spain was still too intolerant of Protestants, so he spent most of his time in Gibraltar. During his second term in Gibraltar, he helped provide the community with clean water, and he thus helped diminish persecution against Methodism. Jackson, "Methodism in Gibraltar," 231–42.

chapel for the purpose of holding meeting, but our request was denied. My father helped to build this chapel and myself and two sisters and a brother were baptized therein.[55]

While looking for a hall in which to hold meetings, we were informed that a permit from the governor was necessary before either an indoor or outdoor meeting was held. On the 14th, we therefore wrote to this individual and solicited the privilege, which was given other ministers to hold religious services. We were referred to Sir George Aderly [Adderley], colonial secretary.[56] With this person we had three interviews. While he was looking over Governor B[righam]. Young's letter of commendation, he said he had read of Brigham Young and his thirty wives.[57] During our last interview we were informed by him that we would have to appear before Stewart Henry Paget,[58] police magistrate, and prove our right to remain on the rock. And he expressed surprise at our being able

---

55. "After meeting, being introduced to Mr. George Alton, Methodist missionary to this place, we desired the privilege to preach to the people from his pulpit, at some convenient time. After many equivocations and apologies, we got a positive denial in as polite a manner as his genteel manners could admit, although my father had been a leading member of this society, and myself and others of the family had been baptized." Stevenson, "Gibralter Mission, Letter No. 6." Latter-day Saint missionaries often relied on the hospitality of other Christian clergy members for places of preaching and worship.

56. Sir George Adderley was a British colonial secretary in Gibraltar. *Colonial Magazine and Commercial-Maritime Journal*, 1:125.

57. Although the doctrine of polygamy was not publicly announced until 1852, rumors of the practice had been circulating much earlier. In 1851, federally appointed officials to Utah Territory had encountered polygamy and published their grievances with the practice. Howard Stansbury and John Gunnison, who had been appointed to make a topographic survey of Utah, also published their observations on polygamy in 1852, but their report was much more positive than that of the officials. These reports gained significant attention in the public press. Whittaker, "Early Mormon Pamphleteering," 117–20; see "Report of Messrs. Brandebury, Brocchus, and Harris, to the president of the United States," 19; Stansbury, *Exploration and Survey of the Valley of the Great Salt Lake of Utah*, 136–38; Gunnison, *Mormons, or, Latter-day Saints*, 67–72.

58. Stewart Henry Paget (1811–69) came from a noble Welsh family and was appointed police magistrate in Gibraltar in March 1840. Roberts, *Eminent Welshmen*, 1:393; *Bulletins of State Intelligence*, 127.

to pass the sentinels unchallenged, etc.[59]

We obtained from Mr. [Horatio J.] Sprague,[60] American consul, a permit to visit on the rock for fifteen days in favor of Elder Porter,[61] and I had a certificate of birth and baptism from the Methodist mission. But Mr. Alton was very reluctant to give a certificate to me now that I had become a "Mormon." I had quite a long dispute with him on the principles of the gospel.

We then went to the court room and the magistrate, after looking at my certificate, said, "You will be allowed, as native born to remain on the rock, but if caught preaching will be made a prisoner immediately. And you, Mr. Porter, by this permit will be allowed to remain fifteen days; your permit will not be renewed, and if you preach you will be cast outside our gates." We left some tracts in the police office and retired to our place of

---

59. "Called at two o'clock at secretary's office, where I was closely questioned. He wished to know if I was a Wesleyan minister or Church of England, &c. My reply was, that as I saw all religions tolerated, I did not expect to be questioned in this free country as to my religion. But I was neither ashamed of my religion, nor its name. I stated I was a minister of the Church of Jesus Christ of Latter Day Saints. This, he said, was new to him; upon which I showed him my papers, bearing Governor Young's name, with the territorial seal affixed; when I received considerable abuse, saying I did not come out in true colors, that Mormons was our true name; he had read about Mormons and Brigham Young and his thirty wives, &c. I then referred him to our true name on my papers, stating we were called by our enemies vulgarly Mormons, and also we were misrepresented by newspaper reports; but I found reason had but little impression." Stevenson, "Gibralter Mission, Letter No. 6."

60. Horatio J. Sprague (1823–1901) was born in Gibraltar, and his father, Horatio Sprague, became the American consul there in 1832. Horatio J. became the consul in 1848, after his father's death. He served in that position until he died in 1901. "Oldest Consul Is Dead," *New York Times*, July 19, 1901.

61. Nathan Porter said the following about being allowed to stay: "In the mean time we were put under rigid examination as to our nationality, and as to how I, claiming to be a foreigner, came into the garrison without a pass. I explained that I was not so instructed nor so requested by the officer at the gate. That ended any further inquiry on that point. He said I would not be allowed to remain in the garrison without a permit. Brother Stevenson claimed to be citizen by birth, as he was born on the Rock. This he sustained by producing the certificate of his christening, obtained from the Methodist Church Record. I applied and obtained a permit to remain in the garrison fifteen days, not to be renewed was inserted." Porter, "Record of Nathan Tanner Porter," 60.

prayer on the top of the rock and offered our complaints to the Lord.[62]

We put out two hundred tracts in various parts of the garrison, and privately taught the people.

Edward Stevenson to George Q. Cannon, July 1, 1885[63]

The morning following our interview with the magistrate we took a walk out into Spain. We found the soil and climate producing oranges, figs, pomegranates, lemons, limes and a great variety of wild flowers; but the indolent Spaniards left nature to do most of the work. Many of them were living in huts similar to Indian *wickeups*. We could not but think that if Utah were favored with so good a climate and rich soil the huts would soon be supplanted by neat cottages and vineyards, and the land made almost like a paradise.

On our return to the lines we were told to call at the magistrate's office. We did so and were informed that the governor had given our letter to him (the magistrate) and that we need expect no aid in spreading "Mormonism" in that stronghold. We were warned to be careful and look out what we were about.[64]

We again called on the American consul, claiming protection for Elder Porter, whose permit was about to expire. He promised to see the magistrate and do all he could for him. On April 1st we called on the American

---

62. "We then proceeded up to the summit of the rock, to our private retreat, which was named Mount Edward, and entered our complaints to a much higher court, and asked the Lord not to do as vile man had done to reject us, but to guide us by the light of his Spirit. After being thus refreshed, we returned to our lonely room, as we had hired a small room for two dollars a month." Stevenson, "Gibralter Mission, Letter No. 6."

63. Edward Stevenson, "Gibraltar, Letter 10, Missionary Experience," *Juvenile Instructor* 20, no. 13 (July 1, 1885): 196. Compare to Edward Stevenson, "Gibralter Mission, Letter No. 7," *Deseret News*, April 30, 1856.

64. "On our return I was invited to call at the police office, as the magistrate wished to see me; a few minutes after we passed the last sentry, a messenger left word for us. This plainly shows our movements are closely watched and known, for no one knew where we were going, except ourselves." Stevenson, "Gibralter Mission, Letter No. 7," 63.

consul, who had just returned from the police station, holding a card in his hand on which were printed our articles of faith. He said, holding up the card and speaking to Elder Porter, "This is the only cause against you, and if Stevenson does not look out he will have to share the same fate as you, although he is a native. Your religion is not wanted here. You have already created jealousy in the churches."[65] He then advised us both to leave the garrison.[66]

Elder Porter's permit being now exhausted a passage was secured for him on a steam packet;[67] but, according to a dream that we had, I was to

65. Porter recorded this dialogue with the consul: "As I entered the Consul's office he arose from his seat and saying, 'Well, I was just going to see the Chief Magistrate. Please sit down. I will be back in a few minutes.' He left having but a few yards to go. He soon returned, and on entering the door held up a pamphlet in his hand saying, 'This is the reason you are not permitted to stay. You have been distributing tracts, and thus caused disturbance among the churches.'

"'Ah, indeed' says I, 'I was not aware that there was a law prohibiting the distribution of religious tracts and references to the Holy Scriptures. Please, is there such law?'

"His countenance dropped with the reply, 'No, not that I am aware of.'

"'And is there any precedent to this charge? Has any person or persons been prohibited from such distribution?'

"'No sir, not that I am aware of.'

"'Then sir, why is this brought against me as a charge?' I looked him straight in the eyes.

"He replied, 'You know what it is.'

"'Yes' says I, 'you mean to say it is religious prejudice.'

"'Yes' says he, 'that is it. The governor consults the ministers and favors them against any thing prejudicial to their welfare religiously.'" Porter, "Record of Nathan Tanner Porter," 62–63.

66. "As I was passing the garrison library, also the sappers library [for British engineers], those tracts I had left was handed me, saying the clergymen had decided they were a nuisance to the library, and would not be allowed to remain. Many who were formerly friends began to look suspiciously upon us, and treat us with disdain, saying we were Mormons and deceived, but always failed to show us wherein, only the learned ministers said we were wrong, and the old apostolic gospel was no longer needed." Stevenson, "Gibralter Mission, Letter No. 7."

67. Nathan Porter recorded his final moments in Gibraltar: "Brother Stevenson accompanied me to the side of the steamer where we shook the parting hand under circumstances to us very trying. We commended each other to God, trusting that

remain and establish the gospel.[68] I immediately went to our place of prayer on the mountain, and while I gazed on my only friend steaming out of the bay up the straits I had rather strange feelings.[69]

Previous to leaving England I was pointed out in a meeting as having been seen in a vision doing a good work in Gibraltar, but was told that I would meet heavy opposition in my labors. I was seen to be baptizing some persons, and heavenly messengers were seen to deliver me from the hands of the wicked.

A Mr. Elliot, who had been reading the Book of Mormon and was inclined to believe my testimony, became prejudiced by the ministers and turned me away from his door. Shortly afterwards he fell twenty feet, broke his leg and otherwise injured his body, which kept him in bed for forty days.

I visited the Jewish synagogue one day in company with a Mr. Delemar, a learned Jew who spoke six la[n]guages. He instructed me to wear

---

in his providence we would meet again in due time. I watched his return to the shore to enter again that forbidding Fortress, whose rulers had rejected us and forbid our testimony being sounded in her halls or on the corners of her streets. This was the 1st day of April 1853. They doubtless thought we were both leaving their quarters, but were April Fooled when they saw him again within the walls." The Latter-day Saint elders seemed to relish the opportunity to deceive the local authorities, given how they had both been treated and how one had been expelled from the British colony. Elder Porter then labored as a missionary in England from 1853 to 1856. Porter, "Record of Nathan Tanner Porter," 63–67.

68. "Finding no other resort but the fulfillment of the manifestations we previously had, which was—Elder Porter would have to go, and I remain alone to establish the work we came to perform, I found a passage home to England for Elder Porter, by paying 20 dollars, which had been previously given me, and I much required to sustain myself." Stevenson, "Gibralter Mission, Letter No. 7."

69. "After taking the parting hand of my only friend on the rock, I retired to Mount Edward to our secret closet, where I saw the last of the steamer bearing my partner away, being troubled concerning his comfort, as he only had a deck passage; but I afterwards learned that the Lord opened the hearts of the officers, who gave him second cabin fare. Truly peculiar were my feelings while I gazed upon the scenes below—the various places of worship, from the Mahomedan and Jew to the various Protestants, not omitting the old mother of all (Catholics)." Stevenson, "Gibralter Mission, Letter No. 7."

my hat in the meeting as it was customary with them so to do. The pulpit was in the center. The ark, in one end of the building, being opened the parchment was taken out. It was rolled on two sticks with bells on the top of them. It was passed around the synagogue and kissed by the worshipers, while a continuous chanting was being kept up by the congregation. A portion was read from the pulpit, contributions were received and then the rolls were returned to the ark, each person bowing in that direction. Meeting was then dismissed.

On the 4th of May I visited the steam packet that brought me to the place, left a Book of Mormon and other reading matter with the clerk and got my mail. As it was raining I sat, by permission, under the porch of a guard house, reading the *Millennial Star*. Several persons became interested in me and asked questions about my belief. Soon an officer stepped up and inquired if I was a Methodist; but as soon as he learned that I was a Latter-day Saint he ordered me put under guard, saying that my religion was one that could not be tolerated in that place. For the first time in my life I was marched into the guard house a prisoner. I there began preaching to the guard, who listened attentively to what I had to say. After some few inquiries concerning what I had been doing in the fortress I was released, and I subsequently sold some books to one of the guard who arrested me, but whose sympathies were aroused in my behalf.

On the 24th of May, the queen's birth-day, there was a grand celebration. The soldiers were marched to the north front, outside of the gates of the fortress. After considerable exercising of the soldiers the firing of cannon commenced from the top of the rock, 1,400 feet high, after which the galleries opened fire about half-way down the rock. Singular, indeed, was it to see fire and smoke gushing out of the perpendicular rock. The shipping in the bay was beautifully decorated with the flags of all nations.

June the 28th was a happy day for me, for at 4 o'clock, a. m., just after gun fire, as per previous arrangement, I met John McCall, a dock-yard policeman, and Thomas Miller, a gunner and driver of the royal artillery,[70]

---

70. Stevenson's journal identifies John McCall as "Elexander" McCall, a native of Scotland. Thomas Miller was born in February 1817 in county Donegal, Ireland. John McCall often did not attend Latter-day Saint meetings because his employer threatened to fire him if he did so, but he was sympathetic towards Latter-day Saint

at the water's edge, we having descended a rope ladder to the shore, and baptized them.[71] These were the first fruits of my labors after being on the rock three months and twenty days.

The Lord only knows the many privations and sacrifices I endured and the lonely hours I spent, living many weeks on the value of three to five cents per day.

Edward Stevenson to George Q. Cannon, July 15, 1885[72]

In the evening of the 28th of June we held a private meeting at the house of Brother Miller. We confirmed the two persons just baptized, and subsequently baptized and blessed some children of this same family.

Soon after this, while distributing tracts, I offered one to the attorney-general and received abuse in return. I also sent a second tract to Rev. Mr. Hambelton, by the hand of his servant. The minister soon returned it in person, throwing it abruptly at me, saying, "We belong to the established church and have no use for your tracts."

I soon found that the priests not only ruled the people but influenced the governor and chief authorities; and in consequence of this influence a card was placed on the door of the barracks which read as follows: "An

---

teachings. Stevenson, diary, March 26, 1854, and table after the March 31, 1854, entry. "These being the first baptized on the rock, after nearly four months' toil, it gave me much joy to open the first furrow in this land of opposition, which has cost me much arduous toil and abuse. In the evening I held a private meeting, and confirmed those baptized at brother Miller's house; his wife and three sons were quite believing." Stevenson, "Gibralter Mission, Letter No. 7."

71. "It is impossible to get to the water in the night, and with difficulty even in the day, where I baptized them privately, but came so near being discovered, that while I stood in the water I saw the guard's hat." Stevenson, "Gibralter Mission, Letter No. 7."

72. Edward Stevenson, "Gibraltar, Letter XI, Missionary Experience," *Juvenile Instructor* 20, no. 14 (July 15, 1885): 215. Compare to Stevenson, "Gibralter Mission, Letter No. 7"; Edward Stevenson, "Gibralter Mission, Letter No. 8," *Deseret News*, May 28, 1856; "Foreign Intelligence," *Millennial Star* 15, no. 52 (December 24, 1853): 841–42; "The Gibraltar Mission," *Millennial Star* 16, no. 11 (March 18, 1854): 174–75.

individual named Stevenson, a Mormonite preacher, is not allowed in the barracks." This was shown to me upon one occasion as I was being marched out of the barracks, although the guard expressed sympathy for me and considered this act as base persecution.

With all this, however, they were not satisfied, but got up the following summons, which was handed me by one of the police:

"City Garrison and Territory of Gibraltar.
To Edward Stevenson, of Gibraltar:

You are hereby required to personally appear before me, Stewart Henry Paget, or any other of her majesty's justices of the peace, in and for the said city garrison and territory, at the police office, on the 30th day of September, 1853, at the hour of eleven in the forenoon of the same day, to answer to the complaint of James McPherson, charging that you have used words profanedly, scoffing the holy scriptures, and exposing part of them to contempt and ridicule. Dated this 29th day of September, 1853."

I was afterwards informed that the complainant was expecting a handsome reward if he got me into trouble. On one occasion I overheard the magistrate who issued the summons say to some ladies that he hoped soon to see me in the stocks.[73]

On the 30th I repaired to the police office. Just before going into court I had the pleasure of bearing my testimony to about fifteen persons, until prohibited by the police. I soon faced my plaintiff, and one good look in his face unnerved him. The following colloquy occurred in the court room:

"Do you know the defendant?"

"Yes, sir."

"When was your first acquaintance with him?"

"Soon after he came here."

"What, did he then give you those books?" (holding up some books I

---

73. "Several were paying attention to my teachings, for I had sold about 40 dollars worth of books, and privately taught a great many, and as some sheep were about to be caught, the wolves in sheep's clothing began to howl." Stevenson, "Gibralter Mission, Letter No. 7."

had sold the plaintiff and for which he failed to pay me.) "Did he wish you to change your religion?"

"Yes, he said I ought to be baptized."

"In what way did he want you to be baptized?"

"By immersion all over in the water."

"Did he speak against the established religion?"

"He said sprinkling little children was not right, as they were not old enough to judge for themselves—they were not accountable."

"Is this all he said?"

"His books say all the churches sprang from the mother of harlots— the abominable Catholic church."

"Can you find it?["]

My books—the Book of Mormon, Voice of Warning[74] and some tracts—were then opened. I now availed myself of the opportunity of opening my Bible at the 17th chapter of Revelation, where it speaks of the mother of harlots. After the judge looked over the text for a short time he remarked, "Oh, this is the Bible."

"Yes, sir," I answered, "all our quotations are from the Bible."

Many officers and spectators began to think that this was a singular way of scoffing at the holy scriptures. The questioning of the plaintiff then continued:

"Did he perform baptism on you?"

"No, but he did on a dockyard policeman and a gunner and driver of the royal artillery."

I was still looking at my Bible, when I was asked, "Do you hear, sir?"

"Yes, sir, all that is said," I replied.

It was then stated that I ought to give bonds to not speak to the military at all, and a bond with penalty was prepared. I was not allowed a defense,

---

74. Parley P. Pratt's *A Voice of Warning and Instruction to All People*, first published in New York in 1837, was one of the most influential Latter-day Saint books of the nineteenth century. It gave a comprehensive overview of church beliefs, including the fulfillment of prophecy, the Book of Mormon, and the Resurrection. Stevenson was probably using the seventh edition, published in Liverpool in 1852. David Rolph Seely, "*Voice of Warning*," in *Encyclopedia of Latter-day Saint History*, 1301; Crawley, *Descriptive Bibliography of the Mormon Church*, 1:69–71, 2:304–5.

neither did they examine other witnesses who had been subpœnaed, as they found their evidence would be in my favor. On my refusal to sign a bond I was taken by the police as a prisoner into the prison room. Soon afterwards the officer came into the room and compromised the bonding by running his pen through some of the lines, rendering it as useless as a blank piece of paper. So to accommodate them I signed it and went on my way.[75] I soon baptized several persons, among whom was a woman who had held me on her knee when I was a child.[76] I organized a branch of the Church.

Edward Stevenson to George Q. Cannon, August 1, 1885[77]

Soon after my arrival in Gibraltar, a Mr. Smith invited me to take dinner with him, at which time he wept with joy for the pleasure it gave him, to eat with a son of one with whom he had enjoyed himself many times over

---

75. "I left my testimony of the gospel with them, also the Book of Mormon, Voice of Warning, and my official documents. The clerk soon followed and was willing to modify the bond, so that it did not materially interfere with my rights; when I signed it, and was set at liberty with a threat that I probably would be indicted for baptizing persons by immersion.

    "Corporal McDonald, who I have previously mentioned received a summons to appear as a witness against me, was at court, but was not called upon as he previously had to appear at his orderly room, where it was ascertained his testimony would be in my favor. This man I soon after baptized. Distributed some tracts and returned to my quiet home, and held a private meeting in the evening, where I sold some books.

    "This difficulty, although designed for evil, resulted in raising friends." Stevenson, "Gibralter Mission, Letter No. 8."

76. An unpublished autobiography by Stevenson identifies a Mrs. Norton as the woman who "dandled me on her knee." The name "Norton" is not in the list of members of the Gibraltar branch that Stevenson put in his journal, so either he did not record her baptism, or else there was a scribal error and Norton was not her actual name. Stevenson, "Life of Edward Stevenson," 5; Stevenson, "Life and History of Elder Edward Stevenson," 2.

77. Edward Stevenson, "Gibraltar, Letter 12, Missionary Experience," *Juvenile Instructor* 20, no. 15 (August 1, 1885): 229. Compare to Edward Stevenson, "Gibralter Mission, Letter No. 9," *Deseret News*, June 18, 1856; and Edward Stevenson, "Gibralter Mission, Letter No. 10," *Deseret News*, July 23, 1856.

twenty-six years before, in the good, old Methodist church. "Why," said he, "your father helped build our good, old church; and used to play the bass viol in the choir, too. Yes, and he sold his property to me for one hundred dollars less than its real value. Can it be possible that you, a minister so well-versed in the good old Bible, the blessed Bible, have come back to us all the way from the land of America—a son of my good old Christian friend, Joseph Stephenson! It seems like a dream. You will doubtless preach for us in the church your good, old Christian father helped to build."

"Yes, Father Smith," I replied, "I am truly his son, and have come from Utah—over 8,000 miles away from my home, about one-third of the way around this world we now occupy. I have left my dear family, and have come as a true minister of the everlasting gospel of Jesus, as did His ancient disciples of old—without purse or scrip.[78] And I assure you Father Smith, it would afford me the greatest pleasure to have the privilege of speaking to my friends in the meeting house where memories arise like green spots in a desert, afresh in my memory, of the good things and favorable impressions made on my mind at the Sabbath schools I used to attend twenty-six years ago. I can well remember the time, although only seven years old, when my mother used to put on my white pinafore, and nicely blackened shoes, and my father bowed down and prayed to the Lord in that house he sold you. I feel to bless them for setting my feet in my youthful days in a Christian life and for the good that I received in this Sabbath school. But my father now sleeps with those who have passed behind the vail, he died when I was but eleven years of age.

"At the age of thirteen, I heard Joseph Smith, the Prophet, preach by the power of the Holy Ghost. He related the heavenly vision with which he was favored;[79] I had a witness of the truth that he had told, although I was

---

78. Following Jesus's New Testament injunction to preach without purse or scrip, Latter-day Saint missionaries in the nineteenth century were instructed to travel without money. They relied on the generosity of local Saints and strangers for their meals and lodging. This practice required great faith, both on the part of the missionaries and on those who helped them. This method of preaching was abandoned as church policy evolved. Jensen, "Without Purse or Scrip?," 3–14.

79. Edward Stevenson heard Joseph Smith speak in Pontiac, Michigan, in 1834. "The Prophet testified with great power concerning the visit of the Father and the Son, and the conversation he had with them." Stevenson, *Reminiscences of Joseph, the Prophet*, 4.

not baptized until some time later.

"I will now relate to you a vision I had. I saw in a very nice, green spot every one who had joined this new Church. They were all dressed in white robes. A messenger, and the only stranger to me, stood by my side. I was the only one who was without the snow-white robe, and this very much amazed me. I asked why this was so, he replied, 'Look! do you see one here who has not been baptized or come in at the door?'

"But I believe as well as do those."

"'You have not yet come in at the door!'"

"This was sufficient for me. I was soon baptized, and was made to rejoice with a testimony of the message which has brought me to this far-off land.

"Many old friends have received and treated me courteously, but the minister not only closed the church doors against me, but himself and some of his co-religionists began to circulate many falsehoods against the truth of the gospel, and the love of many waxed cold."

I thus bore my testimony to the truth, but my father's good old friend closed his house against me and turned as cool as he was warm at first. He became abusive to the servants of God. I told him the consequence of his rejecting the light that he had already acknowledged, and for turning me—a servant of God, from his door, and that the hand of the Lord would speedily follow him to his sorrow.

His wife was reading the Book of Mormon privately, and was with some of the children believing. It was but a short time before Father Smith was stricken and was confined not only to his house, but to his bed. Some time after his wife called my attention to his condition and humiliation. He was not expected to live. Soon after he desired to see me and said if the Lord would only spare his life, he would serve Him better than he ever had done.

I told him that the Lord brought down and raised up; that if he desired to recover and serve Him faithfully, he should get well and the Lord would raise him up to better health. In a few days I was invited to take dinner with him and pray with the family. He was up and around reading, and a very great change had come to him and his house. He was, however, too good to endure, and he shortly burned up some copies of the Church paper and pamphlets, and forbade me to enter his house again. I of course left my testimony, telling him the consequences of his actions. I told him it would now be worse than ever with him. The poor man was very soon again confined to his bed, but not long this time, for he soon died. His family decided to go to England where they said they intended to obey the gospel.

On the 23rd of January, 1854, I had the pleasure of organizing a branch of the Church consisting of ten members, ordaining one Elder and one Priest. We partook of the sacrament and had a joyful time.[80] The branch was named Rock Port Branch of the Church of Jesus Christ of Latter-day Saints.[81]

Edward Stevenson to George Q. Cannon, August 15, 1885.[82]

There was a well-to[-]do free citizen on the rock, a former acquaintance of my childhood, and a great friend of my father when he lived on the stronghold of Gibraltar, whose name was Gilchrist. He was a Methodist, and I had taken considerable pains to inform him concerning our doctrines and had furnished him with a Book of Mormon, Voice of Warning and other books and tracts. He became convinced that sprinkling children was only man's theory and not consistent with Bible doctrine, as Jesus and the disciples taught the people to first believe and repent and then be baptized, not to be baptized and afterwards believe and repent. Mr. Gilchrist acknowledged that I taught the truth, yet he turned me away from his house and was, therefore, more culpable.

At his own request I went to his house one day and taught him for two

---

80. John McLean was ordained an elder, and Thomas Forbes was ordained a priest. Stevenson, "Gibralter Mission, Letter No. 10"; Stevenson, diary, table after the March 31, 1854, entry.

81. See confirmation of this branch in Cottrell, "History of the Discontinued Mediterranean Missions of The Church of Jesus Christ of Latter-day Saints," 62–63; see also, for example, Stevenson, diary, January 29, 1854.

    During the nineteenth century, assigned elders in the far-flung corners of the world were empowered to organize or "plant" branch units within their geographic stewardships by virtue of their priesthood authority with little oversight from church headquarters. Stevenson informed the president of the overarching European Mission of his activities leading the Rock Port Branch, including officiating in priesthood ordinances and ministering to its members.

82. Edward Stevenson, "Gibraltar, Letter 13, Missionary Experience," *Juvenile Instructor* 20, no. 16 (August 15, 1885): 252.

hours, the principles of the gospel. During this time he was called twice to dinner, but he did not go himself, nor did he ask me to partake of a meal, although he was well aware of the meagre diet to which I was compelled to accustom myself.

It appeared to me that he was convinced of the truth of the message that I bore, but was not sufficiently honest to receive it. Finally, as I was leaving him, he offered me fifty cents, saying at the same time that it was not to help me in spreading the imposture, but for my personal use. I told him that I was preaching without purse or scrip, but was unwilling to receive gifts only in the name of a disciple. I returned not again to that house.

At the same time that I was teaching Mr. Gilchrist I was laboring with a soldier named Thomas McDonald, and though he received no more instruction than the former, he accepted the truth and was baptized.[83] One night, he said, after he had retired to rest, he had a dream and a messenger whose hair was nearly white, appeared to him. This searcher after truth then asked his visitor about the Book of Mormon, as they had been talking about that record. It was opened and the messenger simply said, "How plain it is, is it not?"

In the dream he also saw me tired and weary, but hard at work digging the ground. He touched me and asked what I was doing, when I replied that I intended to sow seed and if possible reap a harvest of souls.

This man was the means of bringing several other soldiers of his regiment into the Church.

There was a painful incident came under my observation about this time that I will here just mention: One day I had as usual a parcel of books in my arm and was visiting and teaching wherever I could meet anyone who would listen to my remarks. I called at a shoe shop in the southern part of the rock where I found six men engaged at shoe making. After telling them the object of my visit and giving them some tracts I opened the book of Doctrine and Covenants where it speaks of the martyrdom of Joseph Smith and his brother Hyrum, and read this aloud to the workmen.[84] As I finished reading everything was for a moment as still as death

---

83. Thomas McDonald, born in Scotland in 1828, was baptized on November 19, 1853. Stevenson, diary, table after the March 31, 1854, entry.

84. Doctrine and Covenants 135.

everyone present having ceased to work. In a moment one of the six broke out in an ungovernable rage, saying, "Joe Smith was served just right and ought to have been killed long before he was."

My reasoning with him only served to enrage him more, and his closing remark to me was, "Joe Smith ought to have been cut up into mince-meat."

I gathered up my books and said to him that he was guilty of shedding innocent blood inasmuch as he consented to it in his heart, for which cause the wrath of God would rest upon him, and he should feel His power to the consuming of his body, and that too, in a very short time. He would then know that Joseph Smith was a Prophet of God and that I was a servant of the Almighty.

On the following day he with the others came to his work as usual, but he had not been there long before he began vomiting blood, and before he could be carried to the hospital he was dead. Just before dying he said to his fellow-workmen, "I wrongfully abused that man yesterday."

Thus did the judgment of God speedily follow him.

Edward Stevenson to George Q. Cannon, September 1, 1885.[85]

Soon after organizing a branch of the Church there was quite an agitation regarding the war in the Crimea, England, France and Turkey were allies in a war against Russia, or in the words of Daniel the prophet, the king of the north, (Russia), was arrayed against the king of the south, (Turkey).[86] All this had a tendency to militate against my labors as a missionary in the military garrison of Gibraltar, for the British lion's interests were assailed, and all of its military had war on the brain, which generally has far more effect on the human mind than the spirit of the gospel of peace.

---

85. Edward Stevenson, "Gibraltar, Letter 14, Missionary Experience," *Juvenile Instructor* 20, no. 17 (September 1, 1885): 262.

86. Daniel 11 is a prophecy that says that a king from the north and a king from the south would fight against each other.

The elder John McLain, Corporal Hays[87] and John McDonald,[88] all in the branch just organized, were likely to go on the Mediterranean sea to be engaged in the Crimean war, and the Priest, Sergeant Thomas Forbes,[89] was about to go to Scotland, thus depleting my hard earned little branch, which had a tendency to discourage me in my efforts, if such is possible to a Latter-day Saint Elder engaged in so great a work as saving human souls.

I concluded, however, once more to apply to the governor for liberty to open up a public place of worship, and sent him the following letter:

"Gibraltar, April 24th, 1854.

"To his excellency, Sir Robert William Gardiner,[90] Governor of Gibraltar:

The undersigned, an inhabitant of Gibraltar most respectfully solicits an audience with his excellency, on business of importance. I have the honor to be,

"Your most obedient servant,

"Edward Stevenson."

The next day I received the following:

"The Colonial secretary requests that Mr. E. Stevenson will call at his

---

87. Corporal Peter Hays, born in Scotland in 1827, was baptized on February 3, 1854. He was part of John McLean's regiment, and in the Battle of Inkerman, he received a wound that required his arm to be amputated above the elbow. Jones, "Wars and Rumors of Wars," 33; LeCheminant, "Valiant Little Band," 20; Stevenson, diary, table after the March 31, 1854, entry.

88. The "John McDonald" mentioned here is probably Thomas McDonald. McDonald was hurt three times in one day during the Battle of Inkerman. He had artillery shells explode near him on two separate occasions, catapulting debris against him, and a bullet struck his hand on another occasion. Jones, "Wars and Rumors of Wars," 33; LeCheminant, "Valiant Little Band," 20.

89. Thomas Forbes was baptized on November 15, 1853. Stevenson, diary, table after the March 31, 1854, entry.

90. Sir Robert William Gardiner was born in 1781. He served as Gibraltar's governor from 1848 to 1855, but he had previously been in Gibraltar from 1797 to 1798 as part of Britain's Royal Artillery. He died in 1864. Browne, *England's Artillerymen*, 69–72.

office at 12 o'clock to-day.

"Secretary's Office,
"Gibraltar April 25th, 1854."

I responded to the request and had a favorable reception. The colonial secretary said my case should be duly laid before his excellency, and a reply forwarded to my address.

I was visiting at this time a Prussian whom I had been teaching the gospel, inducing him to read some of our tracts and then compare our doctrines with those taught in the Bible. He was apparently convinced of the truth. I also had some Spaniards investigating our doctrines, and it was manifest to me that if I could obtain permission to open a public place of worship my chances would be increased to spread the gospel among the people.

The Methodists had been making an effort to introduce their gospel into Spain by opening a school there, but as soon as it was ascertained by the inhabitants, who are mostly Catholics, that they were tampering with their religion the innovators had to flee by night out of the country.

I received a very pleasing reply to my letter to the governor through the colonial secretary, Mr. Aderly [Adderley], and therein consent was given me to open a place for public worship. The secretary, however, stated that this garrison was a hard place for religious teachers for a Catholic once had a cat thrown at him while he was holding service. I merely stated that all I expected was the protection of the law.

Subsequently with the assistance of some friends I found a suitable place and began to hold meetings. One evening when I had a few friends in my private room a policeman came with a message for me to appear at the colonial secretary's office on the following day. My reply was that if the secretary had any business with me he would do well to officially notify me of it, otherwise, I would not notice their bidding. The next day I received from the colonial secretary a very polite invitation to visit him at 2 p. m. the next day on business of importance, and to my own interest.

Edward Stevenson to George Q. Cannon, September 15, 1885.[91]

On May 1, 1854, my thirty-fourth birthday, Elder John McLean, Brothers Thomas McDonald and Peter Hays, with their regiment, 1,000 rank and file, marched on board of one of her majesty's men-of-war to sail up the Mediterranean sea and take part in the Crimea war. In the midst of thundering shouts of enthusiasm the gallant ship with her precious burden of souls steamed out of the beautiful bay of Gibraltar to do honor to Briton's flag. A solemn reflection crossed my mind on this occasion with a mental question, who of this one thousand will ever return home again to fathers, mothers, brothers, sisters or wives?

Many tears were shed over the wounded and slain during this cruel war, which lasted about two years.[92] My blessings went with the brave boys in red, especially the three brethren mentioned. These were instructed to remember their prayers as they were in the hands of the Lord who could protect them even in the hour of fierce battle, and also to use their influence to spread the gospel among their comrades. A subsequent letter brought news that Elder McLean had organized a branch of the Church in a Turkish burying ground, and while doing so, bottles and other missiles were thrown at him and his companions. The branch was named the Expeditionary Force Branch of the Church of Jesus Christ of Latter-day Saints.[93]

Frequent letters revealed many of the horrors of warfare, such as being compelled to lie in the trenches before Sebastapool, in a mass of filth and vermin with no one to prepare them a change of linen. Elder McLean stated that he had been in the heavy charges at the battle of Inkerman and Alma.[94] So pressed was the charge from both sides that the soldiers were

---

91. Edward Stevenson, "Gibraltar, Letter 15, Missionary Experience," *Juvenile Instructor* 20, no. 18 (September 15, 1885): 279.

92. It has been estimated that around 750,000 people died during the Crimean War, either from combat or disease. It is unknown how many total Latter-day Saints fought in the Crimean War, but John McLean's Expeditionary Force Branch apparently decreased from twenty-three members to twelve or thirteen, and others died in other branches. Jones, "Wars and Rumors of Wars," 30–34.

93. LeCheminant, "Valiant Little Band," 18–21.

94. The Battle of Alma, one of the earliest battles in the Crimean War, occurred in September 1854 at the Alma River in southwest Crimea, when French and British

crushed together and faced each other with crossed bayonets being unable to use them for some time. He, however, came out with only a slight bayonet wound in the arm which only kept him from duty five days. Brother McDonald was wounded by the bursting of a shell, but with his handkerchief bound up his head and continued the encounter until another shell burst close by and this time disabled him so that he was taken from the field, but soon recovered. Corporal Hays lost his arm, but his life was spared; so the lives of all three of the brethren were spared, while often the ground was strewn with the dead and dying. Thus, even in this war, the hand of the Lord was plainly seen and acknowledged.

Edward Stevenson to George Q. Cannon, October 1, 1885[95]

Soon after receiving permission from the governor to open a public place of worship, I was called upon at my residence by a policeman, and requested to call at the secretary's office. This I refused to do without being notified officially. Soon afterwards I received a polite official notice, which I answered on the following day. I was informed by the secretary that the governor had reconsidered the matter of my holding meetings and had concluded that I should neither preach nor hold meetings. It was a time of war, and he would not allow a new religion to be introduced on the rock of Gibraltar; and if an attempt to do so should be made I would be taken up by the police.

When I took into consideration that several of the brethren I had baptized upon the rock had gone into the Russian war, and that two others were about to go to Great Britain and the spirit of war that prevailed in the garrison, I felt impressed to ask the governor for a free passage to England, which, through the colonial secretary, was cheerfully granted, as I

---

troops defeated the Russian troops, even though the Russians had the advantage of a higher elevation. After the Battle of Alma, the French and British decided not to attack the weakened city of Sevastopol, instead putting it under siege. In November 1854, Russian troops attacked the French and British outside of Sevastopol. The Russians had the advantage of fog and numbers, but they still lost the battle. See Mercer, *Inkerman 1854.*

95. Edward Stevenson, "Gibraltar, Letter [16], Missionary Experience," *Juvenile Instructor* 20, no. 19 (October 1, 1885): 297.

had already learned that the governor had expressed himself willing to give me a free passage on one of her majesty's mail packets, in order to get rid of one who had stirred up so much of a religious excitement.

As I could take my departure at pleasure, the steam packets plying twice a week between that point and England, some twelve hundred miles, I at once began prep[a]rations to leave the few remaining Saints under the care of a proper officer. To my surprise I was again called to the colonial secretary's office, and after going through the inquisition, because I would not compromise principle, my free passage was re[s]cinded, and I was left to depend upon the Lord to open up my way. A saying of the Savior, while instructing His disciples came into my mind:

"Consider the lilies of the field, how they grow; they toil not, neither do they spin; and yet I say unto you, That even Solomon in all his glory was not arrayed like one of these. Wherefore, if God so clothe the grass of the field, which to-day is, and to-morrow is cast into the oven, shall he not much more clothe you, O ye of little faith? Therefore take no thought, saying, What shall we eat? or, What shall we drink? or, Wherewithal shall we be clothed? (For after all these things do the Gentiles seek): for your heavenly Father knoweth that ye have need of all these things. But seek ye first the kingdom of God, and His righteousness; and all these things shall be added unto you. Take therefore no thought for the morrow: for the morrow shall take thought for the things of itself. Sufficient unto the day is the evil thereof." (*Matt.* 6[:]28).

I repaired to the open sea, where I had baptized the first members of the branch, and there washed my feet and cleansed my garments as a witness before God against the cruel authorities of this strong garrison; and felt to rejoice that I was counted worthy to be cast out for the gospel's sake.[96]

You can, perhaps imagine my condition, over eight thousand miles from home, on a little island of only three miles by one half of a mile in size, without purse or scrip and almost friendless.

---

96. In the New Testament, Jesus instructed his followers to shake the dust off their feet as a testimony against the people or places that rejected them (see, for example, Mark 6:11). Some scriptural references also involved the prophets shaking their garments for similar purposes (see Acts 18:6 or 2 Nephi 9:44). In the nineteenth century, many missionaries washed their feet against the people who rejected them,

Edward Stevenson to George Q. Cannon, November 15, 1885.[97]

One night, after retiring to my bed for rest, it was made known to me by vision that my mission on the rock was fulfilled acceptably before the Lord, and I saw a scourge come upon the place soon after my departure, for it appeared to me that I was sailing out of the lovely Bay of Gibraltar on one of her majesty's elegant steam packets.

A short time after I had this vision shown to me I received a letter from a Mr. Lambel, a resident of Li[sb]on, the capital of Portugal. In his communication, Mr. Lambel informed me of the serious illness of his brother-in-law. The doctors had given him up, as it was out of their power to effect a cure. He further stated that he and his family had read a great deal about the Latter-day Saints, and had learned of their faith in the ordinances of the gospel; and by communications from England he had been told of my mission to Gibraltar. He desired me to go to Lisbon and anoint with oil, and pray for this sick man, as they fully believed in the healing of the sick by the laying on of hands, as was customary among the ancient saints of which the Bible tells us.[98] The gentleman furnished me nine pounds English money, with which to pay my passage to Lisbon and return, which was equal to a full fare from Gibraltar to Southampton, England.

Thus was my deliverance brought about. After the governor's unfaithfulness to fulfill his promise, the Lord opened up my way to accomplish what was shown to me by vision. This incident teaches us the lesson that the Lord is good and kind to all who put their trust in Him.[99]

---

and the rite functioned as a curse. In the twentieth century, this practice faded out and was generally discouraged. Weber, "Shake Off the Dust of Thy Feet," 108–39; Belnap, "Those Who Receive You Not," 81–127.

97.   Edward Stevenson, "Gibraltar, Letter 17, Missionary Experience," *Juvenile Instructor* 20, no. 22 (November 15, 1885): 339.

98.   See James 5:14.

99.   Stevenson wrote a few additional letters after he returned to England and America: "Foreign Intelligence," *Millennial Star* 16, no. 29 (July 22, 1854): 457–58; and Edward Stevenson to Brigham Young, July 5, 1854, published as "Mission at Gibraltar," *Deseret News*, September 14, 1854.

4

JESSE HAVEN AND THE CAPE OF GOOD HOPE MISSION

Historical Introduction

After arriving in England in early 1856, Jesse Haven wrote to Franklin D. Richards, president of the British Mission, about the two and a half years he had just spent as a missionary in South Africa. "It is not so easy as one who has not had the experience might suppose, to establish the Gospel in a country where it has not before been preached; where the climate weakens the constitution of persons brought up in a northern clime; where the people speak three or four different languages, and are of all kinds, grades, conditions, and complexions; and where there are only two or three hundred thousand scattered over a country twice as large as England."[1] Despite these difficulties, Haven did his best to fulfill his duties as president of the Cape of Good Hope Mission. There were no church members when he arrived, but during his presidency he created branches of the church.

1. "Foreign Correspondence: Cape of Good Hope Mission," *Millennial Star* 18, no. 12 (March 22, 1856): 191; p. 123 herein.

Jesse Haven. Courtesy of history.lds.org.

Haven and his companions, William Walker and Leonard Smith, were the first to establish a Latter-day Saint presence on the African continent.

Jesse Haven's Early Life, 1814–52

Jesse Haven was born March 28, 1814, in Holliston, Massachusetts, a first cousin of Brigham Young and Willard Richards. In his youth, he began thinking about religion. At thirteen, he aligned himself with Holliston's Congregational Church, where his father was a deacon, and at sixteen, he helped organize a temperance society and a singing school in his neighborhood, which met with derision from his peers. "I mention these circumstances to show that opposition to what I undertook to perform, even in my youthful days, when I knew I was right, instead of discouraging me, made me more zealous," he recounted. In 1833, he left home and pursued various jobs, but it was schoolteaching that he settled on as a profession. When he returned to his hometown in 1837, "the Elders of the Latter Day Saints had been there and left the Book of Mormon. I read it but did not immediately receive it."[2]

However, by the spring of 1838, Haven believed and was baptized by Joseph Ball on April 13. Nine days later, he packed up from his Massachusetts home and headed out to join the main body of Saints at Far West, Missouri. He witnessed the sufferings of his fellow Latter-day Saints in the ensuing months. After relocating to Quincy, Illinois, in 1839, he was sent on a mission with Henry Jacobs back to his native Massachusetts: "Our business was to call on the different branches on our journey east, comfort them as much as possible as it was a time of great excitement about the Church." After his preaching ended, he worked in a shoe business in Massachusetts, where he married Martha Hall in November 1842, and taught school in Rhode Island before once again joining the main body of Saints at Nauvoo, Illinois, in 1843. In 1844, he was part of the Nauvoo Legion[3] and was ordained a mem-

---

2. "The Biography of Jesse Haven," in Haven, journals.
3. The Nauvoo Legion was a unit of the Illinois state militia created in 1840 when the city of Nauvoo was incorporated. It was created to defend both city and state.

ber of the seventy. He left Nauvoo on July 1, 1846, settling in Iowa. In 1848, he was called on another mission, this time to Missouri and the eastern states. That mission ended in 1849, and in 1850, he traveled to Salt Lake City with his wife Martha and "a young lady by the name of Abby Cram," who was sealed to him as a plural wife a week after their arrival. Haven taught school and farmed for two years in Utah before he was called on another mission.[4]

The South African Mission, 1852–55

In early 1852, Joseph Richards stopped in South Africa, known then as the Cape of Good Hope or Cape Colony,[5] on his way to his mission in India by passenger ship. During his brief time there, he distributed tracts and preached sermons.[6] Richards's efforts appear to have had little or no effect on the inhabitants of Cape Colony. It was not until August 1852 that Jesse Haven, William Holmes Walker, and Leonard Ishmael Smith became the first men formally assigned to spread the Latter-day Saint message in the region. William Walker, born in 1820, had been baptized in 1835 and arrived in Salt Lake City in 1847 after serving with the Mormon Battalion.[7] Leonard Smith, born in 1823, had been baptized in 1847 and arrived in the Salt Lake Valley in 1851.[8] Haven, Walker, and Smith left Utah together on September 15, 1852. "I left my family with tears in their eyes; I felt bad when I left—prayed to God to sustain me on my journey, and sustain me in my absence," Haven wrote in his journal.[9] After traveling across the

Joseph Smith called the legion to action in 1844 when tensions were high between Latter-day Saints and dissenters. The name was later used in Utah to refer to a militia of Latter-day Saints. Philip M. Flammer, "Nauvoo Legion," in *Encyclopedia of Mormonism*, 3:997–99; Mike Trapp, "Nauvoo Legion," in *Encyclopedia of Latter-day Saint History*, 826–27.

4. "Biography of Jesse Haven."
5. The Cape of Good Hope, Africa's southernmost point, is located about thirty miles south of Cape Town, South Africa. *Merriam-Webster's Geographical Dictionary*, s.v. "Cape of Good Hope."
6. Cannon, "Mormonism's Jesse Haven," 446.
7. Walker, *Life Incidents and Travels of Elder William Holmes Walker*, 5–15; "Walker, William Holmes," in appendix 2, p. 360 herein.
8. "Smith, Leonard Ishmael," in appendix 2, p. 354 herein.
9. Haven, journals, September 15, 1852.

United States, over the Atlantic, and stopping temporarily in England, they arrived at Cape Town, on the southwest coast of the Cape of Good Hope, and went ashore on April 19, 1853.[10] Shortly thereafter, they ascended Lion's Head, a small mountain of 2,200 feet, and dedicated the land for their preaching. Elder Haven then prophesied that "the Church now organized in the Cape of Good Hope, will roll forth in this Colony, and continue to increase, till many of the honest in heart will be made to rejoice in the everlasting Gospel."[11]

The church did not "roll forth" without considerable opposition. As repeatedly happened elsewhere in the world, the local clergy objected to this new religion in town, doing what they could to stop them, and mobs frequently broke up the Latter-day Saint meetings. Still, Haven and his companions did have their successes; on May 26, 1853, the first two converts were baptized, and a branch was formed in the Cape Town suburb of Mowbray in August. By the end of 1853, William Walker extended his efforts to the settlement of Grahamstown, near the eastern coast of the country, accompanied by John Wesley, one of his converts; and a few months later, Leonard Smith left for Port Elizabeth, also to the east, with Wesley joining him soon thereafter. By the beginning of 1855, there were more than 125 Latter-day Saints in South Africa.[12]

A British colony, South Africa was an ethnically diverse nation. Various African tribes, including the Khokhoi, Zulu, and Xhosa, had inhabited the country for millennia. During the seventeenth century, Dutch colonists established Cape Town, and their descendants formed the Afrikaans-speaking Afrikaner population. The Dutch also brought slaves from Southeast Asia, who formed the Cape Malay population. Around the turn of the nineteenth century, the Cape came under British control, with the first prominent group of English settlers arriving in 1820. Initially, Haven and his companions preached among the English-speaking population—a practice that made sense since Latter-day Saint missionaries in England

10. Wright, "History of the South African Mission," 24–35, 59.
11. Haven, journals, May 23, 1853.
12. Wright, "History of the South African Mission," 59–118; Haven, journals, May 26, 1853.

were meeting with considerable success.[13] Haven later found it important to also preach to the Afrikaner population. He had pamphlets translated into Dutch (or perhaps its linguistic daughter, Afrikaans) in 1854. Haven, his companions, and their new converts visited the Dutch towns of Stellenbosch, Paarl, Malmesbury, and D'Urban in 1854 and 1855. Haven tried to learn Afrikaans, but he never became fluent, and there were not enough bilingual converts to be effective in preaching to Afrikaners. Cultural and religious traditions also made it difficult for those of Dutch descent to heed the Latter-day Saint message. Indeed, during the nearly three-year mission to the Cape of Good Hope, there might have been only one Afrikaner convert.[14]

Besides these European peoples, Haven also mentions "coloured people" in his letters, including the Muslim Cape Malays. There is no evidence of an organized effort to preach among these people, but shortly before his departure, Haven visited a Muslim clergyman. "I then told him of Joseph Smith and of the visions given to him. He was anxious to learn more about him," Haven described. "It is my opinion that many of them will yet receive the Gospel."[15] The other nonwhites, however, were the native African tribes, and there is no evidence of Haven and his companions ministering to them. According to his own words, these peoples "have too much of the blood of Cain in them, for the Gospel to have much effect on their dark spirits"[16]—a reflection of nineteenth-century beliefs on race. In February 1852, Brigham Young had laid out his views, commonly held in America and Europe, of Africans being descended from biblical Cain, the first murderer, and initiated a ban for those of African descent to receive the priesthood.[17] It is unclear, however, to what extent the priesthood ban was an obstacle to Haven's preaching to the native Africans; cultural and linguistic barriers likely played a more substantial role. Missionaries frequently

13. David Cook, "England," in *Encyclopedia of Latter-day Saint History*, 337.

14. Cannon, "Mormonism's Jesse Haven," 446–56.

15. Jesse Haven, "Foreign Correspondence: Cape of Good Hope Mission," *Millennial Star* 18, no. 20 (May 17, 1856): 318; p. 127 herein.

16. Jesse Haven, "Foreign Correspondence: Cape of Good Hope Mission," *Millennial Star* 18, no. 23 (June 7, 1856): 366–67; p. 132 herein.

17. Reeve, *Religion of a Different Color*, 152–58; Mauss, *All Abraham's Children*, 215.

struggled to reach non-European peoples; for example, James Lewis and his companions had difficulties taking their message to the Chinese.[18]

In 1855, word arrived from church leaders in Utah that Haven and his companions were welcome to depart whenever they were ready. On November 27, Walker and Smith boarded the ship *Unity*, which had been purchased by some well-to-do converts, and sailed away the following day with fifteen other members. Circumstances did not permit Haven to leave with them, so he left two weeks later on the *Cleopatra*, but none of the Saints accompanied him on the ship. Local converts took over the leadership of the Cape Town church members.[19]

On his way home from the Cape of Good Hope, Haven spent three and a half months visiting the British Saints in England and Scotland.[20] In May 1856, he and Edward Martin—who had been assigned on a mission to England at the same August 1852 meeting—oversaw more than eight hundred Saints traveling from Liverpool to Boston aboard the ship *Horizon*.[21] After taking the train to Iowa City, Martin, Haven, and the emigrants outfitted to depart for Salt Lake City starting in July 1856. Haven headed a handcart company for three hundred miles, but this group combined with the Martin handcart company, while Haven joined the Hodgetts wagon company.[22] Haven witnessed firsthand the hardships of the Martin handcart company: "I saw much suffering while crossing the plains—women and children travelling in the snow while the thermometer stood below zero. . . . I have been in this church 19 years. I saw more suffering last fall than I ever saw before among the Saints. I was in Missouri when the Church was driven from there and I believe what the Saints suffered there with the exception of those that were taken prisoners was nothing more than a drop to a bucket compared to what those Saints suffered that came in late last fall."[23] He arrived in Salt Lake on December 15, 1856, after a harrowing journey, and he met his three-year-old child,

---

18. See chapter 6, "James Lewis and the China Mission," herein.
19. Wright, "History of the South African Mission," 106–38; *Enduring Legacy*, 8:211.
20. Stephens, "Jesse Haven," 56–59.
21. Sonne, *Ships, Saints, and Mariners*, 98.
22. "Biography of Jesse Haven."
23. Haven, journals, December 15, 1856.

Jesse C. Haven, son of Abby Haven, for the first time.[24]

Though Walker and Smith had left the Cape of Good Hope before Haven, Walker, at least, returned to Utah later than Haven. Walker and Smith reached London on January 29, 1856, and did not tarry long in Britain. They boarded the ship *Caravan* a few weeks after their arrival in England, and they oversaw the emigrating African Saints to America. Smith arrived in the Salt Lake Valley on May 31, 1856.[25] Walker was supposed to head a wagon company to Utah that year, and he had made the necessary preparations to do so, but it was too late in the year, so he stayed behind in the Midwest until the next season and then reached the valley on August 20, 1857.[26] He narrowly avoided the notorious tragedies that Haven witnessed in 1856.[27]

Additional Church Service, 1856–1905

After his return home, Haven quickly became involved in civil and ecclesiastical service in Salt Lake City. He functioned as a chaplain in the Utah Territorial Legislature from 1856 to 1858, and he was also a leader in a militia tasked with defending Utah from Johnston's Army in 1857 and 1858.[28] He was actively involved in the fourteenth quorum of seventy, of which he had been a member since 1844, and he resumed his vocation as a teacher.[29]

In 1862, he moved from his Salt Lake City home to establish a farm in

---

24. "Biography of Jesse Haven"; Stephens, "Jesse Haven," 62–69.
25. "Elder Leonard I. Smith," *Deseret News*, June 4, 1856.
26. "Elder William Walker," *Deseret News*, August 26, 1857.
27. Walker, *Life Incidents and Travels of Elder William Holmes Walker*, 58–63.
28. In 1857, President James Buchanan sent an army of soldiers, under the command of General Albert Sidney Johnston, to suppress a perceived Latter-day Saint rebellion in Utah. The Nauvoo Legion was sent to push back against the approaching army by burning wagons, scattering livestock, and doing other stalling tactics. Johnston's Army finally entered Salt Lake City in June 1858, but the Saints had temporarily relocated southward and left the town empty. Thomas L. Kane, a friend to the church, helped negotiate a peaceful resolution to the conflict. Audrey M. Godfrey, "Johnston's Army," and Richard E. Bennett, "Utah War," in *Encyclopedia of Latter-day Saint History*, 580–81, 1282–84.
29. Stephens, "Jesse Haven," 72–88.

Morgan County, northeast of Salt Lake.[30] Soon after Haven moved there, Brigham Young asked him if he would like to take another mission to Africa. Haven responded, "I should not like to go," because "the climate of Africa is debilitating to both my body and mind, yet I told him that I was ready to do as he said." He was instead appointed to serve as circuit judge in his new home of Morgan County and adjoining Weber and Davis Counties. "The Office of Judge is an office I have no desire to fill, but as I have been appointed to the place by my brethren I will try to do the best I can," he recorded.[31] He became probate judge in 1869 and served until 1878. In addition to these civic duties, he also held a variety of ecclesiastical callings on the branch and stake levels in Morgan County. Haven continued to serve in the church until he died on December 13, 1905.[32]

William Holmes Walker similarly lived the remainder of his life in service to the church. He arrived in Salt Lake in August 1857, and he served a mission to southern Utah in the 1860s. He built mills and homes for his wives in Utah and Idaho and evaded federal authorities who were actively pursuing polygamists. He died on January 9, 1908, in Lewisville, Idaho.[33] Less is known about Leonard Smith. He carried the mail from Salt Lake City throughout Utah and apparently established a farm near Tooele, Utah, where he was shot and killed during an altercation with his nephew in July 1877.[34]

Jesse Haven's Family Life

Jesse Haven married Martha Hall in November 1842, and they were sealed in February 1846 in the Nauvoo Temple. In 1848, Haven and Martha moved to Iowa with four orphans whom they were caring for. It is not

---

30. Stephens, "Jesse Haven," 90–93.

31. Haven, journals, April 23, 1862.

32. Haven died at his grandson's house in Morgan County, Utah, either at Peterson or at Enterprise. A burial notice in the *Deseret News* stated that Haven died "at Preston," but that was likely a misprint. Stephens, "Jesse Haven," 95–110; Jenson, *Latter-day Saint Biographical Encyclopedia*, 4:379; "Interment in Salt Lake," *Deseret News*, December 18, 1905.

33. Walker, *Life Incidents and Travels of Elder William Holmes Walker*, 67–80.

34. "Murder," *Salt Lake Tribune*, July 20, 1877; "Smith, Leonard Ishmael," in appendix 2, p. 354 herein.

known how long they cared for these children, though they probably remained in the Haven family through Haven's mission to the eastern United States. In 1850, Haven and Martha traveled to Salt Lake City with Abigail Cram, and he and Abigail were sealed to each other a week after their arrival.[35] The 1850 census shows a five-year-old Abby and a three-year-old Martha living with Haven and Martha, but it is not clear whether these really were children living with them or simply a census error (they do not appear in the 1860 census).

When Haven left for his mission in 1852, it was the last time he would see his father, John Haven, who died in Salt Lake City in March 1853.[36] In June, however, Jesse Haven's family grew when his wife Abby gave birth to a son, Jesse Cram Haven.[37] Martha, Haven's other wife, followed her husband by becoming a teacher, which might have provided income for the family during his absence, though it is not clear at what point she took up schoolteaching.[38]

When Haven returned home in 1856, young Jesse was more than three years old. In March 1857, he married a third wife, Sarah Taylor, who had traveled west with him in 1856, but they divorced in 1860.[39] Martha bore no children before her death in 1861.[40] Haven and Abby apparently gave birth to a daughter, Marie, in 1857 or 1858, but little is known about her. Haven and Abby faced an ordeal when their son, Jesse Cram Haven, died on April 14, 1879, at the age of twenty-five, leaving behind a wife and two children.[41] Abby died at Enterprise, Utah, on December 4, 1904, and Haven died the following year on December 13, 1905.[42]

Source Note

Between August 1853, four months after Haven and his companions

---

35. "Biography of Jesse Haven"; Stephens, "Jesse Haven," 13, 20, 24.
36. "Biography of Jesse Haven."
37. Haven, journals, December 22, 1853.
38. Barlow, *Israel Barlow Story and Mormon Mores*, 411.
39. Stephens, "Jesse Haven," 76, 81.
40. Stephens, "Jesse Haven," 83.
41. Stephens, "Jesse Haven," 105.
42. Stephens, "Jesse Haven," 110.

arrived in Cape Town, and May 1856, about the time he was preparing to sail from England to America, Haven wrote eleven letters to Presidents Samuel W. Richards and Franklin D. Richards, which were published in the church's *Millennial Star* periodical.[43] The last three of these letters were written while Haven was in the British Isles, and these three are presented in this chapter as they appeared in that publication. The first of these letters describes the missionaries' journey to the Cape of Good Hope and their proselytizing efforts there; the second and third primarily describe the people, cultures, and climate of the country.

43. See the following articles in the *Millennial Star*: "The Cape of Good Hope Mission," vol. 15, no. 43 (October 22, 1853): 695–96; "The Cape of Good Hope Mission," vol. 16, no. 11 (March 18, 1854): 173–74; "Foreign Correspondence: Cape of Good Hope," vol. 16, no. 38 (September 23, 1854): 604; "Foreign Correspondence: Cape of Good Hope," vol. 17, no. 8 (February 24, 1855): 127; "Foreign Correspondence: Cape of Good Hope," vol. 17, no. 22 (June 2, 1855): 347–49; "Foreign Correspondence: Cape of Good Hope," vol. 17, no. 36 (September 8, 1855): 572–73; "Foreign Correspondence: Cape Colony," vol. 17, no. 49 (December 8, 1855): 780–83; "Foreign Correspondence: Cape of Good Hope," vol. 18, no. 7 (February 16, 1856): 111–12; "Foreign Correspondence: Cape of Good Hope Mission," vol. 18, no. 12 (March 22, 1856): 189–91; "Foreign Correspondence: Cape of Good Hope Mission," vol. 18, no. 20 (May 17, 1856): 318–19; "Foreign Correspondence: Cape of Good Hope Mission," vol. 18, no. 23 (June 7, 1856): 366–67.

DOCUMENT TRANSCRIPTS

Jesse Haven to Franklin D. Richards, February 25, 1856[44]

107 Finch Street, Liverpool,
February 25, 1856.
President F. D. Richards.

Dear Brother—I have written a lengthy report of my proceedings since I left G. S. L. City, and also an account of the situation of the Mission at the Cape of Good Hope, and have sent it to the First Presidency in Zion.[45] Instead of sending you a copy of this report, many items of which have already been forwarded to you, I have concluded to extract from it such items as have not appeared in my former communications to the Liverpool Office.[46]

Elders William Walker, Leonard I. Smith, and myself arrived in Liverpool January 4, 1853, on our way from Utah to the Cape of Good Hope. Here we found President S[amuel]. W. Richards ready to lend us all the assistance he possibly could. I must say that his conduct towards the Elders, when they landed in Liverpool, was more like that of a father, than of a young man just emerging into the active scenes of life. His kindness will long be remembered by me, and, considering the multiplicity of business on his hands, I was surprised at the attention which he gave to every call. I remained in Liverpool and its vicinity until January 22nd. Having then obtained means for the further prosecution of my journey, I left Liverpool for London, and wrote to brothers Walker and Smith, who had gone to other parts of England, to meet me there. I remained in London, visiting

---

44. Jesse Haven, "Foreign Correspondence: Cape of Good Hope Mission," *Millennial Star* 18, no. 12 (March 22, 1856): 189–91.

45. This "lengthy report" was thirty-five pages long. Jesse Haven to the First Presidency, January 1856, Incoming Correspondence, Brigham Young Office Files.

46. See note 43, herein.

and preaching among the Saints, who received me with great kindness, until February 11, when, between two and three o'clock, p.m., Elders Walker, Smith, and myself embarked on the barque *Domitia*,[47] bound for the Cape of Good Hope.

As an account of our voyage, arrival at the Cape, and success in preaching, and the organization of Branches and Conferences has been forwarded to the Office in Liverpool before, I will pass over it to matters which more particularly pertain to the mission at the present time.

Many tracts have been circulated,[48] and some preaching has been done among the Dutch in Cape Colony, but only a few have yet received the Gospel. They, as well as other classes of the natives, are much attached to the country, and the idea of leaving it frightens them. Their religion is the Dutch Reformed.[49] Only to suggest the idea that their church is not the true one, causes them to look astonished, and they seem to say—"Is it possible!"

Owing to the prejudices of the Dutch against the English in this

---

47. The small bark *Domitia* was built in 1852. When Haven and his companions traveled on it, they were the only passengers, and they arrived in Cape Town on April 19, 1855. The ship was lost near Gibraltar in 1855. Sonne, *Ships, Saints, and Mariners*, 59–60; Haven, journals, April 19, 1855.

48. During his mission to South Africa, Haven published eleven items describing Latter-day Saint doctrines, including the following four pamphlets: *Some of the Principal Doctrines or Belief of the Church of Jesus Christ, of Latter Day Saints* (Cape Town: W. Foelscher, [1853]); *Celestical [sic] Marriage, and the Plurality of Wives!* (Cape Town: W. Foelscher, [1853]); *On the First Principles of the Gospel* (Cape Town: Van de Sandt de Villiers & Tier, 1853; reprinted in 1855, also translated into Dutch); and *A Warning to All* ([Cape Town]: n.p., [1853]; reprinted in 1855, also translated into Dutch). William Walker also published a few items, and the missionaries brought tracts with them from England as well. Whittaker, "Early Mormon Imprints in South Africa," 404–9; see also Cannon, "Mormonism's Jesse Haven," 450.

49. The Dutch Reformed Church began in the Netherlands in the sixteenth century during the Protestant Reformation, and it spread to South Africa starting in 1652. The religion embraced Calvinistic ideas, such as unconditional election (God has elected whom he will save) and irresistible grace (the elect cannot reject God's grace). The Reformed Dutch Church was a key aspect of European colonialism in South Africa. Gerstner, "A Christian Monopoly," 16–30; *Oxford Dictionary of World Religions*, s.v. "Dutch Reformed Church," 298–99.

colony,[50] if Elders should be sent to labour among them, I would suggest that they be not natives of England. Americans or Scotch would do very well, and a native of Holland still better, for they think much of their mother country, and everything that comes from it.

Through fear of another Kaffir war,[51] the Colonial Parliament have passed a law, that all males in the Colony, between twenty and fifty years of age, shall do military duty, except ministers of religion, and some others. The brethren, who had been ordained to the office of either Elder or Priest, claimed exemption from military duty, as "ministers of religion." They appeared before the committee, appointed by the government to decide such cases, but they refused to decide on their case, and referred it to the Attorney-General. In a few days the brethren were informed that he had decided, that they could not be exempted from doing military duty. I immediately, in company with the brethren, paid this dignitary a visit, and requested the privilege of laying before him the organization of our Church, that he might see that my brethren were exempt from doing military duty, according to law; but he refused to hear me, and said, "I have given you my decision, and if you don't like it, you may take it before the Supreme Court." After this I wrote a letter to the Committee before mentioned, requesting a hearing before them, and had my brethren sign it. As I

50. The Dutch were the first Europeans to colonize Cape Town and Cape Colony, beginning in 1652, but the British took over from 1795 until 1803 and again in 1806. In 1820, many settlers arrived from England to Cape Colony, and in the 1820s and 1830s, the British began passing laws that were difficult for the Afrikaner population, including laws that led to their losing property and slaves. In response, large groups of Dutch descendants left Cape Colony in the 1830s and 1840s to establish homesteads elsewhere in the country. As much as one-tenth of the white population left Cape Town during this period of animosity toward the English. Thompson, *History of South Africa*, 31–69.

51. The Xhosa Wars, also known as Kaffir Wars, were a series of skirmishes between the native African Xhosa people and Europeans beginning in 1778. Now considered offensive, "Kaffir" was a term referring to blacks, especially Xhosa or other native tribes. Both Dutch and British farmers and colonists tried to force the Xhosa off their land, and the Xhosa retaliated to retain it. Eight Xhosa Wars had already occurred when Haven and his companions arrived, with one more occurring in 1877–78. Timothy J. Stapleton, "Cape-Xhosa Wars," in *Encyclopedia of African Colonial Conflicts*, 1:170–77; *Oxford English Dictionary*, s.v. "Kaffir."

left soon after this letter was written, I am not prepared to state the result; but I told the brethren to claim their rights, and if possible get a hearing before some one in authority, for this is the way that the Lord will prove the rulers of the earth, and see if they will do justice to the Saints.

When I left, 176 had been baptized in Cape Colony. Of these about 30 are natives, the remainder English emigrants; 38 had been cut off, one had died, one emigrated to India, and three to Australia, with the intention of going from these places to the land of Zion; twelve have emigrated to America, *via* England, two of whom went before those who lately arrived in London on the *Unity*;[52] leaving now 121 Saints in Cape Colony, in good standing. When I left, the work was still spreading. A number, I believe, would soon be baptized, if there were Elders there to labour among the people. We have ordained some of the brethren to be Elders, and appointed them to preside over the Saints whom we have left behind. I believe that they will prove faithful, and act up to the light which they have.

The Saints are anxious to have more Elders sent to them, and the universal question they asked was—"When do you think that we shall have more Elders from Zion." Of course I could not tell them, but I promised that I would lay their case before the authorities over me.

While in Cape Colony, I paid out about £33 for printing. There has been from £140 to £150 worth of books sent from Liverpool, for the benefit of the mission. I have remitted £40 to the Office in Liverpool by mail; and Elder Walker and myself, since our arrival in England, have paid £45 19s. 9d. There has been collected in the Colony, and remitted to the Liverpool Office, £16 6s. 7d. for the P. E. Fund.[53]

---

52. The ship *Unity* was built in England in 1848. Three Latter-day Saints at Port Elizabeth purchased the ship, and Elders Leonard Smith and William Walker, as well as fifteen emigrating Saints, left aboard the ship on November 28, 1855. Jesse Haven left by himself on December 15 on the ship *Cleopatra*. Buckley, "'Good News' at the Cape of Good Hope," 486; Sonne, *Ships, Saints, and Mariners*, 49, 193.

53. The Perpetual Emigrating Fund originated in fall 1849. It was an organization to help emigrating Saints, as the principle of "gathering" meant that foreign converts were expected to move to the Great Basin. Those who were helped were expected to give back to the fund once they arrived in the Salt Lake Valley, but many of them never did. Fred E. Woods, "Perpetual Emigrating Fund," in *Encyclopedia of Latter-day Saint History*, 910; Carson, "Perpetual Emigrating Fund"; Howard,

When Elder Walker left, agreeable to my instructions, he appointed Elder Edward Slaughter,[54] of Port Elizabeth, book agent for the Eastern Province, and Elders Walker and Smith left in his hands all the books which they had in their possession, belonging to the mission. When I left, I appointed Elder Richard Provis,[55] who lives at Mowbray, general book agent for the whole Colony, until such times as other arrangements are made. The expense of freight, duties, &c., on books sent to the Colony, has been considerable, so that I have been obliged to sell them much higher than they are sold in England. I have given away many pounds worth of books and pamphlets to spread the work, paying for them partly out of my own pocket, and partly by occasional contributions from the Saints of the Cape Conference.

I have kept a strict account, in writing, of everything pertaining to the financial affairs of the mission, and left it in the hands of brother Provis, so that whoever comes after me can see the course I have pursued. I have not been in the habit of trusting out books, except to Elders Walker and Smith, who have acted as agents. After brother Slaughter was appointed agent of the Eastern Province, I sent him a letter of instructions, in which I made the following remark—"I do not make it a practice to trust out any books, &c., except to agents; if I am ever so foolish as to do it, and the persons neglect to pay, I pay it out of my own pocket, and not let the mission suffer for it." My object has been to manage so that the cash and books on hand would at any time pay what the mission owed.

Just before I left, I took an inventory of all the cash, books, pamphlets, &c., which were on hand, also what were in the hands of Elders Walker and Smith, as agents, prizing them at the Liverpool wholesale price; and I found that the amount was about £12 more than the mission was owing to the Office in Liverpool. There were also £9 8s. 11d. worth of pamphlets on hand, which I have had printed in the Colony, and the expense

---

"Economic Analysis of the Perpetual Emigrating Fund."

54. Edward Slaughter (1807–97) was born in England and later moved to South Africa. After being baptized by Leonard I. Smith, he made his way to Utah and later served a mission to Britain in the 1880s. Early Mormon Missionaries database, s.v. "Edward Slaughter."

55. Richard Provis (1825–1907) traveled to Utah in 1860. Mormon Pioneer Overland Travel database, s.v. "Richard Samuel Provis."

of publishing paid. These I have left for the benefit of the mission, which makes upwards of £20 worth of books in the Cape of Good Hope Mission over and above what the mission is owing. For want of proper mail facilities, I have laboured under many inconveniences in forwarding the *Star* and *Journal of Discourses*[56] to my brethren. For the same reason it has been difficult to circulate pamphlets, &c., through the country.

In my instructions to the Saints, I have endeavoured to teach them the first principles of the Gospel, and the gathering, and that it was of more importance to learn how to live their religion, day by day, than to be troubling themselves about doctrines and principles that did not immediately concern them. I have tried to lay before the Saints the object of the P. E. Fund, and urged them to do what they can for it. I have also taught them the principle of Tithing. When speaking on this subject, I have always been impressed upon to say to them, that when they gather to Zion they should not only be willing to pay one-tenth of their property to build it up, but ten tenths, adding themselves, wives, and children, in order to secure the bargain of eternal salvation.[57] This is the way that I understand the revelations of Jesus Christ, which I have made my study since I have been from the body of the Saints.

It is not so easy as one who has not had the experience might suppose,

---

56. *Journal of Discourses* was a semimonthly magazine published in Liverpool from 1853 to 1886. It featured speeches by church leaders in Utah, transcribed by George D. Watt, as well as other reports and forms of public discourse. Crawley, *Descriptive Bibliography of the Mormon Church*, 3:103–8.

57. Devoting all of one's property to the church is known in Latter-day Saint teachings as the law of consecration, and it has shifted in practice throughout the church's history. From 1831 to 1834, the law of consecration was largely a communal endeavor designed to assist the poor and build up communities; living the law involved donating all of one's money, lands, and goods to the church to be administered by the bishop, who would issue a portion (one's "stewardship") in return. Problems forced the system to be modified in 1833 and discontinued by 1834. Due to the struggles of the Saints after their expulsion from Missouri and their failure to keep the law of consecration, they were commanded in July 1838 to pay tithing of one-tenth of "their interest annually" (Doctrine and Covenants 119:4). Lyndon W. Cook, "Consecration, Law of," and Dale Beecher, "Tithing," in *Encyclopedia of Latter-day Saint History*, 241–43, 1249–51; see also Harper, "All Things Are the Lord's."

to establish the Gospel in a country where it has not before been preached; where the climate weakens the constitution of persons brought up in a northern clime; where the people speak three or four different languages, and are of all kinds, grades, conditions, and complexions; and where there are only two or three hundred thousand scattered over a country twice as large as England.[58]

I have often felt, while I have been on this mission, as though the privilege of having the society and counsel of those who preside over me, if only for a few moments, would be invaluable. My situation has often driven me to the throne of grace, and my prayer unceasingly has been, "Lord, give me wisdom, that I may know how to manage the things committed to my care."

As President of the mission, I have not accomplished as much as I could wish, yet, if those who sent me and my brethren are satisfied, I am. If they are not satisfied, and think that I need correction, all I ask is, that I may receive the chastisement with meekness, and kiss the hand that inflicts it.

Having made my report to you, and to the First Presidency of the Church, whose characters I trust I shall ever hold sacred, sustain, and defend, I feel the responsibilities that were placed upon me in August, 1852, rolling off; and when I shall have arrived in Utah, with the Saints now on their way from Africa, I shall consider that the mission appointed to me, nearly three years and a half ago, is fully and completely closed; yet, I trust that I shall ever hold myself ready, at a moment's warning, to take other missions, or do whatever those who preside over me shall be pleased to direct.

If it was not for fear of exhausting your patience, I would continue writing, and express the feelings of my heart, for it is full of gratitude to my Heavenly Father, for the light of the Gospel and the plan of salvation revealed through Joseph the Prophet. I have never enjoyed myself better than when I could stand before Saints and sinners, and declare unto them the Divine mission of our martyred Prophet, saying to them, that he, under

---

58. South Africa has considerably more than "three or four different languages." In addition to the English and Dutch (Afrikaans) languages of European colonists, various African peoples speak (or spoke) numerous native languages, including Zulu, Xhosa, and Swazi. Creole languages based on Portuguese also emerged among Asian slaves. Mesthrie, "South Africa: A Sociolinguistic Overview," 11–26; Thompson, *History of South Africa*, 52.

Christ, would be the leading judge of this generation, for he was sent to this generation, and if they would not believe it, the time would come when they should know it, to their sorrow and condemnation.

Will not I defend the character of the Prophet Joseph? Yes, I will before all men, for he was the instrument in the hands of God of giving me and my brethren the Holy Priesthood, through which we obtain light, knowledge, and salvation. Will I not defend and uphold those men whom he has ordained and left to carry out the work which he commenced? Yes, for on them I am dependent for further light, knowledge, and keys of exaltation, while they also, in connection with him, will be the judges of this generation. May his words, who sealed his testimony with his blood, delivered to the Quorum of the Twelve before his death, ever be fresh in my mind—"There is not one key or power to be bestowed on this Church, to lead the people into the celestial gate, but I have given you, showed you, and talked it over to you; the kingdom is set up, and you have the perfect pattern, and you can go and build up the kingdom, and go in at the celestial gate, taking your train with you."[59] My prayer is that I may be one of this train.

I will here say, in regard to Elder Richard Provis, whom I appointed general book agent at the Cape of Good Hope, that I have given him instructions in the business, and I am perfectly satisfied that all books, pamphlets, &c., sent to him will be seen to and taken care of, and a strict account kept of all moneys received for them, or for the P. E. Fund, and that it will be forthcoming when called for.

I certainly feel interested for the mission and the Saints at the Cape of Good Hope, and wish to do all I can for their benefit. My business is merely to present the situation of the mission to those who preside over me, then leave it for them to act as they think proper.

I remain your brother in the covenant of peace,

J. Haven.

---

59. This quote was attributed to Joseph Smith by Brigham Young, who wrote to Orson Spencer that "Joseph told [it to] the Twelve, the year before he died." "Letter from President Brigham Young to Orson Spencer," *Millennial Star* 10, no. 8 (April 15, 1848): 115.

Jesse Haven to Franklin D. Richards, April 26, 1856[60]

41 Charlotte Street, Glasgow,
April 26, 1856.
President Richards.

Dear Brother—According to a promise in a previous letter, I take my pen to note a few things in regard to the country, climate, and people of the Cape of Good Hope.

The colony is divided into the eastern and western provinces. Cape Town, the largest town in the colony, is in the western province, and situated on the south-west side of Table Bay. On the south side of the town commences the base of Table Mountain, which rises to the height of nearly 3,800 feet above the level of the sea; the upper half is nearly perpendicular.[61] On the west side of the town is a point called the *Lion's Head*, which is nearly as high as Table Mountain, being the highest part of a mountain extending along on the north-west side of the town, which has the appearance, when at sea, of a lion lying on his belly.

Elders Walker and Smith, and myself went on this mountain, on the 23rd day of May, 1853, and organized a Branch of the Church of Jesus Christ of Latter-day Saints, in the Cape of Good Hope, consisting of us three as members. I there and then prophesied that the Church that day organized in the Cape of Good Hope, would roll forth in that land till many of the honest in heart would be made to rejoice in the everlasting Gospel. I rejoice that I tarried there long enough to see this prophecy literally fulfilled.

Cape Town has about 30,000 inhabitants. About one half are coloured people—being of all shades from a jet black to almost a European complexion. A large portion of the coloured population were formerly slaves; but by an Act of the English Parliament, they were emancipated in the

---

60. Jesse Haven, "Foreign Correspondence: Cape of Good Hope Mission," *Millennial Star* 18, no. 20 (May 17, 1856): 318–19.

61. Table Mountain is a peak south of Cape Town that stands about 3,500 feet above sea level. *Merriam-Webster's Geographical Dictionary*, s.v. "Table Mountain."

Modern-day Cape Town. Table Mountain is pictured behind the city, and Lion's Head is at the far right. Courtesy of Pixabay.com.

year 1838.[62] Those of them called Malays, are Mahometans, and according to their religion, they are permitted to have and do have a plurality of wives.[63] Sometimes the English who have emigrated to that colony, intermarry with them, and then adopt their religion. They are generally very quiet people, attending to their own business, though they occasionally practise witchcraft on those with whom they get offended. There is less drunkenness and licentiousness among them than among the whites, or Christians. I called on one of their priests a few days before I left the Cape. He treated me kindly. He said the Mahometans believe there have been six great Prophets on the earth of equal authority, for these six have given the commandments; they are Adam, Noah, Abraham, Moses, Jesus Christ, and Mahomet; Mahomet was the last one; no more are to come.[64] He said

62. When the Dutch colonized Cape Colony in the 1650s, they brought slavery with them. Slaves were imported from other areas in Africa and from southern Asia. In 1807, after England gained control of the cape, the British Parliament banned the slave trade, meaning no new slaves could be brought to British colonies, but slavery continued with those who were already in its clutches. The government enacted various laws to ameliorate the condition of slaves in South Africa until slavery was officially abolished in 1834. Freed slaves went through a state of "apprenticeship" until 1838. See Dooling, *Slavery, Emancipation and Colonial Rule.*

63. Cape Malays are an ethnic group descended from slaves imported from Southeast Asia, and most of them are Muslims. The Koran permits polygamy, especially when it helps widows, but does not expressly encourage the practice. *Modern Muslim Societies*, 32–35.

64. According to Muslim belief, prophets are sent by God to different peoples at differ-

Christ is coming again, and when he comes, we shall all see and understand alike. As he believed in the Old Testament, I asked him if it did not look reasonable that there should be a seventh Prophet, as seven is a Bible number? He acknowledged it looked reasonable, though he had never thought of it before. I then told him of Joseph Smith and of the visions given to him. He was anxious to learn more about him. I gave him a small tract in Dutch, giving an account of the visions of Joseph, as he could not read English, nor converse much in that language.[65] It is my opinion that many of them will yet receive the Gospel. I believe they are the descendants of Abraham by his wife Hagar, that is, those who are the pure blooded Malays.[66] They have long, straight, black hair, skin darker than the American Indian, and none of the Negro features in them. They practise circumcision on their male children, when they are about thirteen years of age; or from thirteen to sixteen. The Malays are scattered more or less through the whole colony. They, and the other coloured inhabitants, form a large portion of the population, perhaps nearly one-half.

The whites are principally English and Dutch, and their descendants. The English language is spoken more or less throughout the whole colony; yet, in many towns and among the scattered farmers in the western province, but very little English is spoken; the white inhabitants being principally of Dutch descent. An Elder, to labour successfully among them in

---

ent times, preaching the same message of the Koran. However, the message from the earlier prophets became corrupted. Muhammad was the last prophet because he preserved the Koran without corruption. *Oxford Dictionary of World Religions,* s.v. "Nabī," 674.

65. Haven had the first third of a pamphlet by Lorenzo Snow, *The Voice of Joseph,* translated into Dutch. He likely used the Liverpool 1852 edition. This part of *The Voice of Joseph* recounts Joseph Smith's early visions, the publication of the Book of Mormon, and the organization of the Church. Whittaker, "Early Mormon Imprints in South Africa," 407; Crawley, *Descriptive Bibliography of the Mormon Church,* 2:369–70, 3:221–22.

66. Genesis 16 recounts the story of Abraham and Hagar. Hagar was the handmaid of Abraham's wife, Sarah, and Sarah gave her to Abraham since she was barren. Hagar bore a son, Ishmael, to Abraham, but it was Sarah's son, Isaac, who would be heir to the Abrahamic covenant described in Genesis 17. Muslim tradition holds that Ishmael is the ancestor of certain Arabian tribes. *Oxford Dictionary of World Religions,* s.v. "Ishmael," 478–79.

spreading the Gospel, should be acquainted with the Dutch language.

The English language is spoken more in the eastern province than in the western. It was settled more by the English, as the whites did not settle there much, until the colony came into the possession of the English, which was in the year 1806.

It is my opinion that there are some honest in heart among the Dutch in that land, who will yet embrace the Gospel.

An Elder to travel among them should be provided with a good horse, saddle, and bridle, and dress respectably. If he goes in this way, he can travel without money, and both him and his horse will be fed and lodged, and he will be provided for much better than he would be were he to go on foot, as has been the practice of Elders in this country and in America; because, if he should go on foot, they would look upon him as some poor vagabond. Their ministers all ride on horse-back, and they expect to see every man that preaches the Gospel, when he travels, ride a good horse; and they have a great respect for preachers of the Gospel.

The winter there, which is at the time of our summer months here, is the rainy season, and the season in which the agriculturist must grow his vegetables and grain, unless he has low moist land, or land that can be irrigated; for the summer is very dry and hot, there being little or no rain.

The rains in the western province generally commence in April, and continue more or less until November; though there are many beautiful, pleasant, fair days in the winter season.

Occasionally there is a light frost on low land in the winter, and sometimes snow on the surrounding mountains. All kinds of tropical fruits grow in the colony, such as oranges, lemons, &c.

Wine and raisins are manufactured from grapes that grow in the country, which are plentiful in the western province, though many vineyards have gone to ruin since the abolition of slavery.[67] The wine is generally cheap, and is much used by those who have emigrated there from Europe, causing much drunkenness, and a hindrance to the spread of the Gospel.

The natives of the country are not so much addicted to drinking as are the emigrants from Europe. The grape is the best fruit that grows at the

67. Wine production also declined after a preferential tariff on wine exports ended in 1826. Thompson, *History of South Africa*, 53.

Cape. It is a great country for flowers. Trees and shrubbery grow rapidly there. There is a tree there called the Gum-tree, brought there, I believe, from Australia or New Zealand. I have seen them, only 10 years old, 80 feet high, and 3 feet in circumference at the bottom. They make excellent timber which is sometimes used for masts for ships. If they would grow in the Valley as they do at the Cape, we could soon have plenty of timber there.[68] I sent some of the seed on when the *Enoch Train* sailed.

The climate of the Cape of Good Hope is weakening to the constitution of all who are raised in a cold climate. I found it had that effect on me. I feel much stronger since I came to this country. The climate is called very healthy for a warm one. The air is pure, and the natives live to a good old age.

I find I am making this communication too lengthy; I will therefore close by promising another slice on the same subject at some future time.

That the Lord may bless you is the prayer of your brother in the kingdom of peace,

J. Haven.

Jesse Haven to Franklin D. Richards, May 13, 1856[69]

41, Charlotte Street, Glasgow,
May 13, 1856.
President Richards.

Dear Brother—In accordance with my promise in my last communication, I take my pen to give you some further items about the country, climate, and people of the Cape of Good Hope.

In my last letter, I spoke more particularly of the Western Province of Cape Colony, I will now speak of the Eastern Province, some parts of which I had the privilege of riding over, a few months before I left.

---

68. Beginning in the 1820s, blue gum trees, *Eucalyptus globulus*, were brought to South Africa from Australia. They grow well in Africa because of the similar climate, but the timber is inferior, and as a nonnative species, they can damage the environment. Bennett and Kruger, *Forestry and Water Conservation in South Africa*, 27–36.

69. Jesse Haven, "Foreign Correspondence: Cape of Good Hope Mission," *Millennial Star* 18, no. 23 (June 7, 1856): 366–67.

The Eastern Province, as well as the Western, is rocky and mountainous; timber and water are scarce, and there is much barren uncultivatable land. Near the sea shore, there are hills and almost mountains of white sand, which, at a distance, look like mountains covered with snow. The inhabitants are far apart. Sometimes I have rode for miles without seeing a house. To find the honest in heart in this part of the world, seems like fulfilling the prophecy of Jeremiah, where he speaks of the fishers and hunters being sent out in the last days—"And they shall hunt them from every mountain, and from every hill, and out of the holes of the rocks." I believe this prophecy, of the old Prophet, was literally fulfilled, in me and my brethren.[70]

In my travels in that part of the country, I beheld much of the effects of the last Kaffir war. Houses and forts are in ruins, being the remains of fires lit by the torch of the savage. The inhabitants were rife with accounts of the cruelties inflicted by the Kaffirs,[71] on those whom they took prisoners; such as flaying them alive; cutting them up inch by inch until they would die; fastening them down to the ground, and there leaving them for the ants to destroy—an insect prevalent in that part of the land—fastening them to a stake or tree, for the purpose of permitting the Kaffir boys to practice throwing the *asseyai* at them, a weapon much used by the Kaffirs in war, and in hunting.[72] The inhabitants are continually in excitement through fear that the Kaffirs will come on them again.

The Kaffirs have a plurality of wives. They buy their wives with cattle, which they have in abundance, though of late, the cattle sickness has been among them, as well as among the whites, and carried off thousands and tens of thousands of their cattle. Among themselves, where they are away from the whites, they go almost entirely, and sometimes wholly, in a state of nudity; yet there is more virtue among the sexes, with them, than there is among the whites. Death is the penalty of adultery. They circumcise

---

70. Jeremiah 16:16.

71. By "Kaffirs," Haven is probably referring to the native Xhosa people, a group of mixed farmers who herded cattle and raised crops. See Thompson, *History of South Africa*, 1–30.

72. The *assegai* is a long, throwable spear used by African tribes. *Oxford English Dictionary*, s.v. "assagai | assegai."

their male children, between the ages of twelve and sixteen years. Some suppose that they are descended from Ishmael; if so, they must have mixed up with some of the African tribes, for they have some of the negro features about them—colour, nearly black, and woolly heads. The men are large and athletic.

There is another class of blacks, called the Fingoes; they are like the Kaffirs in features. Formerly they were the Kaffirs' slaves, but they revolted from them and united with the whites in the last war. They now live among the whites as servants. They have some large villages in the Eastern Province. They also practise circumcision, and have a plurality of wives.[73]

Missionaries are labouring among them, as well as among the Kaffirs, and trying to convert them to modern Christianity, but their success is limited, for the Kaffirs do not like the idea of giving up all their wives except one, which they must do to conform to the "holy religion" of the 19th century.[74]

The English bishop at Natal has a little consistency; he proposes that those who receive the Christian religion, and have already a plurality of wives, should be permitted to keep their wives. I think that this proposition of the bishop's is a choker to some of the "pious, good, sanctimonious" missionaries of that land.

There is a class of blacks in the Cape of Good Hope, called the Hottentots, who are said to be the original natives of that part now occupied by the whites. They are altogether a different race from the Kaffirs and Fingoes; not so dark, but more degraded.[75]

---

73. The Fingo, or Mfengu, people are traditionally considered to be a native group of people who fled from conquering Zulu tribes in the early nineteenth century and joined the Gcaleka group of the Xhosa. The Xhosa enslaved them, and the Fingoes allied themselves with the British and became liberated in the 1830s. Some scholars reject this account as a colonial fabrication and think the Mfengu are actually Xhosa captives. See Stapleton, "Oral Evidence in a Pseudo-Ethnicity," 359–68.

74. Christian missionaries began preaching among the Xhosa in the late 1790s and more permanently beginning in 1816. Missionaries often used native traditions to share their message, and the Xhosa likewise appropriated Christian ideas into their culture; at the same time, however, missionaries tried to quash local traditions they regarded as immoral. Hodgson, "Battle for Sacred Power," 68–88.

75. The Khoikhoi, originally called Hottentots by the Dutch, are a pastoral people of

They are scattered more or less over the Colony, and have mixed up much with the whites by intermarrying, &c.

In the last Kaffir war the body of them joined the Kaffirs.

Missionaries have been labouring among them, trying to convert them to Christianity. They have succeeded in introducing among them some of the licentious customs of our refined cities. Some of the missionaries, in their great zeal to exalt them, have married their women. I think that they, and the Kaffirs and Fingoes, have too much of the blood of Cain in them, for the Gospel to have much effect on their dark spirits.[76]

Much wool is grown in the Eastern Province which is taken to Port Elizabeth on waggons, drawn by oxen—generally from 12 to 18 hitched to one waggon. Port Elizabeth is a seaport, lying on Algoa Bay. The wool is taken from there and shipped to England.

Severe hail storms occasionally occur in the Eastern Province. A farmer informed me that one passed over his farm in October 1854. The hail fell eighteen inches deep, in fifteen minutes, in front of his house, the cloud broke just above his house. His wheat was nearly ready to harvest; but not a vestige of it was left. It killed about thirty sheep for him. The hail stones were about two-thirds the size of hen's eggs. The trees in front of his house, were literally barked by them, which I plainly saw.

If time and circumstances would permit, other items of interest might possibly be related, but I will close for the present.

That heaven's choicest blessings may rest upon you, is the prayer of your brother in the Covenant of peace,

J. Haven.

southern Africa. The term "Hottentot" is now considered offensive. Thompson, *History of South Africa*, 7; *Oxford English Dictionary*, s.v. "Hottentot."

76. See chapter 2, note 69, p. 62 herein.

Part 2

EVANGELIZING IN
THE PACIFIC WORLD

5

BENJAMIN JOHNSON AND THE SANDWICH ISLANDS MISSION

Historical Introduction

A MONTH AND A HALF HAD PASSED FROM THE SPECIAL August 1852 missionary conference before Benjamin Johnson learned that he had been called on a mission to the Sandwich Islands.[1] "At first I could not believe it, but when I found it a reality I was dazed!" he later reflected. "How possibly could I

---

1. The Pacific volcanic island chain of the Sandwich Islands (Hawaii) was occupied by natives sometime before AD 1000 and was explored by James Cook in 1778. Whalers and Christian missionaries came to the island in the nineteenth century. In 1850, the first Latter-day Saint missionaries arrived; the first branch was formed in 1851 on Maui, and by 1854 there were fifty-three branches. When the Utah elders left in 1858 because of the Utah War, the local Saints struggled. Walter Murray Gibson arrived in 1861 and began engaging in unorthodox practices, including selling priesthood offices. He was excommunicated in 1864, and the church later purchased land at Laie, which became the new home for Hawaiian Latter-day Saints. *Merriam-Webster's Geographical Dictionary*, s.v. "Hawaii"; R. Lanier Britsch, "Hawaii," in *Encyclopedia of Latter-day Saint History*, 474–76.

Benjamin Johnson. Courtesy of Church History Library.

be prepared in ten days—or even in ten months—to leave my familys, now separarated 100 miles; . . . and unsettled business almost every where . . . all to be disposed of or thrown away! . . . Reason said— 'No, you cannot go; it is not just to require it under such circumstances.[']" He had three wives and eight living children, and only four years after his arrival in territorial Utah, he already held interests in several business ventures. However, a sense of religious duty had enabled him to pack up and head west in 1848, and this same sense of responsibility prompted him to make tremendous sacrifices and accept the mission call. "I told the Lord I would now commence, and wanted His help."[2]

Benjamin Johnson's Early Life, 1818–52

Benjamin Franklin Johnson was born July 28, 1818, in Pomfret, New York. In 1830, Benjamin's older brothers brought the distinctive message of the restored church of Jesus Christ to the Johnson family. Although Ezekiel Johnson, Benjamin's father, objected to this newfound religion, Benjamin's mother, Julia, embraced the teachings, and the family moved to Kirtland, Ohio, the locus of the Latter-day Saints, in 1833. Benjamin was baptized in March 1835 at the age of sixteen. Shortly thereafter, Johnson had his first proselytizing experience: after his sister was seemingly miraculously healed of a hip injury, he returned to his hometown to preach to his former neighbors, but they had no interest. Benjamin followed the Latter-day Saint migration from Ohio to Missouri and then to Illinois, where he was

---

2. Johnson, "Life Review by Benjamin F. Johnson," 133, in Johnson, papers, box 1, folder 1; p. 149 herein.

called on a mission to Canada in 1840. After his mission, he returned to Kirtland, where a few Saints still resided. He relocated to Ramus, Illinois, about thirty miles east of Nauvoo, in 1842, where he became a member of the Council of Fifty[3] and was taught about plural marriage from Joseph Smith.[4]

Johnson departed from Nauvoo in 1846, stopping in Garden Grove, Iowa, and later in Winter Quarters, now in Nebraska. In 1848, he joined the Willard Richards company to travel west to the Great Salt Lake Valley. When Johnson and his family arrived in Salt Lake City in October 1848, they found the situation dire, as the crickets of the previous summer had decimated the crops. To support his family, Johnson established a harness shop and a drugstore in the city. He became involved in local politics, including Utah's territorial legislature. In 1851, he accompanied Brigham Young on an expedition to southern Utah. Young asked him to make a settlement at Summit Creek, about seventy miles south of Salt Lake City, so Johnson sold his city home and relocated to Summit Creek (now Santaquin)[5] and also nearby Salt Creek (now Nephi),[6] Utah. Johnson retained the ownership of his shops in Salt Lake and also took up a job delivering mail. With all these mercantile, political, and colonizing duties, Johnson felt he did not have the time to attend the special conference session of August 1852. When he later learned that he had been called on a mission to

---

3. The Council of Fifty was an organization that convened under Joseph Smith between March and May 1844. It was intended to function as the kingdom of God, as opposed to the church of God, on earth. The council bolstered Joseph Smith's presidential run in 1844 and discussed potential sites where the Saints could relocate. After Smith's death, Brigham Young likewise convened the council between 1844 and 1846, and again after migrating to Utah. Grow et al., *Joseph Smith Papers, Administrative Records, Council of Fifty*, xxiii–xlv.

4. LeBaron, *Benjamin F. Johnson*, 1–60.

5. Summit Creek was founded by Johnson and others in 1851 and received its name because it was located at the summit between the Utah and Juab Valleys. Its name was changed to Santaquin in 1856. Van Cott, *Utah Place Names*, 331.

6. Salt Creek flows out of the canyon south of Mount Nebo in central Utah. The area was settled in central Utah in 1851. The name of the settlement was changed to Nephi, after a Book of Mormon prophet, but some people of other faiths continued to call it Salt Creek. Van Cott, *Utah Place Names*, 272, 327.

Hawaii at that meeting, he only had ten days to wrap up loose ends of his property and businesses and make preparations for his family.[7]

A History of the Hawaiian Mission

In 1849, Brigham Young sent a few Latter-day Saints to California to join prospectors searching for gold.[8] In 1850, Apostle Charles C. Rich, who oversaw the Saints in the San Bernardino, California, area, asked eleven of these gold seekers, with Hiram Clark as their president, to take the gospel message to the Sandwich Islands.[9] After arriving in Honolulu[10] in December 1850, these elders spread out to labor on the islands of Oahu, Hawaii, Maui, and Kauai. On Maui, George Q. Cannon realized that he would be limited if he tried to teach only the white, or *haole*, population, who were not interested in the missionaries' message and who were outnumbered by native Hawaiians. Therefore, he began to study the Hawaiian language so that he might preach to the native population. He began to have success throughout Maui. Other elders, however, were not so optimistic about their missions, and by April 1851, half of the missionaries had left the islands.[11]

---

7.   LeBaron, *Benjamin F. Johnson*, 62–79.

8.   Latter-day Saints in California were among the first to discover gold, and while gold would be a valuable resource to the Utah settlers, Brigham Young discouraged the Saints from seeking for gold, believing that they should gather in the Great Basin and raise crops. He believed that Sacramento was corrupt and unprofitable, but he did authorize some missionaries to go to California to obtain gold. Arrington, *Great Basin Kingdom*, 64–71; Davies, "Mormons and California Gold," 83–99.

9.   These eleven were George Q. Cannon, Henry Bigler, Thomas Whittle, James Keeler, John Dixon, Thomas Morris, William Farrer, James Hawkins, John Berry, Hiram Clark, and Hiram H. Blackwell. Berry started with the others but returned to Utah. Cannon, *Journals of George Q. Cannon: Hawaiian Mission*, xxxvii.

10. British explorer William Brown visited the area of Honolulu in 1794, and it became a trading center in the Pacific Ocean in the nineteenth century. It became the capital of Hawaii in 1850, the same year that the first Latter-day Saint missionaries arrived. Joseph F. Smith, who later became President of the church, came to Hawaii in 1854, when there were fifty-three branches on the islands. *Merriam-Webster's Geographical Dictionary*, s.v. "Honolulu"; R. Lanier Britsch, "Hawaii," in *Encyclopedia of Latter-day Saint History*, 474–76.

11. Britsch, *Moramona*, 3–17; Cannon, *Journals of George Q. Cannon: Hawaiian*

In August 1851, three more missionaries arrived in Honolulu as rein-forcements to the Sandwich Islands Mission. By the end of 1851, Cannon and James Keeler had established the church throughout Maui, and William Farrer[12] and Henry William Bigler[13] were having moderate success on Oahu. In early 1852, George Q. Cannon began translating the Book of Mormon into Hawaiian in collaboration with Hawaiian convert Jonathan H. Napela, though it would still be two years before the translation was complete. Some of the converts began to depart from their new faith, but still the church continued to grow throughout 1852.[14]

Johnson's Mission to Hawaii, 1852–55

Benjamin Johnson was one of nine missionaries called to the Sandwich Islands in August 1852. The other eight were William McBride, an Ohioan convert of 1841; Nathan Tanner, a former Zion's Camp[15] member who had been baptized in 1831; Thomas Karren, an 1842 British convert

---

Mission, xxxiii–xli.

12. William Farrer (1821–1906) was born in England and baptized in 1841. He traveled to Utah in 1847 and joined gold prospectors in California in 1849. He served a mission in the Sandwich Islands from 1850 to 1854 and nearly served again in 1856, but he returned to Utah for the Utah War. He died in Provo, Utah, in 1906. Journal of George Q. Cannon, People, s.v. "William Farrer."

13. Henry William Bigler (1815–1900) was born in Virginia and baptized in 1837. He went to Utah in 1848 after being part of the Mormon Battalion and staying temporarily in California. He served missions to Hawaii from 1850 to 1854 and again from 1857 to 1858. He died in St. George, Utah, in 1900. Bishop, "Henry William Bigler," 122–36; Journal of George Q. Cannon, People, s.v. "Henry William Bigler."

14. Britsch, *Moramona*, 17–28; Cannon, *Journals of George Q. Cannon: Hawaiian Mission*, xli–lii.

15. Zion's Camp refers to an incident in May and June of 1834 when Joseph Smith led more than two hundred Latter-day Saints from Kirtland, Ohio, to Clay County, Missouri to reclaim lands taken from the Saints by mobs in Jackson County, Missouri. After marching nearly a thousand miles, the Saints met a hostile group of Missourians. Rather than fight to reclaim the land, Smith told his followers to disband and return to Ohio. The expedition failed in its initial purpose, but many veterans of the experience later became prominent leaders of the church. John M. Beck and Dennis A. Wright, "Zion's Camp," in *Encyclopedia of Latter-day Saint History*, 1399–1400.

who had been in the Mormon Battalion;[16] Ephraim Green, an 1841 convert who helped discover gold in California in 1848; James Lawson, originally from Scotland and baptized in 1844; Redick Allred, a Mormon Battalion alumnus who had been baptized in 1833; Reddin Allred, the twin brother of Redick who had also been baptized in 1833; and Egerton Snider, born in Canada and baptized by 1837.[17] This group joined the missionaries traveling to Australia, India, and China as they made their way south through Utah Territory on their way to San Bernardino, California. The Hawaii missionaries sailed from San Francisco and arrived in Honolulu on February 17, 1853, where they were met by Philip B. Lewis,[18] who had assumed duties as president of the mission, and found six hundred converts already on the islands.[19]

For the missionaries, the Hawaii of the 1850s was not the paradise of its modern-day reputation, and they faced significant challenges. Polygamy was an unpopular doctrine and elicited considerable disdain from other Christian clergy. Latter-day Saints, on the other hand, criticized the earlier Protestant and Catholic missionaries for doing an inadequate job of teaching the natives the benefits of Western education and agriculture. The Latter-day Saints tried to establish schools for the Hawaiians, but due to cultural differences and a declining population, these schools did not fare

16. In 1846, around five hundred Latter-day Saint men and eighty women and children left Council Bluffs, Iowa, to march to California to fight for the United States in the Mexican War. This Mormon Battalion arrived in California in January 1847. Most men were discharged from the Battalion in July 1847, but some served until March 1848. Larry C. Porter, Clark V. Johnson, and Susan Easton Black, "Mormon Battalion," in *Encyclopedia of Latter-day Saint History*, 783–85; John F. Yurtinus, "Mormon Battalion," in *Encyclopedia of Mormonism*, 2:935–36.

17. Journal of George Q. Cannon, People, s.vv. "McBride, William," "Tanner, Nathan," "Karren, Thomas," "Green, Ephraim," "Lawson, James," "Allred, Reddick," "Allred, Reddin," "Snider, Egerton."

18. Philip B. Lewis (1804–1877) was born in Massachusetts and was baptized in 1842. He traveled to Utah in 1848. Lewis had helped fund a mission to the Society Islands in 1843 and was assigned to go there in 1851, but Parley P. Pratt appointed him as president of the Sandwich Islands Mission instead. He labored in Hawaii from 1851 to 1855, and he died in Kanab, Utah, in 1877. Journal of George Q. Cannon, People, s.v. "Philip Beesom Lewis."

19. LeBaron, *Benjamin F. Johnson*, 80–83.

much better than their earlier counterparts. Worst of all, the native population plummeted as a smallpox epidemic swept over the islands.[20] Johnson and his companions saw this as an opportunity to manifest the gift of healing that they believed was present on the earth;[21] not heeding quarantine laws, they administered healing blessings, traveling from smallpox victim to smallpox victim, without being vaccinated themselves.[22]

Not everything, however, was so grim on the islands. A few thousand joined the ranks of the church in the Pacific. By October of 1853, Johnson had earned the trust of his fellow missionaries, and the mission presidency placed him on committees to fulfill some of the mission's objectives, including purchasing a press to print the Book of Mormon translation and helping with the less-than-successful church schools.[23] He eventually became first counselor in the mission presidency.[24] One significant endeavor of the mission was to establish an island gathering place for the Saints of the Pacific. Rather than require all the converts to gather to Zion in Utah, church leaders decided it would be wise to create a smaller community there on the islands. Johnson was part of the group that sought a suitable location. Haalelea, a local chief, offered to donate his lands on the island of

---

20. Smallpox was a highly contagious, painful, and often fatal disease, manifested by rashes and pustules. For centuries, Asian nations had practiced inoculation, whereby they inserted smallpox-infected pus or scabs into people's flesh, which diminished the effects of the disease; inoculation was introduced into the Western World in 1721. In 1796, English physician Edward Jenner created a smallpox vaccine by infecting others with cowpox, which made them immune to smallpox. The vaccine was brought to America in 1800 and was endorsed by President Thomas Jefferson. Thanks to the vaccine, smallpox was eradicated worldwide in the 1970s. See Hopkins, *Greatest Killer*.

21. Hawaiian officials ordered for quarantines and vaccinations for smallpox, but the Latter-day Saint missionaries believed that God would bless and heal the people, or at least that it was God's will if they were not healed. Many of the missionaries were not vaccinated or violated quarantine regulations. This negligence made some view the Latter-day Saints unfavorably. Hammond, *Island Adventures*, 141–66; Johnson, "Life Review," 151–52.

22. LeBaron, *Benjamin F. Johnson*, 83–99; Britsch, *Moramona*, 29–34; Hammond, *Island Adventures*, 141–56.

23. LeBaron, *Benjamin F. Johnson*, 86–94; Britsch, *Moramona*, 25–31, 35.

24. Britsch, *Moramona*, 37–38.

Lanai[25] to the church, so Johnson and fellow missionaries Ephraim Green and Francis Hammond scoped out a spot to establish a settlement. During the summer of 1854, they found a spot in the Palawai Valley and named it the Valley of Ephraim. Some Saints moved to the valley to settle and farm. Johnson witnessed the beginnings of the colony at Lanai, but he suffered from an illness, and he departed from Hawaii in January 1855. He arrived at his Utah home on March 26.[26]

Additional Church Service, 1855–1905

Just as Johnson had spent his two years in the Sandwich Islands ministering among the natives of Hawaii, when he returned home, he found himself frequently interacting with the natives of Utah. During his absence, his homes at Summit Creek had been burned to the ground by Indians during the Walker War of 1853–54.[27] As he reestablished homes and farms

25. Lanai is one of Hawaii's central islands. In 1854, the church's Hawaiian mission purchased lands on Lanai as a gathering place for those who joined the church in Hawaii. Most Latter-day Saints were encouraged to gather to Utah, but conditions and laws in Hawaii made that impractical, so the island of Lanai became the gathering place instead, at least temporarily. Lanai had fertile soil, but it was rocky and dry, making it not an ideal agricultural land. As the most faithful Latter-day Saints gathered there, the other Hawaiian branches lost their most active church members and struggled to succeed. Britsch, *Moramona*, 35–49.

26. LeBaron, *Benjamin F. Johnson*, 94–105; Britsch, *Moramona*, 35–42.

27. The Walker War was named after Ute Chief Wakara (known also as Walker). In 1852, the Utah territorial legislature passed three acts intended to end the Ute slave trade with Mexican traders. These efforts, along with the encroachment of settlers on Ute hunting and gathering lands, created a tense environment between settlers and Indians, particularly in Utah County, Sanpete Valley, and other settlements south of the Salt Lake Valley. Atrocities were committed on both sides, and though Brigham Young at times instructed settlers to act only defensively, settlers continued organized assaults on Indians. In an attempt to end the hostilities, Young offered amnesty to the Utes in December 1853. Young also dispatched Indian agent E. A. Bedell to broker a peace with Wakara in March 1854. Dimick B. Huntington, who served as an interpreter, apparently went with Bedell. Young and Wakara met in May 1854 and formally ended the war. Peace, however, was temporary, as settlers continued to encroach on Indian lands and expend shared natural resources. *Acts, Resolutions, and Memorials*, 91–94; Watson, *Life under the Horseshoe*, 11–13; Christy, "Walker War," 395–420; Farmer, *On Zion's Mount*, 84–87.

at Santaquin and nearby Spring Lake, he earned the respect of local Indians by offering them food, protection, and other gifts, even though there were times of turmoil.[28] Johnson even purchased and adopted some Native American children who had been captured by the Ute tribe.[29] In the early 1870s, he and his siblings attempted to build a settlement in Kane County, Utah. After this would-be town, named Johnson, was unsuccessful, he returned to Spring Lake, where he was appointed as a bishop.[30]

In 1882, church leaders asked Johnson to move from Spring Lake to help establish a colony in Arizona. Church President John Taylor then asked him to build up settlements in northern Mexico to enable polygamists to avoid federal prosecution. Johnson relocated to Tempe, Arizona, that year, and while he never permanently settled in Mexico as had been planned, he frequently visited the country.[31] On one occasion in late 1884, he was part of a group sent to preach to the native Yaqui tribe of coastal Mexico. "The Yaquis in physiognomy, dress and mode of living are so like the Hawaians that here on the sea coast I could almost fancy myself again upon the islands," he wrote.[32] After years of hiding, in 1888 Johnson was finally fined seventy-five dollars in Arizona for practicing polygamy. Though he often visited his former homes in Utah, Johnson mainly dwelt in Arizona, where he served as a local patriarch in the church. He died at Mesa, Arizona, on November 18, 1905.[33]

The other eight missionaries sent to the Sandwich Islands in 1852 all

---

28. LeBaron, *Benjamin F. Johnson*, 107–27.

29. The Utes were known for capturing children of other tribes and selling them into slavery, and pioneers often bought Native American children so that the Utes would not kill them. Settlers hoped the adoption of Indian children would protect the children from death and torture and from servitude. They also hoped to civilize a race they regarded as degraded by exposing adopted natives to religion, education, and Western culture. Muhlestein, "Utah Indians and the Indian Slave Trade"; Bennion, "Captivity, Adoption, Marriage and Identity"; LeBaron, *Benjamin F. Johnson*, 123.

30. LeBaron, *Benjamin F. Johnson*, 136–39.

31. LeBaron, *Benjamin F. Johnson*, 149–58.

32. Johnson, "Life Review," 279.

33. LeBaron, *Benjamin F. Johnson*, 168–96.

returned to settle in the Mormon Corridor[34] of Utah and Arizona. William McBride went to California in 1854 to try to get a printing press; he returned to Utah in 1855 and died in Salt Lake City in 1895.[35] Nathan Tanner left Hawaii in 1854 and served a mission to the eastern United States in 1869; he died in Granger, Utah, in 1910.[36] The other six left Hawaii in 1855, just as Johnson had done. Thomas Karren returned to Lehi, Utah, for the rest of his life, dying in 1876.[37] Ephraim Green returned to Hawaii for another mission from 1865 to 1868, when he helped establish the Latter-day Saint settlement at Laie; he died in Rockport, Utah, in 1874.[38] James Lawson likewise served another mission to Hawaii from 1865 to 1867; he died in Salt Lake City in 1912.[39] Redick Allred served in several ecclesiastical callings in Sanpete County, Utah, before dying in the county's town of Chester in 1905.[40] Reddin Allred spent many years in Tooele, Utah, after his return and died in Thatcher, Arizona, in 1900.[41] Egerton Snider died in Salt Lake City in 1867.[42]

Benjamin F. Johnson's Family Life

When Johnson left on his mission, he was married to three wives. He married Melissa Bloomfield LeBaron on Christmas Day of 1841 in Kirtland, Ohio; Mary Ann Hale on November 14, 1844, in Macedonia, Illinois; and Harriet Naomi Holman on March 17, 1850, in Salt Lake City. He also married Flora Clarinda Gleason on February 3, 1846, in Nauvoo, Illinois, but they were divorced in 1849. His first three wives had borne him nine children, eight of them living at the time of his departure.[43]

34. The "Mormon Corridor" is a north-south band of Latter-day Saint settlements in Utah and surrounding states. Michael N. Landon, "Mormon Corridor," in *Encyclopedia of Latter-day Saint History*, 786–87.
35. Journal of George Q. Cannon, People, s.v. "McBride, William."
36. Journal of George Q. Cannon, People, s.v. "Tanner, Nathan."
37. Journal of George Q. Cannon, People, s.v. "Karren, Thomas."
38. Journal of George Q. Cannon, People, s.v. "Green, Ephraim."
39. Journal of George Q. Cannon, People, s.v. "Lawson, James."
40. Journal of George Q. Cannon, People, s.v. "Allred, Reddick."
41. Journal of George Q. Cannon, People, s.v. "Allred, Reddin."
42. Journal of George Q. Cannon, People, s.v. "Snider, Egerton."
43. Johnson, *My Life's Review*, 359–60. His living children at this time were Benjamin

After receiving his mission call in 1852, Johnson made arrangements for his businesses and farms and moved two of his wives, Melissa in Salt Lake City and Mary Ann in Salt Creek, to join his third wife, Harriet, in Summit Creek. Harriet's father, Bishop James S. Holman,[44] agreed to "see to [the] family and property."[45] A year after Johnson's departure, the Indian uprising referred to as the Walker War began in the area. For safety, the entire settlement of Summit Creek was evacuated, initially to Holladay Springs (three miles to the north) and then to Payson (about six miles north of Summit Creek).[46] After the families moved to Payson, one man was killed and two were injured in Summit Creek, and later, the Summit Creek homes were burned to the ground. The Johnson home and crops were a complete loss.[47]

After this significant setback, Johnson's wives and children faced the challenges of finding and securing a safe place to live, caring for livestock, and providing education for their children.[48] Mary Ann and Harriet each gave birth to sons, both named Benjamin Johnson, months after he had left, and Melissa's newborn died shortly after his departure.[49] Melissa wrote about living in a hastily constructed shelter before buying an adobe home and adjoining land in Payson.[50] Despite the trials, they managed to endure

<hr/>

Franklin, Melissa, Julia, Esther, Delcina, and Frances, all from Melissa; Joseph, from Mary Ann; and Huetta, from Clarinda. Harriet bore Benjamin Farland on January 20, 1853, and Mary Ann bore Benjamin Samuel on April 20, 1853. Frances died as an infant while Johnson was on his mission. Johnson, *My Life's Review*, 208, 359–60.

44. James Holman (1805–1873), Johnson's father-in-law, arrived in Utah in 1847, then traveled to Utah again with his family the following year. Mormon Pioneer Overland Travel database, s.v. "James Sawyer Holman."

45. Johnson, "Life Review," 135.

46. Payson was originally named Peteetneet after the Indian chief of the same name. James Pace and others settled the area, thirteen miles south of Provo, in 1850, and the place came to be known as Pacen, later spelled Payson. Van Cott, *Utah Place Names*, 290.

47. Santaquin Ward Manuscript History, 1853; Gottfredson, *History of Indian Depredations in Utah*, 78–82.

48. Melissa L. Johnson to Benjamin F. Johnson, May 8, 1854.

49. Johnson, *My Life's Review*, 360.

50. Melissa L. Johnson to Benjamin F. Johnson, May 8, 1854.

their obstacles. Harriet wrote, "I say that we may rejoice in the sacrifice that we have made. We must consider it the greatest blessing that could be bestowed upon ourselves though it looks like a long time to be parted from each other, but we can realize each other's society which if hadn't happened we would not have known anything about."[51]

After returning from his mission, Johnson married three additional wives: Sarah Melissa Holman, Susan Adeline Holman, and Sarah Jane Spooner; and he had additional children with all six of his wives.[52] In 1860, his first wife, Melissa, died in childbirth.[53] His relationships with his wives were not always harmonious; Mary Ann nearly divorced him in the 1860s.[54] When he moved to Arizona in the 1880s, his five remaining wives chose not to accompany him, and his relocation and subsequent visits to Mexico caused some of them to feel neglected. In return, Johnson felt that his wives treated him coldly.[55] Even so, during the twilight of his life, he reflected, "I can believe that *to some* plural marriage was a *great cross*. Yet I cannot say so from my own experience, for altho in times that tried men's hearts, I married seven wives . . . and there is not one of my children or their mothers that are not dearer to me still than life."[56]

Source Note

Benjamin Johnson began writing a retrospective autobiographical manuscript in 1885 "to record the principal events of my life. From this duty I shrank for years and tried to excuse myself from it. But a voice within my soul has continually urged me to this effort, which has so long appeared onerous. But now, feeling I have no other farther excuse I commenced to write a Life review from my early childhood."[57] Johnson worked on the history off and on until his last entry in 1896. "A Life Review by Benjamin

---

51. Harriet Naomi Holman Johnson to Benjamin Franklin Johnson, no date, Johnson correspondence. Spelling and punctuation corrected for ease of reading.

52. Johnson, *My Life's Review*, 360–61.

53. Johnson, *My Life's Review*, 121.

54. Johnson, *My Life's Review*, 130–33

55. Johnson, *My Life's Review*, 150, 157.

56. Benjamin F. Johnson to George F. Gibbs, 36–37, in Johnson, papers.

57. Johnson, "Life Review," 294.

Johnson" is housed at the Church History Library of The Church of Jesus Christ of Latter-day Saints; it has been published a few times, including as *My Life's Review: The Autobiography of Benjamin F. Johnson* (Provo, UT: Grandin Book, 1997). We have herein reproduced pages 132–89, the portion of his autobiography that relates to his mission to the Sandwich Islands as it appears in the original manuscript. He describes his journey to California and then to Hawaii, preaching on the islands, the smallpox epidemic, finding a place for settlement on Lanai, and the journey back to California and then Utah. For space considerations, we have omitted portions of his writings that are more tangential to the overall story of the mission.[58]

DOCUMENT TRANSCRIPT

Benjamin Johnson, "A Life Review by Benjamin F. Johnson"[59]

At Salt Lake city July 10th 1852 Melissa B.[60] gave birth to our daughter

---

58. See Johnson, "Life Review," to review the omitted portions, which include the following accounts: Johnson's blessing from Jedediah M. Grant (134), rescuing German immigrants from Indian attacks (136–38), a Spanish father attempting to pimp his daughters to Johnson in California (139–41), a disagreement with intoxicated Captain Erskine between San Pedro and San Francisco (142–43), personal clashes with Nathan Tanner and other missionaries (146–48, 162–63), Johnson's role as an attorney in a court case stemming from quarantine laws (151–55), other government issues (155–58), arrival of the printing press (177–78), and Indian troubles on the way home (188–89).

59. Excerpted from "A Life Review by Benjamin F. Johnson," 132–89, holograph, MS 1289, box 1, folder 1, CHL. Also printed in *My Life's Review: The Autobiography of Benjamin Franklin Johnson* (Provo, UT: Grandin Book, 1997), 124–82.

60. Melissa Bloomfield LeBaron (1820–60) married Benjamin F. Johnson on December 25, 1841, in Kirtland, Ohio. The two were sealed to each other twice: first in May 1843 in Macedonia, Illinois, by Joseph Smith, and second in February 1846 in the Nauvoo, Illinois, temple by Amasa Lyman. Johnson, *My Life's Review*, 359.

Frances Bell,[61] and I had taken a boy—Orson Murray[62]—to raise. His father was dead, and his mother and grandfather gave me a writing to ensure my keeping him until 21 years of age. He was a good boy, and we adopted him in our hearts as well as in our home; and business so increased that at the time for October Semi-annual conference I had so much to do and look after that I could not go, and attend Conference.

But the Lord's ways are not as man's ways;[63] and things appearing of so much consequence to man is of no worth to him. And so it proved; for about Oct. 10th I received notice that I was called by the vote of General Conference to a Sandwich Island Mission, and that I had until the 20th to prepare for the start. At first I could not believe it, but when I found it a reality I was dazed! How possibly could I be prepared in ten days—or even in ten months—to leave my familys, now separarated 100 miles; with a U.S. mail contract,[64] and unsettled business almost every where, from north of the city to Manti.[65]—Then my saddlery, with large bill of merchandise just imported, & drug store—all to be disposed of or thrown away! All this,—and only ten days to rent out my farms, gather up my family, dispose of my mail contract, settle all business, and get ready for a start. Reason said—"No, you cannot go; it is not just to require it under such circumstances.["] Three wives with 8 small children—to be increased by two in my absence; and what a loss in means! Such a needless sacrifice! And then—to go among barbarians in a land of license! It was terrible for one so weak as I. "But what shall I do?["] I asked myself; and Faith answers

---

61. Frances Bell Johnson was born July 10, 1852, and died as an infant while Johnson was on his mission. Johnson, *My Life's Review*, 208, 360.

62. Orson Murray died in 1853 while Johnson was on his mission. Johnson, *My Life's Review*, 154–55.

63. Isaiah 55:8 reads, "For my thoughts are not your thoughts, neither are your ways my ways, saith the Lord."

64. In summer 1851, Johnson's brother Joseph obtained a contract to carry mail from Salt Lake City north to Ogden and south to Manti. Johnson sublet the Manti route. Stations were established at Summit Creek, where he built a house for his wife Harriet, and at Salt Creek, where he built a house for his wife Mary Ann. His first wife, Melissa, lived in Salt Lake City. Johnson, *My Life's Review*, 123.

65. Manti, located about 120 miles south of Salt Lake City, was settled in 1849 and was named after a city in the Book of Mormon. Van Cott, *Utah Place Names*, 243–44.

by asking—"from whom did you receive wives and children—farms and houses—goods and cattle? Who redeemed you when you were hopeless of life and name upon the earth? To whom do you owe all you are, all you possess, and all you hope for, but to God? Then why hesitate? when you have professed to be willing even to die for the truth of the gospel?" I could see but little choice between the grave and my mission. But in gratitude to God I said "With the Lord's help I will go; and the cord I cannot untie that holds me from my duty I will cut loose from; for go I will, with the Lord's help.["] I told the Lord I would now commence, and wanted His help.

I started to the city to settle business, and find some one to take my farm at Salt Creek, to dispose of mail contract, Saddlery, Drug Store &c. Faith and Hope grew in my heart. In Salt Lake City those I wished to see on business were the first I met, all dues to me seemed ready, and men I owed and not ready to pay were not pressing; Men living in the north I had no time to visit I met on the street; and the first men I met when looking for renters for my Salt Creek farm were brs. Vickers[66] and Udell,[67] with whom I at once closed an arrangement to take my farm for the term of my absence.[68] . . .

But the idea of leaving my wives and children—more dear to me than life—and for so long a time—Would I ever see them again! A long, tedious and dangerous journey of twelve hundred miles to the coast; then up the coast by sea some 800 miles, and then near 3000 more across the ocean to the Islands![69] . . .

In conversation with Prest Kimball in regard to immoralities of those lands, he gave me a key that I would not forget. I spoke of those who had

66. John Vickers (1822–1919) arrived in Utah in 1852. Mormon Pioneer Overland Travel database, s.v. "John Vickers."

67. David Udall (1829–1910) was born in England and was baptized in 1848. He arrived in Utah in 1852 and settled in Nephi. He served a genealogical mission to Britain in the 1890s. Jenson, *Latter-day Saint Biographical Encyclopedia*, 2:112–13; Early Mormon Missionaries database, s.v. "David Udall."

68. John Vickers and David Udall had just recently arrived in Salt Lake City after crossing the plains when Johnson invited them to settle at Salt Creek (Nephi). They arrived in Salt Lake on September 5, 1852, and left for Nephi on September 20. *Arizona Pioneer Mormon*, 2–3, 282.

69. In reality, there are approximately 700 miles between Salt Lake City and San Pedro,

fallen upon their missions, and expressed a fear for myself. He asked how many wives I had? I said "Three." He asked if they were good, praying women? I said yes. "Well," said he, "no man ever did nor ever will fall that has three good, praying women to hold him." This, as a key of knowledge I wish to record for the benefit of my children.

Our mission was to carry to the world the revelation on plural marriage, to advocate and defend it. We were told to go without purse or scrip, and on arrival in California to sell our teams and send the money home.

I now started teams to move Melissa B. to Summit and to bring Bros. Vickers and Udell to Salt Creek, and by my suggestion Br. Holman was ordained Bishop at Summit. He was also to see to my family and property. Melissa B. and Mary Ann[70] were now moved to Summit and <all> were to remain together there during my absence. I now took an inventory of the improvements on land, grain on hand, houses, horses, oxen, cows, sheep, wagons, stock in trade, farm tools and implements that I left at Summit and Salt Creek to the amount of over $7000.00 after all debts were paid, taking one light spring wagon and a valuable span of horses with me.

On the 22nd of October I was ready and waiting for company, who came and passed, as all were to meet at Salt Creek and start from there on the 24th. . . .

Br. Alexander Badlam[71] who by Prest Young's arrangement was to accompany me to San Barnardino, was with me, and the evening of Oct. 23d we arrived at Br. John Vickers at Nephi, (Salt Creek) and as the company had been already organized, came in as the last wagon of the train, but I felt to be satisfied, confident that through the providence of God I would occupy the place that would be according to his will.

400 miles between San Pedro and San Francisco, and 2,400 miles between San Francisco and Honolulu.

70. Mary Ann Hale (1827–1910) was sealed to Johnson in Nauvoo, Illinois, in November 1844 by John Smith and again in the Nauvoo Temple in February 1846 by Amasa Lyman. Johnson, *My Life's Review*, 359.

71. Alexander Badlam (1809–94) was born in Massachusetts and was baptized in 1832. He had visited northern California twice before Brigham Young requested him to accompany Johnson to California in 1852. Badlam remained in California thereafter and even attempted to minister to the gold-seeking Chinese there before dying in San Francisco in 1894. Bagley, *"Cities of the Wicked."*

We held meetings on our way through the southern settlements, we being over forty in number, appointed to China, Australia, Ceylon, Hindostan, Africa and perhaps other points within the Indies. To the Sandwich Islands there were nine, namely:—William McBride, Nathan Tanner, Thomas Karren, Ephraim Green, James Lawson, Redick and Reddin Alred, Egerton Snyder and B. F. Johnson. . . .

From Parowan[72] we proceeded pleasantly down the Santa Clara.[73] . . .

We were a little short of food, but did not suffer much, and arrived all well, in San Bernardino, and found homes for a time among friends. . . .

At San Bernardino we remained near 3 weeks to recruit our teams and dispose of them, and made my home at Br. Norman Taylor's, by whose two wives, Lorana and Lydia I was treated with great kindness, making all needed clothing for my further journey.[74] I sold my outfit for over $300.00 lent $100.00 to Br. Badlam, and arranged to send to my family by one of the brethren soon to return to Salt Lake whatever I might have left after paying expenses to San Francisco. . . .

From San Bernardino it is about 80 miles to San Pedro on the coast, to which place the brethren of San Bernardino shipped us in open wagons, and the first night—oh, how it did rain, and having no shelter but our blankets, and the last of December, we were soaking wet and miserably cold. The next night we suffered nearly as much; but on the following night, within six miles of San Pedro we stopped at a Spanish Ranch. The

72. Parowan, in Iron County, was the first Latter-day Saint settlement south of Provo. It was originally called Little Salt Lake, after a small semi-salty lake (now a dry lakebed). Parley P. Pratt explored the area in 1850, and it was officially founded a year later as part of the Iron Mission under the direction of Apostle George A. Smith. Van Cott, *Utah Place Names*, 288–89; Janet Burton Seegmiller, "Parowan," in *Utah History Encyclopedia*, 418.

73. The Santa Clara River begins in the Pine Valley Mountains in southern Utah and drains into the Virgin River south of the city of St. George. Van Cott, *Utah Place Names*, 331.

74. Norman Taylor (1828–99) first arrived in Utah in 1847 and then returned east to Winter Quarters. In 1850, he returned to Utah with his wife Lurana Forbush Taylor (1826–84) and his future wife Lydia Forbush (1830–1900). Mormon Pioneer Overland Travel database, s.vv. "Norman Taylor," "Lurana Forbush Taylor," "Lydia Forbush," "Milo Andrus Company (1850)."

proprietor being one of the party of whom the San Bernardino ranch was purchased by Apostles Lyman and Rich. Here we hired a large room at ten dollars per day in which to stay until we could negotiate for our passage up the coast. Here I was appointed with Br. Nathaniel <V.> Jones as agents to negotiate and transact business for the company; and here I began to get an insight into Mexican social and moral life, in a manner I may never forget. . . .

After a short stay here we moved to San Pedro, a small harbor on the coast, Dec. 22d, and here we remained over a week, waiting the arrival of a vessel on which to get passage up the coast. Here we found, also waiting passage, two gentlemen from Boston, physicians, named Williams. The younger was nephew to the other, and he was one of the first known writing mediums in Spiritualism.[75] They seemed refined and cultured, and eminent in their profession. Religion and spiritualism was soon in discussion, and with much assurance they offered to give us demonstrations of power greater than could be found in any religion; and they asked me if I would preside at a meeting if our company would agree to attend, and witness the manifestations of their power, which I agreed to do, conditioned that our company wished it, and the dining hall could be obtained. Being agreeable to the brethren, the room was engaged for the coming evening, and so at the time appointed all were present. There were no opening ceremonies, and as I announced the meeting opened, a feeling came upon me that gave me faith and full assurance that while I exercised my will they could do nothing. I sat while they called for spirits, one after another, until they seemed to exhaust their vocabulary of Spirit names, without answer or demonstration of any kind. At last, chagrined and mortified, they said there was a stronger power present than theirs, whose will had been exercised against theirs, and that under such circumstances they could do nothing; but that they did not regard the man who had placed himself in opposition as a gentleman. I remembered that the Lord had rarely on the earth been regarded as a gentleman. They left the hall mortified and disgusted, and the young man was so chagrined that he rarely spoke through all the time we were together. But at San Francisco, on their arrival, the

---

75. See chapter 2, note 77, p. 66 herein.

public journals were soon full of the mighty things manifest through these men, converts came to the islands the following year and made many converts to spiritualism. Some brethren at Honolulu were captivated by it.

But to return. I spent much time upon the shore in admiration of beautiful shells, or from som[e] higher point watching the sportive seal or sea lion, or the spouting whale in its majesty slowly passing in view; with the wonderful sea weed, like forests and gardens, whose fruit and foliage of great variety in shape, these, with the thousand wonders of the deep gave me pleasant occupation until the arrival of the brig "Fremont," Capt. [John] Erskine,[76] commander, bound for San Francisco, our final point of departure.

Br. Jones and I soon arranged terms of passage for all our party, now numbering 40; and the vessel being limited in accommodations the Captain guaranteed us every facility for comfort in the cabin except the sofa, on which himself would sleep. Upon these conditions we paid passage money and went on board, while he went to Los Angeles for supplies. I was just now afflicted with neuralgia and incipient piles, which tended to greatly weaken and unnerve me. . . .

After ten disagreeable days we landed safely at San Francisco, where we were to raise money to defray expenses to our different fields of labor. But how was it to be done? We rented a house large enough to accommodate all, then, in general council agreed that a Circular Memorial to the people of San Francisco should be written, showing the object of our mission, and ask for donations in money to assist in defraying our expenses. Bros. James T. Lewis, A. M. Musser and Wm Hyde were appointed to draw up this statement memorial, which they zealously strove to do, but did not succeed in a manner satisfactory to themselves and appeared discouraged. Acting then as chairman and sitting by the table, I picked up a pencil and proceeded casually to write as thoughts came to me. One of the committee read the following:—

["]To all to whom this may come greeting:—We the undersigned, missionaries of the Church of Jesus Christ of Latter Day Saints from Salt Lake City, Utah, to the different nations of the Earth, respectfully represent to

---

76.   See "Nason's Line for San Pedro," *Daily Alta California*, December 6, 1852.

the honorable people of San Francisco, that we, like the Apostles of old have left our homes "without purse or scrip," and are now in your midst waiting a passage to our respective fields of labor. We therefore humbly ask you, in the name of our Master to assist us with means to defray expenses incidental to our journey, and the God whom we serve shall reward you a hundred fold." He said, "This is just what we want," and read it aloud, and all agreed that was just what was wanted. I begged the Committee to revise it which they sought to do, but said they could not better it, and asked me to write it over, which I did, carefully. It was given to the brethren, who, two by two, went through the city visiting stores, public houses and business places, to present this memorial and ask for donations. Many responded in small sums of one, two and five dollars; but the amount we must have was not less than six thousand dollars. This was continued for a few days, and having been a member of the Utah legislature I was asked to visit the state legislature then in session in Sacramento[77] and present our memorial and ask for help. I was about to start when Br. John M. Horner,[78] a wealthy L. D. Saint of San Francisco, came and wished us to cease all further efforts to raise money, and said he would furnish us five or six thousand dollars when we were ready to sail. It is but just to say that Thos. S. Williams, who was a member of the Church, gave us $500.00 as also Bros [Quartus] Sparks[79] and others, all of whom later turned away, but gave sums from $10.00 to $50.00. We almost felt to shout "Hosanna" to the Most High.

After 2 weeks pleasant stay in San Francisco, associating with old

77. Located in north central California, Sacramento was first settled in 1839 and became an important trading site during the gold rush. It became California's capital in 1854. *Merriam-Webster's Geographical Dictionary*, s.v. "Sacramento."

78. John M. Horner (1821–1907) was born in New Jersey in 1821 and was baptized by Erastus Snow in 1840. In 1846, he traveled from New York to California on the ship *Brooklyn*, and he became a successful farmer in northern California, but he subsequently fell into great debt. He financially assisted the missionaries called in 1852 as they traveled to Asia and other places in the Pacific. In 1879, he moved to Hawaii, and he died in 1907. He never went to Utah, but he remained in contact with the church throughout his life. Green, "John M. Horner," 244–46, 302–3, 340–42, 344–45.

79. Quartus Strong Sparks (1820–91) was born in Massachusetts in 1820. He traveled on the ship *Brooklyn* to California in 1846, and he practiced law in San Bernardino

fri[e]nds, holding meetings, & conversing with many upon the revelation on plural marriage we heard the ship "Huntress" would sail for Honolulu Feb. 2nd James Lambert Master, with whom we arranged for our passage, and went on board, Feb. 1853.[80]

Our passage to Honolulu occupied sixteen days with weather just rough enough to give us the full benefit of sea sickness. Otherwise it was exceedingly pleasant, and rendered so by the Captain's extreme kindness to us, of which the Lion's share, through his partiality fell to me, for we had no sooner shipped on board than he came to me with the freedom of an old acquaintance or companion. . . .

On our arrival at Honolulu the Captain's friendship did in no degree abate, and as he had friends of long standing among the merchants and business men of the city, he took great pleasure in introducing us to them, and in commending us to the public as missionary gentlemen, and so continued until the day before setting sail, when he invited us and insisted on our coming on board with all our friends, to a turtle soup dinner.[81] After a time of enjoyment, before our farewell, he asked us to sing "When shall we all meet again,"[82] which caused a moisture in his eyes, and made us to feel—"God bless our dear friend Capt. Lambert."

On arrival in Honolulu, which was on Feb. 17, 1853 we found Br. Philip B. Lewis, who was set apart as President of the island mission, oc-

---

and supported the missionary efforts of Parley P. Pratt and Hosea Stout. He was excommunicated in 1857, became an enemy of the church, and remained in California until he died in 1891. Bullock, *Ship Brooklyn Saints*, 219; Lyman, *San Bernardino*, 182, 316–17.

80. The ship *Huntress*, captained by James L. Lambert, was built in Maine in 1850. It left California in late January 1853 and arrived in Honolulu on February 17. Captain Lambert had previously transported a group of Saints from Liverpool, England, to New Orleans, Louisiana. Sonne, *Ships, Saints, and Mariners*, 101.

81. Turtle soup was not unheard of at this time, even in the United States, though it was increasingly viewed as a delicacy. Bronner, *Grasping Things*, 162–63.

82. "When Shall We All Meet Again" was a hymn written by Parley P. Pratt and included in the Latter-day Saint hymnal published in Manchester, England, in 1840. *A Collection of Sacred Hymns*, no. 220, pp. 247–48; Chism, *A Selection of Early Mormon Hymnbooks*, 338.

cupying rooms with Br. Dennis[83] and his wife, a sickly woman, who died on her way home from the mission, plying her needle for their support, while he with all his soul was studying to acquire the native language. The mission was financially in a scanty and humble condition, as was in many ways manifested by the elders who came from their fields of labor to welcome us. . . .

About this time I felt an inspiration to urge the ordination of natives to the priesthood, to assist the foreign elders in preaching the gospel. In this Prest Lewis and Br. Cannon and others were with me, while others opposed; but no sooner were a few ordained and sent than all objections vanished, for they proved far more efficient than we had hoped. Through them the work spread mightily, and many of the best educated were baptized and soon became efficient auxiliaries. . . .

Native elders now in the field were exerting a powerful influence, and it almost seemed as though all the Hawaian people would become members of the Church; but at this time the small pox was getting its start among them. I had never before seen a case of it, and I had no apparent protection by vac[c]ination; and as they continued to flock to us for ministration, there soon came those in the fever, soon developing the disease, to all of whom we ministered. But so soon as it was really known to be small pox the old missionaries left their flocks and fled. Many of the physicians were too frightened to remain and Br. Tanner with some others left us for Hawaii. The health officers began to gather the sick to hospitals and pest houses, to which the natives looked with terror.

Brs. Lewis, Farrar, and I were still together, in the City, and we agreed that by the help of the Lord we would stand by each other, and stay with the native saints. Unlike the others I had no apparent protection, but I felt I was in the line of duty, and in the hands of the Lord, and that I could not afford to desert my post and leave the native brethren alone in their affliction.

But there were trials before us. As soon as some of the natives began to

---

83. Edward Dennis was baptized in Honolulu in 1852 and became an elder in 1853. He donated money and time to the mission and left Hawaii in February 1854. He settled in San Bernardino, California, and departed from the church. Journal of George Q. Cannon, People, s.v. "Edward [Edmund in some sources] Dennis."

die with small pox it struck the people as a panic; and being nearly amphib-ious in their habits, at the appearance of fever they fled to the sea to plunge into the surf,—almost to certain death. This from the first we counselled them not to do, but they would not listen; and before we were aware of it almost the whole native population were sick, dying, or lying dead. Such was the terrible condition of the city that States Prisoners were pardoned on condition they would assist in burying the dead. At first the health of-ficers took them to hospitals or pest houses, and to escape this many fled to the mountains and died in some bye-place. Accompanying Br. Lewis to the hospital at one time to look after some of our brethren, the stench from the dead and dying so overcame me that I was helped from the room to the open air. And going from house to house among the sick we found in yards where perhaps 20 had lived now not a soul alive, while some of the dead were still unburied. Often in one day we used two quart bottles of oil in anointing the sick, for we ministered to all who asked us, feeling they were all our Father's covenant children. I cannot describe the piteous sights we often witnessed. On one occasion coming to a house where lay upon the mats a man and boy too swollen to be recognized, as we ministered to the man he seemed to revive and tried to talk, and I felt sure it was one of our brethren. I looked around and saw a coat which I knew belonged to one of our dearest friends—a most devoted member of the Church. All the rest of his family were dead and he was nearly gone. And so went most of our dearest and most zealous brethren and friends—our most active help in the ministry—and my heart wept, and my whole soul cried out to the Lord for that poor people, and I was in great affliction, and marvelled that the Lord would permit all his most faithful servants to die, so dear to us, and whose help we so much needed, and I pondered the subject prayerfully until the light of the Lord shone upon my understanding, and I saw multitudes of their race in the spirit world who had lived before them, and there was not one there with the priesthood to teach them the gospel, and the voice of the Spirit said to me—"Sorrow not, for they are now doing that greater work for which they were ordained, and it is all of the Lord." So I was comforted, knowing that through the Spirit of Elijah the hearts of the children were now being turned to the fathers in the spirit land.[84] Of the 4000 who died in the vicinity of Honolulu some 400 had received the gospel, embracing the most efficient and the very best of the native saints. . . .

At our conference Oct. 6th 1853 a move was made to procure a printing press, for publishing the Book of Mormon and other works, in the Hawaian tongue; and Prest Lewis, Br. Cannon and I were appointed a committee to devise ways and means for that purpose.[85] At the same time I was called upon, with others, to select & negotiate for a suitable tract of land for the gathering of the Saints. Heretofore the mission had been very poor, and it appeared a great undertaking, especially to raise the money necessary to buy a press and material sufficient for the work before us. But with me it was a principle of faith, and according to prediction that means should come into my hands through the blessing of the Lord, to sustain and comfort my brethren, and to accomplish every purpose pertaining to my mission. Thus far the way had been marvelously opened, and I felt strong faith that we would succeed.

Our general conference was held at Waialuku on East [West] Mauii

---

84.　Malachi 4:5–6 of the Old Testament reads, "Behold, I will send you Elijah the prophet before the coming of the great and dreadful day of the Lord: And he shall turn the heart of the fathers to the children, and the heart of the children to their fathers, lest I come and smite the earth with a curse." Latter-day Saints use the term "Spirit of Elijah" to refer to an interest in and connection to one's ancestors. Latter-day Saints believe that after death, the righteous in the spirit world preach to those who were never able to receive the gospel in their mortal lives. Mary Finlayson, "Elijah, Spirit of," and Walter D. Bowen, "Spirit World," in *Encyclopedia of Mormonism*, 2:452, 3:1408–9.

85.　George Q. Cannon began his translation of the Book of Mormon in January 1852, assisted by Hawaiian convert Jonathan H. Napela. The translation was completed in January 1854, but it was not immediately printed. Church members pooled funds to purchase a printing press, and they ordered one from Boston. When the press arrived in October 1854, no one knew how to use it, so it was sent to California. Cannon printed the translation in San Francisco in an edition of 2,000, finishing it on January 28, 1856. A few copies were bound at the time the printing was completed, and 200 were bound eight months later, most of which were sent to the Hawaiian Islands. How many copies were ultimately bound is not known. Britsch, *Moramona*, 25–28; Crawley, *Descriptive Bibliography of the Mormon Church*, 3:266–70.

at which near 2000 native members were present, there being 6 or 7000
native saints in the mission. East [West] Mauii embraces about one third
of the island, and is one vast mountain rising abruptly from the sea on all
sides except landward, and attaining the height of 14000 feet. In the summit is an abrupt chasm about 10 miles in diameter and some thousands of
feet in depth.[86] To visit this a party was formed, consisting of Prest Lewis,
Brs. Cannon, Hammond,[87] Bigler, myself and others, with horses, mules,
asses and jennys, the provisions being furnished by the natives. With some
natives for guides we set out, the summit being 15 or 20 miles distant. The
ascent occupied nearly two days, and for some miles was gradual, over land
which was the richest and most beautiful of any I had then seen upon the
islands. Here grew many acres of beautiful potatoes, thousands of bushels
of which had in the past been shipped to California, and other markets.
They were of a flesh color, smooth, good size, and much like our present
"early rose." I tried to learn if they were indigenous or from foreign lands,
but the oldest inhabitants could not tell. Thousands of acres were covered
with tomatoes, ground cherries, straw berries, whortle berries[88] &c, and
here was the only place I saw where was growing the famed sandal wood—
burnt as incense in eastern worship.[89] And here was a branch of the church

---

86. Maui, the "Valley Isle," is the second largest of the Hawaiian Islands, formed by
    two adjacent volcanoes that connected to each other, with an isthmus between
    them. The settlement of Wailuku is located on the north shore of the western
    portion of the island (not the eastern, as Johnson wrote). The western portion's
    highest peak is Puu Kukui, at 5,787 feet. The eastern portion is made up of the
    volcano Haleakala, which takes up three-fourths of the island. Its highest peak, Red
    Hill, reaches 10,023 feet, and at the top of Red Hill is a large crater that formed
    not from volcanism but from erosion; it is more than 2,500 feet deep and covers
    an area of nineteen square miles. *Merriam-Webster's Geographical Dictionary*, s.vv.
    "Haleakala Crater," "Maui."

87. Francis A. Hammond (1822–1900) was a sailor born in New York. He was bap-
    tized in 1847 in San Francisco and traveled to Utah in 1848. He served missions
    to Hawaii from 1851 to 1856 and again from 1864 to 1865. Hammond, *Island
    Adventures*.

88. Ground cherries are a fruit similar to tomatoes or tomatillos. *Whortleberry* can refer
    to various berries of temperate areas of the Northern Hemisphere.

89. Several species of sandalwood, a fragrant tree used for incense, grow in Hawaii.
    Between the 1770s and 1820s, sandalwood was greatly exported and exploited.

with their flocks of goats, pigs, fowls &c. who feasted us on our way up and invited us to stay with them on our return, with promise to cook for us a fat goat. The first night brought us up to the frost line, and into the region of rocks, brush, and steep ascent, and to a commodious cave, where we camped for the night. The natives had broiled goat meat and roasted potatoes &c which gave us supper and breakfast, which last was served at break of day. Again we scrambled upward over the few remaining miles before us, which grew steeper and more steep until we were compelled to dismount, lead our mules and pull up by the brush, and there was no intimation to our near approach to the top until we stood upon the very rim of this most awful abyss, almost just beneath us. Here opened to our view a scene sublime, grand and wonderful. Before us was a chasm some thousands of feet deep and 30 miles in circumference, once, to all appearance, the mightiest volcano that ever shook the earth:—where had rolled in majesty not a volcanic caldron but a ten-mile sea of molten fire, which, as we gazed, appeared from our elevation a moving mass and still flowing through a gorge into the sea. But my pen is inadequate to describe the awful majesty of this unparalleled, though now qui[e]scent volcanic crater. And while standing at this great altitude the view stretches away over the mighty deep, taking in all the surrounding islands, which appear but as dots in the watery expanse. And never has any view so impressed me with the majestic greatness of Nature's God and the smallness of finite man.

Of our descent into and exploration of this awful chasm and the dangers encountered in our exit, as also the many interesting incidents attending our visit and return I must not pause to write. Returned to Makawon[90] on the night of the 16th and stayed with Br. John Winchester[91] in company with Brs. Lewis, Cannon and others. Started in early morning for W[ai]luku, 15 miles, and on leaving the road and crossing a broad sand plain we saw large quantities of human bones, apparently spread broadcast far and

---

Rock, *Indigenous Trees of the Hawaiian Islands*, 126–35.

90. Makawao is a town on the north side of the eastern portion of Maui. *Merriam-Webster's Geographical Dictionary*, s.v. "Makawao."

91. John Winchester was baptized in Hawaii in 1851 and provided financial and emotional support to the Sandwich Islands missionaries in the ensuing years. Journal of George Q. Cannon, People, s.v. "John E. B. Winchester."

The Haleakala Crater. This formation is likely near the location Benjamin Johnson is describing. Courtesy of Pixabay.com.

near in every direction—a grim and hideous sight. We learned that here was fought the great battle by Kamahamaha 1st through which the Mauii king became his vassal, as also all the other island Chiefes or kings who were conquered by him about the beginning of this century, since which a constitutional kingdom has been created, and recognized by the governments of Europe & America.[92]

From Wailuku we went to Palia,[93] where the natives took us by whale boat 20 miles to Lahaina,[94] from which point the Committee appointed to obtain a location on which to gather the native saints were to cross the

---

92. King Kamehameha I (c. 1736–1819) was a king who unified the islands of Hawaii. The various islands had their own rulers, but Kamehameha conquered and united them first in 1795 and then more completely in 1810. Britsch, *Moramona*, 9; *Merriam-Webster's Geographical Dictionary*, s.v. "Hawaii."

93. "Palia" might be Kapalua, a settlement on the western shore of Maui, located about ten miles from Lahaina.

94. Lahaina is located on the western shore of Maui. It was particularly prominent in the nineteenth century and is presently a major tourist destination. *Merriam-Webster's Geographical Dictionary*, s.v. "Lahaina."

Channel and explore the island of Lan[a]i, much of which belonged to our friend Halalia,[95] who, I forgot to say, had offered it to us on easy terms, either for occupation or purchase.

We arrived on the 18th and on the 19th the committee consisting of Bros. Hammond, Dennis, McBride, N[athan Tanner] and myself, with Brs. Cannon and Napela[96] started in a whale boat 20 miles across the Channel. After a tedious passage without wind we arrived about 4 o'clock at Mannetta where were a few native houses and the people had collected upon the beach to receive us. We held meeting, baptized a few, and after an early breakfast the following morning upon fish caught by native Brn. through fishing all night in a heavy storm lest we should go hungry, we started to explore this island, which very few foreigners had ever visited. It is nearly circular in shape, and about 20 miles in diameter, and has been upheaved, a melted, dripping mass of molten rock. On all sides, except at the place of our landing the once melted rock stands vertical for some thousands of feet, and its honey combed sides[97] is inhabited by flocks of domestic pigeons in their wild state, with swallows and sea birds as associates. In ascending this island mountain about one mile was rugged and rocky, but another mile of smooth and beautiful grass covered lands brought us to the summit or rim of a basin or valley which as a concave occupied its whole top; and as we gazed down upon it we were charmed with its beauty. Never had I seen a valley of such symmetry and beauty, and as we proceeded, we found the soil very rich, the only question of importance being the needed

95. Levi Haalelea (1822–?) was a high-ranking chief born on Maui. He donated money and land for the Latter-day Saint missionaries. Journal of George Q. Cannon, People, s.v. "Levi Haalelea."

96. Jonathan Napela (1813–79) was one of the *ali'i*, the chiefly class of Hawaii. He served as a district magistrate at the time of his baptism in 1852; he lost his position as a judge after associating with the Latter-day Saints. After his baptism, he significantly helped the missionaries, including collaborating with George Q. Cannon to translate the Book of Mormon, *Ka Buke a Moramona*, into Hawaiian. He served consistently in the church until he died on the island of Molokai in 1879. Journal of George Q. Cannon, People, s.v. "Jonathan (Ionatana) Hawaii Napela."

97. When iron-rich lava cools, it can form columnar basalt, columns of rock with a hexagonal cross section.

supply of water to sustain the population through the dry season. To stay both hunger and thirst we ate the Pabisus, or fruit of a cactus, which is delicious and is much used by the natives. In color it is of a bright red or yellow, and about the size of a turkey's egg. The plant, with its mammoth leaves growing one upon another attains to 20 feet, and its fruit is reached with a forked pole or bamboo.

We were told of springs over a high ridge, from the top of which our descent was over a mile into a deep gorge so steep that much of the way was by steps <cut> out in the hard clay. At the bottom we found a number of small basins dug in the clay banks, filled by the seeping waters. While there two native women came with calabashes, taking water away upon their heads.[98] On our return we found that those two women upon the beach had washed more clothes and made their linen whiter than foreigners would have done with ten times the amount of water, and this trait I often noticed among them.

Exploring the interior portion of the valley, we found beautiful fields of sweet potatoes, with melon vines and beans that had grown year after year, and one bean vine, as it spread over trees and brush, covered, I think, nearly half an acre. It was constantly in bloom, with pods in all stages and bushels of ripe beans loading its branches; near the ground it was 5 inches in diameter. It is said this bean was brought by Capt. Cook.[99] The natives made little use of it, but early ship masters gathered them for ship supplies.

We could not see how to procure water for a settlement, as to construct tanks would be expensive and take time, and then Br. N[athan Tanner] as one of the committee was opposed to any move that interfered with his plan of procuring a ship and emigrating the native saints to the coast, the

---

98. A calabash is a hard-shelled gourd that is dried and used as a container; the term can also refer to similar containers made of other materials. *Oxford English Dictionary*, s.v. "calabash."

99. Captain James Cook (1728–1779) was an English navigator. On his third expedition to the Pacific, in 1778, he became the first European to establish contact with the Hawaiian Islands, which he named the Sandwich Islands, after the Earl of Sandwich. He then traveled to the Pacific Northwest of America and then returned to the Sandwich Islands, where he was killed in February 1779. Journal of George Q. Cannon, People, s.v. "James Cook."

outcome of which may be seen further along.

A storm the night before our leaving for Lahain[a] left the Channel very rough, and on setting sail in the morning we were at once [in a] chopped sea and soon in a dead and sultry calm of tropical heat. The natives plied their oars until exhausted, with little progress. The chopped sea and sultry calm was a terrible ordeal and all became sea-sick—so very sick, and like some others I became unconscious. When aroused from stupor I heard Br. Cannon tell Br. Napela to pray. He stood up in the bow, and in his native tongue and simple faith asked the Lord to have mercy upon his servants there so sick, and send the wind quick or they might die. I knew the wind would come, and it did, in less time than I take to write it, and we soon gladly landed at Lahain[a]. . . .

From a spirit of opposition and other causes the committee deferred for the present efforts relating to a place of gathering for the native saints. . . .

Prest Young again suggested that a place of gathering be obtained upon one of the islands, and so soon as the way opened to commence to gather the saints. Halalia still offers us his choice lands upon the island of Lanai, either to sell at a small price, or to give us to occupy free for a number of years, and this question, by vote of the Conference, was left to be settled by the Mission Presidency. As Prest Lewis feels compelled to remain with our business in Honolulu he lays it upon me, with Br. Karren, to go to La-hain[a] and with Br. Hammond go to Lanai,—select a place, and organize a commencement for the gathering of our native brethren, at once, with Br. E. Green to go with us, and open up and superintend farming works. For this purpose we obtained farm implements, seeds, and necessary outfit, and on the 22d of August 1854 sailed for Lah[aina], arriving after a three day's voyage, and remained with Br. F. A. Hammond until Monday 28th when in a whale boat we crossed the Channel, 20 miles, to Lanai. As I am again sea sick and not strong at best, I feel poorly qualified for climbing up again to the valley. The whole island is but one mountain, the top of which is a beautiful concave or basin, in shape like a saucer, some 10 or more miles in diameter, of which I have written previously. . . .

Although we had spent several days, examining the valley and holding meetings among the natives, looking for a place to start our settlement, which as yet we could not decide upon, even to the day of our departure for Lah[aina]. On this morning I started alone for a walk, without thought as to where or how far I would go, and was glad to see Br. Green coming with me. In him I always had perfect confidence, with warmest friendship, and was glad for his coming. We talked of not having yet agreed upon the place for a town to be established, and wondering how the point would be settled, and were oblivious as to the distance we had come, or the features of that part of the valley over which we were walking, until we came to a tree, and stopped to look around. But when we did, it was with an admiration and an inspiration that filled us both, and I exclaimed "This is the spot we have been looking for!" to which he bore testimony. It was a plot of some hundreds of acres of excellent mesa or table land, sufficiently elevated to overlook the whole beautiful valley. We had walked about one and a half miles which we soon retraced, and made our report to the brethren, who were eager to visit the spot. In eating my breakfast I found myself, for the first time eating *locus*—a large green grasshopper, which I had not noticed until finding them too dry to relish I looked for something more juicy though perhaps equally as nasty. But braced up by a sense of our duties the *nasty* did not trouble us much.

We soon returned to the spot with the other brethren, and all with one voice said "This is the place," and joy seemed to fill all. After a short period of congratulation it was moved that Br. Johnson name and dedicate this spot of ground for the gathering of the native saints; and this being expressed by unanimous vote I named the plot "Joseph" and the valley "Ephraim." We knelt together in the dedication prayer, and on arising all were full of prophecy of good upon this spot; and I well rem[em]ber the words of my prediction—"that through the faithfulness of the elders from this spot salvation should begin to go forth to the children of Joseph upon these lands."[100] We left Br. Green with seed and implements, to commence gathering around him the native saints, to build houses and start agriculture, designing that as soon as the elders now on their way should arrive one or more should be associated with him, and that Br. Karren also should return to his assistance. . . .

---

100. Ephraim was the son of Joseph of Egypt in the Old Testament. In a break with tradition, Joseph's father, Jacob, blessed the younger Ephraim as the firstborn over Manasseh (Genesis 48:13–20). Ephraim's descendants are considered to be a part of the scattered tribes of Israel, and Latter-day Saints believe they will occupy a

My health was now so very poor that Prest Lewis suggested that I return home;—but how can I shirk the fast-increasing responsibilities now upon me! . . .

On the 30th of Dec. a letter came from Apostle Pratt counselling us to ship the Press and material to San Francisco in view of greatly reducing expense of publication. By this I feel a full and honorable release, as our mission liabilities are being paid; but to get money for passage home is now the great question. . . .

The native saints learning I was soon to leave them, came with their small offerings in money—large, considering their poverty—and with tears and sobs said "good bye." I found about $20 in these small sums. I was glad in the hope of again seeing my family, but had not realized how my heart was entwined with these poor people, and it required an effort to subdue my own grief at parting with them. . . .

Tuesday 16th We set sail—so joyful and so sad.[101] . . .

Our cabin was nicely fitted upon the after deck, containing about 20 persons; and with good weather and agreeable social relations we might reasonably hope for a pleasant and cheerful voyage, neither of which were in store for us. No sooner had we taken possession of our berths with hopes of rest and pleasant converse than we found we were associated with libertines, gamblers and renegades of the most prophane and vulgar character. On the 3d day a robbery was committed; some one had entered the Captain's cabin, cut open his carpet bag and stolen a gold watch chain and jewelry to the value of $300.00. While we were known as Mormon missionaries we had hardly spoken to the captain to make his acquaintance; and we could but feel anxious in relation to the matter, when all, both sailors and passengers, were called on deck, the hatchways closed, while the captain and his officers searched on board. When our turn came, with our

significant role prior to the Second Coming of Jesus Christ. According to revelations canonized in the Doctrine and Covenants, Ephraim's descendants bear the responsibility of preaching the gospel and gathering in the scattered house of Israel (Doctrine and Covenants 113:3–6; 133:30–34). Brian L. Smith, "Ephraim," in *Encyclopedia of Mormonism*, 2:461–462; Mauss, *All Abraham's Children*, 18–32.

101. Johnson set sail on the *Susan Abigail* on January 16 or 17, 1855. Johnson, journal, January 12, 1855; December 22, 1855.

baggage on deck, we expected a rigid scrutiny, and felt a tremor of anxiety as the Captain stepped to my side and in a low voice said "Mr. Johnson, we shall only look a little at your things for form's sake. We know you have not the property." When we proceeded to open out everything he would not permit it, and to our surprise, moved away with apparent confidence and respect.—which was marvelous to us. . . .

Cold, sea sick and in peril, we endured these profane and vile fellow passengers and wore out the 22 long days of our passage. But to such a degree did they carry their blasphemous and beastly vulgarity that I rebuked them sharply. They seemed to feel the rebuke and did not again annoy us with their extreme foulness. They were men who had roamed over the world gathering in the vices of all nations, Christian or pagan.

On coming to anchor in the [San Francisco] bay, the Captain of Police was soon on board, to search again for the stolen property, but without finding trace of it. And leaving us, who had more baggage than others until the last, the captain said there was no need for farther search. I insisted that we should be searched, for, should he not find the lost property, he could never know that *we* had not robbed him. But he assured us he should always be perfectly satisfied upon that point, and seemed to take pleasure in giving us information, and in doing all within his power for our accommodation. . . .

We soon found temporary homes with some of the saints, I being invited and kindly cared for by Mother Mowry,[102] whose husband was not in the church; yet I was welcome. In flesh I was thin, and weak in body, but felt I would improve, and did, at once. My stay in San Francesco was very pleasant; apostle Pratt was there and some of the brethren from the islands were waiting to return with him in May. By Br. Pratt, I found our labors upon the islands had been appreciated. He spoke of my pamphlet in reply to the "Polynesian," and said that nothing better had yet been published upon plural marriage;[103] and said the press and material we had procured

---

102. Ruth Mowry (1798–1887) was born in 1798 in Massachusetts. After marrying in 1820, she traveled to California aboard the ship *Brooklyn* in 1846. She went to Utah in 1857 and died in Kaysville, Utah, in 1887. Journal of George Q. Cannon, People, s.v. "Ruth Walkup Mowry (also spelled Mowery)."

103. Benjamin F. Johnson, *Why the "Latter Day Saints" Marry a Plurality of Wives:*

belonged to us according as we had contributed to its purchase. I said I was sent out to work for God and his kingdom; and if I had been faithful I wanted the credit of having "well done." And I could not be paid for leaving a dear family in dollars and cents. I had left the islands, I said, with just money enough to pay my passage at half fare; and as I had money with me due to the "news" "Seer"[104] and tithing office at home, I might use it for my outfit, but would repay every dollar before visiting the city after meeting with my family, then at Payson. . . .

As a steamer that would touch at San Pedro on her way to Panama was soon to leave port, we arranged for our passage; and Br. James Lawson, who had just arrived from the islands, arranged for passage with us. On our way down the coast we encountered the heaviest storm experienced upon the coast, and in a dense fog came near stranding upon the rocks; and such was the storm that when standing on the upper deck, 30 feet above the waters, the waves seemed like mountains above us.

After a cold and perilous passage both by sea and land we arrived at San Bernardino, and found that Capt. Hoopers team, with Capt. Congers mail party would start for Utah in one week; which, for a long period might be the only safe conduct through the hostile indian country. From Capt. Conger I learned that two horses, with pack and riding outfit for each man, with blankets and provisions would be necessary; and with the money due Prest Young and others I bought my horses and outfit. But one of my animals was pronounced unfit for the journey on the evening previous to our start; and this indeed seemed too much. For I had already more than I was able to do to get ready, and I felt I must wait another opportunity. But as usual I prayed that if now was the time for my return, that the way would

---

A Glance at Scripture and Reason, in Answer to an Attack through the Polynesian, upon the Saints for Polygamy (San Francisco: Excelsior Printing Office, 1854). The Polynesian did not publish Johnson's defensive reply, so it was published in San Francisco. This pamphlet went into great detail about Old Testament polygamists and separated polygamy from adultery.

104. While Orson Pratt was a mission president in Washington, DC, he published the periodical the Seer in defense of Latter-day Saint doctrines, particularly polygamy. Eighteen monthly numbers were published in Washington, DC. These eighteen issues were reprinted in Liverpool, along with two additional issues. Neilson, Exhibiting Mormonism, 37–38.

open through some of those who came to visit our camp. I said to those present and who wondered what I would do, that I was in a degree upon their mercy or charity; that I was on my way home from a mission of years, and unless some one would exchange horses, and give me one that would do, for a reasonable difference I must remain, for I could not go around to hunt up a trade; and I must leave the matter with them and the Lord. Br. Thomas Holladay said he had a colt that would carry me if I could ride him, and brought him to me. . . .

At Cedar city[105] I found my brother George[106] and many other warm hearted friends, and at Johnson's Fort[107] my brother Joel H.,[108] and at Parowan Br. James H. Martineau,[109] who accompanied me home, where I arrived March 26th 1855.

But I am again at home with my family in Payson, though worn, weary, weak and thin in flesh. But I know the Angel sent with me by the Prophet and the one promised me on my leaving the islands has been with me to open my way, and I look back with wonder to the many providences that have sustained me upon my mission and upon my return.

105. Parley P. Pratt marked the area of Cedar City for settlement in 1849, and it was settled in 1851. The southwest Utah town was originally called Little Muddy, then Coal Creek, but was ultimately named for the abundance of cedar, or juniper, trees in the area. Cedar City was originally intended to produce iron. Van Cott, *Utah Place Names*, 72; Morris A. Shirts, "Cedar City," in *Utah History Encyclopedia*, 80.

106. George Johnson (1823–1900) arrived in Utah in 1851. Mormon Pioneer Overland Travel database, s.v. "George Washington Johnson."

107. Joel Johnson settled Fort Johnson in 1851. Located about six miles north of Cedar City, it is known today as Enoch. Van Cott, *Utah Place Names*, 128–29.

108. Joel Johnson (1802–82) was baptized in 1831 and served several missions in the eastern United States. He traveled to Utah with his brother Benjamin and their families in 1848. Early Mormon Missionaries database, s.v. "Joel Hills Johnson"; Mormon Pioneer Overland Travel database, s.v. "Joel Hills Johnson."

109. James Martineau (1828–1921) was on his way to California to prospect for gold in 1850, but he stopped in Utah and was baptized in 1851. He initially settled in Parowan, but he later moved throughout Utah and the surrounding region. He died in Salt Lake City in 1921. Godfrey and Martineau-McCarty, *Uncommon Common Pioneer*.

6

JAMES LEWIS AND THE CHINA MISSION

Historical Introduction

"IN 1852 I WAS CALLED ON A MISSION TO CHINA with Hosea Stout and Chapman Duncan," James Lewis reminisced in his closing years in the 1890s. "This was the great trial of my life, in poverty with three helpless children, another was expected any day. I felt my weakness like Sampson shorn of his locks, but my trust was in God my Heavenly Father."[1] Leaving his young wife and three (almost four) children behind in the settlement of Parowan, Utah, was just the beginning of his "great trial." Lewis, Stout, and Duncan spent only six weeks in their assigned mission of China. These missionaries were unable to effectively proselytize among the native Chinese, and the British and American people stationed in Hong Kong[2] would not heed their message. "The heat of the atmosphere

---

1. "Autobiography of James Lewis," 3.
2. The ancient Chinese island of Hong Kong, on the coast of southeast China, came under British rule in 1842 as part of the Treaty of Nanking. It is separated from the

James Lewis. Courtesy of
Hole in the Rock Foundation.

was very oppressive. Being reduced in bad health, owing to change of diet, the manner of preparing it, &c., our spirits were, becoming depressed, and not perceiving a cheering ray of hope in all our labors," Lewis lamented.[3] The three returned to their homes in Utah a little more than a year after they had departed, earlier than most of their colleagues sent out in 1852.

James Lewis's Early Life, 1814–51

Born in Maine on January 12, 1814, James Lewis first heard of the Latter-day Saints and their persecutions after arriving in Missouri in 1840; believing in their doctrine, he was baptized and ordained an elder in February 1842 in Keokuk, Iowa.[4] In 1847, he married Emily Jennison Holman in St. Louis, Missouri.[5] After the Saints relocated to the West, he traveled with the Silas Richards company in 1849; a year later, he was sent to southern Utah to help with the Iron Mission in Parowan.[6] As Iron County was being established, James Lewis was nominated and elected as county recorder,[7] and he also served as second lieutenant in the Iron County militia's cavalry company.[8] A school was started in Parowan in 1851. Lewis was listed on the 1851 census as a teacher, but he apparently was not involved with the local school.[9]

mainland by a harbor, known either as Hong Kong Harbour or Victoria Harbour. In 1860, Kowloon Peninsula, on the north side of the harbor, came under British rule, and more territory was leased to Britain in 1898. These territories of Hong Kong were not returned to Chinese rule until 1997. *Merriam-Webster's Geographical Dictionary,* s.v. "Hong Kong."

3. "Items of the China Mission," *Deseret News,* January 4, 1855; p. 195 herein.
4. "Autobiography of James Lewis," 2.
5. Swapp, "Biography of Emily Jennison Holman Lewis," 7.
6. "Autobiography of James Lewis," 1–3.
7. Shirts and Shirts, *Trial Furnace,* 74, 78.
8. Shirts and Shirts, *Trial Furnace,* 35.
9. Shirts and Shirts, *Trial Furnace,* 107.

James Lewis and the Early Church Mission to China, 1852–53

President Brigham Young and other church leaders discussed sending missionaries to Asia soon after gold was discovered in California in 1848 and political revolutions were roiling Europe.[10] But it wasn't until 1852 that missionaries were called to the nation of China. James Lewis and the other three elders assigned to China that August—Hosea Stout, Chapman Duncan, and Walter Thompson (called shortly thereafter)—were as stunned at their assignment as the other newly called missionaries were at theirs. "To day was the Special Conference held for the purpose of sending Elders abroad. There was about 80 or 90 chosen to day to go forth to different parts of the world," Stout noted in his diary that day. Stout had a long record of serving in Latter-day Saint defensive organizations. In 1838, he had been a member of the Danites,[11] a militant group of church members in Missouri, and in the 1840s, he was chief of police in Nauvoo, Illinois, and a leader in the Nauvoo Legion.[12] "Myself, James Lewis, Walter Thompson and Chapman Duncan were chosen to go to China. The brethren who were chosen all manifest a good spirit & seem to have the spirit of their Calling."[13] Duncan had faced mob violence in Missouri in the 1830s, and like Stout, he had traveled to Utah in 1848.[14] Thompson, on the other hand, had arrived in Utah from his native Scotland only a year before.[15] Lewis and Duncan were then living in southern Utah's Parowan and were

---

10. See Livingston, "Eyes on 'The Whole European World,'" 78–112.

11. Danites, or the Society of the Daughter of Zion, were a private military group organized to defend the Saints during volatile times in Missouri. Although the Danites existed for only a few months in 1838, folklore about murderous Danites followed the Saints even after they had settled in Utah, and fears of Danites showed up in antagonistic propaganda. Ashurst-McGee et al., *Joseph Smith Papers, Documents, Volume 6*, 169–70, 687–88; Alexander L. Baugh, "Danites," in *Encyclopedia of Latter-day Saint History*, 275; David J. Whittaker, "Danites," in *Encyclopedia of Mormonism*, 1:356–57.

12. Brooks, *On the Mormon Frontier*, 1:xiv–xix.

13. Stout, reminiscences and journals, August 28, 1852.

14. Duncan, "Biography of Chapman Duncan," 3–11, 31–40.

15. "Thomson, Walter," in appendix 2, p. 358 herein.

not at the conference.[16] All four men were willing to serve as missionaries at their prophet's request, although Thompson would only make it as far as Southern California due to health problems.

While the missionaries may have been enthusiastic while in Utah, they lost their evangelistic zeal once they arrived in China. This was seemingly due to their lack of preparation for extended missionary life in Asia. When the elders sailed into the Hong Kong harbor, they were struck by the foreignness of their new environment. "We arrived all well, in a strange land and among strange people," Lewis recounted. "We did not find a cordial welcome."[17] The three elders' biggest problem was that none of them spoke Cantonese, the Chinese dialect spoken in the Canton region of southern China, including Hong Kong. The elders assigned to labor in China were seemingly expected to evangelize the Chinese without any missionary training, including language acquisition.[18]

In their defense, it is unclear if Lewis and his missionary companions were actually planning on evangelizing the Chinese-speaking locals or if they instead hoped to convert English-speaking expatriates living in Hong Kong, a British colony. Regardless of their initial intentions, Lewis, Stout, and Duncan quickly realized their linguistic quandary and anguished over the prospect of learning any dialect of Chinese. There were other obstacles as well: whereas traveling without purse or scrip gave biblical legitimacy to the elders in Christian North America and Western Europe, the same Euro-American Latter-day Saint missionary practice proved to be a major liability in Asia. The three Latter-day Saints found the cost of living in Hong Kong prohibitive and the price of Chinese teachers beyond their meager funds. Additionally, traditional Latter-day Saint evangelistic practices added to the elders' lack of success among the residents of Hong

---

16. James Lewis had been a county recorder, and Chapman Duncan had been serving as a tithing clerk in Parowan. Elijah Elmer arrived in Parowan on September 12 from Salt Lake with news that they were going on missions. Godfrey and Martineau-McCarty, *Uncommon Common Pioneer*, 18; Lunt and Lunt, *Life of Henry Lunt and Family*, 54; Shirts and Shirts, *Trial Furnace*, 74, 244.

17. "Autobiography of James Lewis," 4.

18. Hosea Stout to Brigham Young, May 16, 1853, Incoming Correspondence, Brigham Young Office Files.

Kong. Unlike other Euro-American Christian representatives in Asia, the Latter-day Saints did not try to set up schools or offer any social services.[19] To make matters worse, the Taiping Rebellion, which lasted from 1850 until 1864, was raging on mainland China.[20] Natural conditions such as the heat, humidity, and precipitation of Hong Kong added to the elders' discouragement; unaccustomed to the sticky humidity, scorching temperatures, and heavy rains, the elders found it difficult to hold outdoor meetings.

After about six weeks in China, the missionaries lost hope. They were discouraged and at a loss as to how to proceed.[21] "We feel that we have done all that God or man can require of us in this place," Stout lamented. "We have preached publickly and privately as long as any one would hear and often tried when no one would hear."[22] Before they reached their two-month mark in Hong Kong, they determined to pause their missionary labors in China. They returned to America on the *Rose of Sharon* and eventually made their way back to Utah.

Unaware of the linguistic, financial, and social challenges that Lewis and his companions faced in Hong Kong, church leaders in Utah called Cyrus Canfield and Edward Wade to join the missionaries in China during the April 1853 general conference.[23] Canfield and Wade traveled to California

19. See Neilson, "Early Mormon Missionary Work in Hong Kong," 7–11.

20. The Taiping Rebellion was a Chinese civil war that began in 1850. Hong Xiuquan had read some tracts left by Christian missionaries and had a vision that made him believe he was the younger brother of Jesus Christ. Hong established a religious community, the Taiping Tianguo, that forbade opium and alcohol and that pooled all resources into a community fund. He and his followers, known as God worshipers, spread throughout southeast China, preaching their unique form of Christianity, combatting Confucian ideas, and seeking to overthrow the Qing dynasty. Western societies initially favored the idea of a Christian group overthrowing Chinese traditions, but they became less enthusiastic when they realized how eccentric the Taiping group was. The Taiping Rebellion ended in 1864, when Hong Xiuquan died. Spence, *Search for Modern China*, 171–80.

21. Hosea Stout, James Lewis, and Chapman Duncan to Brigham Young, August 27, 1853, Incoming Correspondence, Brigham Young Office Files.

22. Stout, reminiscences and journals, June 7, 1853.

23. "Minutes of the General Conference," *Deseret News*, April 30, 1853. Later that month, on April 17, 1853 (eight months after they called the first four missionaries

on their way to China, but when they arrived on August 26, they learned that the previous missionaries had returned from Hong Kong to California that same month. (Lewis, Stout, and Duncan arrived in San Francisco[24] on August 23, 1853.) Stout recorded, "Elder Cyrus Canfield . . . & Elder E. Wade have been appointed to join us in our mission & had come thus far & meeting us thus returning are left in the same uncertainty that we are not knowing what to do."[25] Stout arrived in San Bernardino, California, on September 11, and Lewis arrived there on October 25. Stout and Lewis left for Salt Lake City in early November and arrived in December.[26]

Additional Church Service, 1853–98

After listening to the reports of Stout and his companions, church leaders decided against sending any elders back to China, and they released the five men from their missionary duties. James Lewis settled back into life in Parowan and served as probate judge in Iron County for ten years.[27] In 1857, Lewis was the major of the First Battalion in Iron County,[28] and on September 11 of that year, he accompanied William H. Dame to try to

to China), the First Presidency and Quorum of the Twelve met together and had a discussion about the role of the apostleship. They discussed if they could ordain other Apostles, in addition to the dozen men in the Quorum of the Twelve. Elder Parley P. Pratt and President Brigham Young offered their opinions that there could be extra-quorum Apostles. President Young then explained, "We want to send a man to China and se[nd] him as an Apostle to build up the K[ingdo]m there and then go thro to the end." Thomas Bullock Minutes (LaJean Carruth shorthand version), April 17, 1853; Historian's Office general Church minutes.

24. Latter-day Saints had arrived in San Francisco in 1846 and built up the town, but most of them left in 1848. Beginning in 1849, thousands of Chinese immigrants arrived in San Francisco to work in the gold mines and elsewhere, inhabiting the communities that had previously been home to many Latter-day Saints. Twenty thousand Chinese arrived in 1852, and sixteen thousand arrived in 1854, but after that the number of immigrants decreased to a few thousand per year until the late 1860s. William E. Homer, "San Francisco, California," in *Encyclopedia of Latter-day Saint History*, 1066–67; Chinn, *History of the Chinese in California*, 22.

25. Stout, reminiscences and journals, August 26, 1853.

26. Stout, reminiscences and journals, August 23–December 8, 1853.

27. "Autobiography of James Lewis," 5.

28. Shirts and Shirts, *Trial Furnace*, 386.

prevent the Mountain Meadows Massacre, but it was too late.[29] He spent the rest of his life around southern Utah: he moved to the settlement of Harrisburg in 1861 to raise cotton; he taught school in Panaca, Nevada, to support his family; and he moved to Kanab in 1871, becoming Kane County's commissioner. In 1882, he was called on a mission to San Juan County in southeast Utah, where he was supposed to once again serve as judge. He was part of the original group that made its way through Hole in the Rock,[30] saying, "The road had been made by the company with great labor and toil of months and was the most rugged I ever traveled."[31] He intended to take his family to the new settlement of Bluff in that county, but he was prevented from doing so because of Native American difficulties; instead, he was released from his mission and settled in Taylor, Arizona, with his family. He returned to Kanab in 1891, where he was called as a patriarch in 1896 and remained until his death in 1898.[32]

When Hosea Stout returned to America in August 1853, he learned that his wife, Louisa, and their baby son had died during his absence. He faced the harsh reality of his situation when he returned home that December: "I gazed upon the sad wreck of all my hopes in silence while my heart sank within me & those around could

Hosea Stout, mission companion to James Lewis. Courtesy of Church History Library.

---

29. Walker, Turley, and Leonard, *Massacre at Mountain Meadows*, 211.

30. In 1879–80, a group of Latter-day Saints were sent to establish a settlement in San Juan County in southeast Utah. They traveled from the Parowan area, and rather than taking roundabout roads to reach the site of their new town, they opted to take a more direct route that included a harrowingly narrow and steep crevice. They had to construct a road in order to get their wagons through, a remarkable feat. See Miller, *Hole-in-the-Rock*.

31. "Autobiography of James Lewis," 6.

32. "Autobiography of James Lewis," 5–6; Mormon Pioneer Overland Travel database, s.v. "James Lewis."

not refrain from mingling their tears with mine for a few moments when we all hastily with drew from a place so full of sad recollections as my *HOME*."[33] Stout helped with the 1856 rescue of the handcart companies, was part of the Nauvoo Legion that resisted the US Army in 1857, became a United States district attorney in Utah, and served in other legal positions before dying in 1889.[34] Chapman Duncan worked for John M. Horner in California immediately after returning from China until 1854, and the rest of his life was spent pursuing various vocations all over Utah; he traded livestock, taught school, farmed, operated a fishery, and mined. He also served another mission to California in 1856 and 1857. He died in Caineville, Utah, in 1900.[35] Though Walter Thompson had been unable to serve in his call to China, he labored in the British Mission in 1875. He was a recorder in Weber County, Utah, where he died in 1877.[36]

James Lewis's Family Life

Before learning of their unsolicited missionary callings, the men were barely eking out a living in pioneer Utah. A week after Lewis departed for his mission, twenty-year-old Emily Lewis gave birth to their fourth child.[37] When the missionaries arrived at the Pacific coast in the spring of 1853, they sent the proceeds from the sale of their wagons and horses to their destitute families back in Utah, thus "starting without purse or scrip as did the Apostles of Christ, to preach the restoration of the Gospel through the Prophet Joseph Smith," in Lewis's words.[38] Later in life, Emily was a nurse and midwife. James and Emily had a total of fourteen children, with twelve living to maturity.[39] In 1857, he was sealed to his second wife, Emma Bateman, in Salt Lake City, and they had one son, but they were eventually divorced.

33. Stout, reminiscences and journals, August 23, 1853.
34. Prince, *Hosea Stout*, 223–340; Stout, *Hosea Stout*, 198–252.
35. Duncan, "Biography of Chapman Duncan," 14–20.
36. Early Mormon Missionaries database, s.v. "Walter Thomson"; "Thomson, Walter," in appendix 2, p. 358 herein.
37. Swapp, "Biography of Emily Jennison Holman Lewis," 9.
38. "Autobiography of James Lewis," 3.
39. Swapp, "Biography of Emily Jennison Holman Lewis," 11.

Source Note

Of the three Latter-day Saints who traveled as missionaries all the way to Hong Kong in 1853, Hosea Stout was the only one to keep a journal of their experiences. Chapman Duncan, one of his two missionary companions, wrote very little about his time in China.[40] But James Lewis wrote a series of six letters to George A. Smith between 1853 and 1855, which describe their proselytizing experiences in some detail and add a perspective not found in Stout's own journal or letters. Lewis devotes much of his writing to summary observations about the Chinese as a people and as a civilization in revolution.

DOCUMENT TRANSCRIPTS

James Lewis to the Editor of the *Deseret News*, February 28, 1853[41]

San Francisco Feb. 28th, 1853.
Editor News,

The Elders arrived here about the 10th of January after a short sojourn at San Bernardino, in good health and spirits, having enjoyed the blessings of the Almighty with his Holy Spirit; being administered to by the saints wherever we have traveled, they being comforted, strengthened, and revived in the principles of the Gospel of Christ, which has caused our hearts to be made glad. Upon our arrival plans were adopted for gathering the

---

40. In a letter to Brigham Young from Union City, California, Duncan said simply, "Bro [Hosea] Stouts information in relation to our mission will probably suffice." Chapman Duncan to Brigham Young, September 24, 1853, Incoming Correspondence, Brigham Young Office Files.

41. James Lewis to *Deseret News*, "Elders Correspondence," *Deseret News*, April 30, 1853.

amount necessary to forward the different missionaries to their distinations.[42] The blessings pronounced upon our heads were not forgotten; still the way seemed dark but we realized that we were engaged in the work of our Father, and if faithful, those promises would not fail. This we have realized. After some exertion without effect among the citizens of this place, the Brethren stepped forward, and the amount freely donated, and our hearts were indeed made glad.[43] The several missionaries have left; the Calcutta and Siam missionaries sailed in ship Monsoon,[44] 29th Jan.; Sandwich Island missionaries ship Huntress 31st; Australian, Barque Pacific,[45] Feb. 2nd. How my heart rejoices in the work of the Lord, as I realize the way opening according to the predictions of the authorities for the Elders to go forth, that those who set in darkness might be made acquainted with the principles of life and salvation.

The China missionaries will leave March 1st for Hong Kong, and from information from that country, the way seems opening for the Gospel by the revolutions which are going on in some of the districts, overthrowing

---

42. Thirty-eight missionaries left Utah for California in October 1852. They were going to China, India, Siam (Thailand), Hawaii, and Australia. Hosea Stout, who was president of the China Mission, was the captain of this missionary company. Britsch, "Church Beginnings in China," 162.

43. The elders collectively needed more than $6,000. For three weeks, they tried to get money from people of other faiths and raised only about $150. T. S. Williams then gave them $500, and wealthy California Latter-day Saint John M. Horner donated several thousand to make up the rest. Britsch, "Church Beginnings in China," 163–64.

44. The *Monsoon*, a clipper ship piloted by Captain Zenas Winsor, was originally built in 1851 in Maine. When the thirteen missionaries bound for the India region sailed away on January 29, 1853, they were apparently the only passengers onboard. Levi Savage and Richard Ballantyne got smallpox but recovered. Sonne, *Ships, Saints, and Mariners*, 147–48.

45. The ship *Pacific*, carrying ten missionaries to Australia, left California on February 2, 1853, under the direction of a Captain Matthews. Some passengers contracted smallpox on the voyage but recovered. The ship rescued some people who were shipwrecked at Christmas Island on February 20. The *Pacific* finally arrived in Sydney, Australia, on March 31, but it remained quarantined for another nine days because of the smallpox outbreak. Sonne, *Ships, Saints, and Mariners*, 163; Crawley, *Descriptive Bibliography of the Mormon Church*, 3:75.

idolatry and establishing the belief in God. This is going on independent of any missionary effort, and the results are in the future relative to the good it may produce to that people, and I judge with some degree of certainty that the Lord is preparing the way for the fullness of the Gospel to go forth among this strange, and till within a few years, comparatively unknown people. If ever there was a time, since the rise of this church, for the saints to rejoice, 'tis the present; for we realize the rapid spread of the gospel in all lands, whither the Elders have been sent; and although the powers of evil keep pace with the truth, yet the onward march of the power and work of God is felt in almost every land and clime beneath the sun. While I reflect that even in this land, where the corrupting influences of evil are spread over the length and breadth thereof, the few saints here feel the influence of the spirit of God which is breathed by their Brethren and Sisters in the Valleys of the Mountains, and many of them feel a deep anxiety to partake, with them, the blessings which they enjoy; feeling that what God has made them stewards over was on the altar for the spread of truth and building up the kingdom, realizing the reward promised to the faithful. The situation of those in this region, who have come here to get rich rather than remain in the Valley, is truly unpleasant, judging from their own statements; all tell of great losses, of their poverty, &c., and almost universally say "*that it would have been better to have remained at Salt Lake, that they are sick of California, that they desire to get back as soon as possible. I am going as soon as I get the means or can settle my business.*" In hearing these sayings I have been often reminded of the sayings of Brother Brigham Young, in his counsels to the saints, and from what I have seen and heard of this country, 'tis the last a saint of God would desire to live in, unless sent by authority to work for the upbuilding of his Kingdom.

If you can I should be glad for my family to have the "News" while I am absent and I will make it right the first opportunity; direct to my address, Iron County.[46]

Respectfully I remain your brother in the bonds of the Gospel,

James Lewis.

---

46. Iron County, in southwestern Utah, was formed in the early 1850s when pioneers went to the area to mine iron ore. It was originally called Little Salt Lake Valley County. The iron mining died out by 1857, but the settlements of Cedar City and Parowan remained. Van Cott, *Utah Place Names*, 200; Ralph M. McAffee, "Iron Mission," in *Encyclopedia of Latter-day Saint History*, 552–53.

James Lewis to Elder George A. Smith, February 18, 1854[47]

Cedar, Feb. 18th, 1854.
Dear Brother:—

A leisure moment I improve to say a few words to you, and the pleasure it affords me to read a line from you is only known to myself, and I am willing to trespass upon my time to exchange what I have experienced while absent for those gems of intelligence which fall from your lips, or are expressed by or through the medium of the pen.

I have often reflected upon the sayings of those who oppose Mormonism, accusing us of wickedness, degradation, and corruption. A visit, however, to many of the eastern cities or California, would quite convince a beholder that there was wickedness, a little degradation, and a small sprinkling of corruption in some other places, besides among the Mormons.

If a person who had but little idea of the ways of the world, of the plans, schemes, and artifices of the different classes of business men, including, with but few exceptions, the clerical gentry, should be set down in San Francisco, and see with what success these different classes "subtract" from the pockets of others, and "add" to their own, by their cunning, their knavery, their villainy, and their religious trickery. In this place, he would suppose he was at least beyond civilization, if he did not hear the people speak in his own tongue. Should he step into some of the most fashionable and thronged buildings, perhaps among the most spacious (though there are many of the same stripe), and see crowds of men gathering and gathered around the different games, which are licensed by the city authorities; see the heaps of gold to tempt the ignorant, to ensnare the unwary, to destroy and blast the reputation of the young; see the eagerness of these licensed thieves to "add" to their already ill-gotten store, he would again say in his heart, "Are these people human, or have I stumbled upon hyenas in the shape of men?"

Passing from these scenes to the most magnificent buildings in the goodly city, and there are many of them, as well as many of other kinds

---

47. James Lewis to editor of *Deseret News*, "Letter," *Deseret News*, March 16, 1854.

(many did I say, yes, whole streets) filled with public prostitutes, so common that many have doubted whether there was a virtuous woman among its inhabitants, so plain and manifest is their corruption. The lower order of this class are ready to assail the passer-by, and if possible taint him or them with their contaminating breath. Debauchery in all its forms is perceptible in all ranks and classes, from the grey-haired sinner to the beardless youth. Licentiousness stalks abroad at noon-day, and waits not for the curtain of night to hide its deformity.

Again is seen, both by day as well as night, the assassin who plunges his weapon into the body of his victim with apparent unconcern, feeling security for his release.

These with thousands of other and minor evils found here, with its political degeneracy truly astonishing, shows evidently that there is corruption in other places besides among the Mormons.[48]

The editors of this goodly city are so fond of this freedom, of these privileges, that one can hardly find a case of villainy, of corruption, or degradation, in all California, but they can find many a line regarding the wickedness and corruption of the Mormons.

This city is built upon made ground, by driving piles, and filling with earth, removed from the hills, by which many of them are entirely removed, and the city extended. Thousands of ships from all parts resort to this point; many of them from the States and England, laden for that

---

48. Hosea Stout did not have overly positive feelings about San Francisco either. In a letter to his wife (tragically not knowing that she had died), he wrote: "We are lonesome and tired of this scrimpt narrow streeted hotch potch, fil[t]hy place; Not wishing to find fault, but it is certainly the most disagreeable place I was ever in, muddy crowded, planked & broken through the side walks, and the fil[t]h eternally sending up a stink offering, makes me think of Salt Lake city with her beautiful clean streets. Then the people, O what a contrast. . . . I believe that this is after all the most respectable city in the Union . . . having the most intelligent and enterprising and liberal people in it. Now I do believe that it would be a good way for us when anonymous letter writers from Utah throw their lying filth to Editors either here or East and they publish them with so much eclat and bombast, that if we had some one in their city who would write what they see 'thar' and we tell on them too, & truth at that it would silence them in a short time, even in a matter of self defence." Hosea Stout to Louisa Stout, February 20, 1853, Hosea Stout papers.

place; then go to India and China for the products of those climes, and return home to enrich their owners. This is become the great mart of the Pacific coast, having a fine harbor, with many advantages naturally, and will, if nothing obstructs its progress, outstrip the eastern cities for wealth and wickedness. Here are gathered thousands of almost every clime, and of course thousands of the vile and vicious.

In this place not long ago thirty-eight elders of the Church of Jesus Christ of Latter Day Saints landed, going to the different parts of the earth, without purse or scrip, to carry the gospel to those who sit in darkness, according to the word of the Lord. They visited the citizens in the name of their master for assistance to pursue their journey to carry joyful tidings to the hearts of the honest among the nations of the reorganization of the Church of Christ, of the revelations of God to man, and what was the reception they met with? They were abused, villified, their characters, and the characters of their leaders branded with wickedness, corruption, and degradation, cast out as evil, having nothing to give the servants of God, but plenty to sacrifice, to devote, to lay at the feet of the French, Spanish, Mexican, and American beauties, who form a large class of the aristocracy of San Francisco.

Did their refusal retard the progress of the men of God[?] No; to other and more noble spirits were reserved the high privilege of giving a portion of their means, to bring joy and comfort to the outcast, the down-trodden, and suffering sons of Abraham. There are many noble spirits in California, and their views of us are far different from the herd, the mass, the ignorant; but the days are fast passing away when ignorance will not shield any one regarding us as a people, or our doctrines.

The anticipation of many there, is, that we are soon to explore and settle the Colorado, step over to Sonora, from thence to the capital (Mexico), revolutionize the country, and possess it;[49] and be ready to look Uncle Sam in the face, claiming our dues, &c., being assured that the Mormons will not long be shut up in the mountains, but will soon be rolling down the hills to the sea coast, spreading east, west, north, and south, with a rapidity truly astonishing. What the people fear, saith the prophet, will surely fall

---

49. In the 1880s, some Latter-day Saints built up settlements in the Mexican states of Sonora and Chihuahua to escape federal prosecution of polygamists, but evidently

upon them.

Our regards with the blessing of the Lord upon his people.

[James Lewis]

James Lewis to Elder George A. Smith, June 3, 1854[50]

Parowan, Iron County, Utah,
June 3, 1854.

A few reflections upon scenes and ideas gathered in other lands may not come amiss. In California there are about 75,000 Chinamen, generally in San Francisco and the mines.[51] They are called the best cooks, washers, and servants in that country. They are capable of performing, and enduring more labor and fatigue than any other people in that land;—have no spirit to retaliate for the many insults and injuries they receive. They, like the Jews, are a distinct people, and work in squads entirely by themselves in the mines, and save every farthing. Their living is brought from China by their own merchants; and all their trading is done among themselves, and they wear their own peculiar costume; few adopt the dress of this country.

In San Francisco whole streets are occupied by them. They have their own hotel keepers, wholesale and retail merchants, grocers, and physicians.

---

the Saints had toyed with the idea of settling in Mexico long before then. When the US Army arrived in Utah in 1858, the Latter-day Saints vacated Salt Lake City and relocated to the settlement of Provo, but evidence suggests they considered going even farther south, all the way to Mexico. President James Buchanan privately relished the thought of the Latter-day Saints settling in Sonora, because with a sizable American presence there, he could potentially annex the region for the United States. MacKinnon, *At Sword's Point, Part 2*, 178–86, 341–45; Shirley Taylor Robinson, "Mexico, Pioneer Settlements in," in *Encyclopedia of Mormonism*, 2:895–97.

50. James Lewis to George A. Smith, June 3, 1854, published as "Chinese in California," *Deseret News*, June 22, 1854.

51. After rebellions and other problems in the nineteenth century, many Chinese left their country. Many of them moved to California for the gold rush. Most of them arrived too late for gold, but they found work in other areas, including helping to build the transcontinental railroad in the 1860s. Spence, *Search for Modern China*, 208–14.

In fact they do their own business, independent of others. After obtaining sufficient to make them independent at home, they usually return. They take little or no notice of strangers, only when for their interest; are greatly addicted to gambling, and have gaming establishments and houses of prostitution publicly open day and night, like their neighbors. Thousands of women are brought from China to this market, hired by the more wealthy of their own countrymen, for ten, and often three dollars per head for each year. On any money advanced for outfit or passage, if not paid the first year, it doubles the second on principal and interest. Young females of from 14 to 16, as well as children, are bought in China at from 30$ to 50$ each, and brought to California to swell the already enormous amount of crime, prostitution, degradation, and corruption.

Thousands of laborers are hired in China for the wages of that country, (a few cents per day) and their passage paid; and they work in the mines their term of service, (generally for years) after which they are sent home; thus one class preys upon another to enrich themselves. I was informed that thousands are thus in bondage, under their different overseers,—sent out for this purpose.

In California there are already large and extensive establishments for the sale of the fine and costly fabrics, as well as many manufactured articles, and paintings of rare workmanship, and of exceeding fine finish, which find their way into the houses, or are worn by the wealthy.

I visited many of their leading men, to ascertain if possible, the situation of their country, and gather books, to forward the work in which I was engaged; but I found they were not disposed to give any information, and seemed surprised that we were desirous of knowing anything about them, tho' few could speak English so as to be understood. They require a high price for information, and carry their distinctness to a great length. In their deal with others, they are very unscrupulous.

I found the Chinese in California with a prejudice of feeling, caused by their ill treatment from its citizens, which is not confined to miners, but includes their legislators. They are traduced, vilified, and abused on every hand. Yet they thrive, increase, and will ere long wield a powerful influence, particularly relating to trade. They are controlled by men of intelligence, and are far from being what Christians call them; for their ideas of the Supreme Being their Father, their government, the laws and obligations they are under to each other, with their code of morals, are in advance of the sectarian world; and have their peculiarities, which seem truly strange to us.

They are rapidly increasing, as many of the barriers are being broken down, which have so long deprived them of associating with other, and neighboring nations. Undoubtedly, upon their return to their own land, they will carry more liberal principles, which, with the extension of the spirit of liberty and reform pervading almost every land, will shortly, under the directing hand of the Almighty, who has said by his servants that when the gospel, the re-organization of his kingdom in the last days, should commence, then his work should begin among all nations. This is truly the case with that people.

After completing our arrangements, we left San Francisco in the barque San Van Hoorne,[52] March 9th, and arrived at Hong Kong after a passage of 49 days.

By letters of same date, we learn that the Indians around Parowan continue friendly, and the inhabitants prosperous; and that they are enclosing the old fort, which was fifty six rods square, with a wall around 112 rods square, to be 12 feet high, and 6 feet thick.

52. The ship *Jan Van Hoorn* (not "*San Van Hoorne*") was a Dutch vessel piloted by Captain Jacob Bouten, who offered to take Stout, Lewis, and Duncan to Hong Kong for eighty dollars each. They had previously almost traveled on the ships *Graf Van Hogendorf* and *Invincible*, but the *Graf Van Hogendorf* was expensive, and the *Invincible* was condemned. The missionaries left San Francisco on March 8, 1853, and arrived in China on April 27. Sonne, *Ships, Saints, and Mariners*, 113–14; Stout, reminiscences and journals, January 25–April 27, 1853.

Lewis later explained this experience: "The different missions were forwarded as fast as passage could be found for them. The China mission was the last, and our passage was $160 each. Our first engagement for passage failed for the vessel could not be insured. Our second effort proved the same. Our third was successful. We obtained passage in the merchant vessel to Hong Kong for $50. apiece, saving $110 each." "Autobiography of James Lewis," 4.

James Lewis to Elder George A. Smith, November 25, 1854[53]

Parowan, Nov. 25, 1854.

I will give a few extracts from our journal of the Chinese Mission.

We landed at Hong Kong on the 28th of April, having arrived in the harbor the day before. After considerable search, we found a room to occupy which had formerly been used for stowing treasure, double barred and bolts, with privilege of eating with the owner, at the rate of one dollar per day each. This being the only chance, our luggage was moved ashore.

The harbor seems little more than an open roadstead, where vessels remain a short time and proceed up the river[54] to Canton,[55] which is 90 miles from this point. From the harbor the city presents quite a handsome appearance, as it is situated at the base of a high mountain,[56] which protects it from a strong south west wind which prevails the most of the year. This is the new city, as a few years ago old Hong [Kong] was abandoned, being situated on the other side of the mountain island, subject to the prevailing winds. The present location is far preferable to the former, on account of improvement in the harbor, &c.

Upon our arrival, the vessel was immediately covered with Chinese either for one pretence or another, designing, however, to steal everything

---

53. James Lewis to George A. Smith, November 25, 1854, published as "Chinese Mission," *Deseret News*, December 14, 1854.

54. This is the Zhu or Pearl River, which drains into the South China Sea. *Merriam-Webster's Geographical Dictionary*, s.v. "Zhu."

55. Canton, known today as Guangzhou, is the capital of Guangdong Province in southeast China and was the first Chinese seaport opened to foreigners. The British began trading opium at Canton, a practice that worried Chinese officials and led to the First Opium War between 1839 and 1842. The 1842 Treaty of Nanking allowed British trade and residence in Canton and four other cities. *Merriam-Webster's Geographical Dictionary*, s.v. "Guangzhou"; Spence, *Search for Modern China*, 150–66.

56. This "high mountain" is Victoria Peak, which stands at about 1,800 feet above sea level. In 1949, church leaders dedicated Hong Kong on this mountain for the preaching of the gospel. *Merriam-Webster's Geographical Dictionary*, s.v. "Victoria Peak"; Britsch, "Asia, the Church in," in *Encyclopedia of Mormonism*, 1:75–81.

they could carry away, for they have the character of being the most skilful thieves in the world, or at least a portion of them. This place is of considerable importance in many respects. The island was ceded to the English at the time peace was ratified after the war.[57] Here is the residence of the governor general of China, and is the great military post in China, and is the terminus of the line of steamers which bring the overland mail from the home government, monthly. To show the rapidity of information, I saw the New York Herald[58] 29 days after its issue, and had the pleasure of reading the President's message.[59] I was informed that this line of steamers would in a few months be continued to Australia and San Francisco.

The British Government affords every facility to their own transmission of intelligence within themselves on matters pertaining to governmental affairs, having war steamers plying from this point along the coast to any point which affords trade or traffic, which in one article within a few years has greatly, and I should say fearfully increased, viz: the opium trade. This drug has spread its deleterious influence over the whole country, and tens of thousands of the inhabitants find a grave through its use yearly.[60]

---

57. As part of the 1842 Treaty of Nanking, which ended the First Opium War, the British took possession of Hong Kong Island to rule it as they "shall see fit." This treaty was the first of several unequal treaties with China, unequal because China had to agree to Britain's terms but Britain did not have to agree to China's terms. Spence, *Search for Modern China*, 158–62; *Oxford Dictionary of World History*, s.v. "Nanjing, Treaty of."

58. The *New York Herald* was an influential newspaper founded in 1835 by James Gordon Bennett, who published it for thirty years. It published sensational stories and became widely popular beginning in the 1840s. It was bought by the *New York Tribune* in 1924. See Crouthamel, *Bennett's New York Herald and the Rise of the Popular Press*.

59. This message is most likely the inaugural address of President Franklin D. Pierce, which Pierce recited from memory on March 4, 1853. It was published in the *New York Herald* as "Inaugural Address" on March 5, 1853.

60. Opium is a drug derived from poppies that has been used for centuries. It has medicinal properties but is addictive and has numerous negative health effects. In the eighteenth century, smoking opium became popular in China, and Chinese officials recognized that it was addictive and had many undesirable consequences. They began making increasingly strict laws against the drug, and in 1813, smoking opium was completely banned. The British objected to these laws

Here are quartered about 1,000 or 1,200 troops of the lower order of English regiments made up of Irish and Scotch, though mostly Irish, with a regiment from the island of Ceylon[61] (blacks). Owing to the heat of the climate, they are only allowed out of barracks in the evening from six to eight o'clock, when they throng the places of prostitution, made so easy of access by license from authority.[62] The city of Hong Kong has probably 10,000 inhabitants of a motley mixture of all nations; of these, it is said, 6,000 are licensed prostitutes. There are about 250 English aside from the troops stationed here; they are the aristocratic nabobs,[63] who reside in that country to make a fortune, and retire from business as soon as this is accomplished.

The vessels in the harbor show that every nation is engaged in the China trade; from this point many ships are clearing; their loading principally consists of smuggled goods brought from other places to be shipped, and within a few years quite a trade has sprung up in granite,[64] found here

---

because they had an economic interest in opium transports. Spence, *Search for Modern China*, 130–32.

61. Ceylon is the nineteenth-century British name for the island nation of Sri Lanka, located off the southeast coast of India. It was a British colony from the beginning of the nineteenth century until 1948. Chauncey W. West and Benjamin F. Dewey spent a few weeks there in 1853, but they were not well received, and Latter-day Saint missionaries would not return until the 1970s. See chapter 7, "Chauncey West and the Siam and Hindoostan Missions," herein. *Merriam-Webster's Geographical Dictionary*, s.v. "Sri Lanka"; Britsch, *From the East*, 555; Britsch, "East India Mission of 1851–56," 157.

62. The three missionaries sent a letter to Brigham Young from San Francisco, mentioning the loose morals of the soldiers: "There are about one thousand soldiers, the most of whom are Irish & Scotch some English some Blacks, from Ceylon. They are closely kept in Barracks, having only from 5 to 8 O'[c]lock P.M. for recess. They are so fond of the Licensed priviledges formed among the Chinese women that they are as corrupt as vicious habits can make them." Hosea Stout, James Lewis, and Chapman Duncan to Brigham Young, August 27, 1853.

63. The word "nabob" refers to high-ranking people, especially British aristocrats who acquired wealth in eastern nations, usually India. *Oxford English Dictionary*, s.v. "nabob."

64. Most of Hong Kong's rocks are igneous, either from volcanoes or from cooled magma underground. During the Mesozoic Era, a convergent boundary formed, where one tectonic plate subducts beneath another. Subduction zones melt the rock underground, forming large magma chambers. Magma chambers feed volca-

in great abundance, shipped to San Francisco to beautify that city. Orders of exact breadth[,] length, and thickness are sent to build a building of any dimensions, which are finished by the Chinese so exact as to fit in every part without sound of hammer.

Here are consuls from all countries, though there are some of them more merchants than consuls, generally doing that business which pays the best. The buildings are built of stone, covered with tile, many of them large and commodious.

[James Lewis]

James Lewis to Elder George A. Smith, December 12, 1854[65]

Parowan, Dec. 12th, 1854.
Brother Geo. A. Smith,

I will again tresspass upon your time, with a few further glimpses of scenes in Asia. After our arrival, we spent a few days in trying to find a location, making our business known; for great enquiries were made regarding our business, because it was not usual for persons to visit that country for other purposes than speculation. In a short time the curiosity of the people was satisfied, and we were ranked with other missionaries. We sought a plan to live, or stay; for we found that unless a man had wherewith to pay his way at quite a high price, he could have the exquisite pleasure of starving. This we were told in plain and positive language. Our only chance was to find some liberal-minded person who cared little for popularity. One came forward, and offered us a room, and gave us much useful information regarding the usages of that country. Our room was in the third story of an old decayed mansion, a portion of which had fallen down; but, as this was

---

noes, but they can also cool over time, forming granite. In the 1850s, following the gold rush, Hong Kong began exporting many products to California, including its abundant granite, which was used for buildings and curbs. Sinn, *Pacific Crossing*, 142, 147–49.

65. James Lewis to George A. Smith, December 12, 1854, published as "Items of the China Mission," *Deseret News*, January 4, 1855.

our only chance, we felt quite at home after our removal, and thanked our benefactor, Mr. [George] Dudell, for he proved friendly to us while we remained in that land.[66] The next business was to find a place to preach; after trying, we found our only chance was the street. Previous to this, we had visited the American consul, Mr. Anthony, who treated us respectfully, saying he knew our principles, and presumed we should have poor success in China; yet he would extend to us all the protection he could; thought we should not be molested, should have to preach in the streets; did not seem to desire we should renew our visit. We visited a number of clergymen of the Baptist and Methodist order,[67] but aside from courtesy it was a mere blank. Our only dependance was in the God of Israel, who sent us; for, thus far, nothing presented any encouragement. The weather was intensely hot.[68] In the middle of the day, the streets were deserted. The soldiers were not allowed out of barracks[,] only from 6 to 8 o'clock p.m. This was the time we fixed upon to preach, and the spot selected was the parade ground.[69] Our appointment being advertized, we began to deliver

---

66. George Duddell (1821–87) was a prominent English auctioneer and landowner in Hong Kong, living there for about thirty years. In 1845, he held a monopoly on the opium trade, and he later also ran a bakery, an icehouse, and other business endeavors. Duddell Street in Hong Kong is named after him. Endacott, *Biographical Sketch-Book of Early Hong Kong*, 152–54; Cameron, *Hong Kong*, 68–70.

  Hosea Stout said this about Mr. Duddell: "Here let me make honorable mention of Mr. George Duddell who furnishes us a house gratis with an ample suit of rooms, where we are happily keeping bachelors hall. He can emphatically be called the first disinterested friend of the China mission, found here." Hosea Stout to Brigham Young, May 16, 1853.

67. The Treaty of Nanking opened up China to Protestant missionaries, who had only been present in limited numbers before then. Baptists opened chapels in Hong Kong as early as 1842, and other churches followed. The Church of England became a prominent church since it was the state church of the British. Welsh, *History of Hong Kong*, 219.

68. During the month of May (when the missionaries spent most of their time proselytizing), Hong Kong currently has high temperatures in the 80s to 90s Fahrenheit (20s to 30s Celsius) with more than 80 percent humidity. The climate was likely slightly different in 1853.

69. The Murray Parade Ground was named after Sir George Murray. It was located next to the army barracks in northern Hong Kong Island. The parade ground is

our message to them; our meetings at first were well attended for that country, where it is not expected that a congregation in the finest chapels will be over fifteen or twenty at most. The people seemed satisfied, yet they said it was not what they expected to hear, for they anticipated an expose of spiritual wives, &c. When they heard the first principles of the gospel, of the re-organization of the church and kingdom of God, they felt disappointed. Our appointments extended to three evenings per week; a few came to our room to inquire more fully into our doctrines, they said, but intending to convince us of our errors; few came oftener than once.

Our object now was to gather all the information we could concerning the language of the Chinese, of their manners and customs, and the extent of the revolution going on in the interior;[70] for this purpose we visited many of them, who could speak a little English. They seemed anxious to know why we came to that country to teach them, when those who could understand and speak our language would not believe us. What reason we had to expect them to believe what we told them, when they could not understand

---

occupied by a Hilton hotel today. Bard, *Voices of the Past*, 210; Snow, *Fall of Hong Kong*, 132.

70. In a letter to Brigham Young, Hosea Stout had this to say about why they didn't preach in China's interior: "Taking all things into consideration, the whole country is in quite a state of excitement, and is considered unsafe to penetrate the interior and even here [in Hong Kong] they say they do not feel very secure." Hosea Stout to Brigham Young, May 16, 1853.

The three missionaries gave this explanation: "We looked to the other parts of China, true we had the privilege of visiting them but what the chance of success? The only safe place was Hong Kong owing to the Revolution spreading through that country. At many of these places the whites were preparing to leave or going on board vessels in the harbor for protection. To go among the Chinese we could not, not being able [to] speak their Language. Thus things continued till we felt that nothing more could be done at present. We could neither turn to the right or left, and having scanty means to remain and no possible resource perceivable for subsistence and the way opened for us to return to this point, where we could wait the counsel of the Presidency regarding our future movements. The Language is only obtained from a living tongue as it cannot be expressed in English owing to the intonations and inflexion of the voice in the same word, for upon the sounds depends the meaning." Hosea Stout, James Lewis, and Chapman Duncan to Brigham Young, August 27, 1853.

us. They seemed to wonder that we did not come as other missionaries, with plenty of money to sustain ourselves, and not become a burden.

In the meantime the editors began an attack upon us, by telling the stories of the Judges,[71] copying from the Tribune, N. Y. Advocate, &c., while other editors stood aloof.[72] The people cared so little for anything in

---

71. These "stories of the Judges" refer to the publications of the "runaway officials" of 1851. When President Millard Fillmore created Utah Territory in 1850, he appointed Brigham Young governor, but he appointed a few non–Latter-day Saints in other positions in Utah: Lemuel G. Brandebury as chief justice of the Supreme Court, Perry E. Brocchus as associate justice of the Supreme Court, and Broughton D. Harris as territorial secretary. Six weeks after the last of these three arrived in Utah, they abandoned their positions and addressed a letter to President Fillmore, claiming the Latter-day Saints in Utah were seditious. They also publicized the practice of polygamy, even before the Latter-day Saints publicly acknowledged it. The officials' claims were published in many newspapers. "Report of Messrs. Brandebury, Brocchus, and Harris, to the President of the United States," in *Utah*, 8–22; Whittaker, "Early Mormon Pamphleteering," 117–18.

72. Hosea Stout recorded this in his journal: "Went to see Mr. Dixon, who showed me this morning paper (Friend of china) containing three lengthy bursts against 'Mormonism.' The first in substance was the stale and discarded account of the celebrated fugitive U. S. officers.

"The Second was a fresh *estampede* from the 'N. Y. Tribune' who had worked himself up into a strange state of excitement least the Mormons should overthrow the U. S. Government by the dangerous & as he says, the newly developed doctrine of Patriarchal Matrimony, and loudly calling on the U. S. to look out and take immediate measures to put a stop to our successful career which is taking deep root in the four quarters of the world.

"The third is from a Religious paper (Advocate & Reflector) which quotes from O. Pratts paper at Washington (The seer) showing the *modus operandi* of a '*Mormon second marriage.*' He is also awfully alarmed and denounces us most unmeasuredly but produces no argument to expose our errors. . . .

"Attended the Theatre at 8 p.m. with C. Duncan while there a singular circumstance occured: a few Persians some of whom was present at our last lecture, were there. One of them came to me and introducing himself, enquired when we would have another lecture. . . . He then spake to the rest of his countrymen in their own language after which he said to me that he was telling them that we were the men who lectured and that we believed in having more than one wife, and they desired to know more about it.

"We never had mentioned the subject but it has been humbuged to day through

the shape of religion, that seldom anything respecting it was allowed. They told us, when speaking upon the subject, that they did not want to hear anything of the system. Our congregations in the meantime were reduced to a cipher—no one attending. We then began to visit the people individually, so that we might clear our garments,[73] and bear a faithful testimony, after having travelled so far. The heat of the atmosphere was very oppressive. Being reduced in bad health, owing to change of diet, the manner of preparing it, &c., our spirits were, becoming depressed, and not perceiving a cheering ray of hope in all our labors. Our books were loaned, and returned without thanks; our endeavors to teach the way of life and salvation was unheeded by the Americans and English. The soldiers turned away because of their officers, and we seemed alone; yet, our hearts were comforted, that bread cast upon the waters might be found after many days.[74]

Health, peace, and happiness are with, and around us. My regards to yourself and family, and my prayer for the faithful in Jesus Christ, our Lord.

Respectfully, &c.,
James Lewis.

this city in consequence of what came out in the papers as above and to day the Persians has been informed on the subject by those who are opposed to us which has had the effect to make them believe we are correct." Hosea Stout, reminiscences and journals, May 21, 1853.

73. This idea is one that is exemplified in the Book of Mormon. Jacob 1:19 says, "And we did magnify our office unto the Lord, taking upon us the responsibility, answering the sins of the people upon our own heads if we did not teach them the word of God with all diligence; wherefore, by laboring with our might their blood might not come upon our garments; otherwise their blood would come upon our garments, and we would not be found spotless at the last day."

74. This phrase comes from Ecclesiastes 11:1: "Cast thy bread upon the waters: for thou shalt find it after many days."

James Lewis to George A. Smith, February 16, 1855[75]

Parowan, Feb. 16, 1855.
Bro. Geo. A. Smith:—

After having visited the people, and, as far as possible, introduced the subject of our mission, we were politely informed, in most instances, that they did not wish to hear of our religion, and desired no reference to the subject. Upon other topics they were free and sociable, but felt to wonder at our presumption in endeavoring to establish our doctrines in Asia under the circumstances in which we placed ourselves; for they looked upon any person in a dependent position as worthy of no regard whatever, & beneath their notice. The other missionaries presented themselves backed by the God of this world,[76] and were received with courtesy and respect, as desirable acquisitions to society; but the servants of the Lord were despised, their company not desired, and their doctrine unheeded by even the lowest caste of the English and American population.

China contains a population of 367 millions, and connect Japan and other countries contiguous to China, and though they have different dialects, about 500 millions of the human race have the same written language.[77] The government of China is Patriarchal, and the religion of their leaders or officers of government is observed by all classes, and the presumption is, that when their leaders change the lower classes will change also. The religion of China is Buddhism,[78] and was introduced by

---

75. James Lewis to George A. Smith, February 16, 1855, published as "China Mission," *Deseret News*, March 14, 1855.

76. In the 1850s, the expression "God of this world" referred either to Satan, as used in 2 Corinthians 4:4, or to money. Davies, *Corpus of LDS General Conference Talks*, s.v. "god of this world."

77. There are many varieties of Chinese that are very different in their spoken form but that use the same writing system. The Japanese borrowed the Chinese *kanji* or characters and modified them to their own use.

78. Buddhism began in India around the fifth century BC and was brought to China by monks about five centuries later. It became very popular after about another five centuries, starting in the 600s AD. It grew continually as monks traveled between India and China, translating sacred texts and spreading ideas. *Oxford Dictionary of World Religions*, s.vv. "Buddhism," "Buddhism in China."

the Tartars[79] at the time the Dynasty was changed, and they became masters of the country, and required the Chinese to wear "tails" as a token of submission;[80] this transpired about 180 years ago. The present revolution is to throw off the Tartar yoke, and return to the religion of their Fathers, (however upon this point there is much speculation.) Yet it is confidently asserted that the present leader of the rebel party claims to be inspired by his Father, (the Almighty) with revelation to rid his country of the Tartars; and it is reported by the missionaries that he believes in visions, dreams, &c. They hold that we are of the same family of spirits, are brethren and sisters, and that Jesus Christ was our brother, and was sent forth to do good to his brethren, and to do what his Father commanded him; so they believe that the present leader is sent forth by his Father to do a great work. They are far from being an ignorant people; the arts and sciences flourish in their way, and their paintings, and mechanical ingenuity in the manufacture of articles more various perhaps than any other country will rank them not behind many nations who boast of their superiority. Their great skill is displayed in imitation which they can accomplish to perfection. The country is not of greater extent than the United States, and to support such a vast population farming must be admirably conducted. They have a mountainous country, and the surface is tilled to their very tops. Much of the soil is irrigated, and produces in great abundance. The principal diet is rice, and other vegetables. They are a quiet and harmless people, and do not interfere with their neighbors. A short time ago the ruins of a church, or synagog[u]e, were discovered near the centre of the empire, in which the books of Moses were found, and sent to England by the missionaries.[81]

---

79. The Tartars mentioned here are the Manchus, a nomadic group who invaded the Ming dynasty during the seventeenth century and overthrew it, establishing the Qing dynasty. They enforced many of their Manchu customs on the Chinese, but over the centuries the Manchus merged with the Chinese. Spence, *Search for Modern China*, 21–48; *Oxford Dictionary of World History*, s.v. "Manchus."

80. These "tails" are queues, long braids worn on the back of the head. They were part of Manchurian culture, and the Manchus imposed the practice on the Chinese when they established the Qing dynasty. The queue was abandoned in the twentieth century. Spence, *Search for Modern China*, 29, 252–53.

81. Judaism had a presence in the city of Kaifeng, China, at least since the twelfth century AD. In 1850 and 1851, some Christian Chinese missionaries traveled to

Chinese history shows that their religion was formerly so much like that of the Jews, that they say the Jews took the form of religion from them.

When I reflect that this vast portion of the human race have the same characters for a language, with a history for so many years back, and comparatively so little known, I am led to wonder, and acknowledge the hand of God in this for some wise purpose.

Respectfully,
James Lewis.

Kaifeng to preach to the Jews there, and they purchased many sacred texts, as well as documents relating to the history of the Kaifeng synagogues. The Torah scrolls that those missionaries acquired might have been copied in the seventeenth century; these writings ended up in various locations. Tokayer and Rodman, *Pepper, Silk & Ivory*, 69–75.

7

CHAUNCEY WEST AND THE
SIAM AND HINDOOSTAN MISSIONS

Historical Introduction

"I CANNOT SAY THAT WE HAVE DONE ANY VERY GREAT THINGS during our mission," Chauncey Walker West reported after returning from his 1852–55 mission to Asia, "but this much I can say, we have done the best that we knew how."[1] From the perspective of gaining converts to the restored gospel, West was right. He did not record baptizing large numbers of converts,[2] and his attempts at preaching were met with great opposition. He had been called to Siam (modern-day Thailand),[3] but he didn't even

---

1. Chauncey W. West to *Deseret News*, "The India Mission, Letter No. 5," *Deseret News*, November 14, 1855. See also Britsch, "The Nobility of Failure," 253–56.

2. West's personal writings do not explicitly mention baptizing anyone, but historian Edward Tullidge recorded that he baptized Martin A. Bransin in Bombay on August 6, 1853. Tullidge, *Tullidge's Histories*, 59, biographical appendix.

3. Siam, known today as Thailand, is a peninsular country in Southeast Asia. It has been populated by, and has fought with, other nearby nations for centuries, and

Chauncey West. Courtesy of Church History Library.

make it to his assigned field of labor during nearly three years away from home. But even though he did not see the proselytizing successes he had hoped for, he saw cultures and places unfamiliar to most nineteenth-century Americans and his fellow Latter-day Saints. West made sacrifices to leave his young family behind in the new Utah Territory, and he traveled by wagon to California, then by ship across the Pacific Ocean to India. He and his companion, Benjamin F. Dewey, were the first Latter-day Saint missionaries to preach in the island nation of Ceylon (modern-day Sri Lanka).[4] On his return, he had a harrowing journey through the coral reefs of Southeast Asia and made a stop in China. Fellow Latter-day Saints regarded these accomplishments as "a great and good work."[5]

Chauncey West's Early Life, 1827–52

Born on February 8, 1827, in Erie County, Pennsylvania, Chauncey

France and other European countries have had a presence there since the seventeenth century. Beginning in 1851, King Mongkut ruled Siam and made significant changes. Although the country has undergone many governmental modifications, it is still a kingdom today. *Oxford Dictionary of World History*, s.v. "Thailand."

4. Ceylon, known today as Sri Lanka, is located off the southeast coast of India. In the fifth century BC, Indians assimilated with the aboriginal population of Sri Lanka to form the Sinhalese population. Sinhalese power ebbed and flowed for millennia until the Portuguese and Dutch took control in the sixteenth and seventeenth centuries. The British renamed it Ceylon in 1796 and made it a colony in the early 1800s. Sri Lanka was granted independence in 1948. *Merriam-Webster's Geographical Dictionary*, s.v. "Sri Lanka."

5. West, "India Mission, Letter No. 5"; p. 256 herein.

Walker West was baptized at age sixteen and moved with his family in 1844 to Nauvoo, Illinois, where he was ordained a seventy at age seventeen. In 1846, he married Mary Hoagland, and his family left Nauvoo. His parents and his older brother died in Winter Quarters, Nebraska, so he and Mary brought his three younger siblings (ages sixteen, thirteen, and five) to Utah, where they arrived in October 1847.[6]

Having traveled west in the first year of Latter-day Saint settlement, Chauncey West became involved in many of the important aspects of building up the new territory. In the spring of 1849, he was one of many people sent to establish Fort Utah (now Provo).[7] Later that year, President Brigham Young sent Apostle Parley P. Pratt to explore new places in southern Utah for settlement. West was part of this expedition, which suffered hardships due to the cold and snow. In January 1850, this group was low on provisions, so Pratt and West traveled swiftly to Fort Utah to send supplies and a rescue party to the rest of the team.[8] After returning from this exploring mission, West continued to live in Salt Lake City.[9]

A History of the India Mission

While Latter-day Saints were relocating from the Midwest and colonizing Utah, they were still spreading their faith around the world. In 1849, British converts George Barber and Benjamin Richey had arrived in Calcutta,[10] India, as sailors and began informally preaching the doctrines of the restored gospel. Following a request from these two sailors, Joseph Richards was sent on a mission to India and arrived in 1851. He baptized a few

6. West, *Chauncey W. West*, 1–9.

7. Tullidge, *Tullidge's Histories*, 56.

8. Smart and Smart, *Over the Rim*, 12, 141–42, 185.

9. West, *Chauncey W. West*, 10–11.

10. Calcutta is an important port town in northeast India. It was occupied by the British from the seventeenth to twentieth centuries. Latter-day Saint missionaries were sent there beginning in 1851, and they were moderately successful, baptizing nearly two hundred people by May 1852. The missionaries mentioned in West's letters were called there in 1852 and labored over the next few years, but the native Indian converts did not stay in the church. *Merriam-Webster's Geographical Dictionary*, s.v. "Calcutta;" Britsch, *From the East*, 8–11, 17–28.

converts and established a branch.[11] In early 1851, Apostle Lorenzo Snow, who was laboring in Italy, sent William Willis and Hugh Findlay[12] to India[13] and Thomas Lorenzo Obray to Malta.[14] Snow had intended to go to India himself, but the vessel he was going to take was damaged.[15] In the spring of 1852, he was called back to church headquarters in Utah along with the other Apostles evangelizing in Europe. Before he left, he expressed his hope that missionary work might spread beyond its Italian mission headquarters. That May, Snow asked the European Saints for additional missionaries for

Hugh Findlay, one of the first Latter-day Saint missionaries to enter India. Public domain.

Bombay, India, before departing for Utah.[16] By May 1852, there were some church members around Calcutta, and Hugh Findlay established a small branch at Poona in September 1852.[17]

Chauncey West's Mission to Asia, 1852–55

Lorenzo Snow's hopes of expanding missionary work in India were realized when the First Presidency called a special missionary conference in Salt Lake City in August 1852. Nine missionaries were called to India: Nathaniel V. Jones, Amos Milton Musser, Truman Leonard, Samuel Amos

---

11. Britsch, *From the East*, 8–13.

12. Hugh Findlay (1822–1900) was born in Scotland and was baptized there in 1844. In 1851, he was assigned as a missionary to India, arriving there in June 1852. He migrated to Utah in 1855, and in 1878, he returned to his native Scotland as a missionary. He died in Fish Haven, Idaho, in 1900. Neilson and Waite, *Settling the Valley, Proclaiming the Gospel*, 308.

13. See Britsch, "East India Mission of 1851–56," 150–76; and Britsch, *Nothing More Heroic*.

14. See Jenson, *Encyclopedic History of the Church*, 465–66.

15. Whittaker, "Richard Ballantyne and the Defense of Mormonism in India in the 1850s," 179–80.

16. Lorenzo Snow to Samuel W. Richards, May 1, 1852, published as Lorenzo Snow, "The Malta Mission: Letter from Elder Lorenzo Snow," *Millennial Star* 14, no. 15 (June 5, 1852): 236–37.

17. Britsch, *From the East*, 8–13.

Woolley, William Fotheringham, William F. Carter, Richard Ballantyne, Robert Skelton, and Robert Owens. Four others were called to go to Siam: Chauncey W. West (as president of the mission), Benjamin F. Dewey, Elam Luddington, and Levi Savage Jr.[18]

Benjamin Franklin Dewey was born in Massachusetts in 1829 and was baptized in 1847, just before traveling with Brigham Young's pioneering company to the Salt Lake Valley. In 1849, he accompanied Jefferson Hunt's wagon train that escorted gold-seeking emigrants to California,[19] and he returned to Utah in 1850.[20] Elam Luddington was born in 1806 and baptized in 1840; he served as a lieutenant in the Mormon Battalion.[21] Levi Savage was born in Ohio in 1820 and was baptized in 1846; he was also a member of the Mormon Battalion and arrived in the Salt Lake Valley in October 1847. He married Jane Mathers in 1848, and she died in 1851. Savage left his one-year-old son in the care of his sister Hannah Eldredge when he left on his mission.[22]

Of the four missionaries called to Siam, Elam Luddington was the only one who actually made it to his assigned mission. Complications from the Anglo-Burmese War[23] and ship schedules prohibited the missionaries from going there, even though West tried repeatedly. West and Dewey preached on Ceylon, but financial constraints prohibited Luddington and Levi Savage from joining them. All four of the elders preached in various parts of

---

18. The conference minutes only list Chauncey West and a Sterne Hotchkiss as being called to Siam. It is not clear why or at what point Hotchkiss was replaced by Dewey, Luddington, and Savage. "Minutes of Conference," *Deseret News Extra*, September 14, 1852; appendix 1, p. 306 herein.

19. Some of these prospectors left Hunt's company to travel through Death Valley, enduring ordeals that gave the region its name. Smart and Smart, *Over the Rim*, 83.

20. Jenson, *Latter-day Saint Biographical Encyclopedia*, 4:698; Sutak, "Jefferson Hunt," 86.

21. Britsch, *Nothing More Heroic*, 286–87.

22. Britsch, *Nothing More Heroic*, 291.

23. The First Anglo-Burmese War occurred in the 1820s, and the Second Anglo-Burmese War began in 1852, when the East India Company complained of grievances committed by the Burmese, although it is in question whether such grievances occurred. The war formally ended in early 1853, when the British claimed territory from Burma without a treaty. Pollak, "Mid-Victorian Coverup," 171–83.

India for a time. Proselytizing in these locations was no easy task. Christian missionaries had incited the local populations against the Latter-day Saints for aspects of their peculiar doctrine, especially plural marriage. The missionaries were often forbidden from preaching to British soldiers. And native Indians would be outcasts and outcastes if they became Latter-day Saints, so they would only stick to this new faith if they were paid to do so—which was impossible for these moneyless missionaries to accommodate.[24] After West and Dewey left, Savage and Luddington stayed behind and preached in Burma (Myanmar).[25] Luddington did eventually make it to Siam, but his only converts were the ship's captain and his wife.[26]

Meanwhile, West and Dewey had a harrowing time making their way back to America. For a time, they worked as sailors for their passage. The ships they traveled on passed through dangerous reef areas in Southeast Asia, and it was a great task to keep the vessels from wrecking on the jagged coral. Dewey was also sick for a great deal of the journey. The missionaries stopped for a time in China, hoping to meet the three elders who had been called to labor there (Hosea Stout, James Lewis, and Chapman Duncan); however, those three had already left Asia due to immense social difficul-

24. India has a caste structure, in which people are born into different ranks of society, each rank being responsible for different tasks. The practice originated with the varna of Hindu religion, which consisted of four different orders: Brahmans, Kshatriyas, Vaisyas, and Sudras; there was also a pseudo-caste, the untouchables. Earlier Christian missionaries had observed that when the natives had converted to Christianity, they were cast out of their castes and societies. Out of goodwill, the missionaries would then employ and pay the converts so that they could live. This led to natives choosing a denomination based on how well it paid. The caste system has changed through the centuries, but it still exists. *Oxford Dictionary of World Religions*, s.vv. "caste," "Varna"; Britsch, *From the East*, 26–27.

25. Burma, whose name changed to Myanmar in 1989, is located in Southeast Asia and is bordered by India, China, and Thailand (formerly known as Siam). In 1852, Matthew McCune and William Adams, Latter-day Saint converts in the British-Indian Army, were sent to Rangoon, Burma, where they preached to their military unit. They established a small branch among soldiers, but they had an extremely hard time preaching to native Burmese. McCune and his family left in 1856 to go to Utah. *Merriam-Webster's Geographical Dictionary*, s.v. "Myanmar"; Britsch, *From the East*, 30–33.

26. Britsch, "East India Mission of 1851–56," 157–58.

ties. While in China, West and Dewey had a few premonitions that might have saved their lives: they left a hotel just before a massive boulder landed on it and killed many inside, and they opted not to board a ship that was soon shipwrecked.[27]

After crossing the Pacific and arriving in California in September 1854, West visited many of the missionaries and settlements in the area until he headed home for Utah the following spring. He arrived in Salt Lake City on July 15, 1855.

Additional Church Service, 1855–70

After returning to Utah in 1855, West played an important part in the church and Utah Territory. He moved to Ogden, about forty miles north of Salt Lake City, where he became a prominent member of the community, building several mills, constructing roads and canals, and serving as presiding bishop of Weber County.[28] In 1857, West was in charge of a regiment of the Weber Military District, and that fall he led units from Ogden to Echo Canyon to block a federal militia sent by President James Buchanan from entering Utah.[29]

The mission to Asia was not to be West's only international mission. In 1862, William H. Hooper and George Q. Cannon were elected as senators from Utah Territory, and they were sent to Washington, DC, to petition for statehood. Church leaders called West to temporarily take over the responsibilities of Cannon, who was president of the European Mission. West traveled with Hooper to New York and then to Washington, DC, where he met President Abraham Lincoln[30] before continuing to England. The

27. "The India Mission, Letter No. 3," *Deseret News*, September 26, 1855; "The India Mission, Letter No. 4," *Deseret News*, October 24, 1855; "India Mission, Letter No. 5"; pp. 230–56 herein.

28. West, *Chauncey W. West*, 16–17; Jenson, *Latter-day Saint Biographical Encyclopedia*, 1:751; Tullidge, *Tullidge's Histories*, 63–64.

29. Roberts and Sadler, *History of Weber County*, 94–95, 100.

30. In a letter to Brigham Young, West nonchalantly recorded "making ma[n]y acquaintance including that of President Lincen." West left New York and joined Hooper and Cannon in Washington because Cannon thought his congressional business would soon finish and that he and West could travel to England together. However, since there were "no prospects that Congress would adjourn soon," West

mission was based out of Liverpool, England, but West also visited France, Germany, Switzerland, Italy, Prussia, Denmark, and Sweden in company with Brigham Young Jr.[31] He returned to Utah in the fall of 1863.[32] In 1866, the Deseret Telegraph Company completed a telegraph line from Salt Lake City to Ogden, and its first message was from Brigham Young to Bishop West and stake president Lorin Farr.[33]

Ogden became the terminus for the Transcontinental Railroad in 1869, and the construction of the railroad gave West some interesting opportunities. Chauncey West and Lorin Farr contracted with the Central Pacific Railroad to employ two thousand men to build the railroad east from Humboldt Wells, Nevada. West was present on May 10, 1869, when the railroad was completed at Promontory Summit.[34] As Latter-day Saints who were gathering to Zion began to travel by train, West was responsible to help supply them with comforts and provisions as they arrived.[35] While working on the railroad, he got sick, so in late 1869 he and his first wife, Mary, traveled

returned to New York to sail to Liverpool. Chauncey W. West to Brigham Young, July 12, 1862, Incoming Correspondence, Brigham Young Office Files.

George Q. Cannon, John M. Bernhisel, William H. Hooper, and Brigham Young Jr. were also part of the group that met Lincoln. At this time, events were taking place that made the church in Utah ambivalent toward Lincoln and his administration. In April 1862, Brigham Young received a telegram from the War Department asking him to send a group to help protect the mail route and the new transcontinental telegraph line. This indicated the president's trust. However, in July 1862, Lincoln signed the Morrill Anti-Bigamy Act, making polygamy illegal, a great blow to the Latter-day Saints. However, by the time of Lincoln's assassination in 1865, their opinion of him was more favorable, in part because he did not enforce the new polygamy laws, likely because of the Civil War. Journal of George Q. Cannon, June 13, 1862; Hubbard, "Abraham Lincoln as Seen by the Mormons," 99–101; Vitale, "Abraham Lincoln and the Mormons," 267.

31. Journal History, October 7, 1863, 2; Tullidge, *Tullidge's Histories*, 65.
32. West apparently didn't serve as mission president for very long. He arrived in Liverpool on July 4, 1862, but Cannon returned and resumed his duties later that same month. West did, however, continue to assist Cannon in his responsibilities, including taking over when Cannon was visiting elsewhere in Europe. Jenson, *Latter-day Saint Biographical Encyclopedia*, 1:47, 752; Tullidge, *Tullidge's Histories*, 65.
33. Arrington, "Deseret Telegraph," 125.
34. "The Proceedings at Promontory Summit," *Deseret News*, May 19, 1869.
35. Cannon, "Change Engulfs a Frontier Settlement," 21, 23.

to California to conduct railroad business, hoping his health would improve in the coastal climate, but he died there on January 9, 1870, at the age of forty-two. Mary died soon thereafter at forty-one.[36] Some traditional stories claim that the town of Farr West, created in 1890 from Harrisville in Weber County, Utah, was named for Lorin Farr and Chauncey West.[37]

As for the other missionaries called to Siam, Benjamin Dewey became a miner and died in the mining community of Chloride, Arizona, in 1904.[38] Levi Savage circumnavigated the world on his return from Asia and became famous for being a captain in the Willie Handcart Company, advising against travel late in the season but supporting the ill-fated pioneers on their journey; he was a farmer and died in Toquerville, Utah, in 1910.[39] Elam Luddington was also a farmer until he died in Salt Lake City in 1893.[40]

Chauncey West's Family Life

Chauncey West married Mary Hoagland, the sister-in-law of George Q. Cannon, in May 1846, and they had a daughter, Margaret, while crossing the plains to Utah. Margaret died as an infant, but Chauncey and Mary had two sons, Chauncey Jr. and Joseph, in their first few years in Salt Lake City.[41] Immediately before leaving on his mission, West sold some of his property to his father-in-law, Abraham Hoagland, who was bishop of the Fourteenth Ward.[42] Little is known about their family life during West's

---

36. West, *Chauncey W. West*, 30; Jenson, *Latter-day Saint Biographical Encyclopedia*, 1:753; "Death of Bishop C. W. West," *Deseret News*, January 12, 1870; Tullidge, *Tullidge's Histories*, 66–67.

37. Taylor, *History of Farr West*, 10. The "West" in the name might have simply come from the town being located west of the earlier settlement of Farr's Fort. Van Cott, *Utah Place Names*, 134.

38. Jenson, *Latter-day Saint Biographical Encyclopedia*, 4:698.

39. Britsch, *Nothing More Heroic*, 291; see Christy, "Weather, Disaster, and Responsibility," 6–74.

40. Britsch, *Nothing More Heroic*, 286–87.

41. "Chauncey Walker West," *Utah Genealogical and Historical Magazine* 2 (January 1911): 9.

42. Salt Lake Recorder's Office, Deeds, 1850–1877, October 13, 1852, 7; Salt Lake City Fourteenth Ward plat map, undated, in Bullock, collection, box 10, folder 10;

absence, but it is supposable that Hoagland and his wife, Margaret, were able to oversee Mary and the two young West sons.

After his return, West married eight more wives: Sarah Covington in 1855, Martha Joiner in 1856, Jenette Nichol Gibson in 1857, Adeline A. Wright in 1858, Angeline Shurtliff in 1866, Mary Ann Covington, Susan H. Covington in 1867, and Louisa Musgrave at an unknown date. He had a total of thirty-five children with all nine wives, nineteen of them living to maturity.[43]

Source Note

Chauncey West wrote five letters about his mission to the *Deseret News*, which were published between August 11 and November 14, 1855. The letters describe a chronological narrative of his mission: the journey to California, sailing across the Pacific and Indian Oceans, proselytizing in India and Ceylon (Sri Lanka), perilous sailing through Southeast Asia and a stop in Hong Kong, and traveling back to Utah. West's writing style is entertaining and even amusing, as he vividly describes such events as monkeys "show[ing] off their gymnastics among the trees" and "the sun hot enough to bake one's brains."[44] It is obvious that the *Deseret News* edited his letters, as West's journal entries and holograph letters have largely nonstandard spelling and grammar; some of his relevant journal entries have been provided in the footnotes, mostly unedited.

Jenson, *Latter-day Saint Biographical Encyclopedia*, 2:364–65.

43. West, *Chauncey W. West*, 32; "Chauncey Walker West," 9–10.

44. West, "India Mission, Letter No. 3"; p. 236 herein.

DOCUMENT TRANSCRIPTS

Chauncey W. West to the Deseret News, August 11, 1855[45]

G[reat]. S[alt]. L[ake]. City, August 11, 1855

At a Special Conference held in Great Salt Lake City, Aug. 28, 1852, we were appointed a mission (in connection with Elders Elam Ludington and Levi Savage)[46] to Asia, the Kingdom of Siam being our place of destination.

On the 20th day of October we bid adieu to our families,[47] friends, and the lovely city of the saints, and started on our mission, being accompanied by 34 other missionaries for different nations of the earth.

We passed thro' the southern settlements in the Territory, holding meetings with the saints.[48] We found them united, and the Spirit of God was in their midst, and they felt their interests were identified with ours in building up the Kingdom of our God. As we were about to leave them, they brought forward their grain for us to feed our animals while crossing the deserts, and oft they would bring more than we could carry. We felt to say in our hearts, may God bless such brethren.

We left Cedar city Nov. 8; had a good time crossing the plains and deserts. December 3, arrived at San Bernardino; found the saints all well, and rejoicing in the truth, glad to make us welcome to their homes and

---

45. Chauncey W. West to *Deseret News*, "The India Mission, [Letter No. 1]," *Deseret News*, August 29, 1855.

46. Perhaps by "we" West was referring to himself and Benjamin F. Dewey, the other missionary assigned to Siam.

47. West left his family affairs in the hands of his cousin Israel Canfield. Chauncey W. West to Israel Canfield, February 9, 1853, in West, journals, 13. West's journal consists of diary entries in the front and a letter book in the back. The journal entries do not have page numbers, but the letters do. We have provided dates for West's journal, and both a date and a page number for letters.

48. They visited the settlements of Nephi, Fillmore, Parowan, and Cedar City. Journal History, October 20, 1852, 2.

firesides, the few days we might stay with them.

Dec. 19, we bid the saints of San Bernardino farewell, and were accompanied by the brethren to San Pedro, a distance of 90 miles. Dec. 29, took passage for San Francisco on board the brig Fremont, in command of Capt. [John] Erskine. Jan. 7, arrived there, and on the 9th, leaving Elder Dewey and others in San Francisco, took steamer for Sacramento city.

From thence I traveled on foot to Mormon Island, Salmon Falls, Greenwood Valley, Mud Spring, Dimond Springs, Hangtown, and Prairie City,[49] holding several meetings by the way; found a number of brethren from the Valley, who contributed liberally to assist on our journey to San Francisco.[50]

Jan. 29 [*sic*], returned to San Francisco. On inquiring for a vessel sailing direct to Siam, we could find none. We were informed by an old sea captain that the only and best way for us would be to sail to the city of Calcutta, and from thence take the overland route thro' the kingdom of Burmah to Siam.

Jan. 28, we took passage in company with the Hindostan Mission, on the ship Monsoon of Boston, Capt. Z. Winzon, for Calcutta. Saturday, 29, weighed anchor, made sail, and bid our native land farewell. Feb. 10, passed the Sandwich Islands, being the quickest passage ever known to those Islands.

March 1, we neared Farewell, on D. Toon's Island, one of the Ladrone

---

49. These towns were gold-rush settlements in central California. Some of them were abandoned, while some of them are still around today; for example, Hangtown is known today as Placerville, the county seat of El Dorado County. Mormon Island was named for the large number of Latter-day Saints from the Mormon Battalion who were in the area at the time of the gold rush. They stayed in California near Sutter's Fort to construct mills. Mormon Island was not a natural island. It was located at a curve in the American River; the north, east, and west sides of the "island" were bounded by the river, while the south side was a man-made canal. *Merriam-Webster's Geographical Dictionary*, s.v. "Placerville"; Berthold, *Story of Mormon Island*.

50. While West was in the mining towns, he preached at several meetings. In a letter to Abraham Hoagland, he recorded: "After I had finished my discourse, and was about to dismiss the meeting a gentleman rose up in the congrigation, and and motioned that thare be a contribution raised to assist me on my journey they made up $72.50, and gave me." Chauncey W. West to Abraham Hoagland, January 26, 1853, in West, journals, 8.

group, in the China Sea. There is on this island a volcanic mountain 2000 feet high.[51] On the 10th we passed along the coast of Coachin China,[52] and on the 19th passed Pirto Pisscany isle,[53] in the China sea, towering 2000 feet above the water, densely crowded with a mantle of beautiful green foliage, which caused it to have a lovely appearance.

March 20, sailed into the straits of Singapore, passed the city of Singapore,[54] near sunset, which lay in the distance some 20 miles; then sailed up the straits of Malacca,[55] and on the 27th sailed into the Bay of Bengal;[56] passed mount Ophir, where it is said Solomon got his gold for ornamenting the temple of Jerusalem.[57]

---

51. The Ladrone Islands, named after a Portuguese word for thief, are known today as the Mariana Islands. They belong to the United States today, but during the 1800s they belonged to Spain. It is difficult to know what island West saw; there is currently no island named D. Toon's Island, and several islands have volcanoes that are about two thousand feet high. Ten of the Mariana Islands are volcanic and are located at the Mariana Trench, the lowest point in the ocean. One tectonic plate is being subducted beneath another, and as it does so, the water in the earth's crust reacts with the earth's mantle, causing it to melt and form magma, which in turn feeds volcanoes. *Merriam-Webster's Geographical Dictionary*, s.vv. "Mariana Islands," "Mariana Trench."

52. Cochin China is the southern portion of Vietnam. The "China" in the name was given to distinguish it from another Cochin in India. *Merriam-Webster's Geographical Dictionary*, s.v. "Cochin China"; *Oxford Dictionary of World History*, s.v. "Cochin China."

53. Pirto Pisscany could be a karst tower, a high, vertical tower made of limestone common in southeast Asia.

54. The island nation of Singapore, with its capital also called Singapore, was acquired by Britain's East India Company in 1819, and many Chinese and other immigrants thereafter populated the area. *Merriam-Webster's Geographical Dictionary*, s.v. "Singapore"; *Oxford Dictionary of World History*, s.v. "Singapore."

55. The Strait of Malacca is a passage of water between Malaysia and the Indonesian island Sumatra. *Merriam-Webster's Geographical Dictionary*, s.v. "Malacca, Strait of."

56. The Bay of Bengal is a portion of the Indian Ocean, located between eastern India and Myanmar. *Merriam-Webster's Geographical Dictionary*, s.v. "Bengal, Bay of."

57. This Mount Ophir could refer to Gunong Ledang in eastern Malaysia, or it could refer to Mount Talakmau on the island of Sumatra. It is unlikely that either of these places is the same Ophir mentioned in the Bible, from whence the navy of Hiram brought back gold, silver, and other precious items for the building of Solomon's temple (see 1 Kings 9–10). The location of the biblical Ophir is unknown.

April 7, we sailed close alongside of Barren island, on which is a volcanic mountain rising 600 feet high. On the top of this mountain are two very sharp peaks, one extending considerably above the other, out of which issues a puff of black smoke every ten minutes, then immediately changes its color to a yellow, and from that to the resemblance of steam. The lava had run from the top of the mountain into the sea, and in appearance resembled stone coal.[58]

The 12th, passed thro' the Andaman islands.[59] Sunday, 24, took a pilot at what is called the Sandheads; here we had to change day and date in journals, it being Monday, 25, in Hindostan, one day later than at home in America.[60]

I would here remark that these Sandheads are extensive deposits of sand and mud, that are continually increasing, being the settling of the muddy waters of the Hoogley.[61]—They extend into the bay about 75 miles.

[Tuesday], 26, we landed in Calcutta, being 86 days out from San Francisco, distant 11,000 miles.

We found a few saints in Calcutta, who were glad to see us and to administer to our wants.[62] The cholera was raging very much when we arrived

Merriam-Webster's Geographical Dictionary, s.vv. "Ophir," "Ophir, Mount."

58. Barren Island is located in the Andaman Islands and is an active volcano in the twenty-first century, although it did not erupt between the mid-nineteenth century and the 1990s. Its lava is generally basaltic, an iron-rich, fluid lava that is black when it cools. Valdiya, *Environmental Geology*, 367–69.

59. The Andaman Islands are located in the eastern part of the Bay of Benghal and belong to India. They have been inhabited by indigenous peoples for millennia; British colonists arrived in 1789, and they established a penal colony in 1858. *Merriam-Webster's Geographical Dictionary*, s.v. "Andaman Islands."

60. It may seem perplexing that they waited until India to change the date, but the International Dateline wasn't formally adopted internationally until 1884, so there were other time-reckoning methods during West's day. *Oxford English Dictionary*, s.v. "dateline."

61. The Hooghly River in northeast India is an important channel that branches off the Ganges River and drains into the Bay of Bengal. *Merriam-Webster's Geographical Dictionary*, s.v. "Hugli."

62. Henry McCune, the son of Latter-day Saint convert Matthew McCune, reported that as a child, he met West and the other missionaries at the wharf in Calcutta. West had experienced a dream the night before about a boy waiting for them, and when he saw young Henry, he said, "This is the little boy that I saw in my dream."

in Calcutta; several hundreds dying daily.

April 29, called on the American Consul, Mr. Hoofniele, whom we found to be very much of a gentleman. He made a great many inquiries, and conversed freely, after which he said, any favor he could bestow upon us he would gladly do; he informed us that we could not go the overland route thro' Burmah to Siam, because the East India Company were carrying on a war with the Burmese, and that no European would be allowed to pass thro' their country; he also said he thought we would be troubled to find a vessel sailing to Siam until fall, when the Monsoons would change.[63] On inquiring among the shipping we found that was the case.

The way to Siam being hedged up for a time, we tho't we would seek a field of labor in some other place. We met in council with the other elders of the mission, and it was decided that Elders Luddington and Savage should go to Burmah, and that br. B. F. Dewey should go with me to the island of Ceylon; and we were to labor in these two places until the way should open to Siam.[64]

May 7.—I left Calcutta with Elders [Truman] Leonard and [Samuel] Woolley for the city of Chincery,[65] up the Hoogley, took passage in a dinga (small native boat);[66] as we went out of the city, we passed the place where

Henry's mother had sent him to meet the elders since no one else was able to. Jenson, *Latter-day Saint Biographical Encyclopedia*, 1:750–51.

63. Monsoons usually occur in Thailand from May to October and can cause rough seas.

64. Financial limitations prevented all the missionaries from going to Ceylon: "We went to the shiping office to ingage our passage to Ceylon. We found the fair [fare] so high that we had not money sufficient to take us all, and it was imposable to get the captain to reduce the fare. We met in council and decide[d] that Elder Dewey and myself should go to Ceylon and Elders Ludington and Savage to Rangoon and labour in that country in connection with brother McCuin." Chauncey W. West to Brother Richards, June 10, 1853, in West, journals, 24.

65. Chinsura is located in northeast India and was colonized by Portuguese and Dutch explorers in the seventeenth century. Truman Leonard and Samuel Amos Woolley visited it in the 1850s, but they were forbidden from preaching in British cantonments. In 1865, Chinsura united with a neighboring town, becoming Hooghly-Chinsura. *Merriam-Webster's Geographical Dictionary*, s.v. "Hooghly-Chinsura"; Britsch, "East India Mission of 1851–56," 156, 172.

66. Dingas were boats used in India, and they had oars or sails or both. The English word *dinghy* is named for this kind of boat. *Oxford English Dictionary*, s.v. "dinghy."

the Hindoos[67] were burning their dead; the stench was awful; we could but just get our breath while passing.

The cholera and yellow fever were sweeping them off so fast that they could not obtain wood sufficient to burn them, and there were to be seen heads, arms, legs, &c., &c., scattered here and there, with the flesh partly burnt off, and the vultures in swarms eating the balance. As we went up the river, we saw hundreds of dead bodies floating down the stream; at the same time, both sides of the river were strewed with men, women and children who were bathing.[68]

We arrived at Chincery in the evening, where we found Elder Richards,[69] and a small branch of the church, waiting to receive us. I tarried three days with the brethren in Chincery, had some good meetings, which made the devil mad, and his emissaries commenced to roar.

March 10, I gave Elders Leonard and Woolley the parting hand, and took passage in a native boat, with Elder Richards for Calcutta, where we landed in the evening; found the brethren all well and in good spirits. May 15, I took passage with Elder Dewey on the steamship 'Queen of the South,' Capt. Davis, for the island of Ceylon. During the day and night five persons were thrown overboard, who died of cholera; on the 16th, nine

67. In nineteenth-century usage, "Hindoo" could refer to the native people of India or to the native religions of India. Hinduism as a religion is very diverse, but some of its common ideas are that of *dharma*, the appropriate way of living; *karma*, the notion that actions have inherent consequences for the future; and *moshka*, the end of the cycle of reincarnation. *Oxford English Dictionary*, s.v. "Hindu | Hindoo"; *Oxford Dictionary of World Religions*, s.v. "Hinduism"; *Oxford Dictionary of World History*, s.v. "Hinduism."

68. Hindus practice *Antyesti*, a sacrament in which the deceased are burned upon a funeral pyre and the cremated remains are placed in a river. Even in modern times, incomplete burnings (because of insufficient wood or money) have remained a problem, as partially consumed bodies are deposited in the water. Combatting the practice is a delicate problem, as the cremations are an important religious tradition. *Oxford Dictionary of World Religions*, s.v. "Antyeṣti, Antyeshti"; Lochtefeld, *Illustrated Encyclopedia of Hinduism*, 1:160–61.

69. Little is known about Joseph Richards, who was probably born around 1801 and was baptized in London in December 1850. He apparently did not travel to Utah and was living in New York in 1884. He likely died before 1890. Britsch, *Nothing More Heroic*, 291; Crawley, *Descriptive Bibliography of the Mormon Church*, 2:363.

more died; a general time of excitement on board. On the 17th, seven died; on the 18th five died; on the 19th, three died.

On the morning of the 20th we arrived at Madras,[70] the capital of South India.[71] We took a boat and went on shore to view the city; on arriving at the water's edge, we found a carriage waiting for us; it had been sent by Capt. Carmel, with whom we had become acquainted while on the passage; he had lost his ship a few weeks before, and was then on his way home to England. We had the carriage for the day, rode round the city and thro' its principal streets, visited two cars of the Juggernaut,[72] and many other heathen curiosities. In the evening went on board; three had died during the day.

May 21, weighed anchor and sailed for Ceylon, where we landed on the morning of the 26th. We found a great prejudice existing among the people, and they were ready to reject us. While walking from the wharf into the town, we fell in company with two gentlemen who entered into conversation with us, during which we told them we were missionaries; they seemed very much pleased to hear that, and said they welcomed us to the island, and then commenced to tell us about the great success of the missionary societies in that country; said we must go and see their minister; after which they asked to what missionary society we belonged; we told

70. Madras, known today as Chennai, is a city on the southeast coast of India, originally a British colonial city. Madras is the capital of the state of Tamil Nadu, which also was once known as Madras. Latter-day Saints Richard Ballantyne, Robert Skelton, and Robert Owens all traveled to Madras as part of their mission in India in the 1850s, but they were forbidden from preaching in cantonments and baptized only about a dozen people. *Merriam-Webster's Geographical Dictionary*, s.v. "Madras"; Britsch, "East India Mission of 1851–56," 155, 172; Jenson, *Encyclopedic History of the Church*, 458–59.

71. The city of Madras was the capital of a political division known as the Madras Presidency, which covered most of southern India from the mid-sixteenth century until the mid-twentieth century. See Thurston, *Madras Presidency*.

72. "Juggernaut" is a variant of the name *Jagannāth*, another name for the Hindu god Vishnu. Hindus hold festivals in which images of the deity are rolled out on large carts. In the late eighteenth and early nineteenth centuries, there were reports of devotees deliberately throwing themselves under the wheels of the carts; but it is more likely that these incidents were simply accidents rather than religious suicides. *Oxford English Dictionary*, s.v. "Juggernaut | Jagannāth"; *Oxford Dictionary of World Religions*, s.v. "Jagannātha."

them to the Lord's; they said they hoped all missionary societies belonged to the Lord, and wished to know to what church or faith; we told them to the Church of Jesus Christ of Latter Day Saints; at which their countenances fell, and they said, "What! not Mormons?" We told them the world gave us that name.[73]

They said they had heard all about the Mormons, and said they could assure us we would meet with great opposition; that they had a pamphlet that told all about Joe Smith and the Mormons. I will here mention that a large number of tracts had been sent from Europe and circulated among the people, filled with the most base lies and misrepresentations.[74]

---

73. Joshua V. Himes disparagingly used the expression "Mormon church" and "Mormonites" as early as 1832. Campbell, *Delusions*, 3.

74. As in other places in the world, many anti–Latter-day Saint tracts were distributed in India and the surrounding areas by various Christian denominations. These included one titled *Mormonism Unveiled* by Charles Saunder (not to be confused with the 1834 work of the same name by Eber D. Howe) and two tracts by Reverend J. Richards. Additionally, local newspapers would often publish antagonistic articles. Missionaries would try to combat the influence of these works by distributing their own tracts and by publishing rebuttals in the local newspapers. Whittaker, "Early Mormon Pamphleteering," 90–95; Crawley, *Descriptive Bibliography of the Mormon Church*, 3:81–83, 89–91.

West recorded this experience in a letter: "We went into the fort and called on several Gentleman and told them that we ware ministers of the Gospel. They seemed to be much pleased at hearing this & said they would do any thing in their power for our comfort they wished us to go and see their minister and he would call for a contribution for us. They would invite us into their houses to rest ourselves. They then would inquire to what church we belonged we would tell them at which they would seem startled and would say 'we can do nothing for you. Our ministers say are a bad people. You are Poligamist.' We also fell in with several gentlemen while traveling from place to place from whom we recived about the same treatment." Chauncey W. West to Brother Richards, June 10, 1853, in West, journals, 25–26.

In another letter he wrote about antagonistic publications: "The public journals of this place will publish all the trash and lies thaey can git or think, against the [church] and will not publish for us in reply. I[n] conversation with one of Editors he said it was very unfair but said he 'if I should publish your replies,' 'I should loose my Christian costermers'. The fact is the Priests govern the people and the people govern the Editors. Truly did John say: she had made all nations drink of

At this moment Capt. Carmel, who furnished us the carriage in Madras, came up and invited us to go and ride with him to the cinnamon gardens,[75] a distance of 4 miles; we accepted the invitation, thinking it would not be gentlemanlike to refuse, after he had manifested so much interest in our welfare; altho' I must say, our minds at that time were in another direction from that of pleasure riding.

The road to the cinnamon gardens was smooth and nice, leading thro' beautiful groves of cocoanut and breadfruit trees,[76] interspersed now and then with small fields of rice. On arriving at the garden, a native hailed us and asked what we wanted. We told him, to view the garden; he then conducted us thro' a narrow lane to a large house, neatly built and well furnished. The owner of the garden was a half caste,[77] and was very kind and affable in all his actions; he accompanied us thro' the garden to a long house where there were a large number of natives peeling and curing the cinnamon. He then took us to the other end of the garden, where he showed us the lemon, orange, plantain, mango, mango steam, nutmeg, clove, and guarver trees;[78] after which he took us to his pine-apple bed,[79] and told us to pick what we wanted. We then went to his house and spent an hour in conversation with him, and found him to be a staunch defender

the wine of the wrath of her fornication." Chauncey W. West to Berrall Covington, September 26, 1853, in West, journals, 97.

75.   These Cinnamon Gardens were apparently a popular nineteenth-century tourist attraction in Sri Lanka (Ceylon). Cinnamon is an important crop in the island nation. Ballou, *Pearl of India*, 103–5.

76.   Both coconut and breadfruit trees are native tropical plants. Breadfruit has a starchy texture reminiscent of bread or potato when it is cooked.

77.   Half-caste refers to someone of mixed race; this half-caste was likely part British and part native Sri Lankan or Indian. *Oxford English Dictionary*, s.v. "half-caste."

78.   Mangosteens (not "mango steam") are a fruit consisting of a purple rind with a white interior. The *guarver* West mentions is probably the *guava*, which is native to Central America and was later taken to Asia. The other fruits and spices mentioned here are native to Asia and are important Sri Lankan crops. Radha and Mathew, *Fruit Crops*, 37–148, 221–24.

79.   Earlier forms of the word *pineapple* used a hyphen; the fruit was so called because it looked like a pinecone. Pineapples grow in patches, with large plants yielding the fruit in the center. The fruit is native to South America but grows well in Southeast Asia. *Oxford English Dictionary*, s.v. "pineapple."

of Catholicism.[80]

On returning to the City, the steamer was about to leave. Mr. Carmel requested us to give him a letter of introduction to some one whom he could call upon for information and instruction when he arrived in England; said he was greatly pleased with our principles; thought we would yet see him in the Valley of the Salt Lake.—We gave him a letter to Elder S. W. Richards, who was then presiding in the British Isles felt very much affected when we parted, and said if he had not lost all he had, and had to borrow money to get home with, he would have assisted us.

In the evening it had got noised around that two missionaries had arrived. Mr. Ripen, a minister of the Presbyterian Church[81] sent a young man to hunt us up, and bring us to his house. We went with the young man; on arriving at his place we met him in the yard, and he gave us a welcome shake of the hand, and said he hailed our arrival with joy; invited us into his parlor (which was furnished in a grand style) asked us to take seats, and then called in his wife, and gave us an introduction to her; after which he commenced to tell us about the different locations of missionary Societies on the Island; of their progress and prosperity, and said he hoped we might be blessed in the good cause.[82]

---

80. Catholic missionaries from Portugal entered Sri Lanka in the early sixteenth century, establishing a lasting Catholic presence. When the Protestant Dutch arrived in the mid-seventeenth century, they sought to counteract Catholicism, but it nevertheless still survived when the British brought religious freedom at the turn of the nineteenth century. Jacobsen, "Creating Sri Lankan Tamil Catholic Space in the South Asian Diaspora in Norway," 117–20.

81. The first Protestants in Sri Lanka arrived in the mid-seventeenth century with the Dutch and their Dutch Reformed Church, but the Dutch didn't do much evangelizing. When the British arrived in 1796, they opened the way for many other Protestant religions. The East India Company often made proselytizing difficult in India, but it was much easier in Ceylon, so many denominations established churches on the island. Melton, *Encyclopedia of Protestantism*, 515.

82. In the eighteenth and nineteenth centuries, missionary societies from European Protestants sprung up in various countries in the world. They were like the Protestant versions of Catholic monastic communities. The missionary societies were often not officially run by the denominations but were run by volunteers from the faiths; the missions generally operated independently of each other. Richard H. Bliese, "Missionary Organizations," in *Encyclopedia of Protestantism*, ed. Hiller-

He then asked us to what church we belonged; we told him to the Church of Jesus Christ of Latter Day Saints, commonly known as Mormons. At hearing this, he seemed to be greatly amazed, and said we could not expect any favor or assistance from him, when our faith differed so widely. He had read some of our works, and considered our doctrines absurd and unscriptural.

We asked him if he would point out some items of our faith that did not agree with the Word of God. He commenced by denying that baptism was necessary to salvation. When he found that he could not sustain his point, admitting the Bible to be the criterion, he flew into a passion, and requested we should work a miracle; we told him we were not sent to work miracles to make the people believe, but to bear testimony of the truth of the Gospel, and that they who rendered obedience thereto should know of its truth. He still contended he should have a miracle done to make him believe; we told him if he could find an account within the Bible where a servant of God ever did a miracle, when called upon by the people, in order to make them believe, we would do one for him. He continued to get more enraged, and asked if we believed in the doctrine of Polygamy; we told him we did;[83] he then cooled down a little, and commenced to talk on that subject; we showed him that Holy men who were acknowledged of the Lord had practised it; he said it was in the dark ages, and the Lord looked over their ignorance. We told him we thought he must be mistaken, it could not be the dark ages, when God condescended to speak with man, and sent His holy angels to instruct him from time to time, and enlightened his mind by dreams and visions; that we believed that one glimpse thro' the vail would teach a man more about the things of God, then the reading of volumes. He commenced to get angry again, and said he did not wish to talk with such men.

We took the liberty to bear our testimony to him of the message which

---

brand, 3:1255–56.

83. Newspapers describing the announcement of polygamy arrived in India three weeks before the missionaries, and Protestants gathered together to discuss how they were going to respond to Latter-day Saint missionaries and their unconventional doctrine. Britsch, "East India Mission of 1851–56," 167–68; see also Whittaker, "Bone in the Throat."

God had sent to man in this day and generation of the world, and cautioned him to be sure and get in the right road, if he wanted to get into the kingdom of God, for Jesus said they would come from the East and West, from the North and South, and set down in the kingdom of God, with Abraham, Isaac, and Jacob;[84] and they were the greatest Polygamists of whom we read. And moreover, in John's revelations there is an account of him having seen the Great City—New Jerusalem descending from God out of heaven, having its twelve gates on which were inscribed the names of the twelve Patriarchs, the sons of the great Polygamist, Jacob; and John says, 'Blessed are they that do his commandments, that they may have a right to the tree of life, and may enter in thro' the gates into the city.'[85] Now sir, said we, if ever you get into that city, you will have to make friends with Polygamists.

{To be continued.}

Chauncey W. West to the *Deseret News*, n.d.[86]

The next day after we arrived at Galle,[87] a piece was published in the newspaper notifying the people that we had come to declare one of Joe Smith's revelations, that we preached a new gospel, that we were polygamists, that they must beware of us and not receive us, for if they did, they would be

84. In Matthew 8:10–11, Jesus commends a centurion for his faith and says, "And I say unto you, That many shall come from the east and west, and shall sit down with Abraham, and Isaac, and Jacob, in the kingdom of heaven"; see also Luke 13:28–29.

85. In Revelation 21:10–12, an angel shows John "the holy Jerusalem, descending out of heaven from God," which "had a wall great and high, and had twelve gates, and at the gates twelve angels, and names written thereon, which are the names of the twelve tribes of the children of Israel." The scripture that West quotes about people entering through the gates is Revelation 22:14.

86. Chauncey W. West to *Deseret News*, "The India Mission, Letter No. 2," *Deseret News*, September 5, 1855.

87. Galle is an important coastal city on the southwest portion of Sri Lanka, serving as the nation's leading port until the 1880s. It has been inhabited for millennia, and as in other places in Sri Lanka, it was occupied by the Portuguese and later the Dutch and British. *Merriam-Webster's Geographical Dictionary*, s.vv. "Galle," "Sri Lanka."

partakers of our evil deeds.

We found it impossible to get a house to hold meetings in, or any person to take us in and feed us. As we had a letter of introduction to a gentleman in Colombo,[88] (Mr. Andra) we concluded to go there, a distance of 70 miles. On arriving at Colombo, he received us kindly, but as he was a lawyer, religion did not trouble him much; however he was a member of the church of England,[89] but he acknowledged to us that he did not believe there was any more salvation in that church than there was out of it, and that he was an infidel in belief. He thought so much of his good name, that he could not afford to keep Mormons long, for fear of being published in the papers; however he let us stop with him for a few days, during which we visited among the people, trying to get a house to hold meetings in, but all to no purpose.

We went to the authorities and tried to get the public hall; they being men who belonged to some of the christian churches, of course we could not have it. We left our testimony with them. We visited both high and low, priest and people, but reasoning and testifying had no good effect upon them; they would not open their doors for preaching, neither would they feed us unless we paid them.[90] Elder Dew[e]y sold his watch to get

---

88. Colombo is the capital of Sri Lanka; it is located on the southwest coast of the island, about fifty-five miles north of Galle. It has been an important port for thousands of years and was taken over by the British in 1796, after occupation by the Portuguese and Dutch. *Merriam-Webster's Geographical Dictionary*, s.v. "Colombo."

89. Around 1818, the Church Missionary Society began preaching in Ceylon. Many Sri Lankans converted, and the church established many schools over the ensuing decades. In the twentieth century, the society separated from the Church of England. J. Gordon Melton, "Church of Sri Lanka," in *Religions of the World*, 708–9.

90. West described these difficulties in Colombo: "We continued to travel from house to house among the people, trying to get a house to hold meetings in, also trying to reason with those that would let us come in. Oftentimes they would shut the door in our face as they saw us coming; as the priests had told them not to receive us into their houses, telling them we were polygamists, and they would be partakers of our evil deeds. Under these circumstances it was impossible to get at the people. They would not so much as give us anything to eat. We were told we would not be allowed to teach if we should find anybody to take us in. The priests had men hired to go from house to house and read the Bible to the people and warn them against

money to purchase food, altho' he did not get half its value.

We were denied the privilege of preaching to the soldiers or visiting them; the low class of Europeans, as well as the half castes and natives, who are educated in the English language; they are dependent on a few speculators and Government men for employment, and if they do anything to displease the priests, they lose their situation, and then starvation will follows [*sic*]. Thus a few great men, with the priests at their head, have the people in fetters, while the priests are rolling in luxury. As for the natives, they are generally an indolent, drunken and filthy people, subsisting on cocoa-nuts and other fruits which grow spontaneously over the island.[91]

After spending several weeks in traveling from place to place, under the burning sun of that clime,[92] we did not feel able to endure such treatment much longer, therefore we concluded to return to Galle and give the people another trial, and if they would not receive us, we would leave and go to a people that would.

The weather being very hot, it took us five days to walk to Galle; we slept upon the ground, and our food was rice and cocoa nuts. We passed thro' 37 native towns and learned something of their sickening, immoral practices and social degradation. The promiscuous intercourse among the sexes is so common that little or no disgrace attends it, even tho' the parties were engaged in the violation of the marriage relations, unless it be with one of the inferior rank in society; then if exposed, the one in superior standing loses reputation;[93] and that most odious practice there prevails,

---

us; at the same time they were circulating tracts which had been written in England against the Church and sent out to this country by the clergy." Chauncey W. West, "Letter," *Deseret News*, December 15, 1853.

91. West said, "The natives and those who have been educated in the Govern[m]ent schools are perfectly under the whites and dare not beleive any thing unless their preists say it is right." Chauncey W. West to Brother Richards, June 10, 1853, in West, journals, 30–31.

92. The average high temperature in Colombo is around 30 degrees Celsius, or the upper 80s Fahrenheit. The temperature remains fairly constant throughout the year. It is a tropical climate, so humidity makes it seem warmer.

93. Encountering these practices would have been shocking for these Western nineteenth-century Latter-day Saints, since they believe in strict chastity and no "intercourse among the sexes" outside of marriage. Bryce J. Christensen, "Chastity,

of a plurality of husbands; a woman may have as many husbands as suits her disposition; they do not all share alike in common, in regard to her favors, but each enjoys her attention exclusively at stated periods, or at her pleasure. When she becomes the mother of a child, *she nominates a father, and he has to maintain it.*[94]

On arriving at Galle, we met with the same reception as before, oftentimes being abused in a most shameful manner. After this we went and saw the American Consul's Agent, Mr. Walker,[95] who did not treat us with respect; he laughed at our papers, and said Governor Young was the man who rode thro' Salt Lake City with sixteen wives;[96] said we had come to the wrong place to preach Mormonism. We bore testimony to him of the gospel which we had to declare to the people; we told him we had been ill-used, and he said that was what we might expect, after which he left us.

We were told by a number of gentlemen afterwards, that he had informed them that we did not belong to America—that the "Mormons" had rebelled against the Government and violated the constitution. This official story being afloat, it also had its influence.

We concluded to leave the island of Ceylon and go to Singapore, but as there were no sailing vessels running to that port, the only chance was to go by the steamers, but they would not take us for less than $50 each.

Law of," in *Encyclopedia of Mormonism*, 1:265–66.

94. Polyandry, the practice of one woman having multiple husbands, was fairly common in Sri Lanka. Usually the husbands were brothers. Sri Lankan men often participated in polyandry because limited family inheritances prevented them from having their own distinct families. The British outlawed polyandry in 1859, but the practice continued. Although Latter-day Saints embraced polygyny, or a plurality of wives, they generally rejected polyandry because they believed that the purpose of marriage was to multiply and because the practice confused the divinely inspired roles of men and women. Hiatt, "Polyandry in Sri Lanka," 583–602; Whittaker, "Early Mormon Polygamy Defenses," 52, 55–56.

95. The American consul was actually J. R. Black. Chauncey W. West to President W. Richards, July 29, 1853, in West, journals, 47; Ferguson, *Planting Directory for India and Ceylon*, 216.

96. The precise number of wives married to Brigham Young is complicated by the fact that many were sealed to him for eternity in a religious ceremony but did not otherwise function as wives in a temporal way. He was sealed to fifty-five wives; sixteen bore him children. Johnson, "Determining and Defining 'Wife,'" 57–70.

Under these circumstances, we saw no chance of getting away. A few days after, the large ship "Penola," from Belfast, Ireland, came in for water, while on its voyage from Australia to Bombay. We concluded if we could obtain a passage, we would go to Bombay[97] and visit br. Findlay, and then sail from there to Siam, and by so doing fulfil a very singular dream which I had a few nights before relative to going to his assistance.[98]

We went on board and found no trouble in getting our passage. We returned on shore and got our trunks, and went on board again. The next evening two gentlemen came on board and told Captain Rany that they hoped he was not going to take us to Bombay; that we were Mormons, and men not worthy to associate with. Captain Rany, who was an Irishman,

97. Bombay, known as Mumbai today, is a coastal city in western India. The Portuguese took over the area in the 1500s and it came under British rule in the 1600s and 1700s. Latter-day Saint missionary Hugh Findlay was called by Lorenzo Snow to Bombay in September 1851, arrived there the following April, and baptized his first convert in May. In September he organized a branch of twelve members in Poona and that winter built a small meeting hall there. By November 1853 "upwards of thirty" had been baptized in Poona. In March 1854 he went to the British cantonment in Belaum, baptizing at least eighteen there before returning to Bombay about the first of the year. In March 1855 he sailed for Hong Kong with seven other Latter-day Saints. During his time in India he published two tracts, one in Marathi. *Merriam-Webster's Geographical Dictionary*, s.v. "Bombay"; Britsch, *From the East*, 9, 12–13; Crawley, *Descriptive Bibliography of the Mormon Church*, 3:52–54, 208–10.

98. West had this dream the night after their interaction with the consul's agent: "Before retiring to bed that night, we called upon the Lord that he would make known unto us what he would have us do; as we had tried every way possible to get the people to receive the gospel, but to no effect. In the night I had a dream; which I will relate, as it is short:—I dreamed that brother Findlay came to me and said he wanted me to go and help him to cut down a large tree: he said it was very large, and he wanted help. I thought I went, and he showed me the tree, and it was very large, and it had been cut into some. We commenced to cut it down and we found it to have a hard shell on the outside, and the middle was soft. We soon cut the tree down, and when it fell it broke all into pieces; at which time I awoke. I could not make out what the dream meant—yet it left a deep impression on my mind." After not acquiring passage to Singapore, he wrote, "We concluded if we could get a passage, we would go to Bombay; we would go and help Elder Findlay cut down the big tree." West, "Letter."

told them, "I don't care a damn what their faith is—they have treated me like gentlemen and they have the appearance of such, and they are going to Bombay with me, if my craft don't sink."

I may here remark, that we might have been able to make arrangements with the Captains of the Steamers for our passage, if the good pious folks had not used influence against us.

After leaving Ceylon, we sailed south-west until we struck the 7th degree of south latitude, where we got the trade winds; we then steered north-east, crossed the Arabian Sea and struck the Malabar[99] coast, 71 miles above Bombay.

The day before getting into Bombay, while sailing along the coast about 10 miles from shore, the ship ran a-ground; the wind was blowing very hard, and the waves were running very high, and when the waves struck the ship they would raise her up, and then she would come down with a tremendous crash, as if she must come to pieces in a very few minutes; and to all human appearance we must be lost in the great deep; as the small boats were so placed that it would take some time to get them overboard, and when they did it was doubtful whether they would ride the sea.

Elder B. F. Dew[e]y and myself went to our room and asked the Lord that the winds would cease blowing, and that He would save us from the fury of the elements. About this time they launched a boat and it filled in a minute; a few minutes after, they put over another boat, and in a few minutes more it was almost a calm.

As we were about to leave the ship, Captain Rany discovered that she was afloat; he called to the carpenter to sound the pumps; he found three feet of water in her hold. The Captain then said he would try and take her into Bombay. He put some of the hands to the pumps and some to hoist the sails, and the next morning, the 25th of July, we landed in Bombay.[100]

We found Elder Hugh Findlay, who was happy to see us after being so

99. The Malabar Coast is located on the southwest coast of India, at the states of Karnataka and Kerala. *Merriam-Webster's Geographical Dictionary*, s.v. "Malabar Coast."

100. After this experience of safely making it into Bombay, West wrote to Willard Richards: "The vessel has been condemned. Thus we see the Lord is powerful to save, and righteous to fulfil his words as spoken by the mouth of his servants the prophets." West, "Letter."

long a time in that benighted land. He had a small branch of the church established in Bombay, and one in Poona, 90 miles thence. We called on Elder Findlay, the President there, to know where he would have us to labor the few months we would tarry with him; he thought it best for me to stop in Bombay and for him and Elder Dew[e]y to go to Poona.[101]

August 1st, Elders Findlay and Dew[e]y left for Poona. I held four meetings a week in Bombay,[102] and also visited a great number of people at their houses, making my own introduction by way of offering them tracts to read. I found that the people acted generally shy, and did not feel free to converse, or to accept of a book to read; I finally took the liberty to ask them the reason of that, and why they rejected us without investigating our principles—that Saint Paul's admonition was "Prove all things and hold fast that which is good."[103] Some of them told me that their minister had told them, they must not read our works, or they would be deceived; that it was such a deception that almost all who allowed themselves to investigate, were caught in the delusion.

Several natives attended my meeting, among whom was one who offered himself for baptism; he was well educated in the English language, and could speak several others; I had hopes he would be a useful man, but

---

101. "We found Elder Findlay, who was very happy to see us after being so long in this country alone and having to contend as it were with priests, the devil, earth and hell combined. He has fought the battle manfully, and has some faithful souls added to the kingdom, who are the fruits of his labors. His health has been poorly for the two last months, and he was very much in want of help, as his labors were too much for him. He is improving in health. The branch of the church in this place numbers 20 members, who are mostly Europeans; and the branch at Poona, 90 miles from this, has about the same number. In both of these places there are a number who are believing and investigating the principles. Br. Findlay finds it very hard to do anything with the natives of this country, as the traditions of their fathers are so great that it seems almost impossible for them to ever give them up. I think we have found br. Findlay's big tree, and we are going to try and help him cut it down." West, "Letter."

102. In a letter published in the *Millennial Star*, West said the church gatherings were held in the Upper Colaba area of Bombay, near the barracks, and "the meetings are moderately well attended, mostly by soldiers." Chauncey W. West, "The Siam Mission," *Millennial Star* 15, no. 44 (October 29, 1853): 716.

103. 1 Thessalonians 5:21.

as soon as he found to his satisfaction that what I had told him was the truth, how that the elders of our church went forth without purse or scrip, and we had not a few thousand lacks of rupees[104] in the Bank of Bombay to draw from to hire the natives to acknowledge our religion, he returned to the church of England, where he said he formerly had two rupees (a piece of money worth 44 cents) a week, but now got three.[105]

The natives of India and more particularly the upper caste, whatever their religion may be, it is made subservient to present interests. The idea of their receiving by immediate revelation a message from God for their implicit obedience, is most foreign from their imaginations; he who comes to them and has no bribe to offer, has no message for them.

The English and American missionaries who have gone to that country have been furnished with plenty of money by the missionary societies at home, and when they found that they could not win the natives with their principles, they have hired them to join their churches, and have written back what great things they are doing in converting the poor heathen.

I have had numbers of them come to me and offer to leave the churches whose names they were then acknowledging and come to ours, if I would only give them a few cents more than they were then getting, at the same time they knew no more about the principles and faith of the church to which they professed to belong, than the brute-beast, and these same people will bow down and worship sticks and stones, gods of their own make, when they think there is no christian seeing them.

Truly have these missionaries fulfilled the saying of the Savior, when he said that they would compass sea and land to make one proselyte, and then he would be twofold more a child of hell than he was before.[106] They

---

104. The rupee is the currency of India; the modern silver rupee was introduced in the 1540s. *Lakh* means one hundred thousand, specifically in reference to rupees. *Oxford English Dictionary*, s.vv. "rupee," "lakh."

105. This man may be the same person whom Edward Tullidge identified as Martin A. Bransin, a member of the Church of England, baptized on August 6, 1853. Tullidge, *Tullidge's Histories*, 59.

106. This refers to Matthew 23:15: "Woe unto you, scribes and Pharisees, hypocrites! for ye compass sea and land to make one proselyte, and when he is made, ye make him twofold more the child of hell than yourselves." The Joseph Smith Translation matches up more with West's rendition, ending with "than he was before, like unto

have taught them to be deceitful and dishonest. The reasons why the native whom I baptized in Bombay did not believe what I told him—that I was sent forth without purse or scrip, and had not money to hire him to be a christian, and that if he joined our church he must do it for the love of the truth—was that he knew that all missionaries with whom he had been acquainted had plenty of money and that at the same time would say they had none.

I would here remark, as the missionaries wish to keep in the good graces of the natives, it is a common thing when they come for money or something which they do not wish to let them have, they say they have none, instead of saying, they cannot let them have it. Hence the natives look for missionaries to tell them these little White lies, as the down easter[107] would say.

On the 7th of September, Elder Allen Findlay[108] from England arrived in Bombay on a mission to that country. After tarrying with me a few days, by request of his brother, Hugh Findlay, he went to Poona to take charge of the work in that place.

October 8th, Prest Findlay and elder Dew[e]y returned to Bombay. It was then autumn, and we thought it time to start for Siam, but could find no ship sailing in that direction, save the mail steamers, and it was impossible for us to obtain a passage on them without money. President Findlay thought it best to give Bombay another fair trial, consequently we circulated a small printed sheet containing some of the articles of our faith; also a notification to the people that we would hold meetings at three different points in the city, naming the places and hours of service.

I went into Fort George[109] to distribute some of these printed sheets,

---

yourselves."

107. A down-easter is someone from Maine or the seacoasts of New England. *Oxford English Dictionary*, s.v. "down."

108. Allan Findlay was born in Scotland in 1830 and was baptized in 1844. He moved to Salt Lake City at some point and died in 1891. Britsch, *Nothing More Heroic*, 283; Crawley, *Descriptive Bibliography of the Mormon Church*, 207.

109. Fort George, named after King George III, was built in Bombay in 1770. By 1862, it was no longer needed and was too small to be used, so it was demolished. *Materials Towards a Statistical Account of the Town and Island of Bombay*, 2:380; Edwardes, *Census of India, Volume X*, part 4, 127–28.

whereupon I was stopped and ordered to be escorted out of the Fort with a guard of soldiers, and myself or any other Mormon forbidden to return. We attended our appointed places of meetings several times, while no one came to hear. We then thought we would leave them without a chance of excuse by visiting them all at their houses, leaving our testimony and offering them tracts to read; and I must say our general reception was either the European aristocratic sneer, or that cold formal orientalism so characteristic of that country.

During this time, the brethren who belonged to the army were called away to Aden[110] in Arabia, when we ordained one elder and one teacher, and furnished them with books and pamphlets, so that they could leave a testimony of the work in that land {where they arrived in safety}.

All this time we had been continually on the lookout for a vessel sailing towards Siam via Singapore, but to no effect; the ships bound for China did not go by Singapore, as they would have to beat[111] from that place all the way up the China sea against the monsoon; but they took what is called the eastern route thro' the straits of Sunda.[112] It was the last of December, and we felt anxious to be on our way.

On being informed that a considerable trade was being carried on between Batavia (on the Island of Java)[113] and Singapore, we concluded to try and get a passage to that port, and trust for our way to be opened from

---

110. Aden is located on the southwest portion of the Arabian Peninsula, in present-day Yemen. It was under British rule as part of India between 1839 and 1937; it had previously been under Portuguese and Ottoman rule. Aden has long been an important seaport because of its location between Europe and India. *Merriam-Webster's Geographical Dictionary*, s.v. "Aden."

111. In nautical terms, "beat" means to sail against the wind. *Oxford English Dictionary*, s.v. "beat."

112. The Sunda Strait is located between the islands of Java and Sumatra in Indonesia, connecting the Indian Ocean to the Java Sea. Numerous volcanic islands, including Krakatoa, are located in the Sunda Strait. *Merriam-Webster's Geographical Dictionary*, s.v. "Sunda Strait."

113. Java is a major island of Indonesia. Batavia is known today as Jakarta, Indonesia's capital; it was named Batavia in the seventeenth century by the Dutch East India Company. Batavia was under Dutch rule until 1942. *Merriam-Webster's Geographical Dictionary*, s.vv. "Batavia," "Jakarta," "Java."

there. After being refused a passage by 14 Captains, only on condition that we would pay them $150 each, we met with Captain Bell of the ship "Cressy,"[114] of London, who said he would give us a chance to ship before the mast and work our passage. Being men who had been raised in the cradle of persecution and hardships, such an offer did not bluff us in the least. We accepted his proposal.

{To be continued.}

{By a slight inaccuracy in the interlining of the manuscript, I was made to say in my first letter, that the brethren contributed liberally to assist "on our journey to San Francisco;" it should have read "on our mission."}

Chauncey W. West to the Deseret News, n.d.[115]

Jan. 9, 1854.—We gave the parting hand to Prest. Findl[a]y, and the brethren in Bombay, and took passage on the ship "Cressa," Capt. Bell, for Java (at this juncture I cannot do justice to my own feelings without expressing my unfeigned gratitude to brother and sister Davies[116] for their unceasing

---

114. The ship *Cressy* was a three-masted bark built in 1843 in England. After making it through the harrowing experience that West describes in these letters, the ship continued to sail for nine more years until it sunk in 1863. Sonne, *Ships, Saints, and Mariners*, 56–57. West and Dewey had previously been refused passage on the *Cressy*, but the captain changed his mind: "I found Bro Dewey who said he had seen the captain of the ship Cressy, and he said he thought he would take us, he said he would like to take us becaus we ware Mericans, he said he was once ship recked on the American coasts and recived great kindness." The next week, Dewey "assertained that we could get a passage by helping all we could to man the vesal. We ware happy to get [such a] chance, after trying for four months." West, journals, December 24 and 28, 1853, and January 2, 1854.

115. Chauncey W. West to *Deseret News*, "The India Mission, Letter No. 3," *Deseret News*, September 26, 1855.

116. Douglas William Davies was a clerk at the government mint in India. He was baptized on May 28, 1852, and his wife, Helen, was baptized on January 9, 1853, both by Hugh Findlay in Bombay. They were both very supportive of the church and the missionaries. "Bro. Davies is a poor man, and has not the means to assist us if he had it he would willingly give it," West recorded. Douglas Davies was not a soldier, so when the other branch members were called away to Arabia, Davies remained. In 1855, the Davieses accompanied Findlay back to Utah, and their daughter was

kindness to us during our sojourn in Bombay).[117]

From Bombay we sailed south-east along the Malabar coast. On the 14th we passed the ancient town of Goar,[118] it being the first town settled by the Portuguese in India. On the 15th passed the town of Calicut,[119] and on the 21st passed the town of Cochin,[120] where several natives came on board, who supplied us with fruits of various kinds.

baptized in Hong Kong on the way. Britsch, *Nothing More Heroic*, 187–88, 194, 205; Chauncey West to Mary West, December 27, 1853, in West, journals, 242.

117. The day before the missionaries' departure from India, they held a church meeting. "At three P.M. we held a meeting and administe[re]d the Sacrament after which Elder Findlay made some remarks expressing his satisfaction with regard to our labou[r]s since we fi[r]st arived and said that he was satisfide that the Lord had directed us to come to Bombay. Also that we arived just in time to realize opposition that had allways been manifested by the people of Bombay. He made a motion that they return us their thanks for our labours and coopperations with them since we had been in their midst and that it be recorded to that efect. The motion was seconded and carr[i]ed una[n]imous. Bro. Davies then said that he was thankful that we come to Bombay for he had rejoiced greatly in our society and had had his faith strengthened greatly by the teachings, and principals which he had received from Elder West, and that he was also thankful that had been permited to do a litle to make us comfortable and would gladly have done more if he had been able. After which I made some remarks expressing my satisfactions with regard to Bro. Findlays movements and labours in Bombay. Also that I was [s]atisfide that his Scurts was clear of the blood of that people. I was followed by Elder Dewey who made some verry appropriate remarks for the acasion After which I closed the meeting by prayer." West, journals, January 8, 1854.

118. Old Goa was established in 1440 on the west coast of India by the king of Bijapur. The Portuguese took control of it in 1510 and used it as the capital of their Indian colony. It was abandoned by the early eighteenth century because of successive cholera epidemics. *Merriam-Webster's Geographical Dictionary*, s.v. "Goa."

119. Calicut, or Kozhikode, is located on the southwest coast of India. It was occupied by the Portuguese in the beginning of the sixteenth century, and the French and British established ports there during the seventeenth and eighteenth centuries until the British acquired it in the 1790s. *Merriam-Webster's Geographical Dictionary*, s.v. "Calicut."

120. Cochin is on the southwest coast of India. Like other towns in India, it was occupied by the Portuguese in the sixteenth century before passing to the Dutch in the seventeenth and ultimately to the British in the late eighteenth century. *Merriam-Webster's Geographical Dictionary*, s.v. "Cochin."

A drawing of Captain Bell's ship, the *Cressy*. Original etched by T. Allom from a drawing by Miss Mary Townsend, 1850–51. Courtesy of Alexander Turnbull Library, Wellington, New Zealand.

Feb. 3.—We crossed the line; the heat of the sun was almost suffocating. On the 14th we spoke[121] the ship "Burlington," of Liverpool, Capt. Gamble, who left Bombay the day before we did; he came on board our ship and counseled with Capt. Bell on the propriety of taking the northeast passage from Java round Borneo,[122] thinking by doing so they would beat several captains into China who left Bombay before us, calculating to take the eastern route. They finally concluded to take the north passage, although a ship had not taken that route for 30 years. On the 24th we sighted the island of Guenna;[123] the 25th, passed the island of Berila Buissa, and entered the straits of Sunday on the 26th in the morning, when six natives from Sumatra[124] came on board

121. In nautical usage, "speak" means to communicate at sea using signals or other methods. This usage does not require a preposition (such as "with" or "to") after the word. *Oxford English Dictionary*, s.v. "speak."

122. Borneo, in southeast Asia, is the third-largest island in the world. Today the island is shared by the nations of Malaysia, Indonesia, and Brunei. During the nineteenth century, it was shared between the British and the Dutch. *Merriam-Webster's Geographical Dictionary*, s.v. "Borneo."

123. It is difficult to determine the location of the islands and other places West mentions in this and ensuing paragraphs. Today there are not Asian islands with a common name of Guenna, Berila Buissa, Batton, Gai, Tuscany, Toquet, Paggonet, Mulwally, or Tonier, nor is there a Kenneeoongon Point or Straits of Benghay in Southeast Asia.

124. Sumatra is the sixth-largest island in the world and is part of the nation of Indo-

with some very nice shells, cocoanuts, and monkeys to sell.

In the evening we arrived at Batavia, where we found there were no vessels sailing to Singapore, with the exception of two Malay juncks,[125] and it was not considered safe for a white man to trust his life with that people; the laws were such that we could not stop there, as no stranger is permitted to tarry in the city unless he has means to take lodgings at some licensed public house, and the landlord has to examine the size of his purse, being responsible for the sustenance of all he has taken in, and obliged to see them conducted from the island. This being the condition of affairs, and Capt. Bell having proposed to let us go on with him to China, it seemed that the only and best chance was for us to accept the offer, and try and make our way from there.

March 1.—We left Batavia and sailed into the Java seas; on the 5th we neared the coast of Borneo, passed the island of Batton, and in the evening entered the straits of Macassar.[126] 6th, sailed between the Bush island and the coast of Borneo; the tide was so strong, with the wind light, we came near running ashore on the island; had to anchor until the tide changed. 7th, we sailed between Borneo and Macassar.

On the night of the 9th we encountered a very severe storm, which carried away the jibboom,[127] and split near half the sails on the ship. On the 10th we were sailing close along the shore of Borneo, found a very stiff tide, and the wind being light, we had to come to anchor.

We were seven days beating trying to round Kenneeoongon Point on the coast of Borneo. We would beat all day, tacking ship[128] between thirty

---

nesia. The kingdom of Srivijaya dominated the island beginning in the seventh century, and it later came under Muslim and European control. *Merriam-Webster's Geographical Dictionary*, s.v. "Sumatra."

125. A junk is a kind of boat native to Southeast Asia; "It is flat-bottomed, has a square prow, prominent stem, full stern, the rudder suspended, and carries lug-sails." *Oxford English Dictionary*, s.v. "junk."

126. The Makassar Strait lies between the islands of Borneo and Sulawesi in Indonesia, connecting the Java Sea and the Sulawesi Sea. *Merriam-Webster's Geographical Dictionary*, s.v. "Makassar Strait."

127. The jibboom extends the bowsprit of a ship. The bowsprit is a pole that extends from the end of the ship. *Oxford English Dictionary*, s.v. "jib-boom."

128. "Tacking ship" refers to changing a ship's direction so that it sails obliquely into the

and forty times, and getting within 3 or 4 miles of the point, and it then would become a calm; and during the night we would drift back to where we were in the morning.

On the fifth day, Capt. Gamble, who was in company with us, rounded the point and went out of sight. On the evening of the seventh, our Capt. got discouraged and thought he could not round the point with his craft, the tide was so strong, and he supposed Capt. Gamble had gone and left him; he swore he would strike across the Selebecean sea[129] and take the eastern route.

As we left the land and got from behind the point in the open sea, we could see the ship Burlington in the distance, the captain of which, as soon as he saw us steering in that direction, mistrusted what was up, and steered after us, and the next morning informed Capt. Bell he had been waiting for him.

About 12 o'clock the wind fell, and it became a calm and continued so until the next day at noon, when they ascertained they had drifted 40 miles from where they were when they left the coast, and they became satisfied that they could not stem the tide and cross the sea with the light winds which they would naturally get at that time of the year, and the only chance would be to go back in order to take the eastern route.

Capt. Gamble finally persuaded Capt. Bell to go back and try and round the point, thinking the tide would not be so bad. We struck the coast some 40 miles below where we left it, and commenced to beat again, and continued for three days, but could not round the point. They discovered as they supposed, a small bay or eddy between the point (which extended into the sea some three miles) and the main land, and concluded to run their ships in there and lay till morning, when they would get the breeze and could round the point, as they would not have far to beat.

About 10 p. m., Capt. Bell discovered that the ship was drifting ashore; about the same time, Capt. Gamble, who was about a mile above us, fired a cannon and made a blue light, which was a signal to us that his ship was

---

wind; by repeatedly tacking, a sailor can make progress against the prevailing wind direction. *Oxford English Dictionary*, s.v. "tack."

129. The Celebes Sea is located east of Borneo, south of the Sulu Sea and the Philippines, and north of Sulawesi. *Merriam-Webster's Geographical Dictionary*, s.v. "Celebes Sea."

near going ashore, and in great danger (I will here mention that they had a list of signals wrote out and each one had a copy).

Capt. Bell gave immediate orders for the three small boats to be let down and manned, made fast to the ship with a line, to row ahead of the vessel and try to tow her off; but we found we could not make any impression upon her, as she had got so near the shore that the swells of the sea had full control of her.

At this time Capt. Gamble shot a rocket, which was a signal that he was out of danger. Capt. Bell saw that our ship was nearing the shore very fast, and finding the water too deep for anchorage, he gave orders for a cannon to be fired and a blue light to be made, as a signal to Capt. Gamble that we were in great danger. In a few minutes more the stern of our vessel commenced to thump on the rock bound coast.

Capt. Bell then gave orders for two cannon to be fired, two rockets to be shot, and a blue light to be made, for a signal to Capt. Gamble that we were ashore, and wanted immediate help; who instanter[130] sent to our help his first mate with two boats well manned. They hitched on with our boats and tried to tow her off, but all to no purpose; the Capt. then gave orders to throw overboard some of the cargo to lighten the stern of the vessel, as he was afraid the rudder would get unshipped. While we were throwing over cargo, she swung round broadside on the shore, where she lay perfectly at the mercy of the swell, which was dashing her against the rocks.

As she struck very heavy in the centre, the Capt. saw something must be done or she would break in two; he therefore sent to the Burlington and got a kedge, (a small anchor) made it fast to a hawser (a large rope) took it out from us the ships' distance and let it down in 270 fathoms[131] water; made the other end fast to the capstan,[132] and commenced to heave and thereby threw her bow off so that she did not strike so hard in the centre; she lay in that position until day light, when the tide commenced to ebb, and the stern swung off.

The night was dark, and not a breath of wind, otherwise she would

---

130. "Instanter" is an adverb meaning "at once," but its usage has decreased significantly since the 1850s. *Oxford English Dictionary*, s.v. "instanter."

131. A fathom is six feet, so 270 fathoms would be 1,620 feet.

132. A capstan is a mechanism around which a rope or cable can coil; by rotating the capstan, an anchor can be raised or lowered. *Oxford English Dictionary*, s.v. "capstan."

have gone to pieces in a very few minutes. At day light it was still a calm, when the two mates, the doctor, the carpenter, Elder Dew[e]y and myself went on shore. We found the land densely timbered, plenty of cocoa nuts, some few berries and large numbers of monkeys, who showed off their gymnastics among the trees; we also saw droves of wild hogs.

While we were traveling in the woods, we came to a wet marshy place, and could discover marks of the feet of the lion and the tiger; having no weapons of war with us, we concluded to beat a speedy retreat.

About 1 o'clock p. m., a good breeze sprung up; we made sale and steered for the point, and rounded it at 4 p. m. While we were beating to round Kenneeoongan point, we crossed the equator twice in each 24 hours; once when we beat up in the day time, and once when we drifted back in the night; the heat of the sun was almost unendurable.

A few day[s] after, she run upon a coral reef, causing a portion more of her cargo to be thrown into the sea to lighten her, so that she could be got off. I will here mention that there was scarcely a day during the passage along the coast of Borneo but what we saw reefs or shoals, consequently had to keep a boat ahead sounding; we sailed nearly three thousand miles in an open boat steering, rowing or throwing the lead, and the sun hot enough to bake one's brains.

On the evening of the 24th we went ashore on Borneo with our Capt. and six seamen accompanied by Capt. Gamble and eight of his men, we saw some natives but they would not come to us, on our return to the vessel we found a fine lot of turtles but their shells were so hard that we broke our spears and did not get many.

March 26th, —while we were ahead sounding, a shark about 20 ft. long came up to the boat, and made a lounge at the man who was throwing the lead, he saw it in time to throw himself down in the boat, when it struck one of the oars with great violence and nearly capsized the boat.

On the 31st the captains thought they had got out of the reefs, as they were in an open sea and neither reef nor island in sight, they therefore concluded to give the men rest and not send any boats ahead. In the evening Capt. Gamble ran his ship on to a reef when under good headway; on seeing the reef he immediately let go his small anchor thinking it might drag along and not bring up the ship so sudden, but the cable broke and hence to him the anchor lost. He then let go one of his large bower anchors which stopped her just in time, as she would touch occasionally when she rocked.

Our captain did not see the reef until the ship touched, but she was under such headway that she went over it although she bumped several times very hard.

April 2nd we lay becalmed between Borneo and several small islands, when a number of small boats made their appearance in various directions and continued to increase until they numbered over one hundred; they were gathering in towards us and from their movements we believed they intended giving us battle and taking our ship if they could; Capt. Bell became much alarmed as Capt Gamble with his ship was several miles ahead.

He then gave orders for the cannons to be loaded with shot, and all the fire arms on board to be put in readiness, also that the cook should fill his boilers with hot water and grease; we had everything ready and waiting their approach, when a little wind sprung up and increased to a stiff breeze when we soon left them and sailed close alongside of the island of Gai, and in the evening came to anchor near the shore of Borneo; during the night we saw large fires on the shore and heard the natives 'hollowing, yelling and making a tremendous fuss.'

On the 4th in the after part of the day there was no wind, we went with Capt. Bell and 6 seamen to the "Burlington" to fit up for an excursion on shore; at 2 p.m. we started, being accompanied by Capt. Gamble and 8 of his seamen, all well armed; shortly after reaching the shore we saw some natives but they seemed afraid and run from us, we walked along the shore for several miles and collected some very fine specimens of coral and shells.

On the 7th of April we lay becalmed between the islands Tuscany, Toquet and Paggonet. We went ashore with Capt. Bell on the latter island; though it had a fine appearance, it was uninhabited, well timbered but very little game; we saw hundreds of turtles but they were very wild; the captain struck his 12 feet long spear into one of them, but it darted off with spear and all.

While we were in the Selebecean sea near the entrance of the straits of Banghey we had sailed for 2 days without seeing a reef or finding anchorage. The captains were in hopes we had got through with reefs and did not send a boat ahead to sound.

On the night of the 11th of April, as pleasant a moonlight night as we could wish to see in a tropical clime, we were sailing with a firm breeze at the rate of 7 knots an hour, the captain was on his lounge on the poop deck,[133] the officers and ourselves were listening to the sweet strains of the violin as played by the third mate, the sailors on the forcastle[134] were singing songs, and all was mirth and glee, thinking we had got through with pulling oars and heaving the lead. All on a sudden the ship ran into a reef, and as the water shallowed gradually and the coral alive and soft, she fastened herself as firm as if she had been in the stocks; when she struck, it was most terrific and not unlike the shock of an earthquake.

The captain immediately gave orders for two cannon to be fired, two rockets to be shot, and a blue light to be made as a signal to Capt. Gamble (who was about a mile to the windward) that we were aground and wanted immediate assistance; he bore down towards us when Capt. Bell sent out a boat and requested him to come and anchor near the stern of our vessel as we had sounded and found the water 7 fathoms deep; he came to anchor about a cable length from our ship, we then passed two nine inch hawsers from his foremast to our capstan and windlass[135] and commenced to heave but without effect, then passed two hawsers from our middlemast[136] to their capstan and windlass; we could not move her, but dragged the anchors of the other ship.

The captain then judged it impossible to get her off without lightening her cargo; he then called his mates and took a survey of the ship and commenced to throw over cargo and continued until we threw out nearly all on board, when all of a sudden she slid off and swung round.

133. The poop deck is located at the very back of a ship and is its highest deck. The word comes from Latinate words for the stern of a ship. *Oxford English Dictionary*, s.v. "poop."

134. In contrast to a poop deck, a forecastle is a deck located at the front of a ship. *Oxford English Dictionary*, s.v. "forecastle."

135. A windlass is a mechanism with a horizontal axis, around which a cord coils so that a weight may be lifted or lowered. It is like a capstan but horizontal. *Oxford English Dictionary*, s.v. "windlass."

136. The middlemast is the primary mast of a ship, located in its center. *Oxford English Dictionary*, s.vv. "middle," "mainmast."

Bales of cotton and other goods could be seen floating in every direction. The next day we made sail and steered on our course. On the 13th we entered the straits of Banghey, passed the beautiful island of Mulwally, noted as being the place where the English planted a small colony in the year A. D. 1700, who were all massacred by the Malays.

At 1 p.m. we were sailing opposite the island of Banghey. Capt. Gamble having only a few days' supply of water on board, wished to go on shore on that island to obtain as much as would last him until he reached China.

Mr. Ausburg gives an account of a stream of fresh water flowing from that island into the straits, at which place he got a supply for his ship in the year 1700. We came to anchor near Banghey point where the stream was said to be, when each sent a boat in search of it; we found the mouth of a small brook, the water of which was quite saltish. The first mate (Mr. Miller) who had command of our boat would not go farther up the stream for fear of the natives; as Mr. Ausburg gives an account of a party of Dutch being massacred there while getting water.

We returned to the ship and reported what we had discovered; the next morning Capts. Gamble and Bell with 2 boats manned with 10 men each, well armed started to explore the stream, we ascended it about three fourths of a mile, when the water became so shallow we could go no further with our boats, we saw native tracks along the banks and passed several boats in which were some cooking utensils and other family necessaries, which seemed to us as if the natives had just fled.

We left a party to guard the boats and ascended the stream one mile farther on foot before we came to fresh water, when it was so shallow we could not go farther with our boats even in high tide and the brush so thick it would be impossible to get our casks up to the water; we then concluded it could not be the stream spoken of by Mr. Ausburg; we returned to the ship and after taking some refreshment we cruised along the shore but could find no stream, it was then conjectured it might be on the other side of Banghey point; during the night the natives came down on the beach in hundreds, howling and yelling in such a terrific manner that the captains gave up the idea of exploring farther.

Capt. Bell thought he could spare Capt. Gamble some water by putting his men on short allowance and make shift with what we had.

We made sail and steered on our course passing the island of Tonier, and about 1 p.m. sailed into the China sea; all hands were rejoicing, thinking we had got out of trouble, but we had not gone far when the Burlington who was ahead run into a sand bank, they fired a cannon and made a blue light to let us know he found bottom again and then raised signals for Capt. Bell to keep to the leeward, which he did and passed the bank; as the wind was blowing pretty strong, Capt. Gamble put on all sail and flung the yards aback, and as the waves and swells would occasionally raise her, he succeeded in backing her off and in a few hours were under way again.

I may here mention that the charts that they had was of little account. The captains believed that many of the reefs had grown since the charts were made. If we were afraid of reefs, sand banks and howling of natives before, we had now to encounter what was more terrific, a "Tiphoon" (a dreadful hurricane)[137] while in the China sea; it is impossible for me to describe the fury of the elements; they were truly awful and terrific, it seemed as if the great deep above and below were about to unite.

The captain being acquainted with these storms which frequent the tropical regions, made preparations for it, by sending down the top yards and masts, and as it was she lay on her side with her bulwarks under water for 36 hours while the waves ran mountains high, oft times dashing themselves over the vessel, and as she was very dry and open on her top side caused by the great heat of the sun, also had received much injury while on the passage, she leaked so that the pumps had to be kept constantly going to keep her afloat, and when the storm abated there were between 4 and 5 feet of water in her hold.

It appeared truly miraculous to all on board that she ever rode the storm. A number of vessels were lost in that sea during the same gale, but through the distinguished favor of our heavenly Father, on the 30th April we beheld the coast of China, and on the 2nd of May came to anchor before the town of Macoa.[138]

{To be continued.}

---

137. "Typhoon" is the name for a hurricane or cyclone when it occurs in Asia and the western Pacific. *Oxford English Dictionary*, s.v. "typhoon."

138. Macao is a Portuguese colonial town on the southern coast of China. The Portuguese settled the area in the 1550s, and they claimed it as their own territory in 1849. It was an important trading port. It has essentially the same status as Hong

Chauncey W. West to the *Deseret News*, n.d.[139]

Macoa is a Portuguese town, and from the sea has an attractive and delightful appearance. We here got a Chinese pilot and on the 3rd of May steered for the mouth of the Canton we came to anchor for the night in Macoa bay, with hundreds of Chinese fishing boats in sight. On the evening of the 4th we came to anchor near the mouth of the river between two high hills, on which were China and Saractars forts each mounting two hundred guns.

On the morning of the 5th we entered the mouth of the river, passing fourteen forts within the first four miles. A more highly cultivated and more beautiful country I never saw than that along the banks of the Canton many of the hills bordering the river flats being cultivated to their summits.[140] The Chinese seem to think it a small affair to carry water in buckets to irrigate their crops on these hills, or to transplant a few thousand acres of rice. On the 6th of May we came to anchor in front of the city Wampoa,[141] the ship's place of destination. Two of the ships company we convinced of the truth; they intended to emigrate to the mountains as soon as they returned to England and got discharged from the ship.

The climate and the great heat of the sun during the passage impaired the health of Elder Dew[e]y, as also that of the capt. who got worse the day we landed at Wampoa, and in a few days he was taken to the hospital at Hong Kong where he died. On the 7th we went to the English Consul to get our discharge from the ship, Capt. Bell being unable to attend to it. After giving it, the Consul told us that we must not go on shore, or we would be taken up and put in the Choca (prison ship).

      Kong, being part of China but having unique laws. *Merriam-Webster's Geographical Dictionary*, s.v. "Macao."

139. Chauncey W. West to *Deseret News*, "The India Mission, Letter No. 4," *Deseret News*, October 24, 1855.

140. Since ancient times, the Chinese have used terrace farming to grow rice and other crops. Step-like terraces have been built onto hills, and small ponds function as rice paddies on the terraces. This agricultural method allows the Chinese to live on higher ground while still farming. Marks, *China*, 148.

141. Whampoa, known today as Huangpu, is located on the Zhu River in southeast China. It is about seventy miles northwest of Hong Kong. *Merriam-Webster's Geographical Dictionary*, s.v. "Huangpu."

We asked him the reason. He said, "the sailors and men from ships who went on shore generally got drunk and beat and knocked the Chinamen about, which caused the Consul and ship masters a great deal of trouble," and remarked that "only a few weeks ago a ship's crew went on shore and were half killed by the natives.["] This we had reason to believe was the case, for we saw the bodies of several Europeans floating about in the river.

We showed him our Gubernatorial recommend and United States passport, at which he seemed considerably astonished and said, "I beg your pardon a thousand times, I thought you were queer looking sailors, and what astonished me most is that you are in possession of such credentials and came before the mast, the reason of which I wish to know."

When we entered into the particulars of our mission he became uneasy, and it was evident that he wished the conversation to close, and as some shipmasters came in about this time he took the advantage, excused himself and left, but not without learning who we were.

In the afternoon we went on shore and traveled through and nearly round the town, and truly it was a picture of social degradation, to say nothing of the inhabitants, whose immoral practices are too low to be described. They were in a great state of excitement about the revolutionists,[142] fearing every day that their city would be attacked. We went on board of ship to stop for the night, as we could not find a place on shore that we considered safe.

May 8th, we fell in with Capt. Dible, of the barque Hiageer, who said his vessel would sail for Hong Kong in two days from that time, and we could have a passage. Capt. Bell gave us liberty to make our home on board his ship until Capt. Dible should sail.

We got a Saupan[143] (a boatman) and went up the river two miles to Bamboo town, which is built mostly on the water, the buildings resting on boats or spiles. Our pilot took us round to the back of the town among the gardens and rice fields. While there a quarrel commenced between several Chinamen who, when we supposed they had exhausted all their

---

142. These "revolutionists" may be participants in the Taiping Rebellion. See chapter 6, note 20, p. 175 herein.

143. A sanpan or sampan, literally meaning "three boards," is a flat-bottomed boat common in China. *Oxford English Dictionary*, s.v. "sampan."

strength in words (for they yelled like hyenas), caught each other by their cues with one hand and commenced to unmercifully beat one another on the head with stones cutting great gashes in their heads from whence the blood ran profusely.

When they had fought until some of them were nearly beaten to death, so that they had to be carried off the ground, some other Chinamen interfered and separated them.[144] While we were returning we observed in the end of the boat a little appartment partitioned off in which was a light burning; we asked the boatman why he had a light burning there, he told us that it was his josh-house and that he kept the light there so that josh could see.[145]

He opened the door and we saw a light burning in the centre, behind which stood a little wooden god on a bench, and before and around it were placed some rice, curry, fish and fruits of various kinds, and a bowl of tea. He said that josh came every night and extracted the best of the articles of

144. West's journal recorded this event occurring on May 7 (not May 8), 1854: "During the forenoon a boat past under the bow and past up some botles of Shamshaw (spirits) to the sailers for which they gave him a blue shirt. Some of them became quite [noisy?] and at last two of them got to fighting. And one of them struck the other when he was down. When the Carpenter told him if he struck him again when he was down he would have a hand in the fuss. At which he told the Carpenter if he was a man to stand out. The Carpenter squared to him and they went at it the blood soon began to fly from their cheeks in various places. They keep at it until their shirts were tower [torn] intirely off ~~of them~~ And when one would knock the other down some of the croud would lift him up again and then they would pick into each other again. At last the Carpenter came off [coolly?] the other man acknowledging him to be the best man." After this incident, "the offi[c]ers had to keep a strict guard during the night to keep the China men from bringing Shamshaw to the Sailers." West, journals, May 7, 1854.

145. *Joss*, a corruption of the Portuguese word *deos* (meaning god), refers to Chinese idols. *Oxford Dictionary of World Religions*, s.v. "joss." West recorded the "josh house" in his journal: "At dusk the second maid [mate] and I went down into a boat to see their josh house. (A house for their God) It was a box some two feet long and one wide with two small dooars, in which ware several images before them stood a brass Candel-stick on the top of that was placed a small Earthern dish of oil with a wick lit which th[e]y keep burning during the night. betwix the images and the Candel stick ware placed victuals of various kinds for josh to eat." West, journals, May 7, 1854.

food, and that he gave him a fresh supply every morning. We asked him if josh was their god; no, he said their god was so good he would not hurt them, but josh was very bad and all the same as our devil, and that they had to do every thing to please him so that he would not hurt them.

In the evening we saw two very long narrow boats with nice silk flags inserted at each end; the boats were filled with men as close as they could sit, each having a paddle which they used with great dexterity, striking all at once. At each stroke came a hearty grunt from every one of them; they propelled the boat with the speed of a swift horse. At each end stood a man beating a drum. We asked a native what they were doing; he said they were making prayers to josh.

It is a common thing through the whole day and night to hear the firing of cannon and guns, and making of various noises, to please josh as they say. When they launch a boat, start on a voyage to sea, or part with a friend, they fire guns and bundles of fire crackers, which they sometimes keep cracking for hours, that they may have good luck, and their friends be blessed and not troubled with josh. When a ship leaves with Chinamen for California, one would almost think by the noises that he was near Sebastopol.[146]

On the 10th we took passage on board the barque Hiageer, Capt. Dible master, for Hong Kong, and had a pleasant passage. The capt. was very kind to us. At 4 p. m. of the 12th we entered the bay of Hong Kong, and at 6 p. m. we came to anchor opposite the city, which is situated at the base of an almost barren mountain. It presented a beautiful appearance from the sea, but when close by it appears more obscure and irregular.[147]

On the 15th we went on shore and made inquiries for Elders Stout, Lewis and Duncan, missionaries to that country, and were informed that they had returned to America.[148] We found ourselves again among perfect

---

146. Sevastopol is a seaport on the southwest portion of the Crimean Peninsula in the Black Sea, and at the time West was on his mission, the Crimean War was raging. West recorded reading about the war in his journal while he was in India: "I spent the fore part of the day in reading the news concerning the war between Russia and Turkey as well as the general political aggatation that seems to provade all Europe." West, journals, December 27, 1853; *Merriam-Webster's Geographical Dictionary*, s.v. "Sevastopol."

147. This "barren mountain" is Victoria Peak.

148. West would have expected Hosea Stout, James Lewis, and Chapman Duncan to

strangers, and destitute of the means to buy food or shelter; but we had the same God to lean upon for support that we had had ever since we left our home in the valleys of the mountains, for we took not a cent with us. Elder Dew[e]y's health continued to get worse, and we could find no person to shelter us from the pitiless storm; the only alternative left was to again go on board ship, which we did in the evening.

16th, constant rain and remained on board. On the 17th we moved on shore and stopped at a Chinese boarding house, that being the best we could do. We found the people had but little regard for "Mormonism," as they called it, or for any other kind of ism but devilism. The word virtue might be expunged from their vocabulary, for their delight appeared to be to wallow in the mire of wickedness and deeds of darkness. Perhaps the inhabitants of the cities of the plains were not much worse.

On the 27th Elder Dew[e]y was taken down apparently with a complication of diseases, fever predominating, and it seemed as if his whole system was a total wreck. In a few days we succeeded in getting the fever broke, which left him very weak.

About this time we became acquainted with a Mr. Jas. Young, a Chinaman by birth, but raised under American influence; he called himself an American, and kept the American Hotel. He was very much of a gentleman in his manners, and we would not have known but what he was an American if he had not told us.

On learning our circumstances, he said we could come and stop with him for a few days, until we could make some other arrangements; we thanked him for his kind offer, and took our trunks to his residence where we received comfortable fare.

On the 6th of June I took passage from Wampoa on the mail steamer Hong Kong, Capt. Williams Master, who gave me a FREE passage. We heard there was a vessel at Wampoa bound for Singapore, which had come in since we left. There were a goodly number of passengers on board, among whom were several sea captains. On learning that I was a Mormon, the

---

still be in China, not knowing the lack of success they experienced. He recorded that he and Dewey "went to the Post office and took out a letter directed to C. Dunken." See chapter 6, "James Lewis and the China Mission," pp. 175–76 herein; Britsch, "Church Beginnings in China," 161–72; West, journals, May 16, 1854.

general topic of conversation was 'Mormons' or 'Mormonism.'

A Mr. Lane requested that I would deliver a short discourse on our faith; I told him I had no objections, if the Captain was willing; he asked the Capt., who said he had no objections, if I would preach the doctrine of the New Testament and not make my discourse from the Book of Mormon, or other 'modern' books.

In opening I stated that Capt. Williams had requested that my remarks should be in accordance with the doctrines of the New Testament, consequently I would endeavor to confine myself strictly to the word of God, and begged leave to make a request of Capt. Williams and the other gentlemen present that they would believe the few words that I might read or quote from the scriptures of truth, saying that I had found many people in my travels who believed the Bible when shut, but when it was opened and read to them they could not believe it meant just what it read, that it must have a spiritual meaning, hence so many different opinions in the world about the plain and pure principles of the doctrines of Christ.

After speaking quite plainly for some time, I bore a faithful testimony of the work of God in this age. When I had closed, Mr. Lane remarked to Capt. Williams that 'he wanted a Bible discourse, and he thought he ought to be satisfied, as Elder West had quoted a good portion of the New Testament,' and asked, what fault do you find with it? 'None at all.' I asked him if he had obeyed the Gospel; he said he had, but not exactly in the same order I set it forth, but that he believed his baptism by sprinkling was just as good as immersion.

Mr. Lane said he had been an infidel for 8 years, but he had to acknowledge there were some very peculiar things about the 'Mormons' which he could not account for, viz: their great prosperity and increase in numbers against such opposition and persecution, and that their leaders could govern such a mixed multitude gathered from all nations with such perfect order; he said there must be a secret spring somewhere.

At this time we came in sight of Wampoa which broke up the conversation. At 5 p. m. we arrived and I landed, leaving a good impression among those on board.

I went on board of our old ship the Cressy, which was in the dock being repaired. The officers were glad to see me (Capt. Bell had gone to the hospital at Hong Kong) and welcomed me to stop with them while I remained in the place.

The next morning I enquired after the vessel sailing to Singapore, but on seeing the Captain I could make no arrangement for our passage, for want of money.

Chauncey W. West to the *Deseret News*, n.d.[149]

June 8th, Mr. James Elister of Virginia, who came up on the steamer with me, invited me to accompany him to the city of Canton, saying that it would not cost me any thing. At 10 a. m. we started in a nice saupan boat, having three men to row and a woman to scull.

We rowed up the river with the tide at the rate of six knots an hour; the scenery was truly delightful; the country on both sides, as far as the eye could reach, was clothed with a mantle of green, interspersed with beautiful groves of fruit and shade trees of various kinds. We passed several large forts on each side of the river, also numbers of China Pago des (monuments) which were beautifully built, and were from 150 to 200 feet high; our boatman said that they had stood for hundreds of years.[150] We passed the entrances into thirteen canals leading from the river into the country, in which we could see immense numbers of boats plying to and fro.

At 1 p. m., we came in sight of the city and began to wind our way among thousands of boats, of all sizes and dimensions, laying from 15 to 20 deep almost obstructing the passage, and so it is for 5 miles above and below Canton. At 2 p. m. we landed in the front of the square where the English church stands; it is beautifully adorned with walks, shades and flower beds.

Our boatman acted as guide and took us to a hotel kept by a Chinaman; here we were treated with great respect, and furnished with a private room adorned with great splendor, after the Chinese style. In the evening our pilot conducted us through the principal streets in the city; the buildings are generally three and four stories high, the streets very narrow and

---

149. Chauncey W. West to *Deseret News*, "The India Mission, Letter No. 5," *Deseret News*, November 14, 1855.

150. Pagodas are Buddhist temples. They hold Buddhist relics and consist of multiple stories with prominent eaves. *Oxford Dictionary of World Religions*, s.v. "pagoda."

thronged with people, nearly all of whom were carrying something from silk and satins to wood, vegetables, fruit, brick and mortar.

At nearly every shop we were importuned to go in and look at their goods, and a dozen or more followed us during our walk trying to get into our good graces by running down other traders, and telling how good and cheap their articles were. The Jews fall far short of the Canton merchants in urging one to trade.

The next morning I concluded to take a walk alone to the English factories, a distance of two miles. I had not gone far before I was surrounded by a crowd of Chinamen who followed me nearly there and back, talking constantly and urging me to trade. On my return I learned that our guide had gone out in search of me, and the landlord said it was a wonder that I got back alive, that it was not safe for an European to travel through the city alone, even in the middle of the day.

After breakfast we visited the markets and several other places of public resort; there appeared to be a great excitement and confusion among the people, which our guide said was caused by the news that the rebels were approaching the city, and would probably attack it that night or next morning.

At 3 p. m. we left Canton and arrived in Wampoa the same evening. When I extended the parting hand to Mr. Elister he gave me $2, and accepted some pamphlets, which he promised to peruse with care and lend to his friends. I again went on board the Cressy, which had come out of dock, and was informed by the officers that they expected to sail for Hong Kong the next day and I could have a passage.

The next morning, about 8 o'clock, we heard a tremendous cannonade at a town about two miles distant on the side of one of the canals, and soon saw the inhabitants running across the fields; in a short time the whole town was in flames. We were informed that the inhabitants had refused to pay tribute, and the government had sent her Mandarene boats to destroy it.[151]

At 5 p. m. we sailed for Hong Kong where we landed on the afternoon

---

151. This battle was a conflict between the British and the Chinese preceding the Second Opium War, which started in 1856. A United States marshal named Cook, stationed at Whampoa, recorded a very similar event occurring in 1855, but since Cook was recalling it years later, it is possible that he simply had the date wrong and that it was the same event West witnessed in 1854: "During the summer of

of June 12. I found Elder Dewey's health about the same as when I left him; he had a severe attack of ague[152] and fever, but had got the chills broken; Mr. Young had been very kind to him. On the 14th I had a conversation with Mr. Miller, who succeeded to the Captaincy on the death of Capt. Bell, and he said we could come on board and remain while his vessel was in port; I thanked him kindly for his offer and returned to Mr. Young's and talked with Elder Dewey, and we agreed to go on board next morning, as we thought it would be more healthy on the water.

On informing Mr. Young that we were going to leave, he said, as it was Saturday, it would be better not to go on board until Monday, that we were welcome to stop and urged us much to do so. He had been so kind to us that we did not like to go against his wishes and concluded to remain.

The next day (Sunday) passed very dull, and about 4 p. m. we concluded to leave our trunks, go out to the vessel and have a little chat with Capt. Miller. We informed Mr. Young of our intentions, but he said we had better remain until after supper, which would be ready in the course of an hour, still we felt impressed upon to go. On reaching the vessel we found Capt. Miller and had a pleasant interview.

The next morning we were informed that Mr. Young's house had fallen down, and on going ashore for our trunks (which we found among the ruins) we learned that in about one hour after we left, while all were at supper, a large rock broke loose from the hill above the house, rolled down and struck the lower story, bringing it down with a crash and covering the inmates in the ruins; some were killed and all more or less injured.[153] Shortly

---

1855, in June or July, there lay . . . from ten to fifteen lorchas engaged in smuggling salt. . . . The number of vessels was thus large at that time, in consequence of the mandarin boats having been sent above Canton to repulse the rebels; but the Government could not keep ignorant of so bold a matter long, and twelve or fifteen mandarin boats, each containing upwards of sixty men, made their appearance one morning soon after sunrise and captured the whole fleet. . . . The mandarin force took the captured fleet to Canton, and the parties having the right to fly the flag subsequently claimed their vessels, which were eventually returned, and the remainder retained by the Government." *Hansard's Parliamentary Debates*, 1606.

152. Ague refers to a disease that causes fever, specifically malaria. *Oxford English Dictionary*, s.v. "ague."

153. West recorded this incident in his journal: "After Dinner we settled with the Land

after getting on board Elder Dewey had another attack of chills and fever.

On the 25th a vessel came in on its way to Singapore, but we could make no arrangements for a passage. The ship we were then stopping in was about ready for sea and Elder Dewey's health was still failing, and, as we both thought he would not regain his health in a tropical clime, after fasting and prayer to know the will of the Lord, we felt that the Spirit dictated that it was our duty to return to America.

The barque Hiageer, Mr. Dibble, master, with whom we came down from Wampoa, was chartered to take Chinamen to California. On seeing him he proposed taking us for one hundred dollars each, payable in San Francisco; being from one third to one half less than the common price for a passage.

The second night on board I dreamed that the vessel was wrecked, and that I saw the crew and passengers in great distress. The next night I twice had the same dream, and a night or two after Elder Dewey dreamed the same thrice. We then became convinced that it was our duty to leave the vessel, but how to get off we did not know; we felt averse to speak to the captain about leaving, for he had been very kind to us and had turned away other passengers who wished to go with him; but the longer we remained on board the more we felt impressed that it was our duty not to remain in the vessel.

As the Capt. was an infidel we knew it would have no good effect to tell him the reason why we wished to leave. The morning before the vessel was destined to sail we informed him that we would like to tarry in China a few days longer (if we could make matters agreeable with him) until the next mail steamer should arrive from the east, as we were looking for letters which we wished to obtain before we sailed; he said he did not wish to hin-

---

Lord. Then took a few of our things. (leaving our chests in the Lanlords care) and went on board of the Cressy. As we thought it would be more healthy on water. In the eavening while the Boarders at the Tavern which we had left were at su[p]per a large Rock rolled down from the hill and struck the foundation of the building and caused the house to fall to peaces when they saw it comming they jumped to run out but as they had to go down a flite of stairs the beam and roof caut them. Dilling [sic] one man (Mr Curry) dead on the spot and caut the Land Lord by his hand between two beams. which smashed it all to peaces holding him till a Gentleman came and pride the timbers apart so that he could draw his hand out. Also ingering [injuring] each person in the room more or less." West, journals, June 18, 1854.

der us if we desired to tarry, but we must be aware that he had laid in stores for us and refused other passengers. Just at this moment three men came and wanted a passage to San Francisco, offering to pay the money down; the captain then said it would be no disappointment to him if we tarried. We then asked him how we could settle for our fare while we had been on board, he replied that we were welcome, that he did not want any thing for it; we thanked him, took our trunks and went on shore.

After being on shore for several days we made arrangements with Capt. McDonald, of the ship "John Grey"[154] of Liverpool, to give us a cabin passage to San Francisco for $150 each, to be paid on our arrival there. On the 8th of July we went on board, and on the 12th we got news, through the papers, of the wreck of the barque Hiageer, Captain Dibble, in the China sea when 7 days out; about one fourth of the passengers were lost, the balance, after suffering severely, were taken off the wreck by a United States frigate.

At 1 p. m. on the 15th of July we weighed anchor and sailed into the China sea. We steered north west until we struck the 45th degree of north latitude, passing through several groups of the Japan islands, where we got a fair wind and steered direct for the port of San Francisco.

On the 15th of August the Chinese passengers, 270 in number, got into a regular quarrel about the division of the rice at meal time, and it was with considerable difficulty that the captain stopped the row. During the quarrel a Chinaman caught a kettle of boiling water and threw it on his opponents, they made a general rush at him, he seized an iron crank and, as he raised it to throw at them, his foot slipped and he fell overboard. The captain gave orders to put the ship in stays,[155] lower a boat and pick him up, but they could see nothing of him; after cruising about some time in search of him, as the sea was considerable rough, they gave him up as lost and hoisted in the boat, when Elder Dewey happened to look down the rudder post and saw him on the top of the rudder.

He was so mad that he would not speak for some time; they threw over

154. The three-masted ship *John Gray* was built in Scotland in 1842. Captain Duncan McDonald was the captain when West and Dewey boarded the vessel in July 1854. The ship was wrecked near England in 1867. Sonne, *Ships, Saints, and Mariners*, 120.

155. Putting a ship "in stays" refers to turning its head windward in tacking. *Oxford English Dictionary*, s.v. "stay."

a rope, which he made fast around him, and hauled him in, to the great joy of his friends but displeasure of his enemies, who would have pitched on to him again if the captain had not interfered.[156]

On the morning of the 6th of September we came in sight of the outer entrance of the bay of San Francisco, and shortly after were hailed by two men-of-war, one French and one English; the captain put the ship in stays and waited until they came alongside, they sent an officer on board to examine the ships papers, as they were on the look out for Russian vessels and did not know but ours were false colors.

On the 7th a pilot came on board, and at 2 p. m. we came to anchor in front of the city of San Francisco; 54 days out.

Elder Dewey's health continued poor, and he had several attacks of the fever and ague, until we reached the northern latitudes when he began to gain strength very fast, and by the time we landed he was enjoying moderate health. We went on shore and made enquires for br. J[ohn]. M. Horner; while in search of him we met an old acquaintance of Elder Dewey, who informed us that Elder P. P. Pratt[157] was in the city. We went immediately to his residence where we found him in company with a number of missionaries who were coming from and going to the Sandwich islands; it was truly a time of rejoicing with us to meet so many of the elders of Israel unexpectedly, and more especially Elder Pratt who was able to give us such counsel as we required.[158]

---

156. West's journal recorded many details about riding on the ship, usually about the weather, but there were a few interesting occurrences: "The men ca[ugh]t a porpoise had some of the liver for dinner it was simler to Hogs liver." West, journals, August 20, 1854.

157. In the spring of 1854, Apostle Parley P. Pratt was called to travel to San Francisco in order to preside over the missions of the Pacific. It was the second time he had been called to do so. While he was stationed in California, he defended the church against the attacks of the local papers. It was also in San Francisco on this mission that he met Eleanor McLean, whom he would later marry and whose estranged husband would kill Pratt in 1857. Pratt left San Francisco to return to Utah in June 1855. Givens and Grow, *Parley P. Pratt*, 339–65.

158. After arriving on shore, West and Dewey "went direct to Bro. John Horners [illegible] ship and inquired for him. We ware informed that he had jest left the city for his place out to mission. We stereted and went out to the mission and caled

The next day we saw br. J. M. Horner who let us have the money to pay Capt. McDonald for our passage. The next consideration was, how are we to repay it? Mr. Q[uartus]. S. Sparks, an old acquaintance of Elder Dewey, offered to settle with br. Horner for him, if he would go to San Bernardino and work at carpentering, and said he would allow him $50 a month during the winter.

Br. Dewey accepted the proposal and, after remaining in San Francisco two weeks, took steamer for San Pedro. On the 20th of September I left San Francisco, crossed the bay to Oakland,[159] and from thence traveled by land to Sacramento, holding meetings by the way; from thence I went to Salmon falls, Eldorado county,[160] and set in to work, for br. Ebenezer Hanks,[161] at repairing his mill race and mining.

---

at Mr Moses whare we ware informed that Pres. P. P. Pratt was in the City. We then returned to the City whare to our joy we found Pres. Pratt[,] Elders Cannon [and] Sparkes And a large number more on their way to the Sandwich Islands on missions it was truly a time of rejoiceing. We spent the ballance of the day and evening in conversing with the brethren and getting the news from home. . . . Made a report to Pres. Pratt of our precedings while on our mission he said we had done jest right And xcepted our report And said I had done right in giving a draft on Bro horner said I had beter see him and tell him all the particulars as I had him And if he did not humer my draft he would. He also said I had come in as he wanted my assistance And he amediately gave me a mission to Sacramento and th[r]ough the state of California." West, journals, September 8, 1854.

159. Oakland is located about six miles east of San Francisco, across its bay. Originally claimed by the Spanish, the city of Oakland was incorporated in 1854. *Merriam-Webster's Geographical Dictionary*, s.v. "Oakland."

160. El Dorado County is located in eastern California, in the Sierra Nevada. *Merriam-Webster's Geographical Dictionary*, s.v. "El Dorado."

161. Ebenezer Hanks (1815–84) was born in New York in 1815 and moved to Adams County, Illinois, where he was baptized around 1841. In 1846, he became a sergeant in the Mormon Battalion, and his wife, Jane, also joined as a cook and washerwoman. They spent a while in Pueblo in present-day Colorado before arriving in Utah in 1847, days after Brigham Young's company. In 1852, he left for a mission to the Society Islands, but when he learned that the French government was hostile to missionaries there, he remained in California and earned considerable money from mining. He also visited California several times before and after that period. He became involved in various political, mercantile, and mining endeavors in southern Utah, including helping to establish the town of Hanksville, where he

I remained in that part of the country until the 1st of December, during which time I earned the sum that I had borrowed of br. J. M. Horner; I sent it to him. I then went to the San Juan valley[162] to visit my brother;[163] here I found Elder [William] McBride who had organized a branch of the Church at that place, and after tarrying two days I accompanied him to Watsonville, in Pathro valley,[164] and lived with br. Wilkins.

From thence we went to Santa Cruz[165] and lived at br. Meador's[166] where we had the pleasure of meeting with Elder Henry Bigler, late from the Sandwich islands; tarried there over the Sabbath, held meetings in the court house and had an interesting time. On the 27th we took the stage for Santa Clara[167] where we arrived in the evening; tarried there until the 30th and attended the general conference, during which we had a good time.

Jan. 1st I started for Eldorado county, where I arrived on the 5th, and on Sunday, the 8th, fulfilled my appointment for preaching at br. Carn's, the next Sabbath in the court house in Auburn, Placer county.[168] On the 20th Elder Nathan Tanner arrived from S. Francisco; the next day we took

died in 1884. Bate, *Ebenezer Hanks Story*.

162. The San Juan Valley is located about eighty miles south of San Francisco.

163. Possibly Israel West (1831–57), who first traveled to Utah in 1847. Mormon Pioneer Overland Travel database, s.v. "Israel West."

164. Watsonville, California, is located about ninety miles south of San Francisco, in Pajaro (not Pathro) Valley. It was founded in 1852. *Merriam-Webster's Geographical Dictionary*, s.v. "Watsonville."

165. Santa Cruz, located about seventy-five miles south of San Francisco, was established as a Spanish mission in the 1790s. It was incorporated as a city in the 1860s. *Merriam-Webster's Geographical Dictionary*, s.v. "Santa Cruz."

166. Moses A. Meder was born in New Hampshire in 1802, and he traveled on the ship *Brooklyn* to California in 1846. He had a successful lumber business, "Stout, Sirrine, & Meder," in Santa Cruz, where he died in 1890. Bullock, *Ship Brooklyn Saints*, 208.

167. Santa Clara is located about forty miles southeast of San Francisco. It started as a Spanish mission in 1777 and was incorporated as a city in 1852. *Merriam-Webster's Geographical Dictionary*, s.v. "Santa Clara."

168. Placer County is located in eastern California, directly north of El Dorado County. Placer, the county seat, was founded in 1848 during the gold rush and was incorporated in 1888. *Merriam-Webster's Geographical Dictionary*, s.vv. "Placer," "Auburn."

a claim of Mr. Orren Smith,[169] to work on shares. We hired six men, bought a team, began to haul the dirt 3-4 of a mile to the water.

We continued to mine until the 1st of April, working week days and holding meetings on Sundays, when we began to make arrangements to start for home. We bought a team and a light carriage, and on the 17th started for the mission of San Juan to join Elder McBride's company for Great Salt Lake.

We arrived at San Juan on the 29th and on the 30th started down the coast for San Bernardino, which place we reached on the 17th, and were again made welcome by the brethren. I spent several days in visiting with my old, tried friend Elder Dewey, who was enjoying good health, and others of my acquaintances.

On the 24th Elder Nathan Tanner and myself entered into a contract with br. Theodore Thorp[170] to haul 40 cwt. of merchandise to G. S. L. City. We rigged out three six mule teams, loaded our freight and, on the 7th of June, left San Bernardino, for Salt Lake, each driving a six mule team, leaving Elder Dewey there. At the big timber on the Mohave[171] we overtook Capt. McBride and company, who were waiting for us, and on the 11th pursued our journey.

The weather, while crossing the desert, was not so warm as we anticipated; we had a good breeze most of the time which raised an almost constant cloud of dust.

On the 23rd we arrived at the Los Vegas springs where we found Elder William Bringhurst and company;[172] it truly made us rejoice to meet these

169. Orrin E. Smith was a shoemaker, born in Connecticut in 1808. He traveled on the ship *Brooklyn* in 1846 and stayed in Hawaii; he went to Utah in 1848 and later returned to California, where he died in 1896. Bullock, *Ship* Brooklyn *Saints*, 217.

170. Theodore Thorpe helped build a sawmill in San Bernardino. He traveled to Utah in 1855. Lyman, *San Bernardino*, 117; Mormon Pioneer Overland Travel database, s.v. "Theodore Thorp."

171. The Mojave Desert in southeast California is east of San Bernardino. The Mojave River flows through the desert. *Merriam-Webster's Geographical Dictionary*, s.v. "Mojave Desert."

172. In 1855, Brigham Young sent thirty missionaries to Las Vegas (at that time in New Mexico Territory) to establish a fort for travelers between Salt Lake City and California and to preach to the Paiute Indians. William Bringhurst (1818–83), a

brethren, many of whom were near to some of us, for with them we had passed through trying scenes during the past history of this Church. We tarried here three days, repairing our wagons and recruiting our teams; a better spirit I never saw prevail, there was a perfect union throughout the camp and they seemed to feel just about right.

On the 26th we pursued our journey, and on the 7th of July reached Cedar City, Iron county, and on the 15th I arrived in G. S. L. City, found my family all well and blessed with the comforts of life.

I cannot say that we have done any very great things during our mission, but this much I can say, we have done the best that we knew how. I feel that we can say in truth that we have kept br. Amasa Lyman's counsel to the missionaries as we were on our way out; he said, "if you can do no more, mind and save one each, that is yourselves."

I feel grateful to my Father in Heaven that my life has been spared to mingle again with the saints in these peaceful valleys, and I now report myself on hand for duty whenever the servants of God call, for the Priesthood is my law.

———

We tender our thanks to br. West for furnishing so interesting an account of his mission, and are aware that he and his fellow laborer accomplished a great and good work, as the gospel has to be preached for the condemnation of those who will reject as well as for the salvation of those who will believe.—ED.

thirty-six-year-old who had been baptized in 1845 and who traveled to Utah in 1847, was appointed as the head of this mission. They arrived in Las Vegas in June 1855, enjoying the natural hot springs in the area. Chauncey West and the other missionaries in his company passed through Las Vegas just a week after Bringhurst and his group arrived. Missionaries were sent to mine lead in the area in 1856, and Bringhurst was unsupportive of the way this new venture was being handled, so he was released as mission president and disfellowshipped from the church. Conflicts between the mining missionaries and the earlier missionaries, as well as insufficient food, led to the abandonment of the settlement in 1857 and 1858. Bringhurst was later reinstated to full fellowship and died in 1883 in Springville, Utah, where he had been serving as bishop. Woods, *A Gamble in the Desert*; David R. Rowberry, "Las Vegas, Nevada," in *Encyclopedia of Latter-day Saint History*, 640–41; *Merriam-Webster's Geographical Dictionary*, s.v. "Las Vegas."

8

AUGUSTUS FARNHAM AND
THE AUSTRALIAN MISSION

Historical Introduction

"THE WORK OF THE LORD IS PROGRESSING SLOWLY, but appearances are favourable," Augustus Farnham wrote to British Mission president Samuel W. Richards from Australia in July 1853.[1] In September 1854, Farnham similarly wrote Samuel's brother and successor, President Franklin D. Richards, "We are not baptizing our hundreds or fifties at one time, the work is moving along slowly but surely."[2] Yet, in December 1853 and January 1855, Farnham wrote nearly the opposite to Church President Brigham Young, telling him that church membership was growing "quite fast."[3] These conflicting accounts make it difficult to know how Farnham, president of

1. "Australian Mission," *Millennial Star* 15, no. 47 (November 19, 1853): 766–67; p. 269 herein.
2. "Australia," *Millennial Star* 16, no. 50 (June 6, 1855): 798–99; p. 273 herein.
3. "Extracts from a Letter to President Young," *Deseret News*, July 27, 1854; "Elders' Correspondence," *Deseret News*, June 6, 1855; pp. 271, 274 herein.

Augustus Farnham. Courtesy of Church History Library.

the Australian Mission, truly felt about his prose-lytizing experiences in the Southern Hemisphere. Compared to the British Isles, where the Richards brothers oversaw Latter-day Saint preaching, the growth of the church in Australia was sluggish. But compared to the missionary efforts in Asia and other parts of Europe, church growth in Australia was substantial. Farnham and his companions were able to establish several branches of the church throughout the colony, and many of their new converts even immigrated to Utah in the ensuing years.

Augustus Farnham's Early Life, 1805–52

Unlike some of his missionary contemporaries, Augustus Alwin Farnham did not write a reminiscence or maintain an extant journal, so comparatively little is known about his life. Farnham was born on May 20, 1805, in Andover, Massachusetts. He married Mary Jane Pottle in Boston in 1840 and was baptized in 1843, after moving to Illinois. In Nauvoo, Illinois, he became actively involved in his new faith, helping with carpentry on the Nauvoo Temple and being ordained a seventy. By June of 1847, he had moved to St. Louis, Missouri, where he served as a counselor to Bishop Nathaniel Henry Felt. He migrated to Utah with the Silas Richards company, arriving in October 1849. Three years after his arrival in Utah, he was called to leave his family and spread the Latter-day Saint message in Australia.[4]

History of the Australian Mission

The Church of Jesus Christ of Latter-day Saints first reached Australia in the early 1840s, when William James Barratt, a seventeen-year-old convert from England, landed in Adelaide[5] in 1840. Andrew Anderson, another

---

4. See "Farnham (Farnum), Augustus Alvin (Alwin)," in appendix 2, p. 328 herein.
5. Adelaide is the capital of the Australian state of South Australia, located on the state's southeast coast. The city was founded in the 1830s. *Merriam-Webster's Geographical Dictionary*, s.v. "Adelaide."

English convert, arrived in Sydney[6] in 1841. Neither of these men, however, was sent to Australia specifically to proselytize; they had already planned to move to the southern continent, as many of the British were doing at the time, and church leaders took advantage of their plans to relocate, commissioning them to preach. Barratt had only one known convert and drifted into different denominations, but Anderson baptized a dozen people by 1844 and established a branch of the church.[7]

In 1851, Apostle Parley P. Pratt, president of the Pacific Mission, appointed John Murdock[8] and Charles Wandell[9] to become the first missionaries officially assigned to Australia. They arrived in Sydney on October 31, 1851.[10] During their first month there, they printed Pratt's tract *Proclamation!*,[11] baptized their first convert in December, met Andrew Anderson, and formed a branch in January 1852. However, Murdock left seven months after his arrival, leaving Wandell in charge. Wandell later made preparations to leave with about thirty of his converts, not knowing that Augustus Farnham and nine others were coming as reinforcements to the missionary effort. These new missionaries arrived in the harbor at Sydney on the ship *Pacific* on March 31, 1853—six days before Wandell sailed for America. Because of a smallpox quarantine, they were kept on the *Pacific*

---

6. Sydney, the capital of the state of New South Wales, was the first city in Australia and was founded in 1788 as a penal colony. It is an important coastal city. *Merriam-Webster's Geographical Dictionary*, s.v. "Sydney."

7. Newton, *Southern Cross Saints*, 23–25.

8. John Murdock (1792–1871) was baptized in 1830. When his wife died in childbirth in 1831, he placed his children into foster care, including the newborn twins into the care of Joseph and Emma Smith. He was sent to preach in Australia in 1851, and he died in Beaver, Utah, in 1871. Newton, *Southern Cross Saints*, 26; Neilson and Waite, *Settling the Valley, Proclaiming the Gospel*, 330–31.

9. Charles W. Wandell (1819–75) was baptized in 1837 and was sent to open Latter-day Saint missionary work in Australia in 1851. In the 1870s, he joined the Reorganized Church of Jesus Christ of Latter Day Saints and returned to Sydney, where he died. He was thus one of the first missionaries for both the LDS and RLDS churches in Australia. Newton, *Southern Cross Saints*, 35; Neilson and Waite, *Settling the Valley, Proclaiming the Gospel*, 350.

10. Newton, *Southern Cross Saints*, 26–28.

11. Parley P. Pratt, *Proclamation! to the People of the Coasts and Islands of the Pacific; of Every Nation, Kindred and Tongue* ([Sydney]: Hibernian Press, [1851]).

for nine more days and were able to contact Wandell only when he came alongside and spoke with them from another boat.[12]

The nine other missionaries traveling to Australia with Farnham were Josiah W. Fleming, an 1837 convert from Virginia; John Hyde, who had emigrated from England in 1850 after his baptism the year before; Paul Smith, another English convert and emigrant of 1850; Burr Frost, an 1842 convert and member of the vanguard 1847 pioneer company; James Graham, baptized in 1839 in Illinois but born in Ireland; William Hyde, a former member of the Mormon Battalion who had already served numerous missions throughout the United States; John S. Eldredge, an 1843 convert from New York who traveled with Brigham Young's 1847 pioneer company; Absalom P. Dowdle, a native of Alabama who was baptized in 1844; and John W. Norton, an 1840 convert from Tennessee.[13]

Augustus Farnham in Australia, 1852–56

After arriving in Sydney, Farnham, as president of the mission, spread his missionary force along the southern and southeastern coast of Australia. William Hyde saw significant success in the Hunter River Valley,[14] while Burr Frost and Paul Smith had fewer converts in Melbourne.[15] Many branches were formed throughout the country. James Graham briefly visited Brisbane in early 1854, but he found the inhabitants unready for the Latter-day Saint message. Farnham published a periodical, *Zion's Watchman*, to present the church's doctrines and defend it from critics.[16]

---

12. Newton, *Southern Cross Saints*, 27–30; Sonne, *Ships, Saints, and Mariners*, 72, 163; Crawley, *Descriptive Bibliography of the Mormon Church*, 3:73–75.

13. See "Fleming, Josiah Wolcott," "Hyde, John," "Smith, Paul," "Frost, Burr," "Graham, James," "Hyde, William," "Eldredge, John Sunderlin," "Dowdle, Absalom Porter," and "Norton, John Warren," in appendix 2, pp. 326–55 herein.

14. The Hunter River is located in eastern New South Wales; it drains into the Pacific Ocean. *Merriam-Webster's Geographical Dictionary*, s.v. "Hunter."

15. Melbourne is the capital of the state of Victoria in southeast Australia. It was originally established in 1835. A branch of the church was established there between 1852 and 1853. *Merriam-Webster's Geographical Dictionary*, s.v. "Melbourne."

16. Newton, *Southern Cross Saints*, 30–32, 57–61. Augustus Farnham created the *Zion's Watchman* to respond to articles by opponents published in Australian newspapers and to defend Latter-day Saint doctrines. The first issue was published in August

In October 1854, Farnham announced that he and William Cooke, a local convert, were going to take their preaching to New Zealand.[17] The Saints at Sydney helped fund the venture, and Farnham and Cooke went to New Zealand with Thomas Holder, another convert who was originally from the area of Wellington, a prominent town that later became New Zealand's capital. Farnham and Cooke had little to no success in Auckland and Wellington, so Farnham headed back to Sydney in December. Cooke, however, found success in the town of Karori, so he stayed there and established a branch before returning to Sydney in March 1856. Farnham was optimistic about preaching to the Maori people, reporting, "As soon as we can get the latter-day faith before the Maori's, it will spread quite rapidly."[18] However, he and Cooke were not able to do so during their time in New Zealand, probably in part because "none of them speak the English language to any perfection."[19]

Farnham and his companions taught the doctrine of "gathering" to Zion to the Australian Saints, and several groups left their homes to travel

---

1853, and the paper continued until May 1856, when Farnham left Australia.

17. New Zealand was originally settled by Polynesians around 1250 and was colonized by the British in 1840; its colonial status ended in 1907. Augustus Farnham and N. William Cooke arrived from Australia in 1854 to preach the restored gospel of Jesus Christ to the white inhabitants. The first Latter-day Saint branch was established in 1855. *Merriam-Webster's Geographical Dictionary*, s.v. "New Zealand"; Newton, *Southern Cross Saints*, 31–32.

18. "Elders' Correspondence," *Deseret News*, June 6, 1855; p. 275 herein. The Maori people arrived in New Zealand from eastern Polynesia in the late thirteenth century. Their traditions explain that their ancestors arrived on canoes from a place called Hawaiki, an event known as the Great Fleet. In the ensuing centuries, they developed a strong warrior culture, organized themselves into *iwi*, or tribes, and hunted large moa birds to extinction. When Europeans began arriving in the late seventeenth century, the Maori reactions were generally friendly. In 1840, British and Maori representatives signed the Treaty of Waitangi, which ceded New Zealand to England and gave the Maori the rights of British subjects. Farnham and his contemporaries did not preach to the Maori, but the restored gospel did become popular among the Maori beginning in the 1880s. Anderson, Binney, and Harris, *Tangata Whenua*; Newton, *Mormon and Maori*.

19. "Elders' Correspondence," *Deseret News*, June 6, 1855; p. 275 herein; Newton, *Tiki and Temple*, 4–7.

to Utah. William Hyde accompanied sixty-three new members aboard the *Julia Ann* in March 1854, and the journey was uneventful.[20] However, in 1855, emigrating Saints from Australia faced challenges aboard ships. In April, seventy-two Latter-day Saints from Melbourne boarded the *Tarquinia*, but that ship kept leaking and was condemned at Hawaii. In September, twenty-eight from Sydney boarded the *Julia Ann* again, but the ship crashed into a coral reef near the Society Islands. Five of the Saints, three of them children, drowned in the accident, and the survivors were stranded on islands of the Pacific for two months.[21] In May 1856, Farnham departed with about 120 Saints aboard the *Jenny Ford*,[22] leaving the mission under the leadership of Absalom P. Dowdle.[23]

Additional Church Service

After arriving home, Farnham was asked in 1857 to build a tabernacle in Bountiful, Utah; the Greek Revival–style building he constructed is one of the oldest Latter-day Saint meetinghouses still in use. He also might

---

20. The bark *Julia Ann* was built in Maine in 1851. On its first trip with Latter-day Saints on board in 1854, the ship left Newcastle, Australia, on March 22 and arrived in San Pedro, California, on June 12, with stops in Tahiti and Hawaii along the way. Sonne, *Ships, Saints, and Mariners*, 124.

21. Though the *Julia Ann* had previously transported Saints safely from Australia, in October 1855 it crashed into a coral reef off the Scilly Isles (known also as Manuae or Fenua Ura), an uninhabited atoll west of the Society Islands. It was carrying fifty-six passengers, twenty-eight of whom were Latter-day Saints. Eliza Harris and Martha Humphries drowned during the initial wreck; children Mary Humphries, ten-year-old Marion Anderson, and six-month-old Lister Harris also died. The castaways found refuge on a reef and later on a sandbar of the atoll. They lived on turtles, coconuts, flour salvaged from the ship, and occasional crabs and sharks. Captain Benjamin Franklin Pond sailed with some of his crew against the wind to the island of Bora Bora in the Society Islands, where he was able to secure a rescue vessel. The stranded Saints resumed their journey from Tahiti to California by spring 1856. See Devitry-Smith, "Wreck of the *Julia Ann*," 5–29.

22. The *Jenny Ford* was built in 1854 in Maine. Sonne, *Ships, Saints, and Mariners*, 114–15.

23. Newton, *Southern Cross Saints*, 30–32; Sonne, *Ships, Saints, and Mariners*, 114–15, 124–25, 185–86.

have brought home alfalfa seed from Australia for use in Bountiful.[24] He died on May 2, 1865, in Farmington, Utah.[25]

The other missionaries called to Australia in 1852 all returned to the Intermountain West between 1854 and 1858, except for John Hyde, who died of cancer in Sydney in August 1853.[26] William Hyde sailed home safely on the *Julia Ann* in 1854 and became a local church leader

The Bountiful Tabernacle, designed by Augustus Farnham. Courtesy of Andy K. Nelson.

at Hyde Park, Utah, which was named for him; he died there in 1874.[27] Burr Frost and Paul Smith left Australia on the *Tarquinia* in 1855.[28] Frost returned to Utah from California with Apostle Amasa Lyman and died in Salt Lake City in 1878;[29] Smith became involved in ecclesiastical leadership in Snowflake, Arizona, where he died in 1912.[30] Two of the returning missionaries were present for the *Julia Ann*'s shipwreck; James Graham died in Salt Lake City in 1857,[31] and John Eldredge died in Charleston, Utah, in 1871.[32] Josiah Fleming accompanied Farnham on the *Jenny Ford* in 1856,

---

24. Roberts, "More of Utah's Unknown Pioneer Architects," 51.

25. See "Farnham (Farnum), Augustus Alvin (Alwin)," in appendix 2, p. 328 herein.

26. Newton, *Southern Cross Saints*, 30.

27. See "Hyde, William," in appendix 2, p. 337 herein; Sonne, *Ships, Saints, and Mariners*, 124; Van Cott, *Utah Place Names*, 196.

28. Sonne, *Ships, Saints, and Mariners*, 186.

29. See "Frost, Burr," in appendix 2, p. 330 herein.

30. See "Smith, Paul," in appendix 2, p. 355 herein.

31. See "Graham, James," in appendix 2, p. 332 herein; Sonne, *Ships, Saints, and Mariners*, 186.

32. See "Eldredge, John Sunderlin," in appendix 2, p. 328 herein; Sonne, *Ships, Saints, and Mariners*, 186.

became a lieutenant in the Black Hawk War of 1865,[33] and died in Provo, Utah, in 1873.[34] Only two missionaries remained in Australia after Farnham left. Absalom Dowdle presided over the Australia Mission until departing on the *Lucas* in 1857, and he died in Weber County, Utah, in 1897.[35] Finally, John W. Norton left Australia in 1858 aboard the *General Wool* and settled in central and southern Utah, dying in Springdale, Utah, in 1863.[36]

Augustus Farnham's Family Life

Farnham married Mary Jane Pottle on July 5, 1840, in Boston, Massachusetts. They were sealed in the Nauvoo Temple in 1846 and had a total of seven children. Their two oldest, Alwin and Ann, died in a fire in 1846, and their fifth, Ruth, died in infancy in 1849 while the family was traveling across Wyoming to Utah.[37] By the summer of 1852, the Farnhams operated a boarding house.[38] When Augustus left on his mission, Mary Jane was able to use the boarding house to support herself and their four surviving children—Sarah, Mary Jane, Emma, and Fenton, ranging in age from seven years to nine months.

One boarder, a "gentile," or nonmember of the church, described Mary Jane Farnham as "a good Mormon in all points, except that she is bitterly opposed to polygamy." She occasionally fed a hungry neighbor

33. The Black Hawk War was a series of skirmishes between whites and Native Americans that started in 1865 and lasted for several years thereafter. Frustrated at the encroachment of settlers onto American Indians' ancestral lands, Antonga, a Ute chief also known as Black Hawk, led various raids against livestock belonging to the Latter-day Saint settlers, forcing them to relocate and build forts to protect their property. Around seventy whites and twice as many Indians were killed during the years of the Black Hawk War. Though Antonga made peace with church members in 1867 and 1868, related skirmishes continued until 1872. See Peterson, *Utah's Black Hawk War*.

34. See "Fleming, Josiah Wolcott," in appendix 2, p. 329 herein; Newton, *Southern Cross Saints*, 149.

35. See "Dowdle, Absalom Porter," in appendix 2, p. 326 herein; Sonne, *Ships, Saints, and Mariners*, 132.

36. Norton, journal, May 27, 1858; "Norton, John Warren," in appendix 2, p. 347 herein.

37. Mormon Pioneer Overland Travel database, s.v. "Ruth Farnham."

38. "A. Farnham's Boarding House," *Deseret News*, August 7, 1852.

boy and provided odd jobs for other women who needed money.[39] Mary Jane supported a women's project to provide clothing for Indian women and children by donating a dollar and thread and rags for carpet in June of 1854.

Farnham returned to Salt Lake City on November 21, 1856,[40] but there were difficulties after his arrival. On April 15, 1857, Mary Jane took the children and joined a wagon train to head back to Boston. She opposed polygamy, disagreed with church leaders, and endured disapproval for boarding "gentiles." After briefly returning to Utah and officially divorcing Farnham in 1859, Mary Jane moved to St. Louis and again ran a boarding house and raised her four surviving children.

Farnham married Caroline Pill in 1858 and had one daughter, Alice, with her. He married another plural wife, Hannah Reese, in 1860 and had a son, Joseph, before dying in 1865.

Source Note

We have provided five letters that Augustus Farnham wrote during the course of his mission. Two of them were written to President Brigham Young in Utah and published in the *Deseret News*.[41] One was written to Samuel W. Richards and another to Franklin D. Richards, who both served as president of the British Mission; these letters were published in the *Millennial Star*.[42] The final letter was written to George Q. Cannon, the editor

---

39. Ferris, *Mormons at Home*, 104–17.

40. "Arrived," *Deseret News*, November 26, 1856.

41. "Extracts from a Letter to President Young," *Deseret News*, July 27, 1854; "Elders' Correspondence," *Deseret News*, June 6, 1855; for the original letters, see Augustus Farnham to Brigham Young, Dec. 24, 1853; and Jan. 12, 1855, Incoming Correspondence, Brigham Young Office Files. Farnham wrote at least six other letters to Brigham Young. See Augustus Farnham to Brigham Young, June 6, 1853; Aug. 14, 1853 (published as "Extracts of a Letter from Elder Augustus Farnham," *Deseret News*, Dec. 8, 1853); July 28, 1854; May 5, 1855; Dec. 4, 1855; and Feb. 11, 1856, Incoming Correspondence, Brigham Young Office Files.

42. "Australian Mission," *Millennial Star* 15, no. 47 (November 19, 1853): 766–67; "Australia," *Millennial Star* 16, no. 50 (June 6, 1855): 798–99. Farnham wrote at least one other letter to Franklin D. Richards; see Augustus Farnham to Franklin D. Richards, May 31, 1855, Incoming Correspondence, Brigham Young Office Files.

THE ZION'S WATCHMAN,

PUBLISHED BY THE AUTHORITY OF THE

Church of Jesus Christ of Latter-Day Saints,

IN SYDNEY.

No. 1.　　　　SATURDAY, AUGUST 13, 1853.　　　　Vol. I.

PROSPECTUS OF
THE "ZION'S WATCHMAN."

——o——

" The Law of the Lord is perfect, converting the Soul :
The testimony of the Lord is sure,
Making wise the Simple."—19 Psalm, 7 v.

To the Saints and all the friends of TRUTH. The "Zion's Watchman"
we intend to issue monthly. We would say to the friends of truth,
who wish to subscribe for the "Watchman," that we design to pursue a course which will shew the difference between the error which
has often been published by the Periodicals of the day, and the *truth*
as it exists with the Saints of God ;—which truths have been revealed from heaven by the Angels of the Lord to the Prophet Joseph
Smith, and which truths are still being revealed to the servants of
God, who still hold the power of the Holy Melchisedic Priesthood
upon the earth at the present day, and are authorised to administer
in its ordinances according to the Law of the Holy Priesthood, which
is withouth father, without mother, without descent, having neither
beginning of days nor end of life, but made like unto the Son of God
—abideth a Priest continually. Peter like, we judge between the
truth and error, and as the Apostles and Elders, by the gift of the
Holy Spirit of truth as it is in Christ Jesus ;—behold the darkness
that rests upon the minds of the people, we as Elders being clothed
with said Priesthood, are deeply impressed with the necessity of dis-
charging the duty laid upon us by the aforesaid authority, to warn
the inhabitants of the earth to repent of their sins, to be baptized for
the remission of the same, and to have hands laid on them for the
gift of the Holy Ghost. That you with us may become the heirs of
God and joint heirs with Jesus Christ in the kingdom of God, and
be redeemed from your sins, and receive salvation thro' the principles of the everlasting gospel as preached by the Prophets and Apostles ever since the world began, and ever will be by all who have
authority to preach the Gospel of Christ. Who have the authority to
preach the Gospel of Christ ? no person except they have been called
of God as was Aaron. How shall they preach except they be sent of
God? Now we have not received the spirit of the world but the

Page from the first edition of *Zion's Watchman*, edited by Augustus Farnham. Courtesy of Internet Archive.

of the *Western Standard*, a Latter-day Saint newspaper published in California.[43] Throughout the five letters, presented here chronologically, Farnham describes arriving in Australia, assigning the elders to their preaching locales, establishing the *Zion's Watchman* periodical, building up the church "slowly but surely," visiting New Zealand, and returning to America aboard the *Jenny Ford*.

DOCUMENT TRANSCRIPTS

Augustus Farnham to Samuel W. Richards, July 25, 1853[44]

Sydney, July 25th, 1853.
President S. W. Richards—

Sir—Before this reaches you, you will have been informed, through brother Capt. Stayner,[45] of our arrival here, and our detention in quarantine. When we got on shore on the 9th day of April, we found that Elder Wandell had sailed with a company for the Valley. My first object was to call the few remaining Saints together, that we might become acquainted, and that I might learn the situation of the colony, and the feelings of the Saints. It soon appeared that the *Deseret News Extra* had caused some excitement, but it was soon manifest also, that truth must prevail.[46]

The next object was the appointing of the Elders, and the raising of

43. "Arrival of Elder A. Farnham with a Company of Saints," *Western Standard*, September 6, 1856; reprinted as "California," *Millennial Star* 18, no. 46 (November 15, 1856): 733–34.

44. "Australian Mission," *Millennial Star* 15, no. 47 (November 19, 1853): 766–67.

45. Thomas Stayner (1802–69) was a Latter-day Saint ship captain. He traveled to Salt Lake City in 1855. Mormon Pioneer Overland Travel database, s.v. "Thomas Collie Stayner"; Newton, *Southern Cross Saints*, 29, 57.

46. This *Extra* included the public announcement of polygamy. See *Deseret News— Extra*, September 14, 1852.

means to convey them to their respective fields of labour.

Elder William Hyde was appointed to the Hunter's River District, and from thence to Moreton Bay;[47] Elders [Burr] Frost and [Paul] Smith, to Victoria;[48] Elders [Absalom] Dowdle and [John] Norton, to Adelaide and Swan River[49] settlement; Elders [James] Graham and [John] Eldridge, to the South Western section of this colony; Elder [Josiah] Fleming remains with me. Elder John Hyde, some eight years ago, received a blow which has terminated in a cancer, disqualifying him for labour. He is now lying in bed.[50]

We held a Quarterly Conference, July 3rd, in the Old Assembly Rooms, King Street, Sydney, at which the Branches at Sydney, William's River,[51] and Melbourne were represented to contain 102 members, including three Seventies, two High Priests, ten Elders, six Priests, three Teachers, and one Deacon.[52] A vote was taken to sustain all the authorities of the

47. Moreton Bay is an inlet of the Pacific Ocean in southeast Queensland, northeast of Brisbane. It is enclosed by Moreton Island. *Merriam-Webster's Geographical Dictionary*, s.v. "Moreton Bay."

48. Victoria, located in southeast Australia, became a state in 1901. It was inhabited by Aboriginal Australians for thousands of years, and British settlements were established there in the early 1800s. Victoria, named for the English queen, broke off from New South Wales as its own colony in 1851, and beginning that same year, immigrants flooded the region due to the discovery of gold. *Merriam-Webster's Geographical Dictionary*, s.v. "Victoria."

49. Swan River is located in southwestern Australia and drains into the Indian Ocean; the city of Perth is located on it. *Merriam-Webster's Geographical Dictionary*, s.v. "Swan."

50. John Hyde died in Sydney in August 1853. Some held the misconception that injuries could cause cancer. They do not, but extra attention to injured body parts may make sufferers aware of unrelated cancers in the same location. Adelson, "Injury and Cancer," 150–73; Newton, *Southern Cross Saints*, 30.

51. The Williams River is located on the coast of New South Wales, about ninety miles north of Sydney. Newton, *Southern Cross Saints*, 31.

52. A quorum is a unit of men with a particular rank of priesthood. On the general level of the church are quorums of apostles and seventies. On local levels are the high priests and elders quorums of the higher Melchizedek Priesthood and the priests, teachers, and deacons quorums of the lower Aaronic Priesthood. Throughout much of the nineteenth and twentieth centuries, seventies quorums were also organized on a local level. Richard E. Turley, "Quorum," in *Encyclopedia of Latter-day Saint History*, 976–77.

Church, which was carried unanimously.

After the afternoon service, the ordination of two Elders, one Priest, and two Teachers was attended to. The Saints feel to give thanks unto their Father in heaven for the privileges and blessings enjoyed during the day.

The work of the Lord is progressing slowly, but appearances are favourable. There is considerable impression made upon the public mind, many people are inquiring, and some few are being baptized, and we hope the time is not far distant when the baptisms will be much more numerous. We realize that the Lord is with us. It is by His Spirit and power that all that is done is accomplished. And it being His work we are engaged in, we feel assured that He will carry it on, until all the honest in heart are gathered from these lands.

We have this day received a letter from Elders Dowdle and Norton, Adelaide; they are well, and prospects appear favourable in that part also.

In consequence of the continued attacks made upon our faith, by the papers, and the utter impossibility of obtaining the insertion of anything in reply, we have determined to issue a monthly paper, to be called *Zion's Watchman*. The public have been notified by a circular.

We wish you to forward us more of O. Pratt's works complete and bound,[53] 200 more Hymn Books,[54] 100 Books of Mormon,[55] 100 Doctrine

---

53. Orson Pratt was a prolific writer of theological and scientific works. In 1851 and 1852, a compilation of sixteen of his pamphlets, written between 1848 and 1851, was published in Liverpool as *A Series of Pamphlets*. The book also included works by William Gibson and John Taylor, but the cover titled it *O. Pratt's Works*, and Pratt's portrait was included near the title page. The pamphlets were influential among Latter-day Saint converts in England. Orson Pratt, *A Series of Pamphlets* (Liverpool: R. James, 1851); Crawley, *Descriptive Bibliography of the Mormon Church*, 2:195–99.

54. Beginning in 1840, the church published hymnals in the British Isles. Although these hymnbooks were originally conceived for European Saints, they became influential collections of songs for Latter-day Saints worldwide and went through substantial revisions. The ninth edition of the British hymnal was published in 1851. *Sacred Hymns and Spiritual Songs, for the Church of Jesus Christ of Latter-day Saints, in Europe* (Liverpool: F. D. Richards, 1851); Crawley, *Descriptive Bibliography of the Mormon Church*, 1:121, 2:241–43.

55. The third European edition of the Book of Mormon was published in 1852. Crawley, *Descriptive Bibliography of the Mormon Church*, 2:311–14.

and Covenants,[56] more Voice of Warning,[57] and Spencer's Letters,[58] 100 O. Pratt's work on Celestial Marriage.[59] You may depend upon us forwarding the money as speedily as possible. I have no doubt, that when these books come to hand, they will give an increased impetus to the work here, and it will require a constant and regular supply of the Standard Works[60] to keep up with the movement. We hope you will be able to supply us with them.

Praying our Heavenly Father to bless you and the Saints, I remain,

Yours, in the New Covenant,

Augustus Farnham.

56. The third European edition of the Doctrine and Covenants was published in 1852. It included 111 sections (revelations) and the Lectures on Faith. Crawley, *Descriptive Bibliography of the Mormon Church*, 2:341–43.

57. Originally published in New York in 1837, the seventh edition of Parley P. Pratt's *A Voice of Warning* was published in Liverpool in 1852. Crawley, *Descriptive Bibliography of the Mormon Church*, 1:69–71, 2:304–5.

58. Orson Spencer, *Letters Exhibiting the Most Prominent Doctrines of the Church of Jesus Christ of Latter-day Saints* (Liverpool: S. W. Richards, 1852) was the fourth edition of a book containing Orson Spencer's replies to a letter by Reverend William Crowell, a Baptist minister, about Spencer's conversion to the church. The edition also included a few of Spencer's other doctrinal letters and a poem by Eliza R. Snow. The first editions were published in 1847 after Spencer became president of the British Mission. Crawley, *Descriptive Bibliography of the Mormon Church*, 1:364–70, 2:358–59.

59. It is not specifically clear what article Farnham is requesting in this letter, but Apostle Orson Pratt published many polygamy defenses in the *Seer*. Neilson, *Exhibiting Mormonism*, 37–38; Whittaker, "Bone in the Throat," 304–14.

60. For Latter-day Saints today, the expression "standard works" refers to the scriptural canon of the Bible, Book of Mormon, Doctrine and Covenants, and Pearl of Great Price. However, in the nineteenth century, the term referred to seminal, important literature in general, both inside and outside of the church. Clyde J. Williams, "Standard Works," in *Encyclopedia of Mormonism*, 3:1415–16; Davies, *Corpus of LDS General Conference Talks* and *Corpus of Historical American English*, s.v. "standard works."

Augustus Farnham to Brigham Young, December 24, 1853[61]

Sydney, Dec. 24th, 1853.

I returned two days since from a tour of some weeks up Hunter's river district, after visiting the different branches of that section—it being the field in which brs. William Hyde and John McCarthy[62] have been laboring. At present, br. Hyde is attending to it by himself. They have been much blest in their labors. Br. Hyde's zeal for the cause of Christ is more than his bodily strength—he does not spare himself in the least, and the extent of his field is so great he is continually on the move.

The work is progressing quite fast, and many good men and women are being added to the Church, thro' his labors. The Lord has abundantly blest him with his Spirit, altho' his bodily health is not such as I could wish it might be.—The labors are very hard in this country, there is so much traveling to do, and the weather is so very warm. The only way of traveling is on foot, yet the brethren are all as active as men can be. The work is spreading over a great extent of country, and the elders are traveling both on the frontiers and in the interior; and the gospel is being preached many miles out from Sydney.

The field is divided into three different conferences. First, Sydney Conference; second, Melbourne; third, Adelaide; which are all prospering as well as I could expect, considering the strong current of opposition which we have to stem. I am in hopes it will stir the people to come out and listen to the truth, that they may understand for themselves, and not be so much bound down by priestcraft.

Since the "Zion's Watchman" has made its appearance, the whole ecclesiastical club is up in arms, and find no place of refuge, where the little fellow is not with them. The elders are so much scattered over the colony, that it has got a wide circulation, for they pass it into every person's hand who will read it and pass it to his neighbor.

---

61. "Extracts from a Letter to President Young," *Deseret News*, July 27, 1854.
62. John McCarthy (1830–98) was a convert from Sydney who survived the shipwreck of the *Julia Ann* and traveled to Utah via San Francisco in 1856. Mormon Pioneer Overland Travel database, s.v. "John McCarthy"; Newton, *Southern Cross Saints*, 30.

If the gospel spreads according to the present prospect, there will be a good work done in this colony in the course of a few years. The field is extensive, and has many more inhabitants than I at first imagined. We have an increase of seven organized branches since the arrival of this mission, and all were in a good and prosperous condition, at the last reports. It is contemplated to send a company of saints over this season, composed of the two Branches of Hunter's river district.—They will number in all, when the company is made up, not far from one hundred, according to the present calculation. I intend to clear the ground if possible, taking the poor first, for the rich can come when they please.[63] It is expected the company will start from Sydney as early as possible in the month of April. Whether we shall ship to San Francisco, to San Diego,[64] or San Pedro, is not yet decided.

It is expected the company will be under the charge of Elder William Hyde, whose health compels his return. It is probable he may regain health before he arrives in the midst of his friends and family. Remember us to all the Saints.

Augustus Farnham.

Augustus Farnham to Franklin D. Richards, September 18, 1854[65]

103 Paramatta Street, Sydney,
Sept. 18, 1854.
F. D. Richards.

Dear Brother—I embrace the opportunity offered me to congratulate you

---

63. In 1854, Farnham organized donations for the Perpetual Emigrating Fund for the Australian Saints. However, he cancelled the endeavor after he received a gentle rebuke from Brigham Young, who believed that circumstances in Australia were better for emigrating Saints than they were elsewhere. Newton, *Southern Cross Saints*, 142.

64. San Diego is located in southern California, near the Mexican border. It was first settled by the Spanish in the eighteenth century, and Robert Field Stockton captured it for the United States in 1846. *Merriam-Webster's Geographical Dictionary*, s.v. "San Diego."

65. "Australia," *Millennial Star* 16, no. 50 (December 16, 1855): 798–99.

upon your safe arrival among the British Saints, and I sincerely pray that the Lord may eminently bless you, in your two-fold capacity of President of the British Mission, and editor of the *Star*.

It gives me pleasure to inform you, that the work of the Lord in these colonies is progressing. We are not baptizing our hundreds or fifties at one time, the work is moving along slowly but surely, more so in the interior than in this city. The principles are winning their widening way into every class of society. In fact, "Mormonism" has made quite an excitement among the people recently, the clergy have awakened in the opposition with renewed zeal and energy, and no course is too mean or despicable for them to pursue, so that they can but prevail upon the people not to listen to the Elders, nor to read our books. The usual ebullitions of calumny and slander, with their concomitants of falsehood, blasphemy, ignorance, &c., are poured forth in a manner alike discreditable to intelligence and honour. At this we are not astonished, for what other weapons could they bring forth against truth and righteousness.

All this does not discourage us in the least, for we know whose we are, and that the work we are engaged in is the work of the Great God. And we feel grateful to our Father in heaven, who has in our weakness made us strong, giving us light, knowledge, and power in the things of His kingdom, so that we have been enabled at all times to rebuke the scorner, silence the gainsayer, and instruct and counsel the Saints.

It is true, the people of these lands are a peculiar people, being generally dead to the interests of religion, caring but little what the true principles of the Gospel are; it may, indeed, be said of them, that their faith is a mere tradition, their worship an empty form, the impression being transitory, ending with the service, when they again devote themselves to gold and pleasure. But withal, there are some as good and honest people in these lands, as can be found on the earth. These must be hunted and fished out and gathered.[66] To accomplish this we are encouraged to labour, but the apathy of the people, and their scattered condition, together with the great opposition manifested by the priests, tend much to embarrass our movements, and to retard the progress of the work.

---

66. See Jeremiah 16:16.

Still the Lord has blessed us and our labours, and we feel assured that He will continue to do so.

We received a letter from Elder William Hyde, on the 14th inst., dated San Pedro, June 13, giving an account of the passage of the *Julia Ann*, and the safe arrival of the company of Saints who left here on March the 22nd.

The desire to leave the confines of Babylon pervades the mass of the Saints here, and they are striving with all their power to gather, so that it is expected that another company will leave here about April or May next.

May God the eternal Father bless you, and prosper His work in your hands, is the earnest desire of your brother in the Gospel.

Augustus Farnham.

Augustus Farnham to Brigham Young, January 12, 1855[67]

{Extracts of a letter from Elder Augustus Farnham to President Brigham Young.}[68]

Australia.
New Castle, Jan. 12, 1855.

As regards the work of the Lord in these lands, it is moving on very steadily, and spreading over a large portion of country. It has, for the last nine or ten months, kept the elders quite busy, as the field is large, and the laborers few. The number of saints is increasing quite fast, and many are making every possible exertion to gather.

So far as we can judge, we consider it best to push them to Zion as quick as circumstances will permit, for this is a very bad pasture in which to herd sheep. Many have closed, and others are closing up their affairs as fast as possible, and wish to get out of this land. When their yearly leases are up, they do not wish to lease again.

If any vessel should happen to be in this port, I may send a company in the spring, and another by the Julia Ann in July.

---

67. "Elders' Correspondence," *Deseret News*, June 6, 1855.
68. See Augustus Farnham to Brigham Young, January 12, 1854, Incoming Correspondence, Brigham Young Office Files.

As respects my New Zealand mission, it occupied nearly three months. Elder William Cooke[69] went with me, and is still in that mission. I traveled thro' most of the towns and villages of any note, and held several meetings in each place. Our meetings were well attended, and in several places quite an interest was manifested; many acknowledged that the work was true, and I have reason to think that there will be a good work done on those Islands among the Europeans.

The natives are a fine race of people, tho' none of them speak the English language to any perfection. We made some effort to get a portion of our works translated, which I am in hopes will soon be done. As soon as we can get the latter-day faith before the Maori's, it will spread quite rapidly. In my opinion there will soon be opposition on that land, as well as in New South Wales,[70] for it is increasing thro' these lands; all right.

The 'Watchman' will give a more full account, both of my travels, and the progress of the work, and the state of affairs with us. I have constantly forwarded them to you, and others in the Valley.

{Not one number has come to the President.}[71]

The elders are all as busily engaged as men can be.—The call is great for preaching in the country, not so much so in the cities. Sydney is our head quarters; it is also the head quarters of the opposition, and they are all at work, but do not gain much ground. They have been met on every side, as

---

69. William Cooke (1827–92) had traveled through Utah in 1852 while he was on his way to search for gold in California. His family remained in Salt Lake City and converted to the church, and after he had continued to Australia to seek gold there, his wife wrote him and advised him to join the Latter-day Saints in Sydney. He left Australia with the Saints in 1856 aboard the *Jenny Ford*. In 1858, he was shot and killed while working as a Salt Lake City jailer. His wife, Sarah Ann Cooke, performed theatrically in the Salt Lake Social Hall and Salt Lake Theater for more than a decade. Newton, *Southern Cross Saints*, 150; Mormon Pioneer Overland Travel database, s.v. "William Sutton Cooke"; Crawley, *Descriptive Bibliography of the Mormon Church*, 3:334–35.

70. New South Wales is a state in southeast Australia, with Sydney as its capital. Captain James Cook named and claimed it for the British in 1770, and it was settled in 1788. The colonies all became part of the Commonwealth of Australia in 1901. *Merriam-Webster's Geographical Dictionary*, s.v. "New South Wales."

71. This *Deseret News* insertion was in a larger font than Farnham's own text.

yet, and will be, I am thinking, and not much to their satisfaction. But the saints are rejoicing in the prospects of the work, and looking forward to the day of release from this wicked people.

Br. Frost is at Van Dieman's Land,[72] and br. Robert Owens[73] is with him. They have been there the last two months.

I shall leave Sydney to go to Victoria and Adelaide, about the 25th of the present month, to visit the branches in those sections, as we have several branches in that region, and many are wishing to gather out this season.

Augustus Farnham to George Q. Cannon, August 23, 1856.[74]

San Pedro, Cal., Aug. 23, '56.
Mr. Editor:—

Feeling to communicate to you at this time, I will give you a short account of my labors, and the progress of the work, as it has been carried forward in Australasia during my mission in that far-off land, for the last three and a half years.

I will briefly state that the gospel has penetrated, and been pushed forward through extensive portions of New South Wales, Victoria, South Australia,[75] Van Dieman's Land and the different Colonies of New Zealand,[76]

---

72. Van Dieman's Land is an old name for Australia's island state, Tasmania, located off the continent's southeast coast. A Dutch navigator, Abel Tasman, named it in 1642. Britain took over in the nineteenth century and renamed it Tasmania; it became part of the Commonwealth of Australia in 1901. In 1854, missionary Robert Owen, who had been laboring in India, went to Tasmania to preach the restored gospel, but he had little success. *Merriam-Webster's Geographical Dictionary*, s.v. "Tasmania."

73. Robert Owen had served in India, and after he finished his labors there, he traveled to Australia as a seaman on the ship *Hyderabad*. Owens left Australia in April 1855 on the ill-fated *Tarquinia*. Britsch, *Nothing More Heroic*, 289–90.

74. "Arrival of Elder A. Farnham with a Company of Saints," *Western Standard*, September 6, 1856.

75. South Australia is located in the center of the southern half of Australia. Though Dutch explorers discovered the area in 1627, it did not become an official settlement until the British established it as a province in 1836. It became a state in 1901. *Merriam-Webster's Geographical Dictionary*, s.v. "South Australia."

76. The New Zealand Constitution Act of 1852 divided New Zealand into six provinces: Auckland, New Plymouth, Wellington, Nelson, Canterbury, and Otago.

where many have obeyed the truth, and in all of which a good foundation has been laid for future progress, so that an abundant harvest cannot fail to be reaped from the labors of faithful and efficient elders who may follow in those fields. Not only are large and spacious halls ready to be opened to receive them, as they go to spread the principles of eternal truth, (which all who have pioneered in the work have so far faithfully labored to do) but in all sections there are families ready to receive them and to minister to their temporal necessities.

In all of these things I acknowledge the hand of Israel's God, and give to Him the glory, who is ever ready to be with and bless his faithful servants, according to his promise, by preceding them in their path, and by opening the hearts of the people to whom they are sent not only to receive them, but also the message of Eternal Truth which they bear. That this is the case is plain to be seen by the gathering of the people from those distant lands to Zion; and I feel that the work in those lands is but in its infancy. That the Lord may bless all His faithful servants who are sent forth to labor in the ministry, is my prayer.

Having been called from my field of labor to gather up a company for Zion, I give you a sketch of our passage across the Pacific.

We left port Jackson,[77] N. S. W., on the 28th of May, and proceeded to sea in good health and spirits. The weather being quite pleasant and the sea calm, we had very little sea sickness. The only disease on board was the whooping cough, which soon ceased, and all was as agreeable as could be expected by a body of passengers gathered from different parts of the Colonies, and crowded together in so small a space.[78] Every exertion was made

---

Mulgan, *Politics in New Zealand*, 192.

77. Port Jackson is a natural harbor located at the city of Sydney. *Merriam-Webster's Geographical Dictionary*, s.v. "Port Jackson."

78. John Jones, who had served as president of the Sydney Branch, kept a journal of the ship *Jenny Ford's* voyage on behalf of Augustus Farnham. Farnham's statement that "all was as agreeable as could be expected" is clearly diplomatic, as Jones recorded numerous instances of the Saints contending with each other over cleanliness, noise, food, drunkenness, and other issues, including complaints that they could not go ashore at Tahiti or Hawaii (though most did go ashore at Tahiti). Passenger James Simmons, a fellow Saint, was particularly quarrelsome and prone to intoxication, and on one drunken occasion, Farnham threatened "that if he would not

by Capt. S. F. Sargent and officers to make us comfortable and happy. They spared no pains to render the situation of all as agreeable as possible.

We arrived at Tahiti[79] on the 22d of June, where we called for the purpose of relieving the Saints who survived the wreck of the *Julia Ann*. We found, however, to our great joy, that they had been assisted by friends, who feel for the sufferings of their fellow-beings independent of sectarian prejudices. The Masonic Fraternity helped them all in their power, and thus rendered their circumstances comparatively comfortable.[80] It gave my heart joy to learn of this act of hospitality on the part of my brethren, the Masons.[81] It being St. John's day[82] a very friendly invitation was sent on

---

be quiet that he would be put in irons." There were troubles among the women as well; on one occasion, "there was a disturbance between Sisters Moyes and Mapstead; Moyes having called the other a whore." Augustus Farnham Immigrating Company journal, June 25, 1856, 57; July 14, 1856, 83; see also Newton, *Southern Cross Saints*, 145.

79. Tahiti is the largest island of the Society Islands in French Polynesia. It was inhabited by Polynesians for about two thousand years before the French claimed the land in 1768. *Merriam-Webster's Geographical Dictionary*, s.v. "Polynesia."

80. As the *Jenny Ford* approached Tahiti, Farnham learned of a Mrs. McGee and her children, who were the last survivors of the *Julia Ann* there, the others having already departed for California. Farnham invited Addison Pratt aboard the ship for a priesthood meeting. "This meeting having been called for considering the case of Mrs McGee and family who tho not members of the Church were the only survivors of the wreck that were left on this Island. It was determined that as our bretheren and Sisters had been assisted to leave through the charity of the Free Masons and Mr McGee being a Mason that therefore they be taken to San Francisco by us. They numbered three and a half passages besides an infant three weeks old." Augustus Farnham Immigrating Company journal, June 23, 1856, 52–54.

81. Freemasonry is a fraternal organization that claims its origins to the stonemasons of Solomon's temple. Masonic lodges sprung up in America in the eighteenth century and increased in popularity. During the 1840s, many Latter-day Saints in Nauvoo, including Joseph Smith and Brigham Young, were involved in the order, but in the 1850s, after the Saints had relocated to Utah, church members and Masons began to distance themselves from each other. Jeffers, *Freemasons*; Homer, "Masonry and Mormonism in Utah," 57–63.

82. St. John's Day, or the feast of John the Baptist, is held on June 24. It is an important day for Masons, as the first Grand Lodge was formed on June 24, 1717, in England. Masons also observe another St. John's Day, the feast of John the Evangelist,

board to Mr. Wilber and myself to join in their celebration; but in consequence of a press of business, neither of us could attend. I was truly glad to meet Elder Addison Pratt[83] here, an old tried friend and brother, from whom I heard intelligence from home which proved a source of consolation to me.[84]

We left Tahiti on the 28th of June, and touched at Honolulu, Oahu, Sandwich Islands, on the 16th of July. We remained only a few hours, but had the satisfaction of meeting with Pres. Silas Smith,[85] Elder John T. Caine[86] and others of that mission, besides several of the saints left there

on December 27. Jeffers, *Freemasons*, 24; "St. John's Day," 6.

83. Addison Pratt (1802–72) was baptized in Kirtland, Ohio, in 1838, and he served missions to the Society Islands from 1843 to 1847 and again from 1850 to 1852. Jenson, *Latter-day Saint Biographical Encyclopedia*, 3:698.

84. In 1843, Joseph Smith sent Addison Pratt, Benjamin F. Grouard, Noah Rogers, and Knowlton F. Hanks on a mission to the Sandwich Islands. Hanks died during the voyage, but the others labored in the Society Islands (French Polynesia), rather than their assigned field of Hawaii. It was the first foreign-language mission in the church. The three missionaries established branches and baptized two thousand people. Pratt served from 1843 to 1847 and again from 1849 to 1852, while Grouard remained in the islands until 1852. However, the French government and Catholic priests in the Society Islands were averse to non-Catholic religious activity, and in March 1852 a new law greatly restricted Latter-day Saint affairs. Pratt and Grouard consequently left the islands in May 1852. Elder James S. Brown left in late 1852 after a scuffle occurred between a French policeman, some Catholic priests, and some local Latter-day Saints, in which the policeman and a priest were killed. In 1856, Apostles Charles C. Rich and Amasa Lyman sent Pratt back. He arrived in Tahiti in June 1856, but the French government prevented him from preaching or visiting other islands. He left the islands four months later. Ellsworth and Perrin, *Seasons of Faith and Courage*; Britsch, *Unto the Islands of the Sea*, 18–21; Early Mormon Missionaries database, s.vv. "Addison Pratt," "Benjamin Franklin Grouard."

85. Silas Smith (1830–1910) traveled to Utah in 1847 and was president of the Sandwich Islands Mission from 1855 to 1857. Neilson and Waite, *Settling the Valley, Proclaiming the Gospel*, 342; Early Mormon Missionaries database, s.v. "Silas Schellinger Smith."

86. John T. Caine (circa 1828–1911) traveled to Utah in 1852, served in the Sandwich Islands Mission from 1854 to 1856, and was Utah's delegate to the US House of Representatives from 1883 to 1893. Early Mormon Missionaries database, s.v. "John Thomas Caine"; Mormon Pioneer Overland Travel database, s.v.

from br. Frost's company; they were all in good health and spirits, and the latter very anxious to get to Zion.

From Honolulu we proceeded with a favorable breeze. The next day our company was thrown into considerable excitement, occasioned by the falling overboard of a young lad, while attempting to draw a bucket of water. The sea was rather rough and the vessel running about ten knots an hour; life buoys were immediately thrown out, the headway of the vessel stopped and a boat launched as quickly as possible; he had, however, floated considerably astern before this could be accomplished, and some thirty minutes elapsed ere he was picked up. When we received him on board safe and sound, we felt to give thanks to our heavenly Father for his remarkable preservation.[87]

The 24th of July—the Anniversary of the arrival of the Pioneers in Great Salt Lake Valley—was celebrated with exercises suitable to the occasion, an account of which is forwarded for the benefit of your readers.[88]

"John Thomas Caine."

87. On July 17, 1856, John Jones recorded, "A little after 9 A.M. all on board were thrown into the greatest consternation by the cry of 'A boy overboard[.']' It soon was ascertained from my son J.R. [John Robert] who was with him at the time that it was Henry Simmonds [Simmons]. He [was] drawing a bucket of water and fell over. We were immediatly hove too. Bouys were thrown over but did not reach him. the Jolly Boat was lowered the painter [a rope] broke and it drifted. The Captains Grey[?] was then lowered <and moved[?]> by 4 Sea Men and McHarse the 2nd Mate they succeeded in rescueing them him and brought the Jolly Boat back with them. The boats being hoisted we again sailed with thankful hearts. The boy was nearly exhausted when the boat reached him he is aged 16 years." The following week, "Prest Farnham made some remarks . . . about young men playing cards. In his remarks he mentioned the name of Henry Simmonds as the person who carried the cards in his pockets and said that [he] had better be careful lest he should fall overboard again." Henry's father did not respond well to the accusation. Augustus Farnham Immigrating Company journal, July 17, 1856, 89–90; July 26, 1856, 111–12.

88. The vanguard company of pioneers arrived in the Salt Lake Valley, July 21–24, 1847. Since that time, Latter-day Saints have observed July 24 in remembrance of the pioneers, with the first recorded celebrations beginning in 1849. Aboard the *Jenny Ford*, the Saints raised the Stars and Stripes, held a parade, fired guns, sang hymns, and made speeches. Newton, *Southern Cross Saints*, 152; Augustus Farnham Immigrating Company journal, July 24, 1856, 97–109; David Kenison,

We arrived at San Pedro on the evening of the 15th inst., having been blessed with a pleasant passage, together with a liberal portion of the Holy Spirit, which caused peace and union to pervade in our midst.

I immediately proceeded to San Bernardino, where I made arrangements for teams to convey the saints to that place, and returned on the 20th inst. I found the saints comfortably encamped in tents, and all doing well. Sister L. Stephens gave birth to a fine healt[h]y boy this morning. The moving of the saints is now going on, and all will shortly be *en route* for San Bernardino.

May the Lord God of Israel bless and prosper you in your efforts to stem the torrent of lies, to unmask error, and diffuse the light and influence of truth abroad.

Your brother in the gospel,
A. Farnham.

"Pioneer Commemorations," in *Encyclopedia of Latter-day Saint History*, 921–22; Olsen, "Celebrating Cultural Identity," 159–78.

APPENDIXES

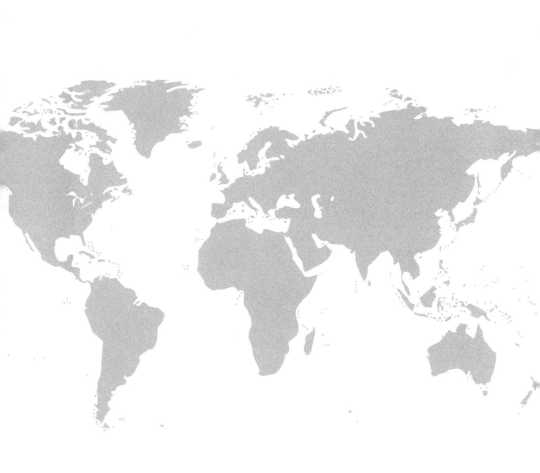

MINUTES OF THE AUGUST 1852 SPECIAL CONFERENCE

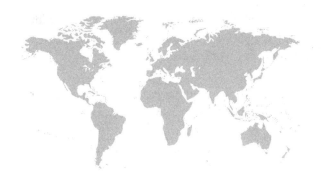

Source Note

MINUTES OF CONFERENCE. FEATURED VERSION PUBLISHED as a *Deseret News* extra in Salt Lake City, September 14, 1852, Church History Library. We have featured only the minutes for Saturday, August 28, when the missionaries' assignments were announced. We have not included the minutes for Sunday, August 29, when Apostle Orson Pratt publicly announced the practice of plural marriage or the related first printing of Joseph Smith's July 12, 1843, revelation on marriage (Doctrine and Covenants 132). See Crawley, *Descriptive Bibliography of the Mormon Church,* 2:354–57.

DOCUMENT TRANSCRIPT

A Special Conference of the Elders of the Church of Jesus Christ of Latter-Day-Saints, assembled in the Tabernacle, Great Salt Lake City, August 28th, 1852, 10 o'clock, a.m., pursuant to public notice.

Present, the First Presidency, Brigham Young, Heber C. Kimball, Willard Richards.

Presiding Patriarch, John Smith.

Of the Twelve Apostles, Orson Pratt, John Taylor, Wilford Woodruff, Geo. A. Smith, Ezra T. Benson, Erastus Snow, and Franklin D. Richards.

Of the First Presidents of the Seventies, Joseph Young, Henry Herriman, Zera Pulsipher, Albert P. Rockwood, Jedediah M. Grant.

Presidency of High Priests quorum, John Young, Reynolds Cahoon, Geo. B. Wallace.

Presiding Bishop, Edward Hunter, and about two thousand elders.

Clerk of Conference, Thomas Bullock.

Reporter, G. D. Watt.

Called to order by Prest. Kimball.

The choir sung a Hymn. Prayer by elder Geo. A. Smith. Singing.

President Kimball presented the business of the conference in the following speech:

We have come together to day, according to previous appointment, to hold a special conference to transact business, a month earlier than usual, inasmuch as there are elders to be selected to go to the nations of the earth, and they want an earlier start than formerly. There will probably be elders chosen to go to the four quarters of the globe to transact business, preach the Gospel, &c.

I recollect reading in one of the revelations in the Book of Doctrine and Covenants, where the Lord says, "If a man, inasmuch as he is an elder, has a desire in his heart to preach the Gospel, he it is that is called to preach the Gospel." On the other hand, the Scriptures or some of the other Revelations of God, say, that many are called, but few are chosen; when a man has that desire in his heart he is called, but perhaps not a great many will be chosen to go forth and preach the Gospel.

I suppose you are all aware, by the information that we have received from our brethren the Apostles, who have lately returned from foreign missions, that the work of God has commenced in many nations of Europe, and upon the islands of the sea; still there are many nations where the Gospel door has not yet been opened in a direct way, though the foundation has been laid for the introduction of the Gospel among them, and indirectly the door has been opened to all nations, that is, it has been opened into the main room, still there are a great many adjacent rooms, leading from that, that have yet to be opened with the smaller keys.

I want to say one thing before we proceed to the business of calling and setting apart those who have to go from this place to the nations, this season; we have made a selection of a considerable number of elders to leave home and go abroad; this may be repugnant to the feelings of some; they may think it is a hazardous undertaking, but at the same time, to go now is nothing to compare with going out to preach the Gospel fifteen years ago, when they had to go not only without purse or scrip, but without any knowledge that there was a friend to take them by the hand when they arrived at their destination; now they cannot go to any part of the world, scarcely, but they will find themselves among the saints.

It is a pleasure to preach the truth, I will say, to those who love to do the will of the Father, as it was with Jesus Christ; for says he, Father, not my will but thine be done; I wish to know nothing but thy will, and that I will do until I spend my life. Did he not do this? He did. You require that same spirit and determination to carry out the same purpose; and I beg and beseech of you, brethren, you that shall be chosen, when you are elected, to go, if you don't live until you get to the United States; for when men are called and set apart to the ministry, to go to the nations of the earth, if they refuse to go it is death to them, that is, to their characters as faithful elders in Israel; they go down and not up, backward and not forward. I merely speak of this from my own experience, for I have had one in this church of upwards of twenty years. I was raised up as it were with the prophet; I lived with him to the day of his death. As to our present prophets and elders, bro. Brigham Young I have lived with, with him I have traveled, and with him

I have suffered. I have eat and slept with him, and been by his side almost my whole life. I could say with propriety, and I can say it with truth, that Joseph Smith was a Prophet of God, a Seer, a Revelator, an Apostle of Jesus, and was ordained directly under the hands of Peter, James, and John; and he died a Prophet, and Hyrum died a Patriarch of Jesus, a father in Israel.

Brother Brigham Young is the successor of Joseph Smith, and a better man never lived upon the earth, nor ever sought the interest of this people more fervently from morning until night, and vice versa, than he has done. Did he not travel in the days of Joseph? He did, from the time he came into the church until the death of Joseph, and so did I. Did we ever hesitate for one moment? No, not for a moment.

Jesus sought to do the will of his Father in Heaven; so it was our duty to do the will of Joseph; and now it is the duty of us all to do the will of Brother Brigham, for he reveals to us the will of God, which is his will. We will do his will as an elder, as a Prophet, as an Apostle of Jesus Christ, holding the same keys that Peter of old held, the same that Joseph Smith held as an Apostle. You all believe this, don't you, without an exception? Well, if this is your faith, if this is your determination, I want you should manifest it by raising your right hands, and saying AYE. {A literal forest of hands was the result of this call, and the spacious hall trembled when a simultaneous aye burst from the mouths of over 2,000 persons.} There it is, and it cannot be any other way.

I say to those who are elected to go on missions, *go, if you never return,* and commit what you have into the hands of God—your wives, your children, your brethren and your property. Let truth and righteousness be your motto, and don't go into the world for anything else but to preach the Gospel, build up the kingdom of God, and gather the sheep into the fold. You are sent out as shepherds to gather the sheep together, and remember that they are not your sheep, they belong to him that sends you; then don't make a choice of any of those sheep, *don't make selections before they are brought home and put into the fold;* you understand *that.* Amen.

Elder Geo. A. Smith said:

What has been said brethren and sisters, is verily true. This kingdom of God has been built up by His distinguished blessings, and the exertion and energy of those whom God has called to bear it off. When men refuse to fulfil their callings, and magnify them in the proclamation of the fullness of the gospel to the nations of the earth, they certainly lay the foundation for their own ruin. When men, on the other hand, become so puffed up in their own estimation as to think that the kingdom of God could not roll forth without their mighty exertions, they fall into transgression; they are fools in Israel, and their greatness will vanish like smoke.

The fact is, God has planned for us the best sieve that could be imagined. He is determined to sift the nations with the sieve of vanity, and he has placed us here on the edge of the mountains, where a little shaking of the winds will cause everything without weight, easily to slide off to the diggings; and in this way the work of sifting is going on daily, and hourly, and yearly, from time to time, according to the nature of the materials that happens to be thrown upon the sieve.

No doubt many of us may be called upon, if not to-day, at some other time, to bear the message of the gospel of salvation to the nations of the earth; for this was one of the commandments of the prophet. He enjoined upon us that we preach the gospel to all nations; that we should send forth the word to all people; this responsibility has been laid upon the priesthood of the church, and they are required to fulfil this commandment. There is not an elder, a priest, a teacher, or a member of this church but what bears a share of this responsibility.

The missions we will call for during this conference, are generally, not to be very long ones; probably from 3 to 7 years will be as long as any man will be absent from his family. If any of the elders refuse to go, they may expect that their wives will not live with them; for there is not a Mormon sister who would live with a man a day, who would refuse to go on a mission. There is no other way for a man to save his family; and in order to save himself he must fulfil his calling, and magnify his priesthood in proclaiming the fullness of the gospel to the nations of the earth; and this, certainly, ought to be the greatest joy to the family of any man, who feels the importance of building up the kingdom, that he is actually considered worthy in these last days to be one of the number to go forth, as one of the horns of Joseph, to push the nations together; to gather out the honest in heart; to run for the prize which we all labor for.

I feel deeply interested in these matters, and I hope and pray that every man who is called upon to go forth on missions to preach the gospel, may have the faith of the church upon their heads, and that they may lift up their voices in faith before the people, that the light of truth may be a lamp in their path, and that by their exertions, and the blessings of God, it may be lighted up in distant nations.

I recollect a little incident in history, that is told of William the conqueror. After he had been king in England twenty years, he became very corpulent. In consequence of a little joke upon his corpulency, by the French king, he declared war, and the declaration was made in these words: "tell my fair uncle I will pay him a visit, and I will bring along tapers enough to set all France on fire." You may suppose we are sending out but a few elders, probably not more than one hundred or one hundred and fifty; but we intend to continue the work; and send out elders enough to set the world on fire, spiritually.

Elder J[ohn]. Taylor remarked,

Bro. George [Smith] was talking about setting the world on fire. I think when the elders have traveled through the world as far as some of us have, and seen the rottenness and weakness of their institutions, the folly and corruption that everywhere prevail, they will find that it is pretty near time as the prophets have said, for it to be burned up, and all its works.

But I suppose it is necessary, before the world is burned up, that the good wheat should be saved, and gathered into the garner, and prepare to take a fresh start in peopling the earth, and placing affairs upon a proper foundation.

There is no person that reflects upon the condition of the world, as it now exists, but his heart must be pained, must be filled with sympathy for the inhabitants of the earth. I have gazed upon their proceedings myself; I have watched their follies, abominations, and corruptions; I have seen them with my own eyes, until I have wept over them. They seem to me to be regardless of God, heaven, hell, eternity, or anything else; and there are thousands and tens of thousands, and millions of people upon the continent of Europe, that would like no better employment, than to go into deadly combat, and destroy one another.

The people talk about how corrupt we, the Latter Day Saints are. If all they say about us be true, it is only a tithing of what you will find in the world. I have told them to look at home; to examine their own firesides, and they would find plenty of corruption and abomination. They are living without God in the world; without hope; and they are dying without hope; consequently they are careless, profligate and reckless.

The Lord has shone upon us; he has lit up a candle of intelligence in our souls; has imparted to us the principles of eternal truth; opened the heavens, and sent his holy angel to put us in possession of principles that will exalt us in the scale of intelligence among men, and raise us up to be associates of the Gods in the eternal worlds.

Then shall we, who have thus been blessed with the visions of eternity; with light and intelligence; we who are filled with the Spirit of God burning in our hearts; who have gazed upon the hidden things of eternity, and contemplated the purposes of God in their majesty and glory; I say, shall we shrink from the task of going forth to snatch these fallen sons of men from everlasting burning?—Should we refuse to do so, it would testify that we had not a single spark of humanity in our bosoms, and were not fit to live in the world; much less to associate with the Gods in the eternal worlds.

I know you have a desire to do these things; but I will tell you, there are many things that are calculated to try the feelings of men.

Those who have to go out, have to put their noses to the grindstone and keep it there, and let them grind at it, and not murmur a word, and then, before it is healed, put it there again, and bear it all the time, and go along without saying anything, for you know it is a sin in the religious world to get angry. You need not attempt to go without faith in God; and you will have need of all the wisdom and intelligence you can command. You cannot go and convert the world all at once, for it is too far sunken in folly and vice. This reminds me of a dream a brother had in France. He said he thought he was trying to kindle a fire on the seashore; every time he attempted to light it, a wave came, and rolled over it, and he could hardly accomplish it until the tide began to recede, and then he considered he would build up a fire when the wood got dry.

You need not think of going abroad into the world, and going, as the Methodists sing, "on flowery beds of ease," for a great many consider you as impostors; and as a general thing, you are looked upon as suspicious characters, to say the least of it; and you will be closely watched. If you go to those foreign nations, your footsteps will be traced; no matter how privately you may make your entrance, or how privately you may take your departure; it will all be known to the police authorities, and they can give all the information required, touching your movements.

It was not more than ten minutes after I had taken the cab and started to the railway station to take my last departure from France, when one of the High Police came to inquire after me. The gentleman with whom I stayed, was a very affectionate friend to me, and he kept the police in conversation for two hours, speaking very highly of me; he told them I was a respectable, high-minded man, &c. The police told him of every place I had been at since I came to Paris; when I came to France; what hotel I staid in, and when I went to England, and how long I staid there; when I went to Germany, and how long I staid there; what books I had printed, &c., &c. He gave my friend a most minute account of every step I had taken, and all this is recorded in the books of the police. They have a congress of police among the nations of Europe, by which they can transmit information about every person who appears as a public character in any of those nations.

This is the way you will be watched. If you go to any of these nations, it will be necessary for you to use the greatest wisdom and prudence, and that you should pray to God to guard you in all things.

This police authority did not come after me until I had finished my work. I suppose they would not have injured me for I had broken no law; but this is their policy: with it we have nothing to do, and I should recommend you strictly to obey all police regulations, and never interfere with any national, civil or police institutions, or regulations. I suppose they might have telegraphed after me if they wished; but I took another course, not, however, knowing that they were after me; I turned off the main route to go by a little seaport town, and I missed the whole concern, and was in France a week longer, and they knew nothing about me. I was out of their track, and came off safe. The Lord blessed me, and I have been blessed as much in these nations, as anywhere else.

You may talk about difficulties, and what you have passed through here and there; but we should not be men, if we did not have difficulties to meet with; and we always feel much better when we have conquered them.

This is the difference between us and the world—they meet with difficulties, and they quash down under them; while we ride over them, and become victorious. This is the reason why there are so many institutions among the Gentiles that come to nought—they meet with difficulties, and fall before them; we meet with the same, but we have a God at the helm, and we triumph over them.

Another elder and myself stayed in a hotel in a small town for about a week—the landlord of which was an infidel. After we had been there two or three days, I told the landlord I was a religious man; he replied, "Oh, you are religious, are you? Religion is a pack of nonsense." I told him I cared as little about most of the religion of christendom as he did; but the one I believed in, I told him, would benefit both body and soul, in time and in eternity. I talked to him a little about it, and he began to feel much interested.

I told him about the success and the prosperity that attended our works; and finally he said, I don't know but I will sell out and go to America, for I am tired of France. I said, I will tell you where you will find a first rate place to settle down in that country; and directed him to Iowa. He spoke to an elder that was with him, after I had gone away, and said, "I don't like the way Mr. Taylor speaks to me." Why? said the elder. "He speaks as though he wants to push me off on one side somewhere, and I want to go where he is; you have got the right religion, and had I have found this, I should have been a religious man."

I talked to another gentleman who came in, who wanted to be introduced to me,—a man of good education, and talked the English language as well as I did. We talked about everything, almost, until religion came on in the conversation. When I was preparing to leave, the gentleman said, "O Mr. Taylor, I wish you would stay three or four days more here, and I will introduce you to a rich sugar manufacturer; and there is a gentleman living in a castle not far from here, I will introduce you to him.["] They felt as sorry at my going away as though I had stayed with them 12 months; and they came more than a mile to see me off, and bid me good bye, and prayed God to bless me, before I left.

You will see many such things as these. I could have introduced the gospel in the whole of that country, had I had time. You will find that the Spirit of the Lord will go before you, and prepare the way. I had men come to me and say, God bless you; you are the man I dreamed about. That is the kind feeling that operates upon the people in those parts, as well as in other parts of the world; the Spirit of the Lord goes before his servants.

I recollect associating with some medical professors, American gentlemen, who had come to Paris for the purpose of attending medical lectures, &c., at *l'Ecole de Medicine,* and visiting the hospitals; and though we were

Mormons, they were glad to have our society, and seemed to feel a desire to associate with us. We talked Mormonism to them, and many other things.

These men came there, remained two or three months, and went away; nobody cared anything about them, only just as much as they paid their way, and that was all. We went there and planted the gospel in the hearts of the people; and they feel as all other people do who are members of this church; the Spirit of God was with them, and we could rejoice in the bosom of our friends, and talk of the things of God, and the blessings he gives to his people. I looked at these doctors, and I said to myself, you poor, miserable creatures; you wander round the world, without the Spirit and blessings of God, and nobody cares for you, whether you live or die; while we come here, to plant the standard of truth in the hearts of the people, and can rejoice with them in its blessings.

If any of you go into those countries, you will find as warm-hearted people as you will find anywhere else. Brothers F[ranklin]. D. Richards and E[rastus] Snow can bear testimony of this. The gospel has the same effect in their hearts, as it has in yours. I won't occupy your time farther. May God bless you in the name of Jesus; amen.

Elder Ezra T. Benson said:

I feel thankful for the privilege to occupy a few moments at this conference, and to give my testimony concerning the work of the Lord in these last days.

I feel thankful that we are here, and that we are blessed with the spirit of truth, which is one of the greatest blessings in the kingdom of God. When we have the spirit of truth dwelling in our hearts, we are ready, and not only ready but willing to do the things that is required at our hands.

We have been hearing, this morning, that there are many that will be called to go to the nations of the earth; I feel that I can say that there is not an individual that will be called upon, if he has the spirit of the Lord, or of Mormonism in his heart, but what will respond to the call with all his soul; he will feel to thank God and his brethren that he is worthy to be called with such an high and holy calling as to be a messenger of salvation; for I do actually know by experience, that there is no calling under the heavens among the children of men, that is so desirable, and so great as to go and preach this gospel.

If a man will magnify his priesthood he can do more in one hour in the vineyard, preaching the gospel, and gathering the saints in one, if he is sent to do so, than he can do here in ten, laboring with his hands for himself, for his family, and for the kingdom of God on the earth. For it is impossible for us to retain the spirit of God,—it is impossible for us to love the Lord, or even keep in good fellowship with this people, unless we do as we are told. Inasmuch as there are honest people in the earth, scattered among the nations, is it pleasing in the sight of God for us to sit down here (unless we are commanded to do so,) and refuse to give them the truth? It is perfectly right to tarry here, and prepare for the saints who are gathering, unless we are commanded otherwise.

I wish to say a few words to those who shall be called upon to go to the nations. The time is now, I feel persuaded of it, for us, elders in Israel, to work while the day lasts,—to work while there is time and opportunity,— while God is softening the hearts of the people; now is the time for the elders to visit the nations, and tell them what they know concerning this great work in the last days; and when we do well for the kingdom of God, we do well for ourselves; when we do well for the people among the nations of the earth, we do well for ourselves; if we go and do as we are told, and that is, to preach what we actually know, and verily believe.

If it be possible, point out one man, an elder in this church, who has gone out to preach the gospel, and has been faithful in the kingdom of God, that has not been blessed, and his family has been blessed. There is not an instance on the records of this church, showing when a man has gone forth to proclaim the truth, that he has not been blessed. The opposite is the case: they have always returned home rejoicing, with their hearts filled with the love of God. Well then, brethren, let us go, if we are called upon, and proclaim the good news, that God is doing a great work in the valleys of the mountains; that God has called his prophet, his apostles, and other servants to proclaim the glad tidings to the children of men, to those who sit in darkness, and the shadow of death.

We have the name of being the best feeling people upon the face of the earth; and I will tell you furthermore, we just have the name of being the best people there is in the world; and the time is not far distant when the nations will seek for counsel at the feet of the servants of God. Why? Because we seek wisdom at the hand of God; because we are led by the revelation of Jesus Christ; because we live humble, and are honest before

God, and he will pour out his blessings upon our heads, to enlighten our minds, and give us visions and revelation, so that we cannot be led estray. I know this from the testimony that I receive.

I can bear testimony that God has been with me. Why? Because I have gone and done just as I have been told. It is because it was my determination, my will, and my desire to do the thing I was sent to do. We had a little to do with mobs it is true.—They undertook to mob me a little, and bro. Grant said, when he heard of it in Washington, he was glad of it. {A voice in the stand, "and so was I."} I was too, because I felt when they were trying to mob me, and seek my life, I was better than they were; if I had not been, they would not have tried to destroy me from the earth. They ran me into bro. Farnsworth's potatoe hole; to be sure, I ran in there, and thought it was a first rate place to hide; I staid there a couple of hours, and reflected upon mobs, upon the things of the kingdom, and called upon my Father in heaven, by the authority of the holy priesthood, and I felt as though I could whip all the mobs in Missouri; if it had been wisdom to do so, and the best course for me to take, I would have gone out and whipped the whole posse of them. {A voice from the stand, "yes, after they had all gone away."}

Many in Kanesville wanted me to wrestle with them. I said, I don't wrestle with any except from Salt Lake; but I can tap you on the head, as I would a little boy, if that will do you any good; but when I see a man from Salt Lake full of good works, I consider it an honor to wrestle with a man of that class; but I don't have any thing to do with the low, degenerated characters who do nothing else but wrestle and gamble; but I said if you don't believe I can wrestle, try me, and I will end you up a few times. They thought I was a very stout man, and it passed off just as well as though I had tried my dexterity upon them.

To close up the whole matter, I feel thankful to God that I am here; I am blessed; and the people here, and that are on the road, are also blessed.

Now is the time for the elders to go forth and preach the gospel; the Lord will soften the hearts of the people; and if mobs are stirred up, it is all for the good of the saints.

When satan begins to grin and show his teeth, you may know there are sheep not far off. Only put your trust in God, and he will keep you, and preserve you as in the hollow of his hand. Be comforted, brethren, whether you go to the nations of the earth, or stay at home. It is just as necessary for men to live humble here, as it is for them to live humble when they go there; for satan is not dead yet, and brother Brigham says he is glad of it. It is necessary he should live on the earth a little while longer, to stir up the saints by way of remembrance of the covenant they have made, and I have become perfectly reconciled concerning the things of the kingdom, and am so from day to day.

Let God do as he pleases, and call whom he pleases, and send whom he pleases abroad, and tell whom he pleases to remain at home, it is all the keeping of his commandments, and one station is as honorable as the other. If a man is told to tarry at home, he is as honorable as that messenger who is going to the nations of the earth. But if we sit down and consult the natural man, consult our own private feelings, and say here is my poor wife, here are my children, and here is my farm that I have earned with my own hands; I know how I came by my hard earned property; how can I go and preach under these circumstances, all my property and all my fair calculations will be knocked into pie. Supposing they are, let them all go; there is plenty more farms, and everything else; we are in the world, and it is filled with the elements, and we have the keys and the power to work and organize them, make them honorable, and contribute to our happiness and earthly comfort.

What is there more honorable than to carry a message of the gospel from this people? You have the prayers and the faith of your brethren, the prayers and the faith of the whole priesthood. Who is there that cannot go and do good under these circumstances? If there are any such men, they are not fit to live upon the earth. If a man is not fit to tarry at home, he is not fit to send abroad; and if he is not fit to send abroad, he is not fit to tarry among the people of God, only to be a scourge and a stumbling block to them.

Then let us rejoice; and if I should give way to my feelings, I should shout glory, hallelujah! and I would call upon every individual to feel that the great God is with them, and he is your Father, and you are his sons and daughters, and have a right to the legacy of eternal life; and not be bowed down in your minds, and say, I don't know, I am afraid I am not worthy to go preaching; if you get the testimony of the Spirit of the Lord, you belong to the great family of God; and if you have the testimony of Jesus abiding in your heart, you may rejoice all the day long.

Have we anything to fear? No! What did the President say the other day? He said, he had not anything to fear; but if he should have any fears, it would be, that this people would sit down and lull themselves to sleep, and forget the kingdom of God. Can a man do this when he feels the Spirit of truth in his heart? No. He will long to go to the nations of the earth, and be willing to be handled like the clay in the hands of the potter. We do not care what his testimony or knowledge has been; it is the abiding witness we want from day to day; it is that which carries a man safe through, according to my experience; it is then that we have no need to fear.

In the days of Nauvoo, there were fears; there was death. The people were afraid this thing and the other would be wrong; that bro. Joseph would get wrong; that we should have to submit to principles and doctrines contrary to the doctrines of Jesus Christ, &c. From the experience we have already had in the kingdom of God, has any person a right now, to such fears, or such a thought for a moment? No. He knows that the principles that have been taught by the Prophet Joseph, brother Brigham, Heber, and Willard, and by every good man in this church, are correct principles; and that these men have been borne off triumphantly over every trial and difficulty they have been called to pass through. The elders, therefore, can go to the nations with their consciences as clear as drifting snow, and with the satisfaction that all is right in Zion, and that we are led by the best men upon the face of this earth. Are you afraid to bear this testimony to this perverse generation? No.—The Spirit of the Lord will back you up and put to silence the slanderers in the Gentile world. I have known it by experience; I have not been insulted in any congregation, when I have taught the principles of God as they are taught in the valleys of the mountains; every dog has been obliged to close his mouth, and has not even dared to exhibit his teeth.

All is right; all is glorious; Mormonism will continue, should it come hot or cold; should it blow high or low; for God sustains it. When you feel so, brethren, you feel right; you feel strong, and ready to combat with your enemies; right is written upon your commissions; you are mighty in the right to do right; so that you are perfectly willing that all the devils in hell should know your works; that God, angels, and your brethren should know; and when you are called home, you will return like lions in strength; you will feel well; you will feel blessed.

While you are gone, prayers are ascending in your behalf, and in the behalf of your families; and every blessing you need is poured out abundantly upon you, and your hearts are filled with gladness.

This is the way to live; in the midst of the saints, in the world; and when the bowels of hell are moved with wrath against you, and devils belch out their fury, you are then ready to withstand them. Suppose bro. Taylor had been guilty of any wickedness in his travels; the whole country would have known it. Just so it is in the U.S. or anywhere else; if a man does not do right, but intends to feed his passions and carnal appetite, it would be better for him to turn round and say, brethren, good bye to Mormonism.

We cannot hide anything from God's Spirit, and from his servants; I know this to be true. Then let us put the rough and ready side out, and let the word be, Come on, all hands, and build up the kingdom of God. This is my determination; and if God will give me strength and wisdom, and the good blessings of my brethren, it is my determination to shape my affairs so, that when I go away, I can be gone any length of time, and not be like the man who went upon the Indian expedition in Utah—he had not got fairly started, before he wanted to return. What's the matter? "O dear, I have married me a wife, and cannot go."

I am glad in my heart, and I say, God bless brothers Brigham, Heber, and Willard; they are the counsel of heaven to this people, and I mean to honor them in the earth, wherever I go; and I would preach down in the bowels of hell the same as I do here, and not be ashamed of it. My story all the time is, Hurrah for Mormonism!

There is a jolly lot of fellows coming on from Kanesville, and other places; eight or ten thousand Mormons will come in here this season. They are a good people. Are the good brethren and sisters here thinking about it? Are they willing to take them by the hand, and say, brother, sister, come to my house, and I will make you welcome to this or to that—to comfort their hearts after the toils of such a journey? They are a good people; as good a people as you are, and just as willing to be counselled. My heart yearns after them, and I want you to feel after them likewise, by rendering them all the assistance in your power, until they are comfortably located.

I only throw out these few hints, that you may be prepared to act, when you receive the proper instructions from your President. There are musicians coming, who perform upon almost all kinds of musical instruments;

the lame are coming; the blind, and the widows, and the fatherless. I did not stop to make any selections; but I said, come on, all of you. We have among them big men and little men, big women and little women; grandfathers and grandmothers; and for ought I know, great grandfathers, and great grandmothers; but if they are not, they will be when they get here; for we have the name of raising the most children, and the best on the earth; and it will be very curious if we do not carry out what they all say we are guilty of.

I told them in Pottawatomie, that we wanted good men to mingle with the saints; we are sent out to preach to a people who wish to do good to their fellow men, and be saved in the kingdom of God; and if you are not willing to obey the gospel, and build up the kingdom, you cannot stand among this people; for God intends to raise up a holy race before him in the last days, to do his will in all things. After we have warned the nations, we will return home, and raise a holy posterity before the Lord; therefore we want good men, and praying men; for I have no confidence in any man who does not pray. It is as much as I can do to live, and pray all the time; and after all, I suppose I may say, like the good old Methodist, I leave undone those things I ought to do, and do the things I ought not.

I do not feel that I have any animosity in my heart, to any man on the earth; if a man will be my enemy, and is determined to be, all I ask of him is to keep out of my way; I will not injure him, but let him get all the glory and exaltation he can, and I will not throw the ashes of a rye straw in his path.

I can feel sensibly, that there has been an increase of union and faith among the people here, since I left here last fall; it is either in me, or in you. (A voice in the stand, it is in both.) It is in both, brother Brigham says. Let this union and this faith continue to increase, until we are brought into the presence of our God; and may this be the happy lot of us all; amen.

President Young remarked:

The morning is far spent, but before we close the morning service, I would like to present before the Conference the names of a few elders who have been selected to take missions.

I suppose the brethren understand the object of this special Conference: it is for the purpose of transacting business pertaining to foreign missions, and of giving to the brethren an opportunity to cross the plains before the cold weather. We shall send them out from this Conference.

I wish to say to the brethren, I am thankful, and I rejoice in the Lord my Savior, for his choice blessings which we enjoy. It was observed by bro. Benson, that bro. Brigham has but one fear concerning this people; it is true.

I do not fear all the devils in hell, or all the mobs that could be raised; but, if I have any fear, it is upon this ground, that the people, in their blessings, should forget the Lord their God. I do not say that this is the case with this people, but if there is danger to be anticipated, it is in the slackness of the people to remember the Lord when the fostering hand of providence is pouring out blessings upon them, and round about them, all the day long.

This has been in former times, when the blessings of the Lord have been poured out upon the people. It is written in the Bible concerning ancient Israel, that they got fat and kicked against the Lord their God. You may understand the expression as you please; they forgot the Lord, and began to trust in the wisdom of man. They forgot their prayers, and the duties they owed to one another; and they fell back into a careless, carnal security, and became like the rest of the world.

This is the only ground on which I would have fear, were I to entertain any. As I have often said, and the same I can say again, it is too late in the day for this people, ever to be cast off, or disowned by the Lord. The work the Lord promised to do is too nigh accomplished, and he has promised to make a short work on the earth. This work has some time since commenced, and if any of the people will not serve their God, and do the work he has given them to do, they will be removed out of the way and that speedily. It is too late in the day for this people to apostatize, and the priesthood to be taken again from the earth; so there is not much ground for fears even in this respect.

A few words to the elders of Israel with regard to the building up of the kingdom of God. Suppose every man who has wanted to go out to preach, (and almost every elder has wanted to go,) suppose they had all gone six years ago last fall, and left Nauvoo entirely destitute of elders, and attended diligently to preaching, up to this time. Would there have been a place prepared for the gathering of the Saints from all the world? No. There would have been no place for the elders to gather them to; there would have been no standard reared or rallying point for the people. Do you preach the gathering of Israel and the redemption of Zion? You do; and when you had got through this, and found all the rest had been neglected, what would be the situation of the elders of Israel? Their mouths would be closed up and sealed; they would not have any more influence among the people, than those doctors and philosophers in France, spoken of by elder Taylor; they came, they tarried, and if they paid for what they had it was all right; they went, and no person cared for them, or sought after them; it would have been the same with the elders of this church.

The whole machinery is in operation and complete; that when the elders go forth to preach the gospel, every man carries with him a two-edged sword; pierces the hearts of the people by the spirit of the gospel which he goes to proclaim; but if the work is in progress only in part, his sword is blunted at once; it has no edge; it is incomplete, and does not pierce the hearts of the people, consequently he had better have staid at home.

Why I make these remarks is, that we may understand that unless this work is in progress, as a whole, it is not complete; we are found wanting, and not prepared to do the work we are called and sent to do. Now it is just as necessary for us to come to these valleys, and build houses, make fences, erect school-houses, rear up places of worship, and prepare for the gathering of Israel, as it is to go and preach to Israel to influence them to gather. The one is just as honorable, and as acceptable in the sight of God, as the other; and those that labor faithfully at home, will be crowned with those that labor faithfully abroad. Those who are selected to remain at home, receive as those who are selected to go abroad.

It is unnecessary for me, for any of the Twelve, or for any of my brethren to rise up here to preach to the elders to infuse the spirit of preaching in them, for we have had to hold them back with a cable rope, as it were, to keep them from going to preach. There is no lack of the spirit of the gospel in the elders of Israel, for we have been teased all the time to give them permission to go out and give vent to the spirit within them; but had we listened to them, you and I would not have had this commodious house to preach in this day. All the elders would have been off preaching, and there would not have been enough left to have made the women and children comfortable.

What is to be done? Obey council. They do, and how far? Enough to scare the whole world. Look at the spirit that is in the midst of this people, and that overshadows them. What influence does this have upon the nations of the earth? It fills them with terror and awe, and when they reflect, and reason, it fills them with astonishment, that there is a people on the earth, in the present confused revolutionary state of the nations, that will hearken to counsel and be of one heart and one mind; they are filled with fear and astonishment, and they dread the union that is among this people more than they dread the Lord Almighty upon his throne. This is a pretty positive proof that this people are willing to hearken to the counsels of heaven.

Bro. Benson proclaims in our hearing that this spirit has increased since he left here last fall. It has, and I expect it has grown in his own bosom; it has in mine. What do you think about it yourselves, brethren, would you not be ready also to acknowledge that the same spirit is increasing in your bosoms, a spirit of love, and union, and of faith in your calling? I think there are a great many who can say, and say it truly, that this Spirit of the Lord has greatly increased in their hearts for six or eight months past, or for a year; were it not so, we should not be found growing in the knowledge of the truth. This is our labor, our business, and our calling to grow in grace, and in knowledge from day to day, and from year to year.

I wish to say to this congregation, and I wish them to say to the families of the brethren who are not here to day, and I would like all the inhabitants of these valleys to hear it; when our brethren who are on the plains, come with their families into this city, or into any of the settlements of the Latter Day Saints, sit down and calmly make a calculation in your own hearts, how you would wish a neighborhood of Latter Day Saints to receive you, if you had been journeying across the plains this season. Ponder it over in your minds, and place yourselves in the situation of a pilgrim traveling across the plains, and after a hard and fatiguing summer's work, now we have got home; imagine yourselves at the doors of your brethren who have plenty. Here are their gardens groaning with the abundance of the products of the earth, with potatoes, beets, and cabbage; here is milk and butter, and fine flour in great quantities; here are the tomatoes and garden vegetables of every description; now you say I have got home to my brother's door, and he has got plenty. What would you wish these brethren to do to you? Ask that same question to your neighbors, and get them to answer it. I can tell you what you would they should do to you; you would wish them to say, come brother or sister into my garden, and help yourselves to some garden sauce; walk in here, and take and eat and make yourselves glad. And if they turn round and say, brother, how shall I pay you for what I get; then you cannot hear that, for it is something that is altogether out of the question? The Lord gave it to me, now come and help me to eat it. That do the emigrant saints, every one of you. I know it is the will of the Lord you should do it; and I know if he should speak to you himself, he would tell you the same thing. I tell you just as it is, and that is just as good precisely, as though another came and told you. Then the brethren will feel joyful; their hearts will be made glad; and they will know that you are actually growing in the knowledge of the truth.

There are a great many coming; bro. Benson says all are coming, even the great grand daddies, and great grand mammies; uncles and aunts, all are coming, and I am glad of it; I rejoice, for it puts us in a position that we can send out elders from this place into all the world; whereas, before, our circumstances needed all the men we had here to prepare for the gathering of the saints. Now the time has come that we can send out our little parties to gather up Israel, and preach the gospel to the nations before the end comes.

The reports we have heard from our brethren are favorable, cheering, and rejoicing to every heart. Those who are coming from the islands of the sea, and from the old countries, where the elders have been sent, those from Pottawatomie and the States are coming home; for the present, this is the place of gathering; here the standard is reared for the Latter Day Saints from all nations, that they may spread out from this place, and fill up other places until all the continent of America, which is the land of Zion, shall be peopled with the saints of the Most High.

Question; when are we going back to Jackson county? Not until the Lord commands his people; and it is just as much as you and I can do to get ready to go, when he does command us.

Bro. [Ezra] Benson and [Jedediah] Grant have been successful in their missions. Bro. Benson says some of the brethren were glad when he was mobbed. I was glad of it; for every mobbing difficulty will add glory upon the heads of the humble, faithful and contrite in heart; it serves to prove and give them experience, it shows them the contrast between the one and the other; all this is preparatory for the saints to enter into their rest, and for the wicked to receive their punishment. Bro. Benson has been successful; and I thank the Lord Almighty, that he turned the key here last fall, and caused a tremendous commotion among the political elements, earthquake, thundering, and lightning, above and below the earth, with great excitement; this gathered a great many more saints than if it had been fair weather all the time. This clashing and noise of the elements stirred up the people in Pottawatomie, and then they wanted to go to the mountains; like bro. George A. Smith in the latter days of Nauvoo, he wanted to go to the mountains, or to California, or to Oregon, he was not very particular; what for? Simply because he was obliged to go somewhere. The saints who are coming now from Pottawatomie, were obliged to leave for the valleys of the mountains, why? Because they had to run somewhere. Do you suppose I am sorry because of persecution? No! I never was in my life; but I have thanked God a thousand times that the devil is not yet bound, for if he had been, the saints would have gone to sleep; and if there could be such a thing, they would have been blotted out of existence, with all their intelligence, and the earth have received them into its bowels. Light, knowledge, truth, wickedness of every kind, the works of the Almighty, and the works of the devil, all conspire to roll on the great work that the Lord Jesus Christ is doing upon the earth; every person and power in their own order.

I do not wish to detain the congregation longer this morning; bro. [Heber] Kimball set before you the object of the meeting, and I have hinted at it. We will now read over a few names that we have selected. May the Lord God of Israel bless you, in the name of Jesus Christ, AMEN.

The clerk read 98 names of individuals who had been proposed to foreign missions.

Singing. Benediction by Geo. A. Smith.

Adjourned for 1 1-2 hour.

———

2 p. m.

Conference called to order by Prest. Young.

Singing. Prayer by Prest. J. Young. Singing.

The following elders were then appointed to their several missions.

EUROPE.—*England.* Daniel Spencer, Charles A. Harper, Isaac Allred, John Van Cott, Mellen Attwood, Cha[u]ncey G. Webb, Charles Smith, Sylvester H. Earl, David Grant, Thomas W. Treat, Benjamin

Brown, James [P]. Park, Perr[i]grine Sessions, Osman M. Duel, John A. Hunt, James Pace, William Burgess, jr.[,] Levi Nickerson, William Glover, Edward Martin, Levi. E. Riter, John S. Fulmer, Richard Cook, John Oakley, William Clayton, William Pitt, John C. Hall, William Woodward, James G. Willie, Daniel D. McArthur, Moses Thurston, John Perry, William Emp[e]y, Spicer Crandell, John Mayer, Elias Gardner, Noah T. Guymon.

Ireland. Daniel Toner, John McDonald.

Wales. Dan Jones, Daniel Daniels, Thomas Jeremy,

France. Andrew L. Lamoreaux.

Germany. George Mayer, George C. Riser, Jacob F. Secrist, William Taylor.

Capital of Prussia. Orson Spencer, Jacob Houtz, Moses Clough.

Norway. Eric G. M. Hogan, Canute Peterson.

Denmark. George Percy.

Gibraltar. Edward Stevenson, Nathan T. Porter.

Asia.—*Hindoostan.* Nathaniel V. Jones, Amos M. Musser, Samuel A. Wooley, Richard Ballantyne, Robert Skelton, William Fotheringham, William F. Carter, Truman Leonard, Robert Owen.

Siam. Cha[u]ncey W. West, Sterne Hotchkiss.

China. Hosea Stout, James Lewis, Chapman Duncan.

Africa.—*Cape of Good Hope.* Jesse Haven, Leonard I. Smith, William Walker.

America.—*Nova Scotia and British Provinces.* John Robinson, A. D. L. Buckland, Benjamin T. Mitchell, Joseph Millet.

West Indies. Jesse Turpin, Darwin Richardson, Alfred B. Lambson, Aaron Farr.

British Guiana. James Brown, Elijah Thomas.

Texas. Preston Thomas, Williams Camp, Washington Jolley.

New Orleans, John Brown.

St. Louis, Horace S. Eldredge.

Iowa. Daniel Miller.

Washington City. Orson Pratt.

AUSTRALIA. Augustus Farnham, William Hyde, Burr Frost, John Hyde, Josiah W. Fleming, Paul Smith, James Graham, John S. Eldredge, Absalom P. Dowdle.

SANDWICH ISLANDS. William McBride, Ephraim Green, Egerton Snider, James Lawson, Thomas Kairnes, Nathan Tanner, Reddick N. Allred, Reddin A. Allred, Benjamin F. Johnson.

Elder O. Pratt said:

The congregation have seen manifested the determination of these brethren who have been appointed to go on their respective missions. If it be the minds of this assembly that all of these brethren whose names have been read shall fulfil their several appointments, you will manifest it by the uplifted hand. (The manifestation was unanimous.)

I will make a few observations by permission. When I see so many of my brethren, feeling a desire to go to the nations, to different parts of the earth, it truly is a cause of great rejoicing to my heart. When I read occasionally, letters and communications that are published in the Millennial Star in regard to the spread of this work among the different nations, it is a cause of joy to me which is indescribable. And when I see the brethren going forth to the different nations, I almost feel as though I wanted to go to all these different places at the same time myself, to go with my brethren and be instrumental with you in trying to build up this kingdom among the nations. There is certainly no work in which the servants of God can be engaged, that is so pleasing and joyful to the mind, as to be engaged in the work of the holy ministry, in trying to persuade the honest in heart among the nations to receive the truth.

This generation have been calling a long time for miracles, but one of the greatest miracles in the last days, in my estimation, is the fact, that scores and hundreds of the missionaries of the Latter Day Saints are traversing the globe, going from nation to nation, upon the principle that the ancient Apostles traveled, namely, *without purse or scrip*. Is not that a miracle? Has there any such thing happened before, for many generations, as people traveling over the whole earth, starting from their homes without purse or scrip? If you should go upon your own business, and the Lord had not a hand in the matter, it would be nine chances out of ten, if you did not perish before you returned; and perhaps, nine chances out of ten, if you ever obtained means to accomplish your journey, and pay your passage from place to place. But where is there an example of any faithful man in this church, since the year 1830, that has gone forth, trusting in the Lord God of Israel with mighty prayer, but what has been sustained, upheld, and preserved to return again in honor, unless they have fallen perhaps by sickness, or have died martyrs in testimony of the truth.

We find, then, that the Lord has actually wrought miracles in scores, and hundreds of instances, in sustaining his servants among foreign nations, in foreign lands, where it would be almost impossible for people that were on their own business to have accomplished anything, or to have traveled among them. What has the Lord said upon this subject? He commands us in a revelation given September 22nd, 1832 as follows: "Therefore let no man among you (for this commandment is unto all the faithful who are called of God in the Church unto the ministry) from this hour, take purse or scrip, that goeth forth to proclaim this gospel of the kingdom." This was a command given 20 years ago this next September. Says one, that looks rather hard. It does not look hard at all, for that same God that gave the commandment is able to bear you up, he is able to sustain you. Perhaps this might have had reference, more particularly, to those who are actually in their fields of labor; this may be the case, for traveling to your field of labor is one thing, and laboring in it is another. There may actually be instances, where an elder is obliged, circumstances being such, to take some means to assist him until he shall arrive at his field of labor, but when he gets there, then depend upon the Lord God of Israel, and the people, to feed and sustain him. I am not going to say, but what it will apply in traveling to the field of his labor, at any rate I would not be afraid to trust the God of Israel to assist me in going to my field of labor, as well as to assist me after having arrived there.

What would be the best thing, then, for these elders who are going forth? As a general thing, I would say to them, if you have any cash, leave it with your wives and children to comfort their hearts, to support them in your absence, and be a blessing to them. And if you can get mules and horses to carry you from here to the States, when you get on the frontiers sell them, and they will bring you in a little cash to carry you through the mobocratic divisions of the country (a voice in the stand "send that back.") The Lord will always provide some way to get along; and the faithful servant of God has nothing to fear only his own weakness, and his own imperfections and follies; these are the things that he has need to fear the most. If an elder gets unfaithful when he is abroad, he is sometimes apt to get into straight places, but if he is diligent in prayer, in doing the work of the Lord, striving in faith to live humbly before him; setting a proper example before his brethren and the people among whom he labors, he will find that the Lord will bear him off victorious; his power will be upon him, and when he administers in the words of life, it will be by the power and wisdom of the Holy Spirit; when he administers in the ordinances of the church the blessings of Jehovah will follow; when he says to the sick, be thou healed in the name of Jesus Christ,—behold! It is done; when he commands, the lame will leap like an hart: the power of the Lord God of Israel will be made manifest through his faithful servants, and they have nothing to fear.

Brethren, I will prophesy that the power of the Lord God of Israel will be with you to a far greater extent, than what has been poured out in days that are passed; and the way will open before you, and the Lord will visit the hearts of the people before you arrive among them, and make manifest to them by visions and dreams that you are the servants of God before they shall see your faces; and you will receive heavenly visions to comfort you, and dreams to give you knowledge of the things of God, if you prove faithful before him. I will prophesy this in the name of the Lord God of Israel, and you will find that his power will be more conspicuously made manifest through your administrations on these missions than has ever taken place since the rise of this church.

How often have I reflected upon the words of the Savior, which were given expressly to his servants; they were not given to the whole church, but to his servants who were engaged in the work of the ministry. He said, "Take no thought for the morrow, what ye shall eat or what ye shall drink, or wherewithal ye shall be clothed. Consider the lilies of the field; they toil not, neither do they spin; yet Solomon or the kings of this world are not arrayed like one of these. And if God so clothe the grass which to-day is, and to-morrow is thrown into the fire, how much more shall he clothe you, if you are not of little faith? Therefore, take no thought for these things." You will find, brethren, if you go forth, trusting in the Lord, that whatever you need, it will be ministered to you in the very moment, and you will return again with your hearts filled with joy, and your bodies comfortably clothed, and means in your pockets to assist your families when you return to them, and with souls as seals to your ministry, with whom you shall rejoice in time and in eternity.

I have oftentimes thought of another saying in the Book of Mormon, concerning the parable of the vineyard, delivered by one of the old, ancient prophets; he said, that "the servants of God shall go forth and labor for the last time;" and the prophecy says, "behold they were few, and the Lord labored with them." Among all the servants, that had labored in previous dispensations, the parable does not condescend to say, that the Lord labored with them, although he no doubt did. But here it is expressly said, that the laborers were few, and the Lord labored with them. And after the vineyard was pruned, and was no more corrupt, he called up his servants and said, behold, you see I have done according to my will, and ye shall have joy with me in the fruit of my vineyard. This truly seems to be characteristic of the way and manner this gospel is going to the nations. It does not go according to the will of man, neither according to his inferior judgment, but according to the will of God. It breaks forth on the right hand, and on the left; and the servants of God are sent forth by his will and authority; and if they are faithful, he has ordained them to labor in his vineyard; and the prophecy says, they will be faithful, and they shall keep the commandments of the Lord of the vineyard, in all things.

Try to have this prophecy fulfilled upon your heads; keep the commandments of the Lord of the vineyard in all things, that his blessings may be upon you; that when you set to your hands with the pruning-knife, to prune and train up the branches of the trees of the vineyard, and dig around their roots, the power of the everlasting God may rest upon you, and the vineyard where you labor. Keep the commandments of the Lord in all things, that you may have joy with him in the fruits of the vineyard, when the work is finished. May he bless you as he did Abraham, and his servants of old, that you may do the work he has appointed to you in faith, and prayer, and perseverance, that you may bring home your thousands, and rejoice in the midst of the mountains.

Elder Franklin D. Richards followed in a short speech, not reported.

Prest. H. C. Kimball motioned that elder Orson Pratt take a mission to Washington to preach the gospel, and preside over the saints in the United States, Upper and Lower Canada, and the British Provinces in North America. Seconded and carried unanimously.

Elder J. M. Grant, and W. W. Phelps severally addressed the audience. Prest. Young said:

I want to say a few words to the congregation before we dismiss, for we shall be under the necessity of separating soon, and probably we shall hold another meeting this evening.

I have heard the exhortations of the brethren who have spoken to day with joy; they seem to be in a good spirit, and certainly, yea most assuredly, there is the most novelty in Mormonism, that there is in anything upon the face of the earth. It is musical, it pleases both the eye, and the ear, and I may say every sense of the man.

When I heard the brethren exhorting those who are going out on missions, I wished them to impress one thing upon the minds of these elders, for it is necessary that it should be uppermost there, which may be the means of preserving them from receiving stains on their characters from which very probably they may never recover. If we get a blight upon our characters before the Lord, or in other words lose ground and backslide by transgression, or in any other way, so that we are not up even with the brethren as we are now, we never can come up with them again; but this principle must be carried out by the elders wherever they go, whatever they do, or wherever they are; one thing must be observed and be before them all the time in their meditations, and in their practice, and that is *clean hands* and *pure hearts*, before God, angels and men.

If the elders cannot go with clean hands, and pure hearts, they had better stay here, and wash a little longer; don't go thinking when you arrive at the Missouri river, at the Mississippi, at the Ohio, or at the Atlantic, that then you will purify yourselves, but start from here with clean hands and pure hearts; and be pure from the crown of the head to the soles of your feet. Then live so every hour; go in that manner, and in that manner labor, and return again as clean as a piece of pure, white paper. This is the way to go, and if you do not do that, your hearts will ache. How can you do it? Is there a way? Yes! Do the elders understand that way? They do. You cannot keep your own hands clean, and your hearts pure without the help of the Lord; neither will he keep you pure without your own help.

Will you be liable to fall into temptation, and be overtaken by sin? Yes; unless you live so as to have the revelations of Jesus Christ continually, not only to live in it to-day or while you are preaching, in a prayer meeting, or in a conference; and when you are out of these meetings when you are guarded more particularly by the Spirit, say, that you can get along without the Holy Ghost; you must have it all the time, on Sunday, Monday, Tuesday, and every day through the week, and from year to year, from the time you leave home until you return, so that when you come back, you may not be afraid if the Lord Almighty should come into the midst of the saints and reveal all the acts, and doings, and designs of your hearts in your missions; but be found clean like a piece of white paper; that is the way for the elders to live in their ministry, at home and abroad.

There are a great many things that could be said here, which would add to the comfort and consolation of us all. A great many principles that could be taught to the elders which they must learn when they go abroad. I will notice one thing with regard to learning. You will hear a great many elders say, if I could go to preaching, I could become a man like many others, I should receive knowledge and understanding, I should be noted, become a great man, and a wise man. Many have such feelings; that they are greater who are in the world preaching the gospel than those who remain here. It is a grand mistake; for if those who have lived with us all the time have not a knowledge of true principles; do not understand the root and foundation of the superstructure, are not filled with knowledge and understanding here, they need not appeal to the gentile world for it; if they have not the foundation within themselves of talent and tact, they need not go abroad for the Spirit of the Lord to instruct them in things they cannot be instructed in here at home, and to obtain improvement where improvement cannot be made.

We may live here year after year, and store up knowledge all the time, and yet not have an opportunity of exhibiting it to others, but if I have knowledge by the Spirit of the Lord, I gain it at the fountain; and if not quite at the fountain head, the nigher I am to that place, the more I get; though I have not the privilege of exhibiting it to the people, it is on hand whenever the time comes it should be used. It is a vain idea to suppose that we can send elders into the world who have not got good common sense, to make men of them; if they have good sense here, they will have it yonder; if they have good sense yonder, they will have good common sense here; whether they are there or here does not alter the foundation that is in them. If the elders have natural ability, and have obtained great wisdom or learning, to go abroad gives them an opportunity to improve upon what they have.

I want to refer to the last speech made here. Bro. Phelps feels very joyful, as the rest of us do. When we hear the glad tidings of salvation among the nations, it gives a spring to our feelings, and fills us with unspeakable joy.

Perhaps in the case before us, as in others, we might say that men become children; we are children in the first place, then become men; and in the second place men become children in their understanding. As to the correctness of the exalted views that bro. Phelps has of myself, I leave it to the congregation to decide for themselves; but to place me on a par with the personages he has named who have overcome, and entered into the presence of God; or even to compare me with Joseph Smith our martyred Prophet is too much; though I expect, if I am faithful, I will be as great as they are now, and so can every other faithful man. But am I now to be compared with these exalted characters? Not at all, not even with Joseph, and he is at present inferior to others bro. Phelps has named. But I expect if I am faithful with yourselves, that I shall see the time with yourselves that we will know how to prepare to organize an earth like this; know how to people that earth, how to redeem it, how to sanctify it, and how to glorify it with those who live upon it who hearken to our counsel.

The Father and the Son have attained to this point already; I am on the way, and so are you, and every faithful servant of God.

One of the greatest queries on the minds of the saints, is, to understand the nature, the principle, or the foundation of our existence. To say nothing about what has been, if you will follow out that which is before you, you can learn all about it. I have a notion to tell you, though I have not time to say much about it now. I will however just tell to you the simple story relating to the exaltation of man in the celestial kingdom of God. We will take Joseph for instance; he is faithful to his calling, has filled his mission to this earth, and sealed his testimony with his blood; he has done the work his Father gave him to do, and will soon come to the resurrection; his spirit is waiting for the resurrection of the body which will soon be; but has he the power to resurrect that body? He has not. Who has this power? Those that have already passed through the resurrection, who have been resurrected in their time and season, by some person else, and have been appointed to that authority just as you elders have with regard to your authority to baptize.

You have not the power to baptize yourselves; neither have you power to resurrect yourselves; and you could not legally baptize a second person for the remission of sins until some person first baptized you and ordained you to this authority. So with those that hold the keys of the resurrection to resurrect the saints; Joseph will come up in his turn, receive his body again, and continue his mission in the eternal worlds until he carries it out to perfection, with all the rest of the faithful, to be made perfect with those who have lived before, and those who shall live after; and when the work is finished, and it is offered to the Father, then they will be crowned, and receive keys and powers by which they will be capable of organizing worlds. What will they organize first? Were I to tell you, I should certainly spoil all the baby resurrection that elder Hyde and others ever preached, as sure as the world.

After men have got their exaltation, and their crowns; have become Gods, even the sons of God; are made king of kings, and Lord of Lords; they have the power then of propagating their species in spirit, and that is the first of their operations with regard to organizing a world. Power is then given to them to organize the elements, and then commence the organization of tabernacles. How can they do it? Have they to go to that earth? Yes, an Adam will have to go there, and he cannot do without Eve; he must have Eve to commence the work of generation, and they will go into the garden, and continue to eat and drink of the fruits of the corporeal world, until this grosser matter is diffused sufficiently through their celestial bodies, to enable them according to the established laws to produce mortal tabernacles for their spiritual children.

This is a key for you. The faithful will become Gods, even the sons of

God; but this does not overthrow the idea that we have a father. Adam is my Father, (this I will explain to you at some future time) but it does not prove that he is not my father, if I become a God; it does not prove that I have not a father.

I am on the way to become one of those characters, and am nobody in the world but Brigham Young. I never have professed to be bro. Joseph, but bro. Brigham, trying to do good to this people. I am no better, nor any more important than another man, who is trying to do good; if I am, I don't know it. If I improve upon what the Lord has given me, and continue to improve, I shall become like those who have gone before me: I shall be exalted in the celestial kingdom, and be filled to overflowing with all the power I can wield; and all the keys of knowledge I can manage will be committed unto me. What do we want more? I shall be just like every other man, have all that I can, in my capacity, comprehend and manage.

I am on my way to this great exaltation; I expect to attain unto it. I am in the hands of the Lord and never trouble myself about my salvation, or what the Lord will do with me hereafter; it is for me to do the will of God to-day; and when to-morrow comes, to enquire what is his will concerning me, then do the will of my Father in the work he has appointed me to do, and that is enough for me. I am serving a God who will give me all I merit when I come to receive my reward, this is what I have always thought, and if I still think so, it is enough for me.

I say to the brethren who are leaving home; when you go from home, leave everything you have got here, don't take anything with you but the Lord and yourselves.

You will want horses to bear you over the plains, but don't carry your wives or your children in your hearts or in your affections with you one rod; dedicate them to the Lord God of Israel and leave them at home; and when you are in England or among other nations, no matter where, when you pray for your families pray for them as being in the Great Salt Lake Valley, and do not bring them close to you as though they were in your carpet bag; pray for them where they are. You must feel, if they live, all right; if they die, all right; if I die all right; if I live, all right, for we are the Lord[']s and we shall soon meet again.

I wish to say to you that are left here, whose husbands and fathers are going away for a season, don't cling to them one particle, but let them go as cheerfully as you would give a weary traveler a cup of cold water. If you live it is all right, and if you fall asleep before they return, it is all right; don't send your hearts after them one step, nor suffer your spirits to cling to them one moment; then you wives in very deed will be blessed, and be help meets to your husbands.

But if a wife should yet cling round a husband's neck and say, O! how I love you, dear husband, and keep him in her embraces, that woman is a dead weight to that man, and not an help to him. Women should be loyal to the cause of God, and help to build up his kingdom by their husbands, in assisting them to fulfil their missions, and if they do not do it they are not a helpmate to their husbands. I know there are a great many here who have had an experience in these things. It is no matter if they are on the other side of the globe, apart, let them long for each other, and there will be a thread of communication between them; the man cannot be useful in his labors while she is all the time weeping and mourning, every day of her life. Let a man suffer his mind to be drawn out all the time after his family and he will become inactive in the work of the Lord.

When you leave, understand it, you have neither wife or children; you have handed them all over to the Lord Jesus Christ. Let the brethren go and say, I will keep my eyes straight before me on the object of my mission, and not look behind me to my family; but I will accomplish my mission, and when I have done, it is all right, I am willing to go home, if the Lord wishes me to do so.

The time is far spent, and it is necessary for our meeting to be brought to a close. May the Lord bless you; and I say he does bless us; we are greatly blessed above all people upon the face of this earth; let us be faithful to God and the covenant we have made, AMEN.

Adjourned till to-morrow 10 a.m.

Benediction by Prest. Young.

MISSIONARIES CALLED IN THE AUGUST 1852 SPECIAL CONFERENCE

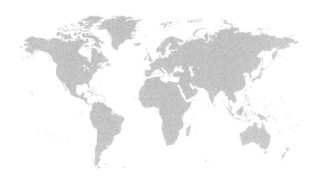

THIS BIOGRAPHICAL REGISTER INCLUDES EVERYONE who was called on a mission in August 1852 or who left with that same group of missionaries. Most of the men in this register were called in August and left in the following weeks. A few missionaries were called but never served, and some of them were called in April 1852 but left with the August group months later.

Biographical entries include basic information, including full name, birth and death information, parents, and dates of key life events. Given the nature of the missionaries' callings, emphasis is given to the religious roles a person played. Many of the men found here married several women. Rather than trace their multiple marriages, the biographical entries simply state the fact of their having practiced plural marriage. Full identifying information is given for geographical places, including county information, with two exceptions: international places are most often listed without county or province, and Salt Lake City is given without full identifying information (Salt Lake Co., Utah Territory). Because of the shifting political designation of the Latter-day Saints' new home in the Intermountain West, listings do not usually distinguish between Deseret, Utah Territory, and Utah; the term *Utah* is used throughout.

Because of space constraints, this biographical register is published without source citations. The files used to compile each biography are available in the General Epistles biographical collection at the Church History Library in Salt Lake City. Additionally, many other resources are available for further biographical research of nineteenth-century Latter-day Saints. Four important electronic resources are maintained by the Church History Department: the Joseph Smith Papers (josephsmithpapers.org/reference/people), the Early Mormon Missionaries database (history.lds.org/missionary), the Mormon Pioneer Overland Travel database (history.lds.org/overlandtravels), and the Journal of George Q. Cannon (churchhistorianspress.org/george-q-cannon/people).

Allred, Isaac (1813–59). Born June 28, 1813, in Bedford Co., Tennessee; son of James Allred and Elizabeth Warren. Baptized in Monroe Co., Missouri, Sept. 10, 1832. Married Julia Ann Taylor in Monroe Co., Oct. 11, 1832. Participated in plural marriage. Served in Camp of Israel, 1834. Began serving mission to Missouri, Dec. 13, 1837. Began serving mission to Missouri and Kentucky, June 11, 1838. Appointed to serve mission to Missouri, ca. 1842. Appointed colonel of the fifth regiment in Nauvoo Legion, 1844. Appointed to fourth quorum of the seventy, Oct. 8, 1844. Elected constable in Kanesville (later Council Bluffs), Pottawattamie Co., Iowa, Aug. 1849. Migrated with Easton Kelsey company to the Great Salt Lake Valley, arriving Sept. 22, 1851. Served mission to England, 1852–55. Died May 11, 1859, in Mount Pleasant, Sanpete Co., Utah.

Allred, Reddin Alexander (1822–1900). Born Feb. 21, 1822, in Bedford Co., Tennessee; son of Isaac Allred and Mary Calvert; twin brother of Redick Newton Allred. Baptized by John Ivie in Missouri, spring 1833. Participated in relief expedition to rescue Joseph Smith from kidnappers, June 1843. Married Julia Ann Bates in Nauvoo, Hancock Co., Illinois, Dec. 21, 1843. Participated in plural marriage. Appointed to fourth quorum of the seventy, Oct. 8, 1844. Migrated to Great Salt Lake Valley in James W. Cummings company, arriving by Oct. 7, 1851. Served mission to Sandwich Islands, 1852–55. Moved to St. Johns, Apache Co., Arizona Territory, by 1880. Served as justice of the peace in Graham Co., Arizona Territory. Died on June 9, 1900; buried in Thatcher, Graham Co.

Allred, Redick Newton (1822–1905). Born Feb. 21, 1822, in Farmington, Bedford Co., Tennessee; son of Isaac Allred and Mary Calvert; twin brother of Reddin Alexander Allred. Baptized in 1833 by John Ivie at Salt River, Ralls Co., Missouri, 1829. Served a mission to Indiana, 1841. Ordained a seventy in 1842. Married Lucy Hoyt, Nov. 26, 1843. Participated in plural marriage. Appointed third sergeant, company A, and staff quartermaster, Mormon Battalion, 1846–47. Migrated to the Salt Lake Valley from California with the Levi W. Hancock/Jefferson Hunt/ James Pace/Andrew Lytle company, arriving in mid-Oct. 1847. Served a mission to the Sandwich Isles, 1852–56. Participated in the rescue of the Willie and Martin handcart companies, Oct. 1856. Counselor to Bishop C. G. Larson in Spring City, Utah, about 1860. Participated in the Black Hawk War in Sanpete Co. Served five terms in the Utah territorial legislature, 1862–64, 1868, 1870. Appointed bishop of the Chester, Sanpete Co., Utah, ward, July 1877. Ordained a patriarch, May 15, 1898. Died Oct. 10, 1905, in Chester.

Atwood, Millen (1817–90). Born May 24, 1817, in Willington, Tolland Co., Connecticut; son of Dan Atwood and Polly Sawyer. Worked as a mason. Baptized in Nauvoo, Hancock Co., Illinois, Aug. 1841. Began serving mission to Wisconsin Territory, Illinois, New York, and Connecticut, July 7, 1842. Ordained a member of 10th quorum of the seventy in Nauvoo, Apr. 20, 1845. Migrated from Winter Quarters, Nebraska, to Great Salt Lake Valley with Brigham Young pioneer company, arriving July 24, 1847. Returned to Winter Quarters. Married Relief Cram in Winter Quarters, Apr. 20, 1848. Participated in plural marriage. Migrated back to Great Salt Lake Valley with Brigham Young company, arriving Sept. 19, 1848. Participated in battle against Indians in Provo, Utah Co., Utah, Feb. 1850. Ordained sixth president of 14th quorum of the seventy in Salt Lake City, by Mar. 9, 1851. Began serving mission to Europe, Sept. 16, 1852. Returned to Iowa; migrated back to Great Salt Lake Valley with James G. Willie company, arriving Nov. 9, 1856. Ordained a high priest, May 9, 1875; served on high council. Appointed bishop of Salt Lake City 13th Ward, Dec. 25, 1881. Died on Dec. 17, 1890, in Salt Lake City.

Ballantyne, Richard (1817–98). Born Aug. 26, 1817, in Whitridgebog, Roxburgshire, Scotland; son of David Ballantyne and Ann Bannerman. Baptized by Elder Henry McCune in Edinburgh, Scotland, Oct. 30, 1842. Emigrated from Liverpool, England, to New Orleans, Louisiana, aboard the *Metoka*, arriving Oct. 27, 1843. Married Huldah Maria Clark, in Winter Quarters, Nebraska, Feb. 17, 1847. Participated in plural marriage. Migrated to the Great Salt Lake Valley in the Brigham Young company, arriving Sept. 20, 1848. Established the first Latter-day Saint Sunday School in the Salt Lake 14th Ward, 1849. Served a mission to India, 1852–54. Led pioneer company from London, England, to the Great Salt Lake Valley, arriving Sept. 25, 1855. Died in Ogden, Weber Co., Utah, Nov. 8, 1898.

Brown, Benjamin (1794–1878). Born Sept. 30, 1794, in Queensbury, Washington Co., New York; son of Asa Brown Jr. and Sarah Moon. Married Sarah Mumford, probably in Pomfret, Chautauqua Co., New York, on Sept. 2, 1819. Participated in plural marriage. Baptized in Westfield, Chautauqua Co., New York, on May 10, 1835. Ordained an elder, probably in Westfield, about 1835. Ordained a seventy in Kirtland, Geauga Co., Ohio, on Feb. 21, 1837. Served a mission in eastern New York, 1837–39. Served a mission in eastern New York and Vermont, 1841. Ordained a high priest in Nauvoo, Hancock Co., Illinois, on July 23, 1843. Served a mission in Cook Co., Illinois; Jefferson Co., New York; and the provinces of Nova Scotia and New Brunswick, Canada, 1843–44. Sent on a tithing mission to Jefferson Co., 1845. Called as a bishop in Winter Quarters, 1846. Emigrated with the Brigham Young company, arriving in the Salt Lake Valley on Sept. 21, 1848. Served as bishop of the Salt Lake Fourth Ward, 1849–66. Served in the British Mission, 1853–55. Served in the pastoral charge of the London, Reading, Kent, and Essex conferences, 1853–54. Ordained a patriarch in Salt Lake City on May 7, 1873. Died in Salt Lake City, May 22, 1878.

Brown, James (1801–63). Born Sept. 30, 1801, in Flat Swamp Creek, Rowan Co., North Carolina; son of James Brown and Mary (Polly) Williams. Married Martha Stephens in Flat Swamp Creek, Mar. 2, 1823. Participated in plural marriage. Moved to Brown Co., Illinois, in 1833, then to Adams Co., Illinois, in 1835, where he served as justice of the peace. Baptized in June 1839 in Adams Co. Served missions to Alabama in 1843, Iowa Territory in 1844, and North Carolina. Served as captain of Company C in the Mormon Battalion. Arrived in Salt Lake City on July 29, 1847. Founded Brownsville, later renamed Ogden, Jan. 1848. Served as bishop of Brownsville, starting in Feb. 1849. Served a mission to British Guiana, 1852–53. Served as an agent for the church in New Orleans, Louisiana, assisting immigrants with transportation to Missouri, 1854. Served as counselor in the stake presidency in Weber Co. Died Sept. 30, 1863, in Ogden, Utah.

Brown, John (1820–96). Born Oct. 23, 1820, near Castalian Springs, Sumner Co., Tennessee; son of John Brown and Martha Chapman. Moved to Perry Co., Illinois, in 1829, where he taught school. Baptized in Perry Co., July 1841. Moved to Nauvoo, Hancock Co., Illinois, Oct. 1841. Ordained an elder by Hyrum Smith, Feb. 9, 1842. Served a mission in southern Illinois, Jan.–Apr. 1843, and in the southern states, May 1843–45. Married Elizabeth Crosby in Monroe Co., Mississippi, May 21, 1844. Ordained a seventy on Nov. 12, 1844, in Monroe Co. Helped lead the Mississippi company from Monroe Co. to Pueblo, Colorado, Apr.–Aug. 1846. Migrated with Brigham Young pioneer company as captain of ten, arriving July 22, 1847. Appointed captain of the company of men (including members of the Mormon Battalion) returning to the United States, Aug. 30, 1847. Returned to Tennessee, winter 1848. With other southern Saints, moved to Winter Quarters in spring 1848. Migrated with Willard Richards company as captain of ten, arriving in the Salt Lake Valley Oct. 16, 1848. Appointed captain of fifty in the Parley P. Pratt company to explore southern Utah, Nov. 23, 1849. Elected to the Utah territorial legislature from Salt Lake Co., Dec. 1851. Ordained president of the eighth quorum of the seventy, Apr. 9, 1852. Captain of exploratory party to southern Utah, June 2, 1852; appointed captain of the company. Elected a representative for Utah and Cedar counties to the territorial legislature, Aug. 1859. Served a mission to England, 1860–62. Ordained bishop of Pleasant Grove Ward, Utah Co., Feb. 2, 1863; served twenty-eight years. Elected mayor of

Pleasant Grove, Feb. 9, 1863; served twenty years. Presided over the Southern States Mission, 1867–68. Ordained a patriarch in Kanab, Kane Co., Utah, Sept. 1, 1893. Died Nov. 4, 1896, in Pleasant Grove.

Buckland, Alondus De Lafayette (1823–54). Born Dec. 11, 1823, in Tunbridge, Windsor Co., Vermont; son of Joseph Mosely Buckland and Hannah Daggett. Baptized Dec. 22, 1845. Sailed on the ship *Brooklyn* with Sam Brannan, arriving in Yerba Buena (now San Francisco), California, July 31, 1846. Married Nancy Laura Aldrich in Yerba Buena, Oct. 10, 1846. Participated in plural marriage. Lived in San Francisco, Stanislaus, and Stockton, California, 1847–49. Emigrated with the Thomas Rhoades gold train, arriving in Salt Lake Valley, Oct. 1849. Living in Davis Co., Utah, 1850–52. Served a mission to Nova Scotia and the British provinces, 1852–54. Arrived at Fort Leavenworth, Kansas, May 11, 1854. Died of cholera near Fort Leavenworth, June 22, 1854.

Edward Bunker (1822–1901). Born Aug. 1, 1822, in Atkinson, Penobscot (now Piscataquis) Co., Maine; son of Silas Bunker and Hannah Berry. Farmer, road builder, and laborer. Baptized Apr. 1845 in Cleveland, Cuyahoga Co., Ohio. Moved to Nauvoo, Hancock Co., Illinois, July 1845. Married Emily Abbott, Feb. 9, 1846, in Nauvoo. Joined the Mormon Battalion. Discharged July 16, 1847, in Los Angeles, California Territory. Rejoined his wife in Winter Quarters, present-day Douglas Co., Nebraska, 1847. Migrated to Salt Lake Valley, Utah Territory, and arrived Sept. 1, 1850. Moved to Ogden, Weber Co., Utah. Participated in plural marriage. Appointed to serve a mission to England, Aug. 28, 1852. Arrived in England, Jan. 5, 1853. Served two years as the District President of the Bristol, Sheffield, Bradford, and Lincolnshire conferences in England, then appointed to preside over the Dundee, Glasgow, and Edinburgh conferences in Scotland for another year. Released from his mission Dec. 8, 1855. Captain of the Edward Bunker company consisting of mostly Welsh Saints that started in Iowa City (outfitting post), Johnson Co., Iowa, traveled to Florence, Douglas Co., Nebraska, and arrived in Salt Lake City on Oct. 2, 1856. Appointed bishop of the Ogden Second Ward, Ogden, Weber Co., Utah. Appointed to serve in the southern Utah cotton mission at the Oct. 1861 general conference. Appointed to preside over and be bishop of the members who located in Santa Clara, Washington Co., Utah, fall 1862. Participated in the United Order. Jan. 1, 1877, formed a temporary organization of member families to move to Mesquite (renamed Bunkerville), Nevada. Ordained a patriarch Sept. 10, 1900. Moved to Mexico, 1901. Died Nov. 17, 1901, in Colonia Morelos, Sonora, Mexico.

Burgess, William, Jr. (1822–1904). Born Mar. 1, 1822, in Putnam, Washington Co., New York; son of William Burgess and Vilate Stockwell. Served as a captain and a colonel in the Black Hawk War in 1832. Baptized Jan. 8, 1835, in Kirtland, Ohio. Married Maria Pulsipher in Lima, Adams Co., Illinois, Sept. 17, 1840. Participated in plural marriage. Served in the Nauvoo Legion in 1841, captain of the third company, fifth regiment, eighth brigade. Ordained to second quorum of the seventy, Oct. 8, 1844. Emigrated in the Brigham Young company of 1848, arriving in Salt Lake Valley by Sept. 24, 1848. Living in Salt Lake City, 1850 and 1860. Called on a mission to England, Aug. 1852; to the Indians at Fort Limhi, Oregon, 1855–56. Moved to St. George, Washington Co., Utah, in 1862, living there during the winters and in Pine Valley, Washington Co., Utah, during the summers until 1880. Moved to Huntington, Emery Co., Utah, in 1886. Died Mar. 14, 1904, in Huntington.

Camp, Williams Washington (1800–75). Born Dec. 11, 1800, in Warren Co., Georgia; son of Cecil (Cecillus) Camp and Mary or Margaret Williams. Married Diannah Greer, about 1821, in Tuscaloosa Co., Alabama. Participated in plural marriage. Baptized in 1842 in Tennessee. Migrated to the Salt Lake Valley in the Shadrach Roundy company, arriving Sept. 1850. Brought slaves with him to Utah. Ordained a high priest on May 29, 1852, in Salt Lake City. Selected and set apart to serve a mission to Texas, Aug. 1852. Served a mission to Las Vegas in 1856. Lived in Salt Lake Co., Utah, 1860–75. Died Nov. 21, 1875, in Salt Lake City.

Carter, William Furlsbury (1811–88). Born May 1, 1811, in Newry, Oxford Co., Maine; son of John Carter and Hannah Knight Libby. Married Sarah York in 1831 in Bethel, Oxford Co. Participated in plural marriage. Baptized Nov. 17, 1834, by Daniel Bean in Newry. Ordained an elder in 1836 in Kirtland, Geauga Co., Ohio. Ordained a seventy, Apr. 9, 1838, in Far West, Caldwell Co., Missouri. Served as drum major in the third regiment, second cohort, Nauvoo Legion, 1841. Ordained a president of the seventy in Nauvoo, Hancock Co., Illinois, Jan. 24, 1843. Ordained one of the seven presidents of the 20th quorum of the seventy, Mar. 18, 1845, in Morleysville, Hancock Co. Served a mission to India, 1852–54. Ordained a high priest, June 1856, in Provo, Utah Co., Utah. Served in the Black Hawk War, May 11–Aug. 29, 1866. Died in Santaquin, Utah Co., Oct. 11, 1888.

Clayton, William (1814–79). Born July 17, 1814, in Charnock Moss, Lancastershire, England; son of Thomas Clayton and Ann Critchley. Married Ruth Moon, Oct. 9, 1836, in Eccleston Parish, Lancastershire. Participated in plural marriage. Baptized by Heber C. Kimball in the River Ribble, near Preston, England, on Oct. 21, 1837. Served as clerk to Heber C. Kimball in 1840. Emigrated on the *North America*, sailing from Liverpool, England, to New York, arriving on Oct. 12, 1840. Arrived in Nauvoo, Hancock Co., Illinois, on Nov. 24, 1840. Member of the high priest quorum in Nauvoo, Apr. 7, 1841. Appointed to the high council of Nauvoo, Apr. 24, 1841. Served as clerk to Joseph Smith, 1842. Served as recorder for the Nauvoo Temple, 1842. Served as treasurer of Nauvoo, 1842. Emigrated with the Brigham Young pioneer company, arriving in Salt Lake Valley in July 1847. Served a mission to England, 1852–53. Served as auditor in Salt Lake Territory, 1870. Died in Salt Lake City on Dec. 4, 1879.

Cluff (Clough), Moses C. (1828–1903). Born Feb. 20, 1828, in Durham, Strafford Co., New Hampshire; son of David Cluff Sr. and Elizabeth (Betsy) Hall. Baptized about 1836 in New Hampshire. Moved to Nauvoo, Hancock Co., Illinois, in 1840. Migrated to the Great Salt Lake Valley, probably working as a teamster for Seth M. Blair company, arriving Sept. 7, 1850. Lived in Utah Co., Utah, in 1850. Called to serve mission to Berlin, Prussia, but was detained in England, lacking a passport. Served a mission to England, 1853–56. Appointed president of the Newcastle upon Tyne conference about 1855. Appointed to the presidency of the Cambridgeshire conference, 1855. Assigned to lead "church herd" of cattle to Utah behind the William B. Hodgetts company, 1856. Married Rebecca Langman, Dec. 25, 1856. Participated in plural marriage. Delivered mail between Provo and Heber City while living in Provo, Utah Co., Utah. Moved to Apache Co., Arizona, by 1880. Died Jan. 30, 1903, in Pima, Graham Co., Arizona.

Cook, Richard (1822–74). Born Dec. 10, 1822, in Cranwell, Lincoln-shire, England; son of John Cook and Charlotte Waddington. Baptized 1840 or Sept. 1841. Married Ellen Haworth on Aug. 13, 1848, in Rad-cliffe, Lancashire, England. Participated in plural marriage. Emigrated from England and arrived in New Orleans, Louisiana, Mar. 11, 1850. Mi-grated from Kanesville (now Council Bluffs), Iowa Territory, with the Milo Andrus company, arriving in Salt Lake City on Aug. 30, 1850. Appointed to serve a mission to England, Aug. 1852. Served as president of the group of emigrating church members who sailed from Liverpool, England, on the ship *Germanicus* on Apr. 4, 1854, and arrived in New Orleans on June 13, 1854. Appointed first counselor of the Robert L. Campbell company that arrived in Salt Lake City, Oct. 1854. Appointed bishop of the South Weber Ward, Davis Co., Utah, 1857–61. Joined the Church of Jesus Christ of Saints of the Most High (Morrisites) in 1861; appointed first counselor to Joseph Morris. Died on May 23, 1874, in Douglas Co., Nevada.

Crandall, Spicer Wells (1822–79). Born Dec. 31, 1822, probably in York, Genesee Co., New York; son of Daniel Crandall and Margaret Mc-Bride. Baptized Mar. 15, 1837, in York, Pike Co., Missouri. Married Sarah Gill in Hancock Co., Illinois, Oct. 15, 1843. Living in Nauvoo, 1846. Wife died; married Irinda Spafford in Macedonia, Pottawattamie Co., Iowa, Oct. 1, 1849. Migrated with the Warren Foote company, arriving in the Salt Lake Valley in late Sept., 1850. Wife died from cholera on the trek; married Sophia Kellogg in Springville, Utah Co., Utah, by Dec. 5, 1850. Served a mission to England, 1852–56. Assisted the Daniel D. McArthur handcart company from Iowa City, Iowa, arriving in the Salt Lake Val-ley, Sept. 26, 1856. Living in Springville, 1860. Served as member of the Springville city council, 1857–59, counselor to Mayor Lorenzo Johnson, 1858–1861. Died in Springville on May 14, 1879.

Daniels, Daniel (1807–79). Born Aug. 9, 1807, in Llain, Llapumsaint, South Wales; son of David Daniels and Dinah Davies. Baptized Oct. 7,

1847. Married Mary Jeremy about 1829 in Carmarthenshire, South Wales. Emigrated from Wales, sailing aboard the *Buena Vista* from Liverpool, England, to New Orleans, Louisiana, arriving on Mar. 19, 1849. Migrated to the Salt Lake Valley as captain of ten with the George A. Smith/Dan Jones company, arriving in late Oct. 1849. Served a mission to Wales, 1852–56. Ordained a high priest, Jan. 22, 1851. Counselor to Thomas Jeremy, branch president of Welsh branch. Served as president of Malad, Oneida Co., Idaho, 1874; bishop of Malad Ward, before 1877. Died Sept. 1, 1879, in Malad.

Deuel, Osmyn Merrit (1802–89). Born Jan. 1, 1802, in Galway, Saratoga Co., New York; son of Lewis Deuel and Mary Barton. Married Mary Whiting by 1830. Participated in plural marriage. Member of the Nauvoo Legion. Ordained an elder in Kirtland, Geauga (Lake) Co., Ohio, on Mar. 17, 1836. Served a mission to New York to promote Joseph Smith's candidacy as president of the United States, 1844. Emigrated with the Charles C. Rich company, arriving in the Salt Lake Valley on Oct. 2, 1847. Second counselor of the North Canyon Ward, 1849–51. Served in the British Mission, 1853–55. President of the Staffordshire Conference, 1854. Captain of ten for the Jacob F. Secrist/Noah T. Guymon company, 1855. Died in Centerville, Davis Co., Utah Territory, on Jan. 11, 1889.

Dewey, Benjamin Franklin (1829–1904). Born May 5, 1829, in Westfield, Hamden Co., Massachusetts; son of Ashbel Dewey and Harriet Adams. Baptized in Winter Quarters by Wilford Woodruff, 1847. Emigrated with the Brigham Young pioneer company, arriving in the Salt Lake Valley in July 1847. Living in Greenwood Valley, California, May 1850. Living in Salt Lake City, Sept. 1850. Ordained a seventy, Oct. 10, 1852. Served a mission in India, Sri Lanka, and Hong Kong, 1852–54. Helped colonize San Bernardino, California, 1855. Married Alzira Smithson in San Bernardino Co., May 9, 1855. Living in Salt Lake Eighth Ward, 1860–80. Living in Indian Secret Mining District, Mohave Co., Arizona Territory, 1900. Died in Chloride, Mohave Co., Feb. 23, 1904.

Dowdle, Absalom Porter (1819–97). Born June 1, 1819, in Franklin Co., Alabama; son of Robert Dowdle and Sarah Ann Robinson. Baptized

Oct. 18, 1844, in Franklin Co., Alabama. Ordained a missionary in Oct. 1844 in Alabama. Married Sarah Ann Holladay in Marion Co., Alabama, ca. 1845. Participated in plural marriage. Traveled to Fort Pueblo, Colorado, in 1846. Presided at Fort Pueblo. Migrated with the Mississippi company arriving in Salt Lake Valley in July 1847. Served a mission to Australia, 1852–57. Presided over mission, 1856–57. Lived in Coalville, Summit Co., Utah, 1857–60. Lived in Provo, Utah Co., Utah, 1860–68. Died in Weber Co., Utah, on June 5, 1897.

Duncan, Chapman (1812–1900). Born July 1, 1812, in Barnet, Caledonia Co., Vermont, or Bath, Grafton Co., New Hampshire; son of John Duncan and Betsy Taylor Putnam. Baptized in Jackson Co., Missouri, Dec. 1832. Married Rebecca Rose, May 1835. Participated in plural marriage. Appointed to serve mission to Virginia, Apr. 1844. Appointed to second quorum of the seventy, Oct. 8, 1844. Migrated to Great Salt Lake Valley in Willard Richards company, arriving Oct. 17, 1848. Served mission to China, 1852–53. Appointed to serve mission to Carson Valley, Utah (later Nevada), 1856. Died on Dec. 22, 1900, in Caineville, Wayne Co., Utah.

Earl, Sylvester Henry (1815–73). Born Aug. 16, 1815, in Scioto Co., Ohio; son of Joseph Earl II and Dorcas Tabitha Wixom. Baptized Feb. 29, 1837. Ordained an elder, Nov. 1837, in Far West, Missouri. Married Lois Caroline Owen, Jan. 28, 1839. Participated in plural marriage. Served a mission in Indiana and Ohio, 1841–42. Ordained a seventy, 1844. Emigrated to the Salt Lake Valley in Brigham Young's pioneer company, arriving in late July 1847. Served a mission to England, 1852–55. Ordained a high priest, May 6, 1856. Living in Pine Valley, Washington Co., Utah, 1870. Died in Middleton, Washington Co., July 23, 1873.

Eldredge, Horace Sunderlin (1816–88). Born Feb. 6, 1816, in Brutus, Cayuga Co., New York; son of Alanson Eldredge and Esther Sunderlin. Baptized June 4, 1836, in New York. Married Betsy Ann Chase in Buffalo, Erie Co., New York, on July 20, 1836. Participated in plural marriage. Moved to Nauvoo, Hancock Co., Illinois, in 1840. Ordained a seventy in 1844. Served as president of the 13th quorum of the seventy in Nauvoo, Dec. 22, 1844. Migrated with the Brigham Young company as company marshal, arriving in the Salt Lake Valley in Sept. 1848. Appointed marshal of the territorial militia, 1848. Served as president of the St. Louis, Missouri, conference and general church agent of emigration and purchasing, 1852–54. Served as a member of the territorial legislature, 1854–62. Served as church emigration agent at New York, 1862–64. Served as mission president of the European mission, 1870–71. Died in Salt Lake City, Sept. 6, 1888.

Eldredge, John Sunderlin (1821-71). Born Apr. 30, 1821, in Brutus, Cayuga, New York; son of Alanson Eldredge and Esther Sunderlin. Baptized in June 1843. Emigrated with the Brigham Young pioneer company, arriving in the Salt Lake Valley by July 24, 1847. Married Sinah Ceneth Chipman in Salt Lake Valley, Mar. 24, 1849. Participated in plural marriage. Served as a president of the 13th quorum of the seventy. Clerk of the American Fork, Utah Co., Utah, branch, 1851. Served as choir director of the American Fork Branch. Served a mission to Australia, 1852–55. Set apart to administer to the sick in the American Fork Branch, Oct. 26, 1856. Died in Charleston, Wasatch Co., Utah, May 5, 1871; buried in American Fork.

Empey, William Adam (1808-90). Born July 4, 1808, in Osnabruck, Canada; son of Adam Empey and Margaret Van Steenbergh. Baptized in Jan. 1839. Married Mary Ann Morgan on Sept. 16, 1829. Practiced plural marriage. Member of the 13th quorum of the seventy, July 4, 1844. Migrated to the Salt Lake Valley with the Brigham Young pioneer company. Assigned by Brigham Young to build the first ferry across the Platte River, 1847. Bishopric member in the 15th Ward, Salt Lake City. Served a mission to England, 1852–54. Called to strengthen the settlements in southern Utah. Died Aug. 19, 1890, in St. George, Washington Co., Utah.

Farnham (Farnum), Augustus Alvin (Alwin) (1805-65). Born May 20, 1805, in Andover, Essex Co., Massachusetts; son of Peter Farnum and Chloe Wilson. Married Mary Jane Pottle in Boston, Suffolk Co., Massachusetts, July 5, 1840. Participated in plural marriage. Moved to Morgan City, Morgan Co., Illinois, by Apr. 6, 1842. Baptized Apr. 21, 1843, probably in Illinois. Served as first lieutenant with the Illinois state militia, by July

19, 1843. Did carpentry work on the Nauvoo temple, 1843–45. Ordained a seventy by Oct. 8, 1844; member of the sixth quorum of the seventy in Nauvoo, Hancock Co., Illinois. Served as president of the 29th quorum of the seventy in Nauvoo, 1845. Moved to St. Louis, St. Louis Co., Missouri, by June 27, 1847. Counselor to Bishop Nathaniel Henry Felt in St. Louis, 1849. Migrated to Utah with the Silas Richards company, arriving in Oct. 1849. Served a mission to Australia, 1852–56. Served as mission president in Australia, 1853–56. One of the first missionaries to New Zealand, arriving in Auckland on Oct. 27, 1855. Left Australia May 27, 1856, with 125 converts. Returned to Utah on Nov. 21, 1856. Designed tabernacle in Bountiful, Davis Co., Utah, 1857. Died May 2, 1865, in Farmington, Davis Co., Utah. Buried in Salt Lake City.

Farr, Aaron Freeman (1818-1903). Born Oct. 31, 1818, in Waterford, Caledonia Co., Vermont; son of Winslow Farr Sr. and Olive Hovey Freeman. Baptized May 19, 1832, in Vermont. Moved to Kirtland, Geauga Co., Ohio, in 1836; to Far West, Caldwell Co., Missouri, in 1838; and to Nauvoo, Hancock Co., Illinois, in 1842. Married Persis Atherton in Nauvoo, Jan. 15, 1844. Participated in plural marriage. Served mission to Indiana in 1844. Ordained a high priest in Nauvoo, Dec. 15, 1844. Migrated with the Brigham Young pioneer company, arriving in the Salt Lake Valley in July 1847. Served a mission to the West Indies and northern states, 1852–53. Presided over the St. Louis, Missouri, conference, 1854. Served as probate judge of Weber Co., Utah, 1859–69. Served a mission to the eastern states, Oct. 1869–Mar. 1870. Lived in Ogden, Weber Co., Utah, 1870–1903. Died in Logan, Cache Co., Utah, Nov. 18, 1903.

Fleming, Josiah Wolcott (1808-73). Born Apr. 25, 1808, in Middleton, Harrison Co., Virginia (now West Virginia); son of William Fleming and Ann (Nancy) Fleming. Married Nancy Bigler in Harrison Co., Virginia, June 3, 1828. Participated in plural marriage. Living in Harrison Co., Virginia, in 1830. Baptized in the North Fork River in Virginia by Jedediah M. Grant, Oct. 1837. Lived in Far West, Caldwell Co., Missouri. Living in Nauvoo, Hancock Co., Illinois, by 1840. Ordained a high priest, Oct. 6, 1843. Migrated in June 1850, possibly with the James Lake company that arrived in the Salt Lake Valley in early Sept. 1850. Living in Salt

Lake City by 1851. Served a mission to Australia, 1852–56; called as counselor to Augustus Farnham, Jan. 7, 1855. Served as a second lieutenant during the Black Hawk War, enlisting Oct. 3, 1865. Died Jan. 6, 1873, in Provo, Utah Co., Utah.

Fotheringham, William (1826-1913). Born Apr. 6, 1826, in Clackmannan, Scotland; son of John Fotheringham and Charlotte Gentle. Baptized in 1847. Emigrated from Liverpool, England, to New Orleans, Louisiana, with his parents, arriving Oct. 28, 1848. Worked as a ship's carpenter in St. Louis, Missouri. Ordained a seventy by Elder Joseph Young, winter 1849–50. Migrated with the Warren Foote company, arriving in the Salt Lake Valley by Sept. 17, 1850. Living in Lehi, Utah, by 1851. Accompanied Brigham Young on a tour of southern Utah, 1852. Served a mission to India, 1852–55. Married Elizabeth Hardy, June 3, 1856. Participated in plural marriage. Accompanied Brigham Young on an exploring trip to the Salmon River (Idaho). Served a mission to South Africa, 1861–64, presiding over the mission. Ordained a high priest by John Blackburn, 1870. Ordained a bishop by Erastus Snow, to serve as bishop's agent in Beaver, Utah, stake, 1877. Served as mayor of Beaver. Ordained a patriarch in 1905 by Francis M. Lyman. Died Feb. 27, 1913, in Milford, Beaver Co., Utah.

Frost, Burr (1816-78). Born Mar. 4, 1816, in Wolcott, New Haven, Connecticut; son of Alpheas Frost and Elizabeth Downs. Married Mary Elizabeth Potter, Aug. 16, 1835, in Connecticut. Participated in plural marriage. Baptized Oct. 18, 1842, by Albert Merrill in Westville, Connecticut. Ordained to eighth quorum of the seventy, 1844. Migrated with the Brigham Young pioneer company as one of two skilled blacksmiths, arriving in the Salt Lake Valley by July 24, 1847. Served a mission to Australia, 1852–54. Migrated to the Salt Lake Valley from San Bernardino, California, with other missionaries in the Amasa M. Lyman company. One of the presidents of 70th quorum of the seventy. Died Mar. 16, 1878, in Salt Lake City.

Fullmer, John Solomon (1807-83). Born on July 21, 1807, in Huntington, Luzerne Co., Pennsylvania; son of Peter Fullmer and Susannah Zerfass. Married Mary Ann Price, May 24, 1837, in Davidson Co., Tennessee. Participated in plural marriage. Baptized on July 29, 1839, by Joseph Smith Jr. in Nauvoo, Hancock Co., Illinois. Clerk for Joseph Smith in Nauvoo, 1841. Became a brigadier general of the Nauvoo Legion, June 3, 1842. Served a mission to Huntington, Luzerne Co., Pennsylvania, 1842–43. Agent for Joseph Smith, by 1843. Participated in exploratory mission to search for settlement sites, Mar. 1, 1845. Admitted to the Council of Fifty, Apr. 1845. Served a mission to Emmett's Camp in 1845. Member of the committee to dispose of property in Nauvoo. Migrated with the Willard Richards company as captain of ten, arriving in Salt Lake Valley, Oct. 19, 1848. Colonel of Nauvoo Legion of Utah, 1849–ca. 1857. Resident of Davis Co., Utah. Served a mission to England, 1852–54. Assigned to guide Mormon emigrants to St. Louis in 1855, leading a group from England to St. Louis, two from Philadelphia, and finally one from New York. Resident of Spanish Fork City, Utah Co., Utah. Moved to Springville, Utah, in 1861. Died Oct. 8, 1883, in Springville.

Gardner, Elias (1807–91). Born Apr. 2, 1807, in Vernon, Oneida Co., New York; son of William Gardner and Nancy Graves. Worked as a shoemaker. Married Harriet Snow Smith, Jan. 1, 1826, possibly in Massachusetts. Wife died, Mar. 1, 1830, in Lee, Berkshire Co., Massachusetts. Married Amy Pritchard, Feb. 13, 1832, in Lee. Baptized on Mar. 21, 1840, by Thomas Dutcher, probably in Portage Co., Ohio. Ordained a seventy on Oct. 7, 1841. Worked as a cooper in Morley's Settlement, Hancock Co., Illinois. Accepted into the Masonic Lodge of Nauvoo, Oct. 3, 1844. Wife died, Nov. 24, 1846, in Winter Quarters, Nebraska. Married Betsy Markham, Dec. 9, 1846, in Winter Quarters. Participated in plural marriage. Migrated to Utah with the Heber C. Kimball company, arriving in the Salt Lake Valley by Sept. 24, 1848. Second counselor to branch president James Pace in Payson, Utah, in 1851. Appointed to serve a mission in England, 1852–54. Participated in rescue parties sent to handcart companies in winter 1856. Died on Feb. 15, 1891, in Annabella, Sevier Co., Utah.

Glasgow, Samuel (1822–90). Born Feb. 6, 1822, in Glasgow, Lanarkshire, Scotland; son of John Glasgow and Elizabeth Campbell. Baptized Dec. 20, 1840, by Reuben Hadlock in Glasgow. Ordained a deacon, May 1, 1842, in Paisley, Refrewshire, Scotland. Married Josina (Josinnah) Bell.

Ordained a seventy, by Jan. 28, 1846. Wife died, June 20, 1847, in Winter Quarters, Nebraska. Married Ann Davis. Migrated with the Warren Foote company, arriving in Utah on Sept. 17, 1850. Served a mission to Scotland, 1852–55. Arrived in New Orleans, Louisiana, on Feb. 28, 1855. Returned to Utah with the John Hindley company, arriving Sept. 3, 1855. Wife died, Oct. 11, 1873. Married Susannah Sarah Farr on Mar. 23, 1874, in Salt Lake City. Lived in Ogden, Weber Co., Utah, by 1860. Died Sept. 15, 1890, in Ogden.

Glover, William (1813–92). Born Aug. 19, 1813, in Kilmarnock, Ayrshire, Scotland; son of William Glover and Catherine Owens. Emigrated to America in 1825. Married Jane Cowen in South Easton, Northampton Co., Pennsylvania, Nov. 13, 1832. Participated in plural marriage. Baptized Sept. 1842. Served as branch president in Easton, Northampton Co., in 1844. Migrated from New York on the *Brooklyn*, arriving in Yerba Buena (now San Francisco), July 31, 1846. Traveled with the Thomas Rhoades company, arriving in the Salt Lake Valley in late Sept. 1849. Served a mission to England, 1852–55. Served as one of the presidents of the 27th quorum of the seventy in England, 1855. President of the *Juventa* company of Saints emigrating from Liverpool, England, to Philadelphia in 1855. Lived in Davis Co., Utah, 1860–92. Died Mar. 31, 1892, in Farmington, Davis Co., Utah.

Graham, James (1804–57). Born Oct. 11, 1804, in Enniskillen, Fermanagh, Ireland; son of Robert Graham and Ann Barrow. Emigrated with his family from Ireland, settling in Pleasant Hill, New Castle Co., Delaware, about 1809. Married first Mary Ann Butler about 1824, probably at New Castle Co. Participated in plural marriage. Baptized probably at Bear Creek, Hancock Co., Illinois, about 1839. Possibly served a mission to Illinois to promote Joseph Smith's candidacy as president of the United States, 1844. Ordained a high priest in Nauvoo, Hancock Co., on Aug. 10, 1844. Migrated with the Howard Egan company as captain of ten, arriving in the Salt Lake Valley on Aug. 7, 1849. Served a mission to Australia, 1853–55. Died on Dec. 9, 1857, in Ogden, Weber Co., Utah.

Grant, David (1816–68). Born July 21, 1816, in Arbroath, Scotland; son of Robert Grant and Isabella Bell Mill. Emigrated aboard the *Riga*, arriving in New Orleans, Louisiana, on July 13, 1839. Baptized on Oct. 20, 1840, in Payson, Adams Co., Illinois, by David Evans. Married Mary Ann Hyde (Bullard) Sept. 18, 1843. Participated in plural marriage. Ordained a seventy. Migrated with the Brigham Young pioneer company, arriving in the Salt Lake Valley by July 21, 1847. Served a mission to England, 1852–56. Living in Salt Lake City, in 1860. Died in Mill Creek, Utah, Dec. 22, 1868.

Green, Ephraim (1807–74). Born Mar. 5, 1807, in Rodman, Jefferson Co., New York; son of Abraham Green and Mary Anna Ross. Baptized in 1839. Married to Malinda Thompson. Migrated to Nauvoo, Hancock Co., Illinois, by 1843. Married Fidelia Thompson by Feb. 6, 1846, in the Nauvoo temple. Ordained to second quorum of the seventy, Feb. 1846. Member of the Mormon Battalion, July 1846–July 1847. Migrated with the Jonathan H. Holmes/Samuel Thompson company to Salt Lake Valley, arrived Sept. 1848. Served a mission to the Sandwich Islands, 1852–55. Laid out the plan for a colony in Lanai, Hawaii, 1854. President of the 16th quorum of the seventy, Feb. 1861. Sealed to Mary DeForrest, Dec. 12, 1863. Served a mission to the Sandwich Islands with wife Mary, 1865. Died Oct. 6, 1874, in Rockport, Summit Co., Utah.

Guymon, Noah Thomas (1819–1911). Born June 30, 1819, in Jackson Co., Tennessee; son of Thomas Guymon and Sarah Gordon. Baptized Mar. 2, 1836. Married Mary Dickerson Dudley in Caldwell Co., Missouri, Dec. 24, 1837. Participated in plural marriage. Ordained a seventy, June 1, 1845, in Nauvoo, Hancock Co., Illinois. Migrated with the Aaron Johnson company, arriving in the Salt Lake Valley on Sept. 12, 1850. Served a mission to Great Britain, 1852–55. Led the company on the ship *Juventa* from Liverpool, England, arriving in Philadelphia on May 5, 1855. Returned to Utah with the Jacob F. Secrist/Noah T. Guymon pioneer company, arriving in the Salt Lake Valley, Sept. 7, 1855. Served as senior president of the 51st quorum of the seventy, May 20, 1857, Springville, Utah. Served as major in the Utah Territorial Militia, June 16, 1857. Called as a president of the

81st quorum of the seventy, Sept. 1884, Emery Co., Utah. Died Jan. 7, 1911, in Orangeville, Emery Co., Utah.

Hall, John Charles (1821–90). Born Oct. 20, 1821, in Faversham, England; son of Thomas Johnson Hall and Charlotte Wright. Baptized Nov. 17, 1847. Served a mission to England, 1852–57. Married Selina DeGrey, Apr. 26, 1853, in Dudley, England. Participated in plural marriage. Probably emigrated aboard the *George Washington*, sailing from Liverpool, England, and arriving in Boston Apr. 20, 1857. Migrated to the Salt Lake Valley in the Jesse B. Martin company, arriving in early Sept. 1857. Served as a private during the Black Hawk War, 1865–67. Living in Rockville, Kane Co., Utah, 1880. Died Mar. 3, 1890, in Rockville.

Harper, Charles Alfred (1817–1900). Born Jan. 27, 1817, in Upper Providence, Montgomery Co., Pennsylvania; son of Jesse Harper and Eleanor Evans. Married Lovina (Lavinia) Wollerton Dilworth, Dec. 19, 1839. Participated in plural marriage. Baptized May 10, 1842. Ordained a seventy by Dec. 31, 1845. Migrated with Brigham Young pioneer company to the Salt Lake Valley, arriving July 23, 1847. Served in Nauvoo Legion of Utah, Oct. 28–Nov. 9, 1850. Served mission to England, 1852–55. Led a company from Liverpool, England, aboard the ship *Juventa*, arriving in Philadelphia on May 5, 1855. Led Charles Alfred Harper company to the Salt Lake Valley, arriving Oct. 28, 1855. Settled at Big Cottonwood Precinct, Salt Lake Co., Utah. Died in Holladay, Salt Lake Co., Utah, Apr. 24, 1900.

Haven, Jesse (1814–1905). Born Mar. 28, 1814, in Holliston, Middlesex Co., Massachusetts; son of John Haven and Elizabeth Howe. Baptized Apr. 13, 1838. Ordained an elder, Jan. 10, 1839. Served a mission to the eastern United States, ca. 1840–42. Married Martha Spring Hall in Northbridge, Worcester Co., Massachusetts, Nov. 24, 1842. Participated in plural marriage. Ordained a seventy at Nauvoo, Hancock Co., Illinois, ca. 1843. Appointed a member of the 14th quorum of the seventy, Dec. 22, 1844, in Nauvoo. Served another mission to the eastern United States, ca. 1847–ca. 1849. Migrated with the Edward Hunter company as captain of ten, arriving in the Salt Lake Valley by Oct. 12, 1850. Presided over the

South Africa mission, 1852–55. Served mission in Scotland after arriving in England, 1856. Leader of a handcart company before merging with Edward Martin company, arriving in the Salt Lake Valley with the William Hodgetts company, 1856. Appointed chaplain of the Utah territorial legislature at Salt Lake City, 1856. Member of the Nauvoo Legion of Utah, 1857–ca. 1862. Appointed a circuit judge of Weber, Davis, and Morgan counties, Utah, 1862. Probate judge of Morgan Co., Utah, 1869–ca. 1876. Served as second counselor of the Weber Ward while simultaneously serving as presiding elder of the Saints in Enterprise, Weber (later Morgan) Co., Utah, 1869–76. Served as a member of the Morgan stake high council, 1877–93. Died Dec. 14, 1905, in Enterprise; buried in Salt Lake City.

Hogan, Erick (Eric) Goudyson Mibben (1802–76). Born June 23, 1802, in Randeberg, Uvdal, Buckerud, Norway; son of Gaute Erickson and Marget Knudsdatter. Christened in Randeberg, July 25, 1802. Married Kari Sondresdatter in Atraa, Telemark, Norway, June 6, 1827. Wife died, 1828. Married Helja Knutdatter Nostebein in Tinn, Telemark, Norway, Mar. 26, 1829. Participated in plural marriage. Emigrated from Norway to LaSalle Co., Illinois, arriving 1838. Anglicized name to Eric G. M. Hogan. Baptized in Iowa, Jan. 1843. Migrated to the Great Salt Lake Valley with Brigham Young company of 1848, arriving Sept. 22, 1848. Called on mission to Norway, 1852. Appointed president of the Norwegian mission, Apr. 10, 1853, and arrived May 10, 1853. Accompanied emigrating Norwegian Saints to the Great Salt Lake Valley, Nov. 10, 1854. Living in Bountiful, Davis Co., Utah, 1860. Died in Bountiful, June 21, 1876.

Hotchkiss, Lawrence Sterne (1816–1904). Born Oct. 9, 1816, in Naugatuck, New Haven Co., Connecticut; son of Thaddeus Hotchkiss and Harriet Ball. Graduated from Dartmouth College and Jefferson Medical College, Philadelphia, Pennsylvania, Mar. 10, 1837. Married Theresa G. Peyre Ferry, June 22, 1842, in Philadelphia. Wife apparently died by 1846. Married Hannah Camilla Free, Feb. 6, 1846. Baptized June 1850, possibly in Iowa. Located at Pottawattamie, Iowa, 1850. Migrated to the Salt Lake Valley, by 1850. Practiced dentistry in Utah. Ordained a seventy by Wilford Woodruff. Divorced, 1852. Called to serve a mission to Siam, 1852, but did not serve. Married Esther R. Candee, Oct. 20, 1852, possibly in

Connecticut. Moved to New Haven Co., Connecticut, by 1858. Buried Aug. 10, 1904, in New Haven.

Houtz, Jacob (1814–96). Born Oct. 12, 1814, in Penn Township, Union Co., Pennsylvania; son of Christian Houtz and Anna Elizabeth Zeller. Married Lydia Mease on Feb. 22, 1838, in Pennsylvania. Participated in plural marriage. Baptized in Oct. 1844. Ordained a member of the sixth quorum of the seventy, Apr. 1846. Migrated with the Daniel Spencer/Ira Eldredge company, arriving in the Salt Lake Valley by Sept. 23, 1847. Appointed second counselor of the Salt Lake Fifth Ward, ca. 1847. Served as second counselor of the Salt Lake Sixth Ward, 1849–50. Called to serve a mission to Berlin, Prussia, 1852. Arrived in Berlin but was deported and spent the rest of his mission in England and probably US, 1853. Served as second counselor of the Salt Lake Eighth Ward, 1856–61. Served a mission to the eastern United States, 1869–70. Elected a member of Springville city council in Springville, Utah Co., Utah, 1871. Died on Dec. 11, 1896, in Springville.

Hunt, John Alexander (1830–1913). Born May 16, 1830, in Gibson Co., Tennessee; son of Daniel Durham Hunt and Nancy Davis. Baptized in Nauvoo, Hancock Co., Illinois, Mar. 15, 1843. Ordained a seventy in Nauvoo, Feb. 1, 1847. Resided with his family in Pottawatomie Co., Iowa, Jan. 22, 1848. Migrated to Great Salt Lake Valley in Aaron Johnson company, arriving Feb. 12, 1850. Called on a mission to Great Britain, Aug. 28, 1852; arrived Jan. 3, 1853. Appointed president of Warwickshire conference, Feb. 10, 1855. Left Liverpool on the *Enoch Train*, arriving in Boston on May 1, 1856. Led the John A. Hunt company, the last to leave Florence, Nebraska, in 1856, arriving in the Salt Lake Valley on Dec. 10, 1856, after suffering much hardship. Ran mail station at Devil's Gate, summer 1857. Married Elizabeth Tilt in Salt Lake City, Sept. 22, 1859. Resided in Grantsville, Tooele Co., Utah Territory, 1859–64. Moved to St. Charles, Bear Lake Co., Idaho. Served as county commissioner for Tooele and Bear Lake Counties. Called as first bishop of St. Charles Ward, Aug. 25, 1877, serving until 1895. Died Jan. 23, 1913, in St. Charles.

Hyde, John (1803–53). Born June 4, 1803, in Stockport, Cheshire, England; son of Robert Hyde and Ellen Maycock. Baptized by June 1, 1849. Emigrated from Liverpool, England, to New Orleans, Louisiana, aboard the *North Atlantic*, arriving Nov. 1, 1850. Ordained a seventy. Served a mission to Australia, 1852–53. Died near Sydney, Australia, on Aug. 27, 1853.

Hyde, William (1818–74). Born Sept. 11, 1818, in present-day York, Livingston Co., New York; son of Heman Hyde and Polly Wyman Tilton. Baptized Apr. 7, 1834. Served mission to Illinois, Indiana, and Michigan, Nov. 1839–Feb. 1840. Ordained to quorum of the seventy, Apr. 7, 1840. Began serving mission to Maine, Apr. 1840. Married Elizabeth Howe Bullard in Hancock Co., Illinois, Feb. 25, 1842. Participated in plural marriage. Served mission to Vermont, Oct. 1842–June 1843; to eastern states, Sept. 1843–Aug. 1844; to Mississippi and Alabama, Jan. 1845–Mar. 1845. Ordained a president of the eighth quorum of the seventy, Oct. 8, 1844. Joined Mormon Battalion, July 16, 1846; appointed sergeant of company B. Migrated from California Territory to Great Salt Lake Valley with Levi W. Hancock/Jefferson Hunt/James Pace/Andrew Lytle company, arriving by Oct. 16, 1847. Appointed to serve mission to Australia, Aug. 1852. Appointed a president of the 44th quorum of the seventy, May 1857. Appointed bishop of Hyde Park, Cache Co., Utah, July 1, 1860. Led William Hyde company from Nebraska Territory to Great Salt Lake Valley, arriving Oct. 26, 1864. Ordained a patriarch, June 27, 1873. Died in Hyde Park, Mar. 2, 1874.

Jeremy, Thomas Evans (1815–91). Born July 11, 1815, in Llanegwad Parish, Carmarthenshire Co., Wales; son of Thomas Jeremy and Sarah Evans. Married Sarah Evans, Mar. 16, 1838, Carmarthenshire Parish, Wales. Baptized Apr. 3, 1846, by Dan Jones in Carmarthenshire, Wales. Participated in plural marriage. Emigrated from Liverpool, England, aboard the *Buena Vista*, arriving in New Orleans, Louisiana, Apr. 19, 1849. Migrated July 14, 1849, to Salt Lake Valley, arriving Oct. 1849. Served mission to Wales, 1852–55. Presided over the districts of Western Glamorganshire, Llanelly, and Carmarthen, 1853. Sustained counselor of the church in Wales, June

26, 1853. Served a second mission to Wales; appointed president of the Welsh mission, Jan. 20, 1861. Released Mar. 26, 1864. Appointed member of the Salt Lake Stake high council, Oct. 9, 1864. Ordained a patriarch, 1887. Died Apr. 17, 1891, in Salt Lake City, Utah.

Johnson, Benjamin Franklin (1818–1905). Born on July 28, 1818, in Pomfret, Chautauqua Co., New York; son of Ezekiel Johnson and Julia Hills. Baptized in Kirtland, Geauga Co., Ohio, spring 1835. Ordained an elder in Far West, Caldwell Co., Missouri, Mar. 10, 1839. Served mission to eastern United States and Upper Canada, 1840–41. Married Melissa B. LeBaron in Kirtland, Dec. 25, 1841. Participated in plural marriage. Ordained a high priest at Ramus, Hancock Co., Illinois, ca. 1843. Admitted to Council of Fifty, spring 1844. Migrated with Willard Richards company to the Great Salt Lake Valley, arriving Oct. 10, 1848. Appointed captain in Nauvoo Legion of Utah, May 1849. Appointed member of the provisional state of Deseret house of representatives, 1849. Presided over Summit Creek Branch in Utah Co., Utah, 1851–52. Served Mission to Sandwich Islands, 1852–55. Presided over Santaquin Branch in Utah Co., 1856–58. Presided over Spring Lake Branch in Utah Co., 1862–77. Served mission in Utah, 1877; instructed Saints on importance of temple work. Served as bishop of Spring Lake Ward in Utah Co., 1877–82. Ordained a patriarch in Arizona Territory, Jan. 7, 1883. Served mission to Yaqui Indians, 1884. Died on Nov. 18, 1905, in Mesa, Maricopa Co., Arizona.

Jolley, Washington Lafayette (1831–89). Born May 14, 1831, in Dresden, Weakley Co., Tennessee; son of Reuben Manning Jolley and Sarah Pippen. Living in Nauvoo, Hancock Co., Illinois, in 1842. Baptized in 1842 by Peter Hawes. Moved to Iowa, May 1846. Migrated with the Warren Foote company, arriving in the Salt Lake Valley on Sept. 17, 1850. Living in Pleasant Grove, Utah Co., Utah, in 1851. Living in Salt Lake 13th Ward, 1851. Called on a mission to Texas, Aug. 1852. Married Emily Knight, Apr. 3, 1854. Led a group of Texas Saints to the Salt Lake Valley, arriving Sept. 21, 1854. Living in Payson, Utah Co., Utah, in 1860. Called on a mission to the southern states, Sept. 22, 1860, returning to Utah with the David H. Cannon company, arriving in Payson Aug. 15, 1861. Called as a member of the cotton mission to southern Utah, Oct. 19,

1862. Served as major of the Washington battalion in the Iron Co., Utah, military district in 1865. Living in Washington, Washington Co., Utah, in 1870–80. Died on Nov. 8, 1889, in Washington.

Jones, Dan (1810–62). Born on Aug. 4, 1810, in Caerfallwch, Wales; son of Thomas Jones and Ruth Roberts. Married Jane Melling in Denbigh, Wales, Jan. 3, 1837. Immigrated to United States, ca. 1840. Baptized on Jan. 19, 1843, in Mississippi River. Served mission to Wales, 1845–49. Presided over the church in Wales, 1845–49. Appointed to preside over the Merthyr Tydfil conference, 1846. Migrated with the George A. Smith/ Dan Jones company, captain of the Welsh Saints and marshal, arriving in the Salt Lake Valley between Oct. 25 and 29, 1849. Elected first mayor of Manti, Sanpete Co., Utah, Apr. 1851. Ordained a high priest by 1851. Served a second mission to Wales, 1852–56. President of church's Welsh principality, 1854–56. Captain of the Dan Jones company (later called John A. Hunt company) for a time, 1856. Died on Jan. 3, 1862, in Provo, Utah Co., Utah.

Jones, Nathaniel Vary (1822–63). Born Oct. 13, 1822, in Brighton, Monroe Co., New York; son of Samuel Jones and Lucinda Kingsley. Baptized Apr. 6, 1842. Served mission to eastern states, 1843–44. Ordained to seventh quorum of the seventy, Oct. 8, 1844. Married Rebecca M. Burton in Nauvoo, Hancock Co., Illinois, Mar. 14, 1845. Participated in plural marriage. Served in Mormon Battalion. Migrated to Great Salt Lake Valley with Howard Egan company, arriving Aug. 7, 1849. Appointed to serve mission to Asia, Aug. 28, 1852. Ordained a high priest, Sept. 14, 1852. Ordained bishop of Salt Lake 15th Ward, Sept. 14, 1852. Served mission to Calcutta, 1853–55. Appointed president of Calcutta Mission, Apr. 29, 1853. Served mission to England, 1859–61. Died on Feb. 15, 1863, in Salt Lake City.

Karren, Thomas (1810–76). Born on May 1, 1810, in Onchan, Isle of Man, England; son of Thomas Kerran and Catherine Clark. Worked as a baker and farmer. Married Ann Ratcliffe, May 5, 1833, in Liverpool, England. Baptized May 7, 1842, in England. Immigrated to the US, possibly on the *Isaac Allerton*, arriving in New Orleans, Louisiana, late Mar. 1844.

Migrated to Nauvoo, Hancock Co., Illinois. Enlisted with the Mormon Battalion at Mount Pisgah, Iowa; served with E company. Became ill and wintered over in Pueblo, Colorado, 1846–47. Migrated to Utah with the Mormon Battalion sick detachments company, arriving in July 1847. Traveled to Garden Grove, Iowa, to reunite with his family, migrating again to Utah in 1850. Assigned by Brigham Young to settle what became Lehi, Utah Co., Utah, 1850. Served a mission to the Sandwich Isles (Hawaii), 1852–55. Participated in plural marriage. Appointed to various city positions in Lehi. Served as counselor to Bishop David Evans in Lehi. Died Apr. 4, 1876, in Lehi.

Lambson, Alfred Boaz (1820–1905). Born Aug. 27, 1820, in Royalton, Niagara Co., New York; son of Boaz Lambson and Polly Walworth. Moved from Kinderhook, Branch Co., Michigan, to Nauvoo, Hancock Co., Illinois, in 1843. Baptized Apr. 4, 1844, in Nauvoo. Ordained a seventy on Apr. 13, 1844, in Nauvoo. Left Nauvoo on June 4, 1844, to serve a mission in Virginia. Called back to Nauvoo after the murder of Joseph Smith, arriving on Dec. 21, 1844. Married Melissa Jane Bigler, Nov. 25, 1845, in Nauvoo. Assisted with the building of wagons in Winter Quarters, Nebraska, 1845–47. Migrated to Utah with the Daniel Spencer/Perrigrine Sessions company, arriving Sept. 25, 1847. Appointed to serve a mission to the West Indies, Aug. 1852. Arrived in Jamaica, Jan. 10, 1853. Returned home because of opposition and finished mission in Michigan. Lived in Florence, Nebraska, 1856–66, outfitting and blacksmithing emigrant wagon trains. Returned to Utah in 1866. Died on Feb. 26, 1905, in Salt Lake City.

Lamoreaux, Andrew Losey (1812–55). Born Mar. or Oct. 17, 1812, in Scarborough or Pickering, York, Ontario, Canada; son of John McCord Lamoreaux and Abigail Ann Losey. Married Isabell Rodgers Wilson in Markham, York, Ontario, Canada, Oct. 12, 1833. Participated in plural marriage. Baptized in June 1837 in Ontario. Ordained an elder in Kirtland, Geauga Co., Ohio; signed the Kirtland Camp constitution, Mar. 1838. Received into the high priest quorum in Nauvoo, Hancock Co., Illinois, on Dec. 17, 1843; 10th quorum of the seventy on Oct. 8, 1844. Remained in Nauvoo to protect the property of those who remained; participated as captain in the "battle of Nauvoo," Sept. 1846. Migrated with the Willard Richards company, arriving in the Salt Lake Valley, Oct. 10, 1848. Elected to represent Davis Co. in the territorial government, Aug. 21, 1852. Presided over the French Mission, 1852–55. Died June 13, 1855, in St. Louis, Missouri.

Lawson, James (1820–1912). Born July 20, 1820, in Kinross, Scotland; son of David Lawson and Margaret Anderson. Baptized in Scotland, Sept. 10, 1840. Married Margaret Thomson (Thompson) in Glasgow, Scotland, Apr. 28, 1841. Wife died in Glasgow, Oct. 4, 1842. Emigrated on the ship *Metoka* from Liverpool, England, to New Orleans, Louisiana, arriving Oct. 27, 1843. Arrived in Nauvoo, Hancock Co., Illinois, May 14, 1845. Ordained a seventy in Nauvoo, May 18, 1845. Migrated to Utah with the Daniel Spencer/Perrigrine Sessions company, arriving ca. Sept. 25, 1847. Appointed to mission in Iron Co., Utah, and, with others, smelted the first iron that was discovered in that region. Served missions in Sandwich Islands (Hawaii), 1852–55, 1865–67. Presided over church in Molokai, 1854–55. Married Elizabeth Ann Noon in Salt Lake City, Oct. 10, 1855. Participated in plural marriage. Served mission in Carson Valley, Utah (later Nevada). Ordained a patriarch, 1903. Died in Salt Lake City, Sept. 14, 1912.

Leonard, Truman (1820–97). Born Sept. 17, 1820, in Middlesex, Ontario Co., New York; son of Truman Leonard Sr. and Roxanna Allis. Baptized Mar. 25, 1834. Served a mission to Ohio and New York in 1843. Married Ortensia White, Jan. 1, 1846, in Nauvoo, Hancock Co., Illinois. Participated in plural marriage. Migrated to Salt Lake Valley from Kanesville (later Council Bluffs), Iowa, with the William Snow/Joseph Young company, arriving by Oct. 4, 1850. Ordained a seventy on June 11, 1843, by Noah Packard. Served a mission to India, 1852–55. Emigrated from Liverpool, England, on the *Enoch Train*, arriving in Boston May 1, 1856. Migrated to Utah in the Daniel D. McArthur handcart company, leaving Iowa City, Iowa, on June 11, 1856, and arriving on Sept. 26, 1856. Appointed senior president of the 56th quorum of the seventy, Sept. 1854. Member of Deseret Brass Band. Died Nov. 20, 1897, in Farmington, Davis Co., Utah.

Lewis, James (1814–98). Born Jan. 12, 1814, in Gorham, Cumberland Co., Maine; son of James Lewis and Hannah Harding. Moved to Missouri in 1840. Baptized and ordained an elder, Feb. 1842, in Keokuk, Iowa. Served a fund-raising mission to the eastern states, 1843. Returned to St. Louis, Missouri, 1844. Ordained a seventy, Feb. 22, 1845. Married Emily Jennison Holman, May 9, 1847. Participated in plural marriage. Immigrated to the Salt Lake Valley in the Silas Richards company, arriving in the Salt Lake Valley in late Oct. 1849. Served a mission to southern Utah, 1850; to China, 1852–54. Elected representative to the territorial legislature, 1855–57. Probate judge of Iron Co., Utah. Removed to Kanab, Kane Co., Utah, in 1871. Elected commissioner of Kane Co., 1872. Worked in the St. George Temple, 1879–82. Called on a mission to San Juan, Utah, 1882; appointed judge of San Juan Co. Lived in Taylor, Apache Co., Arizona, until 1891. Removed to Kanab, Oct. 1891. Called as a patriarch Sept. 8, 1895. Died May 28, 1898, in Kanab.

Luddington, Elam (1806–93). Born on Nov. 23, 1806, in Litchfield Co., Connecticut; son of Elam Luddington and Aseneth (Sena) Munger. Living in New York City, New York, by 1834. Baptized May 16, 1840, in Nauvoo, Hancock Co., Illinois, possibly by Joseph Smith. Married Mary Elizabeth Clark, May 16, 1841, in Nauvoo. Participated in plural marriage. Proselytized in New Orleans, Louisiana, 1841–43. Served a mission to Quincy, Illinois, June 1844; to New Orleans, fall 1844. Ordained a high priest on Sept. 15, 1844. Served a mission to Mississippi, 1844–45. Member of the Mormon Battalion, July 1846–July 1847. Migrated to Utah with the Mormon Battalion sick detachments, arrived July 29, 1847, with his wife, daughter, and mother. Appointed a city marshal, assessor, and collector for Salt Lake City, winter 1849. Served a mission to Siam, 1852–55. Appointed as president of East India Mission and Calcutta Branch. Member of Captain Killan's company, Utah War, 1857–58. Died Mar. 3, 1893, in Salt Lake City.

Martin, Edward (1818–82). Born Nov. 18, 1818, in Preston, England; son of John Martin and Ann Slater. Baptized by Orson Hyde on Oct. 14, 1837. Married Alice Clayton, ca. 1840. Participated in plural marriage.

Emigrated aboard the *Sheffield* from Liverpool, arriving in New Orleans, Louisiana, Mar. 30, 1841. Ordained a seventy in Nauvoo, Hancock Co., Illinois, Oct. 9, 1844. Appointed a president of the 24th quorum of seventy in Nauvoo, Apr. 9, 1845. Served in the Mormon Battalion. Migrated to the Salt Lake Valley with the Levi W. Hancock/Jefferson Hunt/James Pace/Andrew Lytle company, arriving by Oct. 16, 1847. Served a mission to England, 1852–56. Captain of the Edward Martin handcart company, 1856. Died Aug. 8, 1882, in Salt Lake City.

Mayer, George (1805–96). Born Mar. 2, 1805, in York Co., Pennsylvania; son of Abraham Mayer and Elizabeth Lauck. Married Ann Yost in Bucyrus, Crawford Co., Ohio, Mar. 4, 1828. Participated in plural marriage. Served in the military in Bucyrus, Ohio, 1830. Baptized in Logansport, Cass Co., Indiana, Nov. 11, 1843. Ordained elder, Mar. 5, 1844. Ordained a seventy, Jan. 12, 1845. Appointed senior president of the Nauvoo 32nd quorum of the seventy, Dec. 21, 1845. Migrated to Great Salt Lake Valley in the Heber C. Kimball company, arriving Sept. 24, 1848. Served mission to Germany and Switzerland, 1852–55. Served mission to Las Vegas, New Mexico Territory (now Nevada), 1856–57. Appointed president over the quorums of the seventy in Spanish Fork, Utah. Ordained a high priest, Dec. 10, 1893. Ordained a patriarch, Apr. 19, 1896. Died in Spanish Fork, July 24, 1896.

Mayer, John (1811–92). Baptized Nov. 7, 1813, in Burslem, Staffordshire, England; son of William and Frances Mayer. Married Sarah Minshall, 1831, in Saint Giles, Newcastle-under-Lyme, Staffordshire, England. Practiced plural marriage. Baptized before Dec. 1, 1838. Emigrated from Liverpool, England, aboard the *Champion*, arriving with his family in New Orleans, Louisiana, Dec. 6, 1843. Migrated with the Warren Foote company, arriving in the Salt Lake Valley on Sept. 17, 1850. Worked as a bricklayer and mason. Served a mission to Great Britain, 1852–55. Settled in Los Angeles, California, 1861. Died Jan. 23, 1892, in Los Angeles, California.

McArthur, Daniel Duncan (1820–1908). Born Apr. 8, 1820, in Holland, Niagara Co., New York; son of Duncan McArthur and Susan

McKeen. Baptized 1838. Married Cordelia Clark, June 14, 1841; she died June 14, 1844. Ordained to 10th quorum of the seventy, Oct. 8, 1844. Married Matilda Caroline Fuller, Dec. 14, 1845. Participated in plural marriage. Migrated from Winter Quarters, unorganized US territory (later in Omaha, Douglas Co., Nebraska) to Great Salt Lake Valley with Brigham Young company, arriving by Sept. 24, 1848. Appointed to mission in England, by Aug. 29, 1852. Led Daniel D. McArthur company from Iowa City, Johnson Co., Iowa, to Great Salt Lake Valley, arriving Sept. 26, 1856. Appointed major in Nauvoo Legion of Utah, 1857. Called to settle southern Utah, by Oct. 9, 1861. Became bishop of Third Ward, St. George, Washington Co., Utah, Mar. 22, 1862. Assisted Saints coming to Great Salt Lake Valley, 1863, 1868. Called as presiding bishop in southern Utah, Sept. 15, 1869. Called on mission to Europe, by Apr. 7, 1877. Set apart as president of St. George stake, Dec. 17, 1888. Ordained a patriarch, June 1901. Died in St. George, June 3, 1908.

McBride, William (1807-95). Born Mar. 22, 1807, in Sugar Creek, Greene Co., Ohio; son of James McBride and Margaret Jane Andrew. Married Elizabeth Harris Ball Boorham, Sept. 1, 1831, at Randolph, Montgomery Co., Ohio. Participated in plural marriage. Baptized Oct. 28, 1843, by Henry Elliot. Ordained a president of 26th quorum of the seventy, 1845. Migrated with the Willard Richards company, arriving in the Salt Lake Valley, Oct. 10, 1848. Served a mission to the Sandwich Islands, 1852–55. Led the William McBride company, arriving in the Salt Lake Valley July 21, 1855. Served as presiding elder of Santaquin, Utah Co., Utah, branch, 1858–65. Served as a major in the Nauvoo Legion of Utah, 1866. Ordained patriarch of the Pima, Arizona, stake, 1877. Died Mar. 6, 1895, in Salt Lake City.

McDonald, John Kilpatrick (1797-1874). Born Jan. 5, 1797, in Donaghadee, Ireland; son of William McDonald and Agnes (Nancy) Kilpatrick. Cabinet maker. Married Rachel Burck Taffee, Apr. 1823, in Lurgan, Ireland. Immigrated to Canada about 1831; lived in Quebec. Lived in Philadelphia, Pennsylvania, in 1834. Lived in Pittsburgh, Allegheny Co., Pennsylvania, 1838–42. Baptized June 1842 by John E. Page, probably in Pittsburgh. Living in Nauvoo, Hancock Co., Illinois, in fall 1842. Went to St. Louis, Missouri, for work; returned to Nauvoo by June 29, 1844. Ordained a seventy on Apr. 9, 1845, in Nauvoo, Illinois. Worked on the Nauvoo Temple and built wagons for the migration to Utah. Traveled to Utah with the Ezra T. Benson company in 1849; returned east (possibly to Nebraska or Iowa) to his family. Moved to Utah with the Warren Foote company, arriving Sept. 17, 1850. Called to serve a mission to Ireland and England, 1852–56. Served as the president of the Belfast Conference and Londonderry Branch in Ireland. Wife died by Apr. 29, 1863. Married Sarah Johnson, Dec. 26, 1863, in Salt Lake City. Participated in plural marriage. Died Aug. 31, 1874, in Salt Lake City.

Miller, Daniel Arnold (1809–81). Born Aug. 11, 1809, in Lexington, Greene Co., New York; son of James Gardner Miller and Ruth Arnold. Moved to Quincy, Adams Co., Illinois, ca. 1829. Married Clarissa Pond, Dec. 29, 1833. Baptized Sept. 1839. Moved to Hancock Co., Illinois, 1840. Ordained a high priest, Nov. 1840. Appointed bishop in Columbus, Adams Co., Illinois, Oct. 27, 1840. Member of the Nauvoo Legion. Served mission in Indiana, 1843–44. Wife died, Sept. 1, 1844. Married Hannah Bigler, Hancock Co., Illinois, Dec. 29, 1844. Participated in plural marriage. Moved to Iowa Territory, 1846. Appointed bishop, or manager, of Council Bluffs, Iowa, July 21, 1847. Immigrated to Great Salt Lake Valley with William Perkins company; arriving Sept. 4, 1848. Accompanied Apostle George A. Smith to begin settlement in Little Salt Lake Valley (later Parowan), Utah, Dec. 1850. Served mission to Iowa, 1852; assigned to bring ammunition, books, and other items back to Utah. Director of Farmington Co-op, 1869–81; director, and later president, of Davis Co. Co-op, 1876–81. Died in Providence, Cache Co., Utah, Dec. 4, 1881. Buried in Farmington, Davis Co., Utah.

Millett, Joseph (1832–1911). Born Dec. 12 or 22, 1832 or 1833, in Ernestown, Ontario, Canada; son of Artemas Millet and Susannah Peters. Baptized by Apr. 1, 1842. Married Sarah E. Glines, Mar. 26, 1854, in Lowell, Massachusetts. Family moved to Kirtland, Geauga Co., Ohio, 1834. Moved to Nauvoo, Hancock Co., Illinois, by Apr. 1843. Migrated to Salt Lake Valley with the David Evans company, arriving Sept. 15, 1850. Served a mission to Nova Scotia and the British provinces, 1852–53; to

New England, 1854. Returned to Salt Lake Valley with the Canute Peterson company, arriving Sept. 19, 1856. Settlement mission to southern Utah, 1866–75. Moved to Arizona, 1878. Died on Oct. 11, 1911, in Cedar City, Iron Co., Utah.

Mitchell, Benjamin Thomas (1816–80). Born Jan. 12, 1816, in Muncy, Lycoming Co., Pennsylvania; son of Abraham Mitchell and Annie Colpetzer. Married Sarah Treicbach in Portage, Wood Co., Ohio, Apr. 26, 1835. Participated in plural marriage. Baptized June 15, 1836. Worked as stonecutter for Nauvoo Temple. Ordained to third quorum of the seventy, Oct. 6, 1844. Migrated to the Great Salt Lake Valley with Heber C. Kimball company, arriving Sept. 24, 1848. Served mission to Nova Scotia and British provinces, 1852–54. Led the Benjamin Thomas Mitchell company to the Great Salt Lake Valley, arriving Aug. 5, 1854. Oversaw stonecutting for Salt Lake Temple, 1854–64. Called as bishop of Salt Lake 15th Ward, Dec. 24, 1856. Appointed a captain of the Nauvoo Legion of Utah. Died in Salt Lake City, Mar. 9, 1880.

Musser, Amos Milton (1830–1909). Born May 20, 1830, in Donegal, Lancaster, Pennsylvania; son of Samuel Musser and Anna Barr. Baptized May 24, 1851, at Kanesville, Iowa. Migrated to the Salt Lake Valley with the Easton Kelsey company, arriving Sept. 1851. Served a mission to India, 1852–56. Labored in England and Wales, 1857. Married Ann Leaver, Jan. 31, 1858. Practiced plural marriage. Ordained a president of the 57th quorum of the seventy, Feb. 1858. Held many business and civic positions. Called as traveling bishop, 1858–76; appointed trustee-in-trust for the church, 1873. Served a mission in the eastern states, 1876. Wrote the pamphlet *Fruits of Mormonism* and the periodicals *Utah Farmer* and *The Palantic.* Worked in the Church Historian's Office, 1896; sustained as an Assistant Church Historian, 1902. Died Sept. 24, 1909, in Salt Lake City.

Nickerson, Levi Stillman (1814–1853). Born Apr. 2, 1814, in Springville, Susquehannah Co., Pennsylvania; son of Freeman Nickerson and Hulda Chapman. Baptized June 1833. Member of Camp of Israel. Ordained to priesthood, fall 1835, in Kirtland, Geauga Co., Ohio. Assisted in moving the Saints from Missouri, winter 1838–39. Married Mary Ann

Neyman, June 1840. Appointed to a mission with his father in Peoria, Illinois, July 1840. Ordained as a president of the fourth quorum of the seventy, Oct. 8, 1844. Migrated to Utah with the Edward Hunter company, arriving Oct. 1, 1850. Appointed to a mission in Europe, Oct. 13, 1852. Died Dec. 15, 1853, in Kanesville (now Council Bluffs), Iowa.

Norton, John Warren (1810–63). Born May 12 or 13, 1810, in Franklin Co., Tennessee; son of William Norton and Hester, Esther, or Easter James. Cotton grower and processor, and farmer. Married Dorothy Osborn, Oct. 17, 1830, in Franklin Co., Tennessee. Moved to Shelby Co., Tennessee, about 1835. Baptized Aug. 12, 1840. Moved to Tippah Co., Mississippi. Moved to Nauvoo, Hancock Co., Illinois, early 1846. Moved to Lee Co., Iowa. Wife died in Lee Co., Sept. 6, 1846. Moved to Mount Pisgah settlement, Union Co., Iowa. Married widow Martha Ann Covington Gay, 1846 or 1847. Migrated to Utah Territory with the John Brown company and arrived Sept. 29, 1851. Divorced. Probably ordained a high priest Apr. 6, 1852. Appointed to serve a mission to Australia and arrived in Sydney, Australia, Mar. 3, 1853. Returned from mission, late 1850s. Resided in Provo, Utah Co., Utah Territory, by Sept. 13, 1860. Moved to Nephi, Juab Co., Utah. Married widow Ann Jackson Baxter, Oct. 17, 1863, and moved to southern Utah. Died Nov. 28, 1863, in Springdale, Washington Co., Utah.

Oakley, John Degroot (1819–90). Born Nov. 12, 1819, in Flatlands, Kings Co., New York; son of Ezra Oakley and Elizabeth Degroot. Baptized in North River at New York City, Sept. 4, 1840. Ordained a seventy, Oct. 8, 1844. Married Mary Madalena McCormall Patterson in Nauvoo, Hancock Co., Illinois, Feb. 16, 1845. Member of Nauvoo Legion. Migrated to Great Salt Lake Valley with Edward Hunter/Joseph Horne company, arriving Sept. 29, 1847. Served mission to England, 1852–56. Participated in rescue companies that assisted struggling companies across plains, 1856. Died on May 4, 1890, in Snowflake, Apache Co., Arizona Territory.

Owens, Robert (1818–83). Born July 10, 1818, probably in Dover, Kent Co., Delaware; son of Edmund H. Owens and Margaret Turner. Married Catherine Ann Williams, 1837. Participated in plural marriage. Baptized and ordained a seventy, Sept. 21, 1844. Appointed to 34th quorum of the seventy, Feb. 5, 1846. Served in Mormon Battalion, 1847. Migrated to Great Salt Lake Valley in Levi W. Hancock/Jefferson Hunt/James Pace/ Andrew Lytle company, arriving by Oct. 16, 1847. Appointed to serve mission to India, Aug. 1852. Died on Nov. 8, 1883, in Los Angeles, California.

Pace, James (1811–88). Born June 15, 1811, in Rutherford Co., Tennessee; son of James Pace and Mary Ann Loving. Married Lucinda Gibson Strickland in Murfreesboro, Rutherford Co., Tennessee, Mar. 20, 1831. Participated in plural marriage. Baptized by Dominicus Carter, Apr. 14, 1839. Ordained a seventy in Nauvoo, Hancock Co., Illinois, Oct. 1840. Served mission to Illinois, 1843; to Arkansas, 1844. Appointed to fourth quorum of the seventy, Oct. 8, 1844. Appointed as a president of 17th quorum of the seventy, Jan. 12, 1845. Enlisted in Mormon Battalion, July 16, 1846. Led Mormon Battalion veterans to Great Salt Lake Valley in Levi W. Hancock/Jefferson Hunt/James Pace/Andrew Lytle company, arriving by Oct. 16, 1847. Led James Pace company to Great Salt Lake Valley, arriving Sept. 23, 1850. Appointed branch president in Payson, Utah Co., Utah, by 1851. Appointed to serve mission to England, Aug. 28, 1852. Appointed to presidency of Bedfordshire conference, by Jan. 1854. Appointed to serve mission to southern Utah, Oct. 1861. Elected president of United Order in Washington Co., Utah, by Dec. 22, 1876. Moved to southern Arizona Territory, Nov. 1882. Died Apr. 6, 1888, in Thatcher, Graham Co., Arizona Territory.

Park, James Pollock (1821–89). Born Dec. 21, 1821, in Cambuslang, Scotland; son of Andrew Park and Jane (Jean) Pollock. Immigrated to Canada, by 1842. Baptized in Canada, 1844. Appointed to ninth quorum of the seventy at Nauvoo, Hancock Co., Illinois, Oct. 8, 1844. Ordained an elder, ca. 1845. Appointed to serve mission to Canada, ca. 1845. Enlisted in Mormon Battalion at Council Bluffs, Iowa Territory, July 16, 1846. Migrated to Great Salt Lake Valley in Ebenezer Brown company, arriving Oct. 10, 1848. Married Agnes Findley in Big Cottonwood, Utah, Sept. 21, 1849. Participated in plural marriage. Served mission to British Isles, 1852–57. Presided over Saints emigrating from Liverpool, England, to Boston on ship *George Washington*, spring 1857. Led Christian Christiansen company to Great Salt Lake Valley, arriving Sept. 13, 1857. Appointed as a president of 61st quorum of the seventy at Millcreek, Salt Lake Co., Utah, Feb. 25, 1859. Appointed to serve in cotton mission in Washington Co., Utah, Oct. 19, 1862. Died on Dec. 30, 1889, in Fairfield, Utah Co., Utah.

Parry, John (1799–1855). Born June 22, 1799, in Bishops Frome, Herefordshire, England; son of Richard Parry and Elizabeth Price. Married Anne Williams in Ashperton, Herefordshire, England, Nov. 14, 1822. Baptized in Herefordshire, England, Mar. 8, 1840. Ordained a seventy, Mar. 17, 1840. Arrived in New York on ship *North America*, Oct. 12, 1840. Migrated to Great Salt Lake Valley with Charles C. Rich company, arriving Oct. 2, 1847. Appointed to Salt Lake stake high council, Sept. 8, 1850. Served mission to British Isles, 1852–55. Died on July 19, 1855; buried in Mormon Grove, Atchison Co., Kansas Territory.

Peterson (Petersen), Canute (Knud) (1824–1902). Born May 7, 1824; christened May 9, 1824, in Ulvik, Hordaland, Norway; son of Peder Jonsen and Herborg Knudsdatter. Emigrated 1837. Moved to LaSalle Co., Illinois, in 1837. Baptized at Fox River Settlement, La Salle Co., Illinois, Sept. 12, 1842. Ordained a seventy in Nauvoo, Hancock Co., Illinois, May 13, 1845. Appointed to serve mission in Wisconsin, Nov. 1844–45. Married Sarah Ann Nelson in Council Bluffs, Iowa, July 3, 1849. Migrated to Great Salt Lake Valley with the Ezra T. Benson company, arriving Oct. 25, 1849. Appointed to settle Dry Creek (now Lehi), Utah, July 1850. Appointed a mission to Norway, Aug. 28, 1852. Returned to Utah in the Canute Peterson company, arriving Sept. 16, 1856. Participated in plural marriage. Served as counselor to Bishop David Evans in Lehi, Utah, 1863–67. Called to settle in Sanpete Co., Utah; appointed bishop of Ephraim Ward in 1867. Served as representative in Utah legislature, 1876–82. Appointed to preside over Scandinavian mission, 1871–73. Sustained as stake president of Sanpete, Utah, stake, July 4, 1877. Sustained as a patriarch, Nov. 20, 1897. Sustained as president of the South Sanpete, Utah, stake, Dec. 9, 1900. Died in Ephraim, Sanpete Co., Utah, Oct. 14, 1902.

Piercy, George (also known as Hans Peter Olsen) (1821–65). Born June 17, 1821, in Forshayn, Foroe Island, Denmark; son of Ole Justinussen

(Gustinussen) and Ane Marie Svendsen. Worked as a sailor. Baptized Apr. 20, 1849. Migrated to Utah by 1851. Appointed mission to Denmark, Aug. 1852, and spent ten months on the island of Bornholm. Appointed president of Copenhagen, Denmark, conference, Oct. 6, 1853. Brought group of Scandinavian converts from Copenhagen, Denmark, to Hull, Yorkshire Co., England, Jan. 1854. Appointed captain of Saints who sailed from Liverpool, England, on the ship *Benjamin Adams*. Married Catherine Ingreberg (Ingeborg) Neilson, Feb. 1854. Arrived in New Orleans, Louisiana, on Mar. 22, 1854. Migrated to Great Salt Lake Valley as captain of Hans Peter Olsen company, arriving Oct. 5, 1854. Moved to American Fork, Utah Co., Utah, by 1856. Appointed to Carson Valley, Utah (now Nevada), 1856. Appointed to Muddy Mission in 1865 and settled at St. Joseph, Yavapai Co., Arizona. Died in St. Joseph, Oct. 24, 1865.

Pitt, William (1813–73). Born Aug. 16, 1813, in Dymock, Gloucestershire, England; son of Robert Pitt and Hannah Hill. Baptized June 13, 1840. Married Caroline Smith, Apr. 28, 1841, in West Bromwich, Staffordshire, England. Emigrated from Liverpool, England, to New Orleans, Louisiana, with wife and two children, arriving Apr. 26, 1842. Elected captain of the Nauvoo Brass Band, 1842. Worked as a carpenter and painter on the Nauvoo Temple, 1844–45. Served in the Nauvoo Legion. Wife died Feb. 14, 1844, in Nauvoo, Illinois. Ordained a seventy, 1844. Married Cornelia Melvina Devine in Nauvoo, Illinois, Dec. 12, 1844. Migrated to the Great Salt Lake Valley in Edward Hunter company, arriving Oct. 13, 1850. Served mission to England, 1852–55. Migrated to Great Salt Lake Valley in Richard Ballantyne company, arriving Sept. 25, 1855. Wife died in Salt Lake City, Aug. 21, 1860. Married Mary Jane Collins in Salt Lake City, Dec. 12, 1861. Died Feb. 21, 1873.

Porter, Nathan Tanner (1820-97). Born July 10, 1820, in Corinth, Orange Co., Vermont; son of Sanford Porter and Nancy Aretta Warriner. Baptized in Jackson Co., Missouri, June 15, 1832. Ordained elder, Oct. 6, 1841. Appointed mission to eastern states, fall 1841. Campaigned for Joseph Smith for president of the US, June 1844. Migrated to the Great Salt Lake Valley in Charles C. Rich company, arriving Oct. 2, 1847. Married Rebecca Ann Cherry, Nov. 12, 1848. Departed on mission to Gibraltar,

Oct. 13, 1852; arrived Apr. 1853 but was soon deported. Continued mission in England. President of the Worcestershire conference of British Isles mission, 1855. Migrated to Great Salt Lake Valley in William B. Hodgetts company, arriving Dec. 10, 1856. Participated in plural marriage. Acting superintendent of Centerville, Davis Co., Utah, Sabbath Schools. Mission to eastern states, 1869, 1872. Counselor to Bishop William R. Smith in Centerville. On Davis stake high council, June 17, 1877. Ordained a patriarch, June 1894. Died in Centerville, Apr. 9, 1897.

Pratt, Orson (1811–81). Born Sept. 19, 1811, in Hartford, Washington Co., New York; son of Jared Pratt and Charity Dickinson. Baptized Sept. 19, 1830. Ordained elder, 1830, and called on mission. Ordained high priest and proselytized in eastern United States, beginning Feb. 2, 1832. Member of Camp of Israel. Ordained member of the Quorum of the Twelve Apostles, Mar. 6, 1835. Married Sarah Marinda Bates, July 4, 1836. Participated in plural marriage. Served a series of short missions, traveling hundreds of miles. Served a mission with other apostles to the British Isles, 1839–41; dedicated Scotland for missionary work. Migrated to Great Salt Lake Valley in Brigham Young company, arriving July 21, 1847. Appointed president over all branches in England, Scotland, Wales, Ireland, and adjacent countries, 1848 and 1856. Migrated with family to Great Salt Lake Valley in James W. Cummings company, Sept. 30–Oct. 30, 1851. Editor of *Millennial Star*, 1850 and 1856–57. Served mission to Austria, 1865. Published mathematical work, *New and Easy Method of Solutions of the Cubic and Biquadratic Equations*, 1866. Went to New York in Apr. 1869 to publish Book of Mormon in the Deseret Alphabet. Appointed Church Historian, Jan. 1874. Speaker of Utah House of Representatives, 1874. Served mission to Europe to publish new edition of Book of Mormon, 1878. Died in Salt Lake City, Utah, Oct. 3, 1881.

Redfield, Harlow (1801–66). Born Sept. 25, 1801, in Killingworth, Middlesex Co., Connecticut; son of Levi Redfield and Wealthy Stevens. Married Caroline Foster in present-day Madison, New Haven Co., Connecticut, Dec. 23, 1824; she died, 1834. Baptized Dec. 1831. Married Alpha Luranda Foster in Killingworth, Oct. 11, 1835. Appointed member of high council at Kirtland, Geauga Co., Ohio, Sept. 1837. Ordained a high priest in Nauvoo, Hancock Co., Illinois, Apr. 8, 1841. Migrated with Aaron Johnson company to the Great Salt Lake Valley, arriving Sept. 12, 1850. Appointed counselor to Bishop Elias Blackburn in Provo, Utah Co., Utah, Mar. 19, 1851. Elected an alderman of Provo, Apr. 1851. Appointed member of high council in Utah Co., 1852. Appointed to serve mission to Siam, 1852, but did not serve. Died Aug. 3, 1866, in Salt Lake City.

Richardson, Darwin Charles (1812–60). Born on June 29, 1812, in Denmark, Oxford Co., Maine; son of Bernice Richardson and Olive Harnden. Baptized by Stephen Burnett, Sept. 1833. Participated in Camp of Israel, 1834. Appointed to first quorum of the seventy, Feb. 1835. Married Jane Cyrene Cobleigh in Lisbon, Grafton Co., New Hampshire, Sept. 2, 1839. Participated in plural marriage. Migrated to Great Salt Lake Valley in Daniel Spencer/Perrigrine Sessions company, arriving by Sept. 25, 1847. Appointed to serve mission to West Indies, by Aug. 29, 1852. Led Darwin Richardson company to Great Salt Lake Valley, arriving Sept. 30, 1854. Died on Nov. 13, 1860, in Salt Lake City.

Riser, George Christian (1818–92). Born July 16, 1818, in Wertemburgh, Germany; son of Christopher Riser and Barbary Hoofman. Immigrated to Ohio in 1831. Married Christiana Kull in Marion Co., Ohio, Jan 10, 1841. Baptized in Nauvoo, Hancock Co., Illinois, Dec. 12, 1842. Practiced plural marriage. Ordained a seventy, 1844. Served mission to Ohio, 1844. Migrated to Great Salt Lake Valley in Abraham O. Smoot company, arriving Sept. 29, 1847. Served mission to Europe, 1853–55. President of German Mission, 1854–55. First counselor to Bishop F. Kesler, 1856. Died in Salt Lake City, Utah, Jan. 24, 1892.

Riter, Levi Evans (1805–77). Born Jan. 1, 1805, in Uwchlan Township, Chester Co., Pennsylvania; son of Michael Riter and Elizabeth Neide. Married Rebecca Woolerton Dilworth, Nov. 24, 1830. Participated in plural marriage. Baptized by Jan. 1, 1845. Ordained a bishop of the First Ward, Winter Quarters, Oct. 1846. Migrated with Jedediah M. Grant/Joseph B. Noble company, arriving in Salt Lake Valley, Oct. 2, 1847. Ordained a high priest, Apr. 6, 1852. Served mission to England, 1852–53. Served mission as colonist in Carson Valley, Utah (later Nevada), May 7, 1856.

Served as counselor to Bishop Samuel A. Woolley. Died in Salt Lake City, Apr. 13, 1877.

Robinson, John (1792–1878). Born Dec. 27, 1792, in Cushing, Lincoln Co., Maine; son of Simon Robinson and Hannah Hyler (Hiller). Married Abigail Parsons in Cushing, July 9, 1814. Captain of ship, *Milo*, near Cushing. Baptized in Maine, by Apr. 17, 1844. Migrated to Nauvoo, Hancock Co., Illinois, before Aug. 22, 1844. Ordained a seventy, before Jan. 20, 1846. Migrated to Utah with the Edward Hunter/Joseph Horne company, arriving Sept. 29, 1847. Ordained bishop of the West Jordan Ward in the Salt Lake Valley, Jan. 20, 1852. Served mission in Nova Scotia and British provinces, ca. 1852–53. Moved to Weber Co., Utah, before Sept. 5, 1857. Wife died, Nov. 1, 1857. Died in Burch Creek (later South Ogden), Weber Co., Utah, Feb. 16, 1878; buried in Uintah, Weber Co., Utah.

Savage, Levi, Jr. (1820–1910). Born Mar. 23, 1820, in Greenfield, Huron Co., Ohio; son of Levi Savage and Polly Hayes. Baptized June 12, 1846. Private in the Mormon Battalion, 1846–47. Migrated to Great Salt Lake Valley in Levi Hancock company, arriving Oct. 16, 1847. Married Jane Mathers, in Utah, Jan. 23, 1848. Ordained a seventy, Oct. 19, 1848. Wife died, Salt Lake City, Dec. 28, 1851. Served mission to Siam, 1852–53, and Burma, 1853–56. Part of the Willie handcart company. Married to Ann Brummel Cooper, Oct. 31, 1858. Died Dec. 13, 1910, in Toquerville, Washington Co., Utah.

Secrist, Jacob Foutz (1818–55). Born Sept. 19, 1818, in Quincy, Franklin Co., Pennsylvania; son of Solomon Secrist and Mary Foutz. Married Ann Eliza Logan in Waynesboro, Franklin Co., Pennsylvania, Mar. 15, 1842. Baptized June 1, 1844. Migrated to Salt Lake Valley with Edward Hunter/Jacob Foutz company, arriving Oct. 1, 1847. Served mission to Germany, 1852–55. Died on the Little Blue River, Kansas Territory, July 2, 1855.

Sessions, Perrigrine (1814–93). Born June 15, 1814, in Newry, Oxford Co., Maine; son of David Sessions and Patty Bartlett. Married Julia Ann Killgore in Newry, Sept. 21, 1834. Participated in plural marriage.

Baptized Sept. 17, 1833. Served missions to Maine, 1839–40, 1841–44, 1873–75. Migrated to the Great Salt Lake Valley in Daniel Spencer/Perrigrine Sessions company, as captain of fifty, arriving Sept. 24–25, 1847. Served mission to England, 1852–54. Captain of Perrigrine Sessions pioneer company, 1854. Died June 3, 1893, in Bountiful, Davis Co., Utah.

Skelton, Robert Hodgson (1824–95). Born Nov. 28, 1824, in Burgh, England; son of Thomas Skelton and Mary Hodgson. Emigrated from Liverpool, England, to New Orleans, Louisiana, in Oct. 1848, on the *Lord Maidstone*. Baptized Mar. 1849. Migrated to the Great Salt Lake Valley in Ezra Taft Benson company, arriving Oct. 25–29, 1849. Served in Nauvoo Legion of Utah during the Walker War, 1850. Ordained a seventy, Feb. 3, 1851. Helped settle Tooele, Tooele Co., Utah. Served mission to India, 1852–56. Presided over East India mission, 1855–56. Married Angeline Gollaher, Feb. 16, 1857. Practiced plural marriage. Served as mayor of Tooele and as a member of the Utah legislature, 1856–57. Served as counselor in Tooele bishopric. Died Feb. 1, 1895, in Tooele.

Smith, Charles (1819–1905). Born July 10, 1819, in Ipstones, Staffordshire, England; son of John Smith and Ann Varley. Baptized Dec. 13, 1840. Appointed to preach the gospel in England, 1841–42. Married Sarah Price, Jan. 3, 1842, in Liverpool, England. Practiced plural marriage. Immigrated to New Orleans, Louisiana, aboard the ship *Swanton*, arrived Mar. 16, 1843. Private in the Nauvoo Legion. Migrated to the Salt Lake Valley with the Heber C. Kimball company, arriving Sept. 24, 1848. Served a mission to England, where he was appointed to take charge of the Derbyshire, Leicestershire, and Nottinghamshire conferences, 1852–55. Moved to St. George, Utah, Apr. 6, 1862. Ordained patriarch of the St. George stake, Mar. 16, 1903. Died Nov. 28, 1905, in St. George.

Smith, Leonard Ishmael (1823–77). Born Mar. 10, 1823, in Hamilton Co., Illinois; son of Randolph Smith and Ann Henson. Baptized May 1, 1847. Ordained to the 14th quorum of the seventy, June 14, 1848. Married Ann King Shanks, Feb. 10, 1852. Participated in plural marriage. Migrated to the Great Salt Lake Valley in 1851. Served mission to the Cape of Good Hope, South Africa, 1852–56. Counselor in South African mission presidency, May 23, 1853. Appointed president of the 41st quorum of the seventy, Mar. 2, 1857. Carried the mail from Salt Lake City south as far as Fillmore, Utah. Murdered by his nephew in Batesville, Tooele Co., Utah, July 19, 1877; buried in Salt Lake City.

Smith, Paul (1820–1912). Born Apr. 28, 1820, in Great Kelk, Yorkshire, England; son of Paul Smith and Maria Greenwood. Married Jane Wharram, in Howden, Yorkshire, England, 1841. Participated in plural marriage. Baptized Dec. 31, 1848. Immigrated to the US on the *Silverpool*, Mar. 2, 1850. Migrated to Great Salt Lake Valley in James W. Cummings company, arriving Oct. 7, 1851. Served mission to Australia, 1852–55. President of the Snowflake, Navajo Co., Arizona, stake high priests quorum, 1880. Served in the St. George Temple. Ordained a patriarch, 1892. Died July 23, 1912, in Snowflake.

Snider, Egerton (1826–67). Born Jan. 9, 1826, in Toronto, Ontario, Canada; son of John Snider and Mary Herron (Herrin). Baptized by 1842. Moved to Nauvoo, Hancock Co., Illinois, by 1842. Moved to Utah by 1848. Served in Utah territorial militia in William McBride company in Sept. 1850. Married Mary Jane McBride in Utah, Oct. 15, 1850. Served mission to the Sandwich Islands, 1852–55. Died Jan. 7, 1867, in Salt Lake City.

Spencer, Daniel (1794–1868). Born July 20, 1794, in West Stockbridge, Berkshire Co., Massachusetts; son of Daniel Spencer and Chloe Wilson. Married Sophronia Eliza Pomeroy in West Stockbridge, Jan. 21, 1823. Participated in plural marriage. Baptized Mar. 3, 1840. Presided over Richmond and West Stockbridge Union Branch, 1841. Served missions to Canada, Indian Territory, and Massachusetts, 1842–44. Elected member of Nauvoo City Council, Hancock Co., Illinois, by 1843. Elected mayor of Nauvoo, 1844. Ordained a high priest in Nauvoo, Oct. 6, 1844. Served as bishop of Ninth Ward at Winter Quarters (later in Omaha, Douglas Co., Nebraska). Led Daniel Spencer/Perrigrine Sessions company to Great Salt Lake Valley, arriving Sept. 23, 1847. Served as president of Salt Lake stake, 1849–52, 1856–68. Appointed member and treasurer of Perpetual Emigrating Fund Company by Sept. 27, 1850. Began service as member of

Utah territorial legislature, 1851, and as part of Utah territorial legislature council, 1861. Served mission to England, 1852–56. Died in Salt Lake City, Dec. 8, 1868.

Spencer, Orson (1802–55). Born May 13, 1802, in West Stockbridge, Berkshire Co., Massachusetts; son of Daniel Spencer and Chloe Wilson. Served as a Baptist pastor, 1829–41. Married Catharine Curtis, Apr. 13, 1830. Baptized May 1841. Served mission to Connecticut, 1843. Ordained a high priest in Nauvoo, Hancock Co., Illinois, Oct. 6, 1844. Elected mayor of Nauvoo, Feb. 3, 1845. Wife died near Keosauqua, Van Buren Co., Iowa Territory, Mar. 12, 1846. Served mission to England, 1846–49; presided over British Mission, 1847–49. Married Martha Knight of Lancaster, Lancashire Co., England, Apr. 1847. Participated in plural marriage. Led the Samuel Gully/Orson Spencer company to the Great Salt Lake Valley, arriving Sept. 23, 1849. Appointed chancellor of the University of Deseret, Feb. 28, 1850. Member of the Utah territorial legislature, 1851. Served mission to Prussia, England, and Germany, 1852–53. Served mission to Cincinnati and St. Louis, 1854–55; editor of the *St. Louis Luminary*; president of the church in the Ohio and Mississippi Valleys. Died in St. Louis, Oct. 15, 1855. Final burial in Salt Lake City.

Stevenson, Edward (1820–97). Born May 1, 1820, in Gibraltar, British Overseas Territory; son of Joseph Stevenson and Elizabeth Stevens. Emigrated from Gibraltar to US on ship *Canning*, arriving in New York July 16, 1827. Baptized by Japhet Fosdick at Silver Lake, Michigan, Dec. 20, 1833. Married Nancy Areta Porter in Nauvoo, Hancock Co., Illinois, Apr. 7, 1845. Participated in plural marriage. Ordained a seventy by Joseph Young, Feb. 7, 1845. Migrated with Charles C. Rich company to Great Salt Lake Valley, arriving Oct. 2, 1847. Appointed to serve mission to Gibraltar, Aug. 28, 1852. Served missions in United States and Canada, 1857–58, 1869–70, 1872, 1877–78, 1883–84. Divorced Nancy Areta Porter in Salt Lake City, July 3, 1869. Set apart for mission to US and Europe, Feb. 1886. Crossed Atlantic Ocean nine times and Great Plains eighteen times as missionary. Selected as one of the first seven presidents of the seventy, Oct. 7, 1894. Died Jan. 27, 1897, in Salt Lake City.

Stout, Hosea (1810–89). Born Sept. 18, 1810, in Mercer Co., Kentucky; son of Joseph Stout and Anna Smith. Married Samantha Peck, Jan. 7, 1838. Baptized in Caldwell Co., Missouri, Aug. 24, 1838. Wife died, Nov. 29, 1839. Appointed clerk of high council in Nauvoo, Hancock Co., Illinois, Mar. 8, 1840. Married Louisa Taylor, Nov. 29, 1840. Participated in plural marriage. Elected colonel of fifth regiment, second cohort in Nauvoo Legion, June 23, 1843. Selected as chief of police in Nauvoo, by Oct. 1844. Ordained an elder, Oct. 4, 1844. Ordained a president of 11th quorum of the seventy, Oct. 8, 1844. Migrated with Brigham Young company to Great Salt Lake Valley, arriving Sept. 23, 1848. Appointed attorney general of the provisional state of Deseret, by Mar. 1850. Served mission to China, 1852–53; wife and infant son died, Jan. 1853. Elected speaker of House of Representatives in Utah territorial legislature, Dec. 1856. Appointed to settle southern Utah, Oct. 8, 1861. Appointed foreman of St. George high council, Washington Co., Utah, May 1864. Appointed to Salt Lake stake high council, 1870. Died on Mar. 2, 1889, in Big Cottonwood, Salt Lake Co., Utah.

Tanner, Nathan (1815–1910). Born May 14, 1815, in Greenwich, Washington Co., New York; son of John Tanner and Lydia Stewart. Baptized Sept. 1832. Member of Camp of Israel, 1834. Married Rachel Winter Smith, in Bolton, New York, June 1836. Appointed as a president of fourth quorum of the seventy, Oct. 8, 1844. Migrated to the Great Salt Lake Valley with the Willard Richards company, arriving Oct. 10, 1848. Served mission to the Sandwich Islands, 1852. Freighted between Salt Lake and Los Angeles, California. Died Dec. 17, 1910, in Granger, Salt Lake Co., Utah.

Taylor, William (1823–1910). Born Sept. 2, 1823, in Hale, Westmorland, England; son of James Taylor and Agnes Taylor. Baptized Mar. 2, 1841. Ordained a seventy on Feb. 26, 1845. Married Lovina Chandler by June 1847. Participated in plural marriage. Migrated to the Great Salt Lake Valley in Edward Hunter/Joseph Horne pioneer company, arriving Sept. 29, 1847. Served mission to Germany, 1852. Member of the French

Mission presidency, 1854. Located in the Big Cottonwood Ward, Salt Lake Co., Utah, 1862. Died in Holladay, Salt Lake Co., 1910.

Thomas, Elijah (1815–1906). Born Jan. 22, 1815, in West Rockingham, Richmond Co., North Carolina; son of Henry Thomas and Esther Covington. Baptized Feb. 14, 1844. Ordained a seventy, Nov. 1844. Member of the Mormon Battalion, 1846–47. Married Mercy Murray Day in San Francisco, California, 1848. Participated in plural marriage. Migrated to the Salt Lake Valley in the Ebenezer Brown company, arriving Oct. 10, 1848. Served a mission to British Guiana. Returned to the Salt Lake Valley in the David H. Cannon company, arriving by Aug. 16, 1861. Living in St. George, Washington Co., Utah, by June 1870. Living in Leeds, Washington Co., Utah, in June 1900. Died Oct. 14, 1906, in St. George.

Thomas, Preston (1814–77). Born Feb. 15, 1814, in Rockingham, Richmond Co., North Carolina; son of Daniel Thomas Jr. and Nancy Ann Morehead. Married Sarah Ann Jane Morehead in Tennessee, May 10, 1838. Participated in plural marriage. Baptized Jan. 13, 1844. Served mission to southern states, 1847–48. Served mission to Texas, Nov. 1848–July 1849; Nov. 1849–50. Migrated to the Great Salt Lake Valley in John Brown company, arriving Sept. 29, 1851. Again served mission to Texas, 1852. Led subsequent companies arriving in the Great Salt Lake Valley, Nov. 1853 and Sept. 1856. Served mission to Texas, 1854–56. Served as adjutant in Nauvoo Legion of Utah, 1857. Served mission to southern states, 1869–56. Died July 10, 1877, near Franklin, Franklin Co., Idaho.

Thomson, Walter (1825–77). Born Aug. 10, 1825, in Barony, Glasgow, Scotland; son of John Thomson and Margaret Thomson. Baptized Jan. 4, 1841. Married Agnes Ross in Rowe, Dunbarton, Scotland, Nov. 13, 1847. Served as clerk of Glasgow conference, 1849–50. Emigrated with wife and two children from Liverpool, England, arriving in New Orleans, Louisiana, Mar. 20, 1851. Migrated to the Great Salt Lake Valley in Morris Phelps company, arriving Sept. 26–Oct. 1, 1851. Ordained a seventy, Feb. 22, 1852. Called on mission to China, but fell ill and stayed in California, 1852–53. Served as Weber Co., Utah, recorder, 1869. Died June 13, 1877, in Ogden, Weber Co.

Thurston, Moses (1817–73). Born Sept. 13, 1817, in present-day Belmont, Waldo Co., Maine; son of John Thurston and Rebecca French. Baptized by William Anderson in Bureau Co., Illinois, June 2, 1842. Ordained an elder, Sept. 1842. Appointed to 26th quorum of the seventy, Apr. 9, 1845. Married Lucy Jane Leonard in Winter Quarters, Nebraska, ca. 1846. Migrated to Great Salt Lake Valley in Jedediah M. Grant/Willard Snow company, arriving Oct. 4, 1847. Traveled to unorganized US territory (later in California) in William D. Huntington company to mine gold, May 7, 1850. Appointed to serve mission to Europe, Oct. 13, 1852. Led Moses Thurston company from Mormon Grove, Atchison Co., Kansas, to Great Salt Lake Valley, arriving Sept. 19, 1855. Served mission to Muddy Valley, 1868. Held office in militia. Died on Aug. 5, 1873, in Salt Lake City.

Toner, Daniel (1800–1881). Born Feb. 1, 1800, in Letterkenny, Ireland; son of James Toner and Catherine O'Donell. Married Biddy Donell. Lived in Montgomery and Grimes counties, Texas, 1845–50. Baptized Apr. 1849. Called to serve mission to Ireland, Aug. 28–29, 1852. Arrived in England, Apr. 1, 1853. Migrated to the Great Salt Lake Valley in Jacob Croft company, arriving Oct. 11, 1856. Migrated to Spanish Fork, Utah Co., Utah, by Aug. 24, 1860. Married Anne Mary Peterson by Aug. 4, 1870. Died May 12, 1881, in Spanish Fork.

Treat, Thomas Wight (1803–70). Born Apr. 3, 1803, in Schuyler, Herkimer Co., New York; son of Charles and Amy Treat. Married Mary M. Lawyer in Nauvoo, Hancock Co., Illinois, Dec. 8, 1842. Enlisted in Mormon Battalion in Miller's Hollow (later Council Bluffs), Iowa Territory, July 16, 1846; discharged in present-day Los Angeles, California, July 16, 1847. Wife died, by 1849. Migrated to Great Salt Lake Valley in Thomas Rhoades company, arriving Sept. 1849. Appointed to serve mission to England by Aug. 29, 1852. Arrived in England on ship *American Union*, Jan. 5, 1853. Departed from England on ship *Jersey*, June 29, 1853. Migrated to Great Salt Lake Valley in Canute Peterson company, arriving by Sept. 23, 1856. Married Caroline Elizabeth Dyer Winter in Marriott-Slaterville, Weber Co., Utah, Mar. 14, 1863. Died on Dec. 8, 1870, in Ogden, Weber Co.

Turpin, Jesse (1816-54). Born June 22, 1816, in Panther Creek, Stewart Co., Tennessee; son of James Turpin and Nancy Ann Tatum. Baptized Apr. 14, 1836. Served mission to Virginia, Apr. 24, 1837. Ordained a seventy, Apr. 14, 1840. Served mission to eastern states, 1840. Married Eliza Ann Boggess, Dec. 24, 1840. Served mission to his family in Kentucky, winter 1844–45. Married Jane Louisa Smith, Apr. 16, 1846. Participated in plural marriage. Migrated to the Great Salt Lake Valley in Brigham Young company, arriving Sept. 20, 1848. Served mission to West Indies, Oct. 13, 1852. Left West Indies and continued mission in the middle states, Feb. 1853. Died June 22, 1854, while returning from mission, near Fort Leavenworth, Kansas.

Van Cott, John (1814-83). Born Sept. 7, 1814, in Canaan, Columbia Co., New York; son of Losee Van Cott and Lavina Pratt. Baptized Sept. 1845. Married Lucy Levinia Sackett, by June 15, 1847. Participated in plural marriage. Ordained a seventy, Feb. 25, 1847. Migrated to the Great Salt Lake Valley in Daniel Spencer/Perrigrine Sessions company, arriving Sept. 23 or 24, 1847. Served mission to England, Oct. 13, 1852. Presided over British Mission, Sept. 1853. President of the 41st quorum of the seventy, 1857. President of the Scandinavian Mission, Sept. 16, 1859. Served as a member of the Utah House of Representatives, 1864–65. Died Feb. 18, 1883, in Salt Lake City.

Walker, William Holmes (1820-1908). Born Aug. 28, 1820, in Peacham, Caledonia Co., Vermont; son of John Walker and Lydia Holmes. Baptized 1835. Married Olive Hovey Farr in Nauvoo, Illinois, Nov. 1, 1843. Participated in plural marriage. Ordained member of the 13th quorum of the seventy, Aug. 1844. Enlisted in the Mormon Battalion, July 16, 1846. Migrated to the Great Salt Lake Valley in the Mormon Battalion sick detachments and the Spencer-Eldredge company, arriving Sept. 1847. Served mission to Cape of Good Hope, South Africa, 1852–57. Appointed to a mission to southern Utah, 1861. Ordained a high priest and patriarch, May 20, 1892. Died Jan. 9, 1908, in Lewisville, Fremont Co., Idaho.

Webb, Chauncey Griswold (1811–1903). Born Oct. 24, 1811, in Hanover, Chautauqua Co., New York; son of James Webb and Hannah Griswold. Baptized in New York, Nov. 27, 1834. Ordained a seventy at Kirtland, Ohio, Feb. 28, 1835. Married Eliza Jane Churchill in Kirtland, Sept. 15, 1835. Participated in plural marriage. Appointed one of the presidents of 25th quorum of the seventy in Nauvoo, Hancock Co., Illinois, Oct. 24, 1845. Built wagons and later handcarts for church members migrating to Utah, including wagon used by Brigham Young. Migrated to the Great Salt Lake Valley with the Brigham Young company, arriving Sept. 1848. Served a mission to England, 1852–55. Assigned by Brigham Young to go to Chicago, Cook Co., Illinois, to build sixty wagons and carriages for the YX Company, Apr. 21, 1857. Died Apr. 7, 1903, in Salt Lake City.

West, Chauncey Walker (1827–70). Born Feb. 6, 1827, in Erie Co., Pennsylvania; son of Alva West and Sally Benedict. Married Mary Hoagland in Nauvoo, Hancock Co., Illinois, May 1, 1846. Participated in plural marriage. Migrated to Great Salt Lake Valley in Edward Hunter/Joseph Horne company, arriving Sept. 29, 1847. Served mission to Asia, 1852–54. Served as presiding bishop of Weber Co., Utah, by May 29, 1856. Served in Utah house of representatives, 1856–62, 1864–69. Died Jan. 9, 1870, in San Francisco Co., California.

Willie, James Grey (1814–95). Born Nov. 1, 1814, in Murrell Green, Southampton, England; son of William Willie and Mary Sutton. Baptized July 12, 1842. Married Elizabeth Ann Pettit in Nauvoo, Hancock Co., Illinois, June 13, 1846. Participated in plural marriage. Migrated to the Great Salt Lake Valley in Jedediah M. Grant/Joseph B. Noble company, arriving Oct. 2, 1847. Served a mission to England, 1852–56. Captain of the James G. Willie handcart company that arrived in the Salt Lake Valley, Nov. 9, 1856. Served as bishop of Salt Lake Seventh Ward, 1856–59. Called by Brigham Young to help settle Cache Valley in northern Utah. Settled in Mendon, Utah, 1867. Member of bishopric in Mendon, 1884–90. Served as a patriarch, 1892–93. Died Sept. 9, 1895, in Mendon.

Woodward, William (1833-1908). Born Jan. 4, 1833, in Bushey, Hertfordshire Co., England; son of William Field and Sophia Woodward. Baptized in Watford, Hertfordshire Co., June 21, 1848. Emigrated from Liverpool, England, to Kanesville (later Council Bluffs), Iowa, arriving Apr. 9, 1850. Migrated to Great Salt Lake Valley as a teamster in the John Reese freight train, 1851. Appointed to serve mission to England, Aug. 29, 1852; returned in James G. Willie company, 1856. Married Harriet Hogan in Great Salt Lake City, Feb. 1, 1857. Participated in plural marriage. Migrated to present-day Franklin, Franklin Co., Idaho, Apr. 14, 1860. Appointed justice of the peace of Franklin, by Dec. 28, 1868. Served missions to England, 1873, 1904. Appointed president of the 18th quorum of the seventy, Dec. 29, 1874. Ordained a high priest, Feb. 1901. Died on Nov. 22, 1908, in Franklin.

Woolley, Samuel Amos (1825-1900). Born Sept. 11, 1825, in Newlin, Chester Co., Pennsylvania; son of John Woolley and Rachael Dilworth. Baptized Oct. 7, 1840. Married Catherine Elizabeth Mehring, May 21, 1846. Participated in plural marriage. Migrated with Brigham Young company to the Great Salt Lake Valley, arriving Sept. 21, 1848. Ordained a seventy, Oct. 8, 1845. Served mission to India, 1852–56; to eastern US (Ohio, Pennsylvania, Kentucky, and Michigan), 1869–70. Appointed bishop of the Salt Lake Ninth Ward, 1865. Ordained a patriarch. Died on Mar. 23, 1900, in Salt Lake City.

BIBLIOGRAPHY

2013 Church Almanac. Salt Lake City: Deseret News, 2014.

Acts, Resolutions, and Memorials, Passed by the First Annual, and Special Sessions, of the Legislative Assembly, of the Territory of Utah, Begun and Held at Great Salt Lake City, on the 22nd Day of September, A.D., 1851. Great Salt Lake City: Utah Legislative Assembly, 1852.

Adelson, Lester. "Injury and Cancer." *Case Western Reserve Law Review* 5, no. 2 (Winter 1954): 150–73.

Allred, Alma. "The Traditions of Their Fathers: Myth versus Reality in LDS Scriptural Writings." In *Black and Mormon*, edited by Newell G. Bringhurst and Darron T. Smith, 34–49. Urbana: University of Illinois Press, 2004.

Anderson, Atholl, Judith Binney, and Aroha Harris, eds. *Tangata Whenua: An Illustrated History*. Wellington: Bridget Williams Books, 2014.

Arizona Pioneer Mormon: David King Udall, His Story and His Family. Tucson: Arizona Silhouettes, 1959.

Arrington, Leonard J. "The Deseret Telegraph—A Church-Owned Public Entity." *Journal of Economic History* 11, no. 2 (Spring 1951): 117–39.

Arrington, Leonard J. *Great Basin Kingdom: An Economic History of the Latter-day Saints,*

1830–1900. Cambridge, MA: Harvard University Press, 1958.

Ashurst-McGee, Mark, David W. Grua, Elizabeth A. Kuehn, Brenden W. Rensink, and Alexander L. Baugh, eds. *Documents, Volume 6: February 1838–August 1839*. Vol. 6 of the Documents series of *The Joseph Smith Papers*, edited by Ronald K. Esplin, Matthew J. Grow, and Matthew C. Godfrey. Salt Lake City: Church Historian's Press, 2017.

Augustus Farnham Immigrating Company journal, 1856 May–August. MS 7779. Church History Library, The Church of Jesus Christ of Latter-day Saints, Salt Lake City.

"Autobiography of James Lewis." MS 11365. Church History Library, The Church of Jesus Christ of Latter-day Saints, Salt Lake City.

Bagley, Will. *"Cities of the Wicked": Alexander Badlam Reports on Mormon Prospects in California and China in the 1850s*. [Spokane, WA]: Arthur H. Clark, 1999.

Ballou, Maturin M. *The Pearl of India*. Boston: Houghton, Mifflin, 1895.

Barclay, David E. "Revolution and Counter-revolution in Prussia, 1840–50." In *Modern Prussian History: 1830–1947*, edited by Philip G. Dwyer, 66–85. New York: Routledge, 2013.

Bard, Solomon, ed. *Voices of the Past: Hong Kong, 1842–1918*. Hong Kong: Hong Kong University Press, 2002.

Barlow, Ora H. *The Israel Barlow Story and Mormon Mores*. Salt Lake City: Ora H. Barlow, 1968.

Barrett, Gwynn W. "Dr. John M. Bernhisel: Mormon Elder in Congress." *Utah Historical Quarterly* 36, no. 2 (Spring 1968): 143–67.

Bate, Kerry William. *The Ebenezer Hanks Story*. Provo, UT: M. C. Printing, 1982.

Belnap, Daniel L. "'Those Who Receive You Not': The Rite of Wiping Dust off the Feet." *International Journal of Mormon Studies* 5 (2012): 81–127.

Bennett, Brett, and Fred Kruger. *Forestry and Water Conservation in South Africa: History, Science and Policy*. Acton, Australia: Australian National University Press, 2015.

Bennett, Richard E. "'The Upper Room': The Nature and Development of Latter-day Saint Temple Work, 1846–55." *Journal of Mormon History* 41, no. 2 (April 2015): 1–34.

Bennion, Michael Kay. "Captivity, Adoption, Marriage and Identity: Native American Children in Mormon Homes, 1847–1900." Master's thesis, University of Nevada, Las Vegas, 2012.

Berthold, V. M. *The Story of Mormon Island*. N.p.: 1929.

Bishop, Guy. "Henry William Bigler: Mormon Missionary to the Sandwich Islands during the 1850s." *Hawaiian Journal of History* 20 (1986): 122–36.

Bitton, Davis. "Mormonism's Encounter with Spiritualism." *Journal of Mormon History* 1 (1974): 39–50.

Black, Susan Easton. "*St. Louis Luminary:* The Latter-day Saint Experience at the Mississippi River, 1854–1855." *BYU Studies* 49, no. 4 (2010): 157–73.

Black, Susan Easton. "The University of Nauvoo, 1841–45." *Religious Educator* 10, no. 3 (2009): 189–206.

Bradshaw, Jeffrey M. "Freemasonry and the Origins of Modern Temple Ordinances." *Interpreter: A Journal of Mormon Scripture* 15 (2015): 159–237.

Britsch, R. Lanier. "Church Beginnings in China." *BYU Studies* 10, no. 2 (Winter 1970): 161–72.

Britsch, R. Lanier. "The East India Mission of 1851–56: Crossing the Boundaries of Culture, Religion, and Law." *Journal of Mormon History* 27, no. 2 (Fall 2001): 150–76.

Britsch, R. Lanier. *From the East: The History of the Latter-day Saints in Asia, 1851–1996.* Salt Lake City: Deseret Book, 1998.

Britsch, R. Lanier. *Moramona: The Mormons in Hawaii.* Laie, HI: Institute for Polynesian Studies, 1989.

Britsch, R. Lanier. "The Nobility of Failure." In *Brigham Young University 1998–99 Speeches,* 253–56. Provo, UT: Brigham Young University, 1999.

Britsch, R. Lanier. *Nothing More Heroic: The Compelling Story of the First Latter-day Saint Missionaries in India.* Salt Lake City: Deseret Book, 1999.

Britsch, R. Lanier. *Unto the Islands of the Sea: A History of the Latter-day Saints in the Pacific.* Salt Lake City: Deseret Book, 1986.

Bronner, Simon J. *Grasping Things: Folk Material Culture and Mass Society in America.* Lexington: University Press of Kentucky, 1986.

Brooks, Juanita. *On the Mormon Frontier: The Diary of Hosea Stout, 1844–1861.* 2 vols. Salt Lake City: University of Utah Press, 1964, reprinted 1982.

Brown, Lisle G. "'Temple Pro Tempore': The Salt Lake City Endowment House." *Journal of Mormon History* 34, no.4 (Fall 2008): 1–68.

Browne, James Alex. *England's Artillerymen. An Historical Narrative of the Services of the Royal Artillery, from the Formation of the Regiment to the Amalgamation of the Royal and Indian Artilleries in 1862.* London: Hall, Smart, and Allen, 1865.

Buckley, Jay H. "'Good News' at the Cape of Good Hope: Early LDS Missionary Activities in South Africa." In *Go Ye into All the World: The Growth and Development of Mormon Missionary Work,* edited by Reid L. Neilson and Fred E. Woods, 471–502. Provo, UT: Religious Studies Center; Salt Lake City: Deseret Book, 2012.

Bulletins of State Intelligence, &c. Westminster: F. Watts, 1840.

Bullock, Richard H. *Ship* Brooklyn *Saints: Their Journey and Early Endeavors in California.* Sandy, UT: 2009. M273.41 B938s 2009. Church History Library, The Church of Jesus Christ of Latter-day Saints, Salt Lake City.

Bullock, Thomas. Collection, 1830–1939. MS 27307. Church History Library, The Church of Jesus Christ of Latter-day Saints, Salt Lake City.

Cameron, Nigel. *Hong Kong: The Cultured Pearl.* Hong Kong: Oxford University Press, 1978.

Campbell, Alexander. *Delusions. An Analysis of the Book of Mormon; with an Examination of Its Internal and External Evidences, and a Refutation of Its Pretences to Divine Authority.* Boston: Benjamin H. Greene, 1832.

Campbell, Eugene E. *Establishing Zion: The Mormon Church in the American West, 1847–1869.* Salt Lake City: Signature Books, 1988.

Cannon, Brian Q. "Change Engulfs a Frontier Settlement: Ogden and Its Residents Respond to the Railroad." *Journal of Mormon History* 12 (1985): 15–28.

Cannon, George Q. *The Journals of George Q. Cannon: Hawaiian Mission, 1850–1854.* Edited by Chad M. Orton. Salt Lake City: Deseret Book, 2014.

Cannon, Jeffrey G. "Mormonism's Jesse Haven and the Early Focus on Proselytising the Afrikaner at the Cape of Good Hope, 1853–1855." *Dutch Reformed Theological Journal* 48, no. 3 (September 2007): 446–56.

Cannon, Joseph A. "George Q. Cannon and the *Western Standard*: Defending Utah's Pioneers in Print from the California Coast." *Pioneer* [no vol., no no.] (Summer 1998): 22–25.

Carson, Scott Alan. "The Perpetual Emigrating Fund: Redemption, Servitude, and Subsidized Migration in America's Great Basin." PhD dissertation, University of Utah, 1998.

Chinn, Thomas W., ed. *A History of the Chinese in California: A Syllabus.* San Francisco: Chinese Historical Society of America, 1969.

Chism, Shane J., comp. *A Selection of Early Mormon Hymnbooks, 1832–1872: Hymnbooks and Broadsides from the First 40 Years of The Church of Jesus Christ of Latter-day Saints.* Tucson: 2011.

Christensen, Rex LeRoy. "The Life and Contributions of Captain Dan Jones." Master's thesis, Utah State University, 1977.

Christy, Howard A. "The Walker War: Defense and Conciliation as Strategy." *Utah Historical Quarterly* 47, no. 4 (Fall 1979): 395–420.

Christy, Howard A. "Weather, Disaster, and Responsibility: An Essay on the Willie and Martin Handcart Story." *BYU Studies* 37, no. 1 (1997–98): 6–74.

A Collection of Sacred Hymns, for The Church of Jesus Christ of Latter-day Saints, in Europe, selected by Brigham Young, Parley P. Pratt, and John Taylor. Manchester: W. R. Thomas, 1840.

The Colonial Magazine and Commercial-Maritime Journal. Vol. 1, *August–December, 1842.* London: Fisher, Son, & Co., 1842.

Constantine, Stephen. *Community and Identity: The Making of Modern Gibraltar since 1704.* Manchester: Manchester University Press, 2009.

Cottrell, Ralph L., Jr. "A History of the Discontinued Mediterranean Missions of The Church of Jesus Christ of Latter-day Saints." Master's thesis, Brigham Young University, 1963.

Crawley, Peter L. *A Descriptive Bibliography of the Mormon Church.* 3 vols. Provo, UT: Religious Studies Center, 1997, 2005, 2012.

Crouthamel, James L. *Bennett's* New York Herald *and the Rise of the Popular Press.* Syracuse, NY: Syracuse University Press, 1989.

Daily Alta California. San Francisco. 1847–1891.

Dalton, Lloyd Meeks, Murry L Dalton, and Sandy Dalton Haacke, comps. *Ancestors and Descendants of George Frederick Lewis & Mary Adalaide Huff.* N.p.: 1996.

Davidson, Karen Lynn, David J. Whittaker, Mark Ashurst-McGee, and Richard L. Jensen, eds. *Histories, Volume 1: Joseph Smith Histories, 1832–1844.* Vol. 1 of the Histories series of *The Joseph Smith Papers,* edited by Dean C. Jessee, Ronald K. Esplin, and Richard Lyman Bushman. Salt Lake City: Church Historian's Press, 2012.

Davies, J. Kenneth. "Mormons and California Gold." *Journal of Mormon History* 7 (1980): 83–99.

Davies, Mark. *Corpus of LDS General Conference Talks.* Online database, 2011, http://lds-general-conference.org/.

Davies, Mark. *Corpus of Historical American English.* Online database, 2011, http://corpus.byu.edu/coha/.

Daynes, Kathryn M. *More Wives Than One: Transformation of the Mormon Marriage System, 1840–1910.* Urbana: University of Illinois Press, 2001.

Dennis, Ronald D. *The Call of Zion: The Story of the First Welsh Mormon Emigration.* Provo, UT: Religious Studies Center, 1987.

Dennis, Ronald D. *Defending the Faith: Early Welsh Missionary Publications.* Provo, UT: Religious Studies Center; Salt Lake City: Deseret Book, 2003.

Dennis, Ronald D., ed. *Prophet of the Jubilee.* Provo, UT: Religious Studies Center, 1997.

Dennis, Ronald D., ed. *Zion's Trumpet: 1853 Welsh Mormon Periodical.* Provo, UT: Religious Studies Center; Salt Lake City: Deseret Book, 2014.

Dennis, Ronald D., ed. *Zion's Trumpet: 1854 Welsh Mormon Periodical.* Provo, UT: Religious Studies Center; Salt Lake City: Deseret Book, 2015.

Dennis, Ronald D., ed. *Zion's Trumpet: 1856 and 1857 Welsh Mormon Periodical.* Provo, UT: Religious Studies Center; Salt Lake City: Deseret Book, 2017.

Deseret News. Salt Lake City. 1850–.

Devitry-Smith, John. "The Wreck of the *Julia Ann.*" *BYU Studies* 29, no. 2 (Spring 1989): 5–29.

Dooling, Wayne. *Slavery, Emancipation and Colonial Rule in South Africa.* Scottsville, South Africa: University of KwaZulu-Natal Press, 2007.

Duncan, Chapman. "Biography of Chapman Duncan, 1812–1900." MS 6936. Church History Library, The Church of Jesus Christ of Latter-day Saints, Salt Lake City.

Early Mormon Missionaries database. LDS Church History Department. https://history.lds|.org/missionary/.

Edwardes, S. M. *Census of India, Volume X: Bombay* (Town and Island). Part IV: History. Bombay: Times of India Press, 1901.

Encyclopedia of African Colonial Conflicts, edited by Timothy J. Stapleton. Santa Barbara, CA: ABC-CLIO, 2017.

Encyclopedia of Latter-day Saint History. Edited by Arnold K. Garr, Donald Q. Cannon, and Richard O. Cowan. Salt Lake City: Deseret Book, 2000.

Encyclopedia of Mormonism. Edited by Daniel H. Ludlow. New York: Macmillan, 1992.

The Encyclopedia of Protestantism. Edited by Hans J. Hillerbrand. New York: Routledge, 2004.

Endacott, G. B. *A Biographical Sketch-Book of Early Hong Kong*. Hong Kong: Hong Kong University Press, 2005, originally published in 1962.

An Enduring Legacy. Vol. 8. Salt Lake City: Daughters of Utah Pioneers, 1985.

Farmer, Jared. *On Zion's Mount: Mormons, Indians, and the American Landscape*. Cambridge, MA: Harvard Univeristy Press, 2008.

Ferguson, A. M. & J., comps. *The Planting Directory for India and Ceylon*. Colombo: 1878.

Ferris, B. G. *The Mormons at Home; With Some Incidents of Travel from Missouri to California, 1852–3*. New York: Dix & Edwards, 1856.

Ferris, Marc. *Star-Spangled Banner: The Unlikely Story of America's National Anthem*. Baltimore: Johns Hopkins University Press, 2014.

"Franklin D. Richards and His Missions." *Tullidge's Quarterly Magazine* 4, no. 2 (July 1883): 577–600.

Gerstner, Jonathan N. "A Christian Monopoly: The Reformed Church and Colonial Society under Dutch Rule." In *Christianity in South Africa: A Political, Social, and Cultural History*, edited by Richard Elphick and Rodney Davenport, 16–30. Berkeley: University of California Press, 1997.

Givens, Terryl L. *People of Paradox: A History of Mormon Culture*. New York: Oxford University Press, 2007.

Givens, Terryl L., and Matthew J. Grow. *Parley P. Pratt: The Apostle Paul of Mormonism*. New York: Oxford University Press, 2011.

Godfrey, Donald G., and Rebecca S. Martineau-McCarty, eds. *An Uncommon Common Pioneer: The Journals of James Henry Martineau, 1828–1918*. Provo, UT: Religious Studies Center, 2008.

Godfrey, Matthew C., Mark Ashurst-McGee, Grant Underwood, Robert J. Woodford, and William G. Hartley, eds. *Documents, Volume 2: July 1831–January 1833.* Vol. 2 of the Documents series of *The Joseph Smith Papers*, edited by Dean C. Jessee, Ronald K. Esplin, Richard Lyman Bushman, and Matthew J. Grow. Salt Lake City: Church Historian's Press, 2013.

Gordon, Sarah Barringer. *The Mormon Question: Polygamy and Constitutional Conflict in Nineteenth-Century America.* Chapel Hill: University of North Carolina Press, 2002.

Gottfredson, Peter, ed. *History of Indian Depredations in Utah.* Salt Lake City: Skelton Publishing, 1919.

Green, Doyle L. "John M. Horner: California's 'First' Farmer." *Improvement Era* 54, nos. 4 and 5 (April and May 1951): 244–46, 302–3, 340–42, 344–45.

Grow, Matthew J. "A Providential Means of Agitating Mormonism: Parley P. Pratt and the San Francisco Press in the 1850s." *Journal of Mormon History* 29, no. 2 (Fall 2003): 158–85.

Grow, Matthew J., Ronald K. Esplin, Mark Ashurst-McGee, Gerrit J. Dirkmaat, and Jeffrey D. Mahas, eds. *Administrative Records, Council of Fifty, Minutes, March 1844–January 1846.* Vol. 1 of the Administrative Records series of *The Joseph Smith Papers*, edited by Ronald K. Esplin, Matthew J. Grow, and Matthew C. Godfrey. Salt Lake City: Church Historian's Press, 2016.

Hammond, John J. *Island Adventures: The Hawaiian Mission of Francis A. Hammond, 1851–1865.* Salt Lake City: Signature Books, 2016.

Hansard's Parliamentary Debates: Third Series, Commencing with the Accession of William IV. Vol. CXLIV. London: Cornelius Buck, 1857.

Harper, Steven C. "'All Things Are the Lord's': The Law of Consecration in the Doctrine and Covenants." In *The Doctrine and Covenants: Revelations in Context*, edited by Andrew H. Hedges, J. Spencer Fluhman, and Alonzo L. Gaskill, 212–28. Provo, UT: Religious Studies Center; Salt Lake City: Deseret Book, 2008.

Haven, Jesse. Journals, 1852–1892. MS 890. Church History Library, The Church of Jesus Christ of Latter-day Saints, Salt Lake City.

Hays, J. N. *Epidemics and Pandemics: Their Impacts on Human History.* Santa Barbara, CA: ABC-CLIO, 2005.

Hedges, Andrew H., Alex D. Smith, and Richard Lloyd Anderson, eds. *Journals, Volume 2: December 1841–April 1843.* Vol. 2 of the Journals series of *The Joseph Smith Papers*, edited by Dean C. Jessee, Ronald K. Esplin, and Richard Lyman Bushman. Salt Lake City: Church Historian's Press, 2011.

Hiatt, L. R. "Polyandry in Sri Lanka: A Test Case for Parental Investment Theory." *Royal Anthropological Institute of Great Britain and Ireland* 15, no. 4 (December 1980): 583–602.

Historian's Office general Church minutes, 1839–1877. CR 100 318. Church History Library, The Church of Jesus Christ of Latter-day Saints, Salt Lake City.

Hodgson, Janet. "A Battle for Sacred Power: Christian Beginnings among the Xhosa." In *Christianity in South Africa: A Political, Social, and Cultural History*, edited by Richard Elphick and Rodney Davenport, 68–88. Berkeley: University of California Press, 1997.

Homer, Michael W. "*Il Libro di Mormon*: Anticipating Growth beyond Italy's Waldensian Valleys." *Journal of Book of Mormon Studies* 11, no. 1 (2002): 40–44.

Homer, Michael W. "Masonry and Mormonism in Utah, 1847–1984." *Journal of Mormon History* 18, no. 2 (Fall 1992): 57–96.

Hopkins, Donald R. *The Greatest Killer: Smallpox in History, with a New Introduction*. Chicago: University of Chicago Press, 2002.

Howard, Heather Fay. "An Economic Analysis of the Perpetual Emigrating Fund." PhD dissertation, Cornell University, 2008.

Hubbard, George U. "Abraham Lincoln as Seen by the Mormons." *Utah Historical Quarterly* 31, no. 2 (Spring 1963): 91–108.

Hunter, J. Michael. "Starting a Pioneer Newspaper: The Deseret News." *Pioneer* 53, no. 1 (2006): 8–17.

Irving, Gordon. *Numerical Strength and Geographical Distribution of the LDS Missionary Force, 1830–1974*. Salt Lake City: Historical Department of the Church of Jesus Christ of Latter-day Saints, 1975.

Jackson, Susan Irene. "Methodism in Gibraltar and Its Mission in Spain, 1769–1842." PhD dissertation, University of Durham, 2000.

Jacobsen, Knut A. "Creating Sri Lankan Tamil Catholic Space in the South Asian Diaspora in Norway." In *South Asian Christian Diaspora*, edited by Knut A. Jacobsen and Selva J. Raj, 117–32. Farnham, UK: Ashgate, 2008.

Jansen, Marius B. *The Making of Modern Japan*. Cambridge, MA: Belknap Press of Harvard University Press, 2000.

Jeffers, H. Paul. *Freemasons: A History and Exploration of the World's Oldest Secret Society*. New York: Citadel Press, 2005.

Jensen, Richard L. "Without Purse or Scrip? Financing Latter-day Saint Missionary Work in Europe in the Nineteenth Century." *Journal of Mormon History* 12 (1985): 3–14.

Jenson, Andrew. *Encyclopedic History of the Church of Jesus Christ of Latter-day Saints*. Salt Lake City: Deseret News, 1941.

Jenson, Andrew. *Latter-day Saint Biographical Encyclopedia*, 4 vols. Salt Lake City: Andrew Jenson Historical Co. and Andrew Jenson Memorial Association, 1901–36.

Johnson, Benjamin F. Correspondence, 1851–1966. MS 15610. Church History Library, The Church of Jesus Christ of Latter-day Saints, Salt Lake City.

Johnson, Benjamin F. Papers, 1852–1923. MS 1289. Church History Library, The Church of Jesus Christ of Latter-day Saints, Salt Lake City.

Johnson, Benjamin F. *Why the "Latter Day Saints" Marry a Plurality of Wives: A Glance at Scripture and Reason, in Answer to an Attack through the Polynesian, upon the Saints for Polygamy.* San Francisco: Excelsior Printing Office, 1854.

Johnson, Jeffery Ogden. "Determining and Defining 'Wife': The Brigham Young Households." *Dialogue: A Journal of Mormon Thought* 20, no. 3 (Fall 1987): 57–70.

Johnson, Melissa L. Letter, Summit, Utah, to Benjamin F. Johnson, Sandwich Islands, May 8, 1854. MS 7094. Church History Library, The Church of Jesus Christ of Latter-day Saints, Salt Lake City.

Jones, Dan. "The Martyrdom of Joseph and Hyrum Smith." MS 153. Church History Library, The Church of Jesus Christ of Latter-day Saints, Salt Lake City.

Jones, Dan. "The Martyrdom of Joseph Smith and His Brother Hyrum," edited by Ronald D. Dennis. *BYU Studies* 24, no. 1 (Winter 1984): 78–109.

Jones, Zachary R. "'Wars and Rumors of Wars': United Kingdom Latter-day Saints and the Crimean War, 1853–1856." *Mormon Historical Studies* 14, no. 1 (Spring 2013): 29–43.

Journal History of The Church of Jesus Christ of Latter-day Saints. Church History Library, Salt Lake City.

Journal of Discourses. 26 vols. Liverpool: F. D. Richards, 1855–1886.

The Journal of George Q. Cannon. https://www.churchhistorianspress.org/george-q-cannon.

Juvenile Instructor. Salt Lake City. 1860–1929.

Kline, Mary-Jo, and Susan Holbrook Perdue. *A Guide to Documentary Editing.* 3rd ed. Charlottesville: University of Virginia Press, 2008.

Knoblock, Glenn A. *The American Clipper Ship, 1845–1920: A Comprehensive History with a Listing of Builders and Their Ships.* Jefferson, NC: McFarland, 2014.

Latourette, Kenneth Scott. *The Great Century: North America and Asia, A.D. 1800–A.D. 1914.* Vol. 6 of *A History of the Expansion of Christianity.* Grand Rapids, MI: Zondervan, 1970.

LeBaron, E. Dale. *Benjamin F. Johnson: Friend to the Prophets.* Provo, UT: Benjamin F. Johnson Family Organization, 1997.

LeCheminant, Wilford Hill. "'A Valiant Little Band': LDS Soldiers in the Crimean War." *Ensign* 11, no. 1 (January 1981): 18–21.

Leonard, Glen M. *Nauvoo: A Place of Peace, a People of Promise.* Salt Lake City: Deseret Book, 2002.

"Light on the Lutheran Church in Germany." *The Lutheran Witness* 37, no. 17 (August 20, 1918): 260–61.

Livingston, Craig. "Eyes on 'The Whole European World': Mormon Observers of the 1848 Revolutions." *Journal of Mormon History* 31, no. 3 (Fall 2005): 78–112.

Livingston, Craig. *From Above and Below: The Mormon Embrace of Revolution, 1840–1940.* Salt Lake City: Greg Kofford Books, 2013.

Lochtefeld, James G. *The Illustrated Encyclopedia of Hinduism.* New York: Rosen Publishing Group, 2002.

Lunt, Vern, and Rachel Petty Lunt, comps. *Life of Henry Lunt and Family (Together with a Portion of His Diary).* Cedar City, UT: Reprinted for Lunt Reunion, 1970. Typescript in Church History Library, The Church of Jesus Christ of Latter-day Saints, Salt Lake City.

Lyman, Edward Leo. *San Bernardino: The Rise and Fall of a California Community.* Salt Lake City: Signature Books, 1996.

MacKinnon, William P., ed. *At Sword's Point, Part 2: A Documentary History of the Utah War, 1858–1859.* Norman, OK: Arthur H. Clark, 2016.

Maffly-Kipp, Laurie F. "Assembling Bodies and Souls: Missionary Practices on the Pacific Frontier." In *Practicing Protestants: Histories of Christian Life in America, 1630–1965,* edited by Laurie F. Maffly-Kipp, Leigh E. Schmidt, and Mark Valeri, 51–76. Baltimore, MD: Johns Hopkins University Press, 2006.

Maffly-Kipp, Laurie F. "Looking West: Mormonism and the Pacific World." *Journal of Mormon History* 26, no. 1 (Spring 2000): 40–63.

Maffly-Kipp, Laurie F., and Reid L. Neilson, eds. *Proclamation to the People: Nineteenth-Century Mormonism and the Pacific Basin Frontier.* Salt Lake City: University of Utah Press, 2008.

Marks, Robert D. *China: Its Environment and History.* Lanham, MD: Rowman and Littlefield, 2012.

Materials Towards a Statistical Account of the Town and Island of Bombay. Bombay: Government Central Press, 1894.

Mauss, Armand L. *All Abraham's Children: Changing Mormon Conceptions of Race and Lineage.* Urbana: University of Illinois Press, 2003.

Mauss, Armand L. "Casting Off the 'Curse of Cain': The Extent and Limits of Progress since 1978." In *Black and Mormon,* edited by Newell G. Bringhurst and Darron T. Smith, 82–115. Urbana: University of Illinois Press, 2004.

Melton, J. Gordon, ed. *Encyclopedia of Protestantism.* New York: Facts on File, 2005.

Mercer, Patrick. *Inkerman 1854.* London: Osprey, 1998.

Merriam-Webster's Geographical Dictionary. 3rd ed. Springfield, MA: Merriam-Webster, 2001.

Mesthrie, Rajend. "South Africa: A Sociolinguistic Overview." In *Language in South Africa,* edited by Rajend Mesthrie, 11–26. Cambridge University Press, 2002.

Millennial Star. Liverpool, England. 1840–1970.

Miller, David E. *Hole-in-the-Rock: An Epic in the Colonization of the Great American West.* 2nd ed. Salt Lake City: University of Utah Press, 1966.

Mitchell, Michael. "The Mormons in Wilhelmine Germany, 1870–1914: Making a Place for an Unwanted American Religion in a Changing German Society." Master's thesis, Brigham Young University, 1994.

Modern Muslim Societies. New York: Marshall Cavendish, 2011.

Monson, Farrell Ray. "History of the South African Mission of The Church of Jesus Christ of Latter-day Saints, 1853–1970." Master's thesis, Brigham Young University, 1971.

Moore, R. Laurence. *Religious Outsiders and the Making of Americans.* New York: Oxford University Press, 1986.

Morgan, Dale L. *The Great Salt Lake.* Indianapolis: The Bobbs-Merrill Company, 1947.

Mormon Pioneer Overland Travel database. Latter-day Saint Church History Department. https://history.lds.org/overlandtravels/.

Muhlestein, Robert M. "Utah Indians and the Indian Slave Trade: The Mormon Adoption Program and Its Effect on the Indian Slaves." Master's thesis, Brigham Young University, 1991.

Mulgan, Richard. *Politics in New Zealand.* 3rd ed., updated by Peter Aimer. Auckland: Auckland University Press, 2004.

My Life's Review: The Autobiography of Benjamin F. Johnson. Provo, UT: Grandin Book, 1997.

Nash, John D., comp. "Isaac B. Nash Family Histories & Documents." July 2004. Manuscript in family possession.

Neilson, Reid L. *Early Mormon Missionary Activities in Japan, 1901–1924: Strangers in a Strange Land.* Salt Lake City: University of Utah Press, 2010.

Neilson, Reid L. "Early Mormon Missionary Work in Hong Kong: The Letters of James Lewis to Apostle and Church Historian George A. Smith, 1853–1855." *Mormon Historical Studies* 17, nos. 1 and 2 (Spring and Fall 2016): 1–35.

Neilson, Reid L. *Exhibiting Mormonism: The Latter-day Saints and the 1893 Chicago World's Fair.* New York: Oxford University Press, 2011.

Neilson, Reid L. "Proselyting on the Rock of Gibraltar, 1853–55: The Letters of Edward Stevenson to the *Juvenile Instructor* in 1885." *BYU Studies Quarterly* 55, no. 1 (2016): 95–132.

Neilson, Reid L., Justin R. Bray, and Alan Johnson, eds. *Rediscovering the Sites of the Restoration: The 1888 Travel Writings of Mormon Historian Andrew Jenson, Edward Steven-*

son, and Joseph S. Black. Provo, UT: Religious Studies Center; Salt Lake City: Deseret Book, 2015.

Neilson, Reid L., and Nathan N. Waite, eds. *Settling the Valley, Proclaiming the Gospel: The General Epistles of the Mormon First Presidency*. New York: Oxford University Press, 2017.

The New International Encyclopædia. 2nd ed. 25 vols. New York: Dodd, Mead, 1930.

Newton, Marjorie. *Mormon and Maori*. Salt Lake City: Greg Kofford Books, 2014.

Newton, Marjorie. *Southern Cross Saints: The Mormons in Australia*. Laie, HI: Institute for Polynesian Studies, 1991.

Newton, Marjorie. *Tiki and Temple: The Mormon Mission to New Zealand, 1854–1958*. Salt Lake City: Greg Kofford Books, 2012.

New York Herald. New York City. 1835–1924.

New York Times. New York City. 1851–.

Norton, John W. Journal. Typescript, MS 14686. Church History Library, The Church of Jesus Christ of Latter-day Saints, Salt Lake City.

Olsen, Steven L. "Celebrating Cultural Identity: Pioneer Day in Nineteenth-Century Mormonism." *BYU Studies* 36, no. 1 (1996–97): 159–78.

The Oxford Dictionary of World History. 3rd ed. Oxford: Oxford University Press, 2015.

Bowker, John, ed. *The Oxford Dictionary of World Religions*. Oxford: Oxford University Press, 1997.

Oxford English Dictionary, 3rd ed. Oxford: Oxford University Press, 1971.

Palmer, A. Delbert, and Mark L. Grover. "Hoping to Establish a Presence: Parley P. Pratt's 1851 Mission to Chile." *BYU Studies* 38, no. 4 (1999): 115–38.

Parrish, Alan K. "Beginnings of the *Millennial Star:* Journal of the Mission to Great Britain." In *Regional Studies in Latter-day Saint Church History: British Isles*, edited by Donald Q. Cannon, 133–49. Provo, UT: Department of Church History and Doctrine, 1990.

Paulsen, David L., Roger D. Cook, and Brock M. Mason. "Theological Underpinnings of Baptism for the Dead." *BYU Studies Quarterly* 55, no. 3 (2016): 101–16.

Penney, Sherry. *Patrician in Politics: Daniel Dewey Barnard of New York*. Port Washington, NY: Kennikat Press, 1974.

Peterson, John Alton. *Utah's Black Hawk War*. Salt Lake City: University of Utah Press, 1998.

Plewe, Brandon S., ed. *Mapping Mormonism: An Atlas of Latter-day Saint History*. 2nd ed. Provo, UT: BYU Press, 2014.

Plewe, Brandon S. "The State of the Church in 1852." *Mormon Historical Studies* 16, no. 1 (Spring 2015): 233–43.

Pollak, Oliver B. "A Mid-Victorian Coverup: The Case of the 'Combustible Commodore' and the Second Anglo-Burmese War, 1851–1852." *Albion: A Quarterly Journal Concerned with British Studies* 10, no. 2 (Summer 1978): 171–83.

Porter, Nathan Tanner. "The Record of Nathan Tanner Porter." Typescript, MS 15250. Church History Library, The Church of Jesus Christ of Latter-day Saints, Salt Lake City.

Pratt, Parley P. *A Voice of Warning and Instruction to All People, Containing a Declaration of the Faith and Doctrine of the Church of the Latter Day Saints, Commonly Called Mormons.* New York: W. Sandford, 1837.

Prince, Stephen L. *Hosea Stout: Lawman, Legislator, Mormon Defender.* Logan, UT: Utah State University Press, 2016.

Radha, T., and L. Mathew. *Fruit Crops.* New Delhi: New India Publishing Agency, 2007.

Reeve, W. Paul. *Religion of a Different Color: Race and the Mormon Struggle for Whiteness.* New York: Oxford University Press, 2015.

Reilly, Thomas H. *The Taiping Heavenly Kingdom: Rebellion and the Blasphemy of Empire.* Seattle: University of Washington Press, 2004.

Religions of the World: A Comprehensive Encyclopedia of Beliefs and Practices. Edited by J. Gordon Melton and Martin Baumann. Santa Barbara, CA: ABC-CLIO, 2010.

"Report of Messrs. Brandebury, Brocchus, and Harris, to the president of the United States." In *Utah: Message from the President of the United States Transmitting Information in Reference to the Condition of Affairs in the Territory of Utah,* 8–22. 32d Cong., 1st sess., 9 January 1852, H. Ex. Doc. 25.

Roberts, Allen D. "More of Utah's Unknown Pioneer Architects: Their Lives and Works." *Sunstone* 1, no. 3 (Summer 1976): 42–56.

Roberts, B. H. *A Comprehensive History of the Church of Jesus Christ of Latter-day Saints, Century I.* 6 vols. Salt Lake City: The Church of Jesus Christ of Latter-day Saints, 1930.

Roberts, Richard C., and Richard W. Sadler. *A History of Weber County.* Salt Lake City: Utah State Historical Commission, 1997.

Roberts, T. R. *Eminent Welshmen: A Short Biographical Dictionary of Welshmen Who Have Attained Distinction from the Earliest Times to the Present.* Vol. 1. Cardiff and Merthyr Tydfil: Educational Publishing, 1908.

Robertson, Craig. *The Passport in America: The History of a Document.* New York: Oxford University Press, 2010.

Rock, Joseph F. *The Indigenous Trees of the Hawaiian Islands.* Honolulu: E. Herrick Brown, 1913.

Rogers, Aurelia Spencer. *Life Sketches of Orson Spencer and Others, and History of Primary Work.* [Salt Lake City]: Geo. Q. Cannon & Sons, 1898.

Sadler, Richard Wallace. "The Life of Orson Spencer." Master's thesis, University of Utah, 1965.

Salt Lake Recorder's Office. Deeds, 1850–1877. MS 17753. Church History Library, The Church of Jesus Christ of Latter-day Saints, Salt Lake City.

Salt Lake Tribune. Salt Lake City. 1871–.

Sanger, William D. *The History of Prostitution: Its Extent, Causes, and Effect throughout the World.* London: Sampson Low, Son, 1858.

Santaquin Ward, Nebo Stake. Santaquin Ward Manuscript History and Historical Reports, 1853. LR 8765 2. Church History Library, The Church of Jesus Christ of Latter-day Saints, Salt Lake City.

Scharffs, Gilbert W. "*Das Buch Mormon*: The German Translation of the Book of Mormon." *Journal of Book of Mormon Studies* 11, no. 1 (2002): 35–39.

Scharffs, Gilbert. *Mormonism in Germany: A History of The Church of Jesus Christ of Latter-day Saints in Germany between 1840 and 1970.* Salt Lake City: Deseret Book, 1970.

The Second Supplement to the Penny Cyclopædia of the Society for the Diffusion of Useful Knowledge. London: Knight & Co., 1858.

The Seer. Washington, DC. 1853–54.

Shaffer, Donald R. "Hiram Clark and the First LDS Hawaiian Mission: A Reappraisal." *Journal of Mormon History* 17 (1991): 94–109.

Shirts, Morris A., and Kathryn B. Shirts. *A Trial Furnace: Southern Utah's Iron Mission.* Provo, UT: Brigham Young University Press, 2001.

Sinn, Elizabeth. *Pacific Crossing: California Gold, Chinese Migration, and the Making of Hong Kong.* Hong Kong: Hong Kong University Press, 2013.

Smart, William B., and Donna T. Smart, eds. *Over the Rim: The Parley P. Pratt Exploring Expedition to Southern Utah, 1849–1850.* Logan, UT: Utah State University Press, 1999.

Smith, Bathsheba W. "Autobiography of Bathsheba W. Smith." MS 8606. Church History Library, The Church of Jesus Christ of Latter-day Saints, Salt Lake City.

Smith, Joseph, et al. History, 1838–1856. Vols. A1–F1. Church History Library, The Church of Jesus Christ of Latter-day Saints, Salt Lake City. https://josephsmithpapers.org.

Smith, Marilyn Austin, comp. "The Story of Eliza Ann Dibble and Her Three Husbands, Orson Spencer, Henry W. Jackson, and Julius A. C. Austin." N.p.: 1995.

Snow, Philip. *The Fall of Hong Kong: Britain, China and the Japanese Occupation.* New Haven: Yale University Press, 2003.

Snow Smith, Eliza R. *Biography and Family Record of Lorenzo Snow.* Salt Lake City: Deseret News, 1884.

Sonne, Conway B. *Ships, Saints, and Mariners: A Maritime Encyclopedia of Mormon Migration, 1830–1890.* Salt Lake City: University of Utah Press, 1987.

Spence, Jonathan D. *The Search for Modern China.* New York: W. W. Norton, 1999.

Spence, Jonathan D. *The Taiping Vision of a Christian China, 1836–1864.* Waco, TX: Baylor University Press, 1998.

Spencer, Daniel. Diaries. MS 1566. Church History Library, The Church of Jesus Christ of Latter-day Saints, Salt Lake City.

Spencer, Orson. *The Prussian Mission of the Church of Jesus Christ of Latter-day Saints.* Liverpool: S. W. Richards, 1853.

Spencer, Seymour H. *Life Summary of Orson Spencer.* Salt Lake City: Mercury Publishing, 1964.

"St. John's Day." *Masonic Standard,* June 20, 1903.

St. Louis Luminary. St. Louis, MO. 1854–1855.

Stansbury, Howard. *Exploration and Survey of the Valley of the Great Salt Lake of Utah, Including a Reconnoissance of a New Route through the Rocky Mountains.* Philadelphia: Lippincott, Grambo, 1852.

Stapleton, Timothy J. "Oral Evidence in a Pseudo-Ethnicity: The Fingo Debate." *History in Africa* 22 (1995): 359–68.

Stephens, Calvin R. "Jesse Haven: A Biography." Typescript, MS 27764. Church History Library, The Church of Jesus Christ of Latter-day Saints, Salt Lake City.

Stevens, Michael E., and Steven B. Burg. *Editing Historical Documents: A Handbook of Practice.* Walnut Creek, CA: Altamira Press, 1997.

Stevenson, Edward. Diary, Edward Stevenson Collection, 1849–1922. MS 4806. Church History Library, The Church of Jesus Christ of Latter-day Saints, Salt Lake City.

Stevenson, Edward. "The Life and History of Elder Edward Stevenson." MS 1054. Church History Library, The Church of Jesus Christ of Latter-day Saints, Salt Lake City.

Stevenson, Edward. *Reminiscences of Joseph, the Prophet, and the Coming Forth of the Book of Mormon.* Salt Lake City: by the author, 1893.

Stevenson, Joseph Grant. "The Life of Edward Stevenson, Member of the First Council of Seventy, Friend of the Prophet Joseph Smith and the Three Witnesses." Master's thesis, Brigham Young University, 1955.

Stout, Hosea. Papers, 1832–1875. MS 16397. Church History Library, The Church of Jesus Christ of Latter-day Saints, Salt Lake City.

Stout, Hosea. Reminiscences and journals. MS 8332. Church History Library, The Church of Jesus Christ of Latter-day Saints, Salt Lake City.

Stout, Wayne. *Hosea Stout: Utah's Pioneer Statesman.* Salt Lake City: Wayne Stout, 1953.

Sutak, Tom. "Jefferson Hunt: California's First Mormon Politician." *Journal of Mormon History* 36, no. 3 (Summer 2010): 82–117.

Swapp, Lettie Young. "Biography of Emily Jennison Holman Lewis." MS 20135. Church History Library, The Church of Jesus Christ of Latter-day Saints, Salt Lake City.

Talbot, Christine. *A Foreign Kingdom: Mormons and Polygamy in American Political Culture, 1852–1890.* Urbana: University of Illinois Press, 2013.

Taylor, Brian L. *History of Farr West*. N.p.: 1980. M277.9228 F239h 1980. Church History Library, The Church of Jesus Christ of Latter-day Saints, Salt Lake City.

Temperley, Harold. "The Treaty of Paris of 1856 and Its Execution." *Journal of Modern History* 4, no. 3 (September 1932): 387–414.

Thompson, Leonard. *A History of South Africa*. New Haven: Yale University Press, 2000.

Thurston, Edgar. *The Madras Presidency, with Mysore, Coorg and the Associated States*. Cambridge: Cambridge University Press, 1913.

Times and Seasons. Commerce/Nauvoo, IL, November 1839–February 1846.

Tokayer, Marvin, and Ellen Rodman. *Pepper, Silk & Ivory: Amazing Stories about Jews and the Far East*. Jerusalem: Gefen Publishing House, 2014.

Toronto, James A. "'A Continual War, Not of Arguments, But of Bread and Cheese': Opening the First LDS Mission in Italy, 1849–67." *Journal of Mormon History* 31, no. 2 (Summer 2005): 188–232.

Torpey, John. "Leaving: A Comparative View." In *Citizenship and Those Who Leave: The Politics of Emigration and Expatriation*, edited by Nancy L. Green and Francois Weil, 13–32. Urbana: University of Illinois Press, 2007.

Tullidge, Edward W. *Tullidge's Histories, (Volume II), Containing the History of all the Northern, Eastern, and Western Counties of Utah; also the Counties of Southern Idaho*. Salt Lake City: Juvenile Instructor, 1889.

Tullidge, Edward W. *The Women of Mormondom*. New York: N.p., 1877.

Ulrich, Laurel Thatcher. *A House Full of Females: Plural Marriage and Women's Rights in Early Mormonism, 1835–1870*. New York: Alfred A. Knopf, 2017.

Utah: Message from the President of the United States, Transmitting Information in Reference to the Condition of Affairs in the Territory of Utah, January 9, 1852. Washington, DC: N.p., 1852.

Valdiya, K. S. *Environmental Geology: Ecology, Resource, and Hazard Management*. New Delhi: McGraw Hill Education [India] Private Limited, 2013.

Van Alfen, Peter G. "Sail and Steam: Great Salt Lake's Boats and Boatbuilders, 1847–1901." In *Great Salt Lake: An Anthology*, edited by Gary Topping, 204–28. Logan, UT: Utah State University Press, 2002.

Van Cott, John W. *Utah Place Names: A Comprehensive Guide to the Origins of Geographic Names*. Salt Lake City: University of Utah Press, 1990.

Vitale, Gary. "Abraham Lincoln and the Mormons: Another Legacy of Limited Freedom." *Journal of the Illinois State Historical Society* 101, nos. 3 and 4 (Fall and Winter 2008): 260–71.

Walker, Ronald W., Richard E. Turley Jr., and Glen M. Leonard. *Massacre at Mountain Meadows: An American Tragedy*. New York: Oxford University Press, 2008.

Walker, William Holmes. *The Life Incidents and Travels of Elder William Holmes Walker and His Association with Joseph Smith, the Prophet.* N.p.: Elizabeth Jane Walker Piepgrass, 1943.

Watson, Kaye C. *Life under the Horseshoe: A History of Spring City.* Spring City, UT: Spring City Corporation, 1987.

Weber, Samuel R. "'Shake Off the Dust of Thy Feet': The Rise and Fall of Mormon Ritual Cursing." *Dialogue: A Journal of Mormon Thought* 46, no. 1 (Spring 2013): 108–39.

Welsh, Frank. *A History of Hong Kong.* London: HarperCollins, 1993.

Welsh Mormon History. Center for Family History and Genealogy, Brigham Young University. http://welshmormon.byu.edu.

West, Chauncey W. Journals, 1853–54. MS 6074. Church History Library, The Church of Jesus Christ of Latter-day Saints, Salt Lake City.

West, Franklin L. *Chauncey W. West: Pioneer-Churchman.* N.p.: 1965.

Whitney, Orson F. *History of Utah.* Vol. 4, *Biographical.* Salt Lake City: George Q. Cannon & Sons, 1904.

Whittaker, David J. "The Bone in the Throat: Orson Pratt and the Public Announcement of Plural Marriage." *Western Historical Quarterly* 18, no. 3 (Summer 1987): 293–314.

Whittaker, David J. "Brigham Young and the Missionary Enterprise." In *Lion of the Lord: Essays on the Life and Service of Brigham Young,* edited by Susan Easton Black and Larry C. Porter, 85–106. Salt Lake City: Deseret Book, 1995.

Whittaker, David J. "Early Mormon Imprints in South Africa." *BYU Studies* 20, no. 4 (Summer 1980): 404–9.

Whittaker, David J. "Early Mormon Pamphleteering." PhD dissertation, Brigham Young University, 1982, reprinted Provo, UT: BYU Studies, 2003.

Whittaker, David J. "Early Mormon Polygamy Defenses." *Journal of Mormon History* 11 (1984): 43–63.

Whittaker, David J. "Richard Ballantyne and the Defense of Mormonism in India in the 1850s." In *Supporting Saints: Life Stories of Nineteenth-Century Mormons,* edited by Donald Q. Cannon and David J. Whittaker, 175–212. Provo, UT: Religious Studies Center, 1985.

Williams, Gwyn A. *Madoc: The Making of a Myth.* London: Eyre Methuen, 1979.

Woods, Fred E. *A Gamble in the Desert: The Mormon Mission in Las Vegas (1855–1857).* Salt Lake City: Mormon Historic Sites Foundation, 2005.

Woods, Fred E. "A Gifted Gentleman in Perpetual Motion: John Taylor as an Emigration Agent." In *Champion of Liberty: John Taylor,* edited by Mary Jane Woodger, 177–92. Provo, UT: Religious Studies Center; Salt Lake City: Deseret Book, 2009.

Woods, Fred E. "Nathaniel H. Felt: An Essex County Man." In *Regional Studies in Latter-day Saint Church History: The New England States*, edited by Donald Q. Cannon, Arnold K. Garr, and Bruce A. Van Orden, 219–36. Provo, UT: Religious Studies Center, 2004.

Wright, Evan P. "A History of the South African Mission: Period 1, 1852–1903." 1977. M276.8 W948h. Church History Library, The Church of Jesus Christ of Latter-day Saints, Salt Lake City.

Young, Brigham. Office Files. CR 1234 1. Church History Library, The Church of Jesus Christ of Latter-day Saints, Salt Lake City.

INDEX

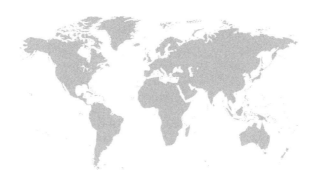

ABOUT THE EDITORS

Reid L. Neilson is the Assistant Church Historian and Recorder and managing director for the Church History Department of The Church of Jesus Christ of Latter-day Saints in Salt Lake City. He completed his PhD in religious studies at the University of North Carolina at Chapel Hill.

R. Mark Melville has a bachelor's degree in English linguistics, with minors in editing and geology, from Brigham Young University. He was an editorial assistant at BYU Studies before working for the Church History Department of The Church of Jesus Christ of Latter-day Saints.